Negotiating Cooperation

THE UNITED STATES AND CHINA,

1969 – 1989

ROBERT S. ROSS

Negotiating Cooperation

THE UNITED STATES AND
CHINA, 1969–1989

STANFORD UNIVERSITY PRESS

STANFORD, CALIFORNIA

Stanford University Press
Stanford, California
© 1995 by the Board of Trustees of the
Leland Stanford Junior University
Printed in the United States of America

CIP data appear at the end of the book

Stanford University Press publications are
distributed exclusively by Stanford University
Press within the United States, Canada,
Mexico, and Central America; they are distributed exclusively by Cambridge University Press
throughout the rest of the world.

Original printing 1995
Last figure below indicates year of this printing:
04 03 02 01 00 99 98 97 96 95

Research for this book was supported by a
grant from the Social Science Research
Council program in Advanced Foreign Policy
Studies, with funds provided by the Ford
Foundation, and a postdoctoral fellowship in
chinese Studies from the Henry M. Jackson
School of International Studies, University of
Washington.

For Betsy

Acknowledgments

During the course of the research for and writing of this book, I benefited from the assistance and generosity of many friends and institutions. I began the research with the financial support of a postdoctoral fellowship in the China Program of the Henry M. Jackson School of International Studies at the University of Washington. My colleagues there provided an ideal intellectual setting for developing and writing a book on U.S.-PRC relations. Additional support was provided by a two-year advanced research fellowship in foreign policy studies from the Social Science Research Council (with funds provided by the Ford Foundation), which enabled me to spend 1990 as a Guest Scholar at the Foreign Policy Studies program at the Brookings Institution. This opportunity enabled me to conduct most of the interviews for this book and provided me with a stimulating environment comprised of colleagues who shared my interest in U.S. foreign policy and U.S.-PRC relations.

This book could not have been written without the help of the many current and former American and Chinese government officials who generously took the time to discuss their experiences. Many of them met with me on two and sometimes three occasions. I should note that as a group, these were dedicated officials who had given the greater part of their lives working for the good of their respective countries and for U.S.-China relations. The following are the Americans who agreed to be interviewed: William Abnett, Elliott Abrams, Morton Abromowitz, Richard Allen, Donald Anderson, Richard Armitage, Harold Brown, Zbigniew Brzezinski, Harvey Feldman, Carl Ford, Gerald Ford, Charles Freeman, William Gleysteen,

Marshall Green, Alexander Haig, Richard Holbrooke, Benjamin Huberman, Arthur Hummel, Samuel Huntington, William Huston, Alfred Jenkins, James Kelly, Paul Kreisberg, James Lilley, Winston Lord, Mark Mohr, Michel Oksenberg, Lionel Olmer, Mark Pratt, Frank Press, Stapleton Roy, James Schlesinger, Peter Murphey, Peter Rodman, William Rogers, Alan Romberg, William Rope, Yoshi Ogawa, Thomas Shoesmith, Gaston Sigur, Michael B. Smith, Richard Smyser, Richard Solomon, Helmut Sonnenfeldt, Roger Sullivan, Harry Thayer, Leonard Unger, Cyrus Vance, H. Reiter Webb, Richard Wich, Paul Wolfowitz, and Leonard Woodcock.

I am particularly grateful to Leonard Woodcock and Michel Oksenberg, who also allowed me to read the transcript of their joint oral history of U.S.-PRC relations during the Carter administration. I am also grateful for the contributions of many Chinese colleagues who answered my numerous questions and helped make this book possible.

The staff at Stanford University Press deserves special appreciation. Muriel Bell and John Feneron were a pleasure to work with throughout the publication process. They kept me on schedule while cheerfully fielding my numerous questions. Peter Dreyer was an exceptionally fine editor. He greatly improved the grammar, style, and content of the manuscript while maintaining uncommon sensitivity to the argument.

Many friends also took the time to read the manuscript and provide valuable criticism and extensive suggestions for its improvement. I am grateful to Thomas Bernstein, Thomas Christensen, B. Michael Frolic, Banning Garrett, Paul Godwin, Steven Levine, Andrew Nathan, Michel Oksenberg, Ross Terrill, and Allen Whiting for their time and efforts. This is a far better book because of their contributions. I also benefited from the excellent and valuable research assistance of Li Chengyuan and Wang Zhi.

My family receives my greatest thanks. My parents have been consistent supporters of this project. I regret my father, Theodore Ross, could not have seen this project come to completion. He was always full of questions and eager to know about the manuscript while it was on its way to becoming a book. Although Alex and Rebecca know about China firsthand, they are still too young to read this book. Emily is now old enough to read my writings, but she has been wise to stick to mysteries and sports books. Nonetheless, all of my children have had to endure my long visits to China and their father's preoccupation with U.S.-PRC relations. Once again, my wife, Betsy Glaser, deserves the most thanks. Despite the conventional wisdom, writing a book is not a solitary process. Friends and family share in the various stages of the writing process. Betsy has been more involved in every stage of my work than anyone. And she has shared in the process with remarkable patience and good humor, while offering constant friendship. I have dedicated this book to her.

R.S.R.

Contents

Negotiating Cooperation

THE UNITED STATES AND CHINA,

1969 – 1989

Introduction

It has become nearly a truism to say that in the 1970s and 1980s, the United States and the People's Republic of China developed cooperative relations in order to enhance their security against the threat to both from the Soviet Union. This was clearly the case. U.S.-PRC rapprochement in the early 1970s and in the ensuing twenty years was characterized by perceptions in Washington and Beijing that the USSR was intent on unlimited expansion, and that it was necessary to establish as large a coalition as possible to compel Moscow to limit its ambitions. China and the United States were the two largest countries opposing the USSR, and they sought each other's assistance to bolster their respective Soviet policies.

But like most truisms, this description of U.S.-PRC relations during the 1970s and 1980s obscures more than it reveals. Although the common threat encouraged Washington and Beijing to cooperate, it does not explain how they were able to cooperate. Initiating and sustaining cooperation is never easy, because it not only requires that both sides have common interests but also requires that their conflicts of interests be either insignificant or manageable. More often than not, there are significant preexisting and ongoing bilateral conflicts, so that establishing and sustaining cooperation requires mutual adjustment and extensive negotiations. Cooperation is neither spontaneous nor self-perpetuating. Maintaining cooperative relations requires considerable effort by both parties.

It has also become the conventional wisdom that for most of the years of U.S.-PRC cooperation, Washington and Beijing agreed to "shelve" or "put aside" conflictual issues in the interest of maximizing cooperation against the Soviet Union, and that when conflict did occur, it was because of either diplomatic mismanagement or the intrusion of domestic politics into diplomacy—left to their own devices, pragmatic policy makers would finesse bilateral conflicts in the interest of developing cooperation against the Soviet threat. But as is often the case with a conventional wisdom, this description of U.S.-PRC relations during the 1970s and 1980s is wrong, despite Henry Kissinger's insistence that only he and Richard Nixon understood that Taiwan was not an important issue in U.S-China relations, and that China was interested in availing itself of U.S. strategic power in its struggle against the Soviet Union.[1]

Taiwan was the most conflictual issue in U.S.-PRC relations throughout the 1970s and 1980s, and Washington and Beijing never "agreed to disagree" or to "sweep it under the rug." Indeed, at no time during the 1970s and 1980s was there agreement between Beijing and Washington that as long as cooperation was imperative, the status quo in U.S.-Taiwan relations was temporarily acceptable. Rather, in the midst of cooperation, there was ongoing conflict, requiring continuous negotiations and mutual adjustment. This book is a study of those negotiations. It explains how the United States and China negotiated cooperation.

Negotiating for Cooperation

Cooperation is never cheap. Establishing and maintaining it entails a cost, insofar as coping with an immediate and significant threat often requires that other objectives go unrealized.[2] In these circumstances, the underlying issue requiring negotiation in all cooperative relationships is how to distribute the burden of cooperation. While it may often be obvious that the parties will succeed in cooperating, it is rarely obvious how they are to share the cost.

Security relationships characterized by cooperation against a common threat usually involve a status-quo state and a dissatisfied state. While pursuing its strategic interest of maintaining security cooperation, the dissatisfied state seeks to impose a greater burden of cooperation on the status-quo state by achieving some or all of its objectives in bilateral conflict over particular interests.[3]

During U.S.-PRC cooperation in the 1970s and 1980s, the primary point of contention was U.S. policy on the conflict between mainland China and Taiwan. Throughout this period, the United States was the status-quo state, and China was the dissatisfied state. It was

China's task to maintain, and at times consolidate, U.S.-PRC cooperation against the Soviet threat, while simultaneously trying to reorder U.S.-Taiwan relations. Washington's objective was to yield as little as possible to Chinese demands, while also trying to maintain, and at times consolidate, U.S.-PRC strategic cooperation.

Throughout the twenty years of U.S.-PRC security cooperation, the burden of cooperation gradually and significantly shifted. Despite Washington's efforts to maintain the status quo, Chinese leaders managed to consolidate various aspects of U.S.-PRC relations while weakening critical aspects of U.S. policy toward Taiwan, so that by the end of the 1980s, China had succeeded in imposing upon the United States a larger share of the burden of cooperation.

Yet Chinese success did not occur as part of a gradual, even process. In persistently demanding change in U.S. policy toward Taiwan, China was sometimes successful, but at other times it failed to elicit U.S. concessions. Moreover, there was nothing inevitable about the changes in U.S.-Taiwan relations during the 1970s and 1980s. There was no way to predict in 1970 what compromises the United States would have to make, and what costs Beijing would have to endure, in order for the two sides to develop cooperative relations over the ensuing twenty years. Similarly, there was no way to predict in 1970 how much cooperation would develop; it was not inevitable that the two sides would be able to manage their conflicts well enough to develop cooperative military, economic, and educational ties by the mid 1980s. Instead, the course of U.S.-PRC negotiations was shaped by a number of factors that interacted in different ways at different times to produce various periods during the era of cooperation, each characterized by distinct negotiating dynamics, and to create the ultimate distribution of the cost of cooperation at the end of twenty years.

The outcome of any negotiation is primarily determined by the relative resolve between the two sides to incur the cost of reduced cooperation. The side that has the most to offer and the least to lose is said to have the greater leverage in the negotiations. Ultimately, the distribution of the costs of cooperation will reflect this dynamic. This was just as true of U.S.-PRC negotiations during the 1970s and 1980s as of any other set of bilateral negotiations.[4]

Nevertheless, the negotiations between Washington and Beijing reflected the dynamics of a particular subset of negotiations, insofar as China and the United States were strategic partners rather than adversaries. These were not adversarial negotiations in which the two sides bargained in the context of threats of arms races and armed conflict. There was always the assumption in Beijing and Washington that there would be cooperation—this truism about U.S.-PRC relations is correct. Rather, the issue was how little or how much cooperation there would be. Thus, instead of facing the risk of escalated adversarial relations, China and the United States weighed the benefit of cooperation, expressed in terms of enhanced security, against the cost of cooperation, expressed in terms of compromise over conflictual issues, and the cost of reduced cooperation should negotiations fail. In this context, relative resolve was determined by the cost each would incur should negotiations fail and cooperation diminish. This distinct aspect of U.S.-PRC relations determined the factors affecting the leverage of each side in the negotiations.[5]

In the context of cooperative relations, the most important factor affecting the cost to the United States and China of reduced cooperation, and thus their respective negotiating positions, was their relative security situation vis-à-vis the Soviet threat. Simply put, at any particular time, the state that was better able to adjust to reduced cooperation was in the better position to call its security partner's bluff. If it were the United States, it could maintain the status quo in its Taiwan policy, and thus resist assuming a greater share of the cost of cooperation; if it were China, it could reduce the burden of cooperation by compelling the United States to distance itself from Taiwan. During the twenty years of cooperation, the bargaining position of the two states frequently changed.[6]

Assessments in Washington and Beijing of the Soviet threat at any particular point in time were accordingly one decisive factor determining each country's resolve, and thus the outcome of U.S.-PRC negotiations. Changes in threat perception affected a state's security, and thus its willingness either to resist or to accept compromise in the interest of cooperation.

But an equally important factor shaping bilateral negotiations is each state's assessment of its counterpart's resolve, which enables each state to establish the relative resolve of the two parties, the ultimate determinant of bargaining power and negotiating positions. To establish a counterpart's resolve, a state cannot rely only on its counterpart's policy statements or even more subtle bilateral signals, for both are subject to manipulation in an effort to enhance the credibility of a bluff. Policy makers must therefore not only assess the security of their own state in order to determine its need for cooperation and its ability to endure conflict; they must also make an assessment of their security partner's security to determine its resolve to endure reduced cooperation. Unlike signals, a state's security situation is not subject to manipulation, which makes it a better indicator of resolve.[7]

Beijing thus not only assessed Sino-Soviet relations in formulating its U.S. policy but also had to assess U.S. security vis-à-vis the Soviet Union, trying to determine whether or not it could compel the United States to change its Taiwan policy. Although because of the considerable strategic asymmetry between the Soviet Union and China, and because the unrelenting hostility between the two countries reduced the chances of significant change in China's security situation, Washington was less sensitive to Sino-Soviet relations, it nevertheless had to look for changes in Chinese security as well as in U.S.-Soviet relations to determine its negotiating posture.

In such circumstances, appraisals of a counterpart's resolve are not based solely on an assessment of its bilateral relationship with the common adversary. Chinese analysis of U.S. security, for example, considered not only the trend in U.S.-Soviet relations and U.S. and Soviet defense spending, but also such issues as the trend of the U.S. economy, alliance relations, and policy toward regional conflicts involving the superpowers. Each country sought information that would help it to determine the resolve of its security partner to resist compromise.

But estimates of the respective security situations of the two countries were not mere variables in U.S.-PRC relations that policy makers in Washington and Beijing simply plugged into a strategic equation to devise their respective negotiating policies, thus leading to a predictable outcome of U.S.-PRC negotiations. Security assessments are ultimately subjective calculations defying absolute measurement. Hence, senior policy makers can differ over their country's security situation, and the same policy maker can change his or her views over time. Individuals matter; they make what are ultimately personal evaluations of the strategic environment, and on this basis make policy.

In U.S.-PRC relations, leaders mattered because the extensive debate in the 1970s and 1980s in the United States over the seriousness of the Soviet threat and the importance of pursuing superpower détente was reflected in presidential transitions or, alternatively, because a particular president's view on these issues changed over time. Moreover, there tended to be a corresponding view of China's strategic importance. Statesmen less concerned about the Soviet threat tended to discount China's strategic importance in U.S. security. Thus, at various times, shifting leadership views of the Soviet

Union affected an administration's willingness to conciliate Chinese interests in order to consolidate U.S.-PRC cooperation.

Similarly, because an assessment of another country's security position is also subject to disagreement, policy makers can differ over the necessity for compromise insofar as they differ over their counterpart's readiness to compromise. American policy makers who believed that the Soviet threat to China was so severe that Beijing had "nowhere else to go" and had no choice but to maintain good relations with the United States were less inclined to make significant compromises to secure Chinese cooperation than policy makers who believed that Chinese leaders could either ease tension with the Soviet Union or withstand the pressures of increased isolation.

Moreover, this tendency to differ over a security partner's security situation and its consequent negotiating strategy can cause escalated bilateral tension. If leaders of the two states reach different conclusions about the security predicament of one of them, and its corresponding need to compromise, there will be disagreement over which state must bear the burden of cooperation, causing tension to escalate. In the language of game theory, the escalated tension is the result of one state possessing incomplete information about its counterpart, which leads it to an incorrect assessment of the payoff structure. In consequence, the state with incorrect information believes its counterpart is bluffing when, in fact, it has sufficient resolve to prefer reduced cooperation to compromise. Thus, the misinformed state believes the two sides are in a game of "chicken," when its counterpart in fact has a "dominant strategy," so that they are in a game of "called bluff."[8]

Emphasis on the role of perceptions of strategic issues in choosing policy options discounts the importance of bureaucratic politics on the formation of negotiating positions. Although this study of U.S.-PRC negotiations acknowledges the importance of differences among the foreign policy elite, it explains these differences as a function of different strategic perspectives rather than conflicting bureaucratic interests. It argues that these differences ultimately reflect a debate over the country's strategic posture, which is the chief executive's prerogative, not an issue decided by bureaucratic battles. Moreover, the role of the chief executive is especially important in U.S.-PRC relations. For both Washington and Beijing in the 1970s and 1980s, U.S.-PRC relations involved policy on alignment with a major power against the primary threat and sensitive issues in both domestic and international politics—policy toward a long-term ideological adversary, and, for the United States, toward a long-term ideological ally, Taiwan. The chief executives in the two countries thus made the ultimate decisions, not lower-level of- ✕ ficials waging policy battles in the bureaucracy, and to the extent that there were winners and losers in the bureaucracy, the outcome tended to reflect the chief executive's decision, which was based on his policy preference rather than a particular bureaucrat's skill in forging bureaucratic alliances.[9]

The role of idiosyncratic leadership style especially affects policy-making stability in democratic countries, where there is regular leadership turnover. In contrast, in communist countries there is greater leadership stability, except during political successions. Although the absence of an institutionalized succession mechanism tends to lead to gerontocracy and periodic succession crises, it also yields extended periods of predictability in foreign policy. In China, during the 1970s and 1980s, there were only two preeminent leaders—Mao Zedong and Deng Xiaoping—so that there was relatively greater continuity in evaluating the costs and benefits of cooperation and compromise.

Regardless of which country was more affected by contending leadership perspectives, these arguments that idiosyncratic leadership perspectives on the strategic environment or on the strategic importance of a particular country can influence negotiating policy toward security partners nonetheless assume that leaders are foreign policy realists who make policy based on perceptions of national interest. This is often a powerful and sufficient explanation of state behavior. Nonetheless, at other times it can only serve as a first cut at the material. Although senior foreign policy makers, including heads of state, usually prefer to develop foreign policy in the context of international developments, they often opt to be domestic realists rather than international realists, sacrificing immediate foreign policy objectives to domestic ambition. Negotiating positions can thus be shaped by the domestic political implications of either compromise or rigidity on important foreign policy issues rather than solely by strategic considerations. Ultimately, the leadership with the most domestic flexibility may be the state that incurs the greater cost of an agreement.[10]

This dynamic affects both the United States and China. In the United States, presidents not only have to win reelection every four years but must also consider the impact of controversial foreign policy decisions on their ability to attract support for policies requiring congressional approval. In China, the preeminent leader clearly has far more latitude in making foreign policy than a U.S.

president. But during the succession from one preeminent leader to another, domestic politics in China tend to have an even greater influence on Chinese foreign policy than presidential elections have on U.S. foreign policy, albeit occurring at less frequent intervals. Because China lacks an institutionalized succession arrangement, and because the cost of political defeat in China is often so high, at the height of the succession, in the absence of a preeminent leader who can establish order among contending politicians, all significant issues, including foreign policy issues, become subordinate to political survival.[11]

Finally, any discussion of bargaining between security partners must consider inherent bilateral asymmetries, irrespective of relative strategic circumstances at any particular time. Although relative bargaining power may change over time, the range is constrained by these bilateral asymmetries. Thus, at times the weaker of the two parties may develop greater leverage, but it still may lack the leverage necessary for negotiating superiority or even parity. In U.S.-PRC relations, despite China's impressive size and military capability, and despite its importance to U.S. security, it remained a significantly weaker state in international affairs and in its ability to contend with Soviet power, regardless of short-term improvements in its relative security. Even during the best of times, this fact severely limited China's negotiating leverage with the United States. It also enabled Washington to impose the foreign policy costs of U.S. domestic instability on Beijing when Chinese leaders might reasonably have expected U.S. security considerations to compel the United States to conciliate Chinese interests in order to promote greater cooperation.

Policy is thus often the result of many distinct factors influencing the policy-making process. But the relative significance of each can vary over time. It would be a mistake, for example, to assume that domestic politics always influences the making of foreign policy. Its precise role is a function of a leader's particular political circumstances at a particular time. Similarly, perspectives on the strategic environment or on the value of cooperation may or may not change with leadership transitions. The only constant in policy making in U.S.-PRC relations is that leaders first considered the strategic environment when making policy, and, all things being equal, they preferred to make policy on the basis of international considerations.

Using these various negotiating and policy-making perspectives, this book examines how China and the United States managed to develop and consolidate cooperative relations during the 1970s and

1980s, despite the existence of significant conflict of interest over Taiwan. It examines how Washington and Beijing conducted negotiations over Taiwan, and the compromises they had to make to sustain cooperation. It explains why Washington and Beijing made certain compromises, when they made them, and why, at other times, they tolerated the status quo. It also explains why the negotiations sometimes became acrimonious, and why the acrimony eventually subsided. In this respect, each chapter is a separate case study of U.S.-PRC negotiations, each examining the impact of a distinct combination of internal and external factors on the behavior of the negotiators and the outcome of the negotiations.

In the aftermath of normalization in 1979, U.S.-PRC relations extended beyond discussions between a handful of senior leaders on both sides of global security and Taiwan. Negotiations over economic, military, and educational ties brought new actors into the arena. As might be imagined, the negotiations in these areas reflected significantly different dynamics than those addressing strategic issues and Taiwan; the interests at stake, the balance of resolve, and the level at which decisions were made were accordingly very different in each issue area. Analyses of negotiations over establishing and developing cooperation in these other areas provide revealing comparisons to analysis of the negotiations over Taiwan and U.S.-PRC security cooperation. Equally important, the discussions of cooperation in these other areas underscore just how successful U.S. and Chinese diplomats were in overcoming the obstacles to cooperation. By the mid 1980s, only fifteen years after the United States and China took the first tentative steps toward ending twenty years of intense hostility, cooperation had become an established and institutionalized feature of U.S.-PRC relations.

This book is therefore not only a study of how the United States and China formulated negotiating policies and resolved their differences, thereby developing the basis for extensive cooperation in wide-ranging areas. It is also a comprehensive history and analysis of U.S.-PRC negotiations over the issues most crucial to defining the course of relations during a critical period in the international affairs of the two countries.

Understanding the Taiwan Issue

Full appreciation of the difficulty Washington and Beijing encountered in developing compromise solutions to conflicts of interest requires understanding of each country's interest in Taiwan.

The North Korean invasion of South Korea in June 1950 funda-

mentally affected the long-term development of U.S.-PRC relations.[12] Reacting to what he believed was a direct challenge to U.S.
commitments to resist Soviet-led expansion, President Harry Truman intervened directly in the Chinese civil war, announcing that
the U.S. Navy was freezing the hostilities and would prevent attacks
by either party, thus defending Taiwan and Generalissimo Chiang
Kai-shek's Kuomintang (Nationalist Party), the rulers of the Republic of China (ROC), from attack by the armed forces of the newly
established People's Republic of China. Truman also said that the
United States would continue to recognize the Republic of China as
the legitimate government of China. In later years, the United States
increased its commitment to the defense of Taiwan. In 1954, President Dwight Eisenhower signed the Mutual Defense Treaty, formally committing the United States to defend Taiwan, and in later
years, particularly during the 1960s, when Taiwan served as an important base for military operations in Indochina, the U.S. military
presence on Taiwan grew.

Truman's decision to intervene militarily and diplomatically in
the Chinese civil war challenged a vital interest of the People's Republic of China, creating a major and increasingly serious obstacle
to developing even a minimal working dialogue between Beijing
and Washington. In the spring of 1950, the Chinese People's Liberation Army was making final preparations for what would have been
the final battle of the civil war, and total victory over its longtime
ideological, political, and military adversaries, only to be frustrated
when the United States, the leader of the "imperialist bloc," came
to the defense of the Kuomintang. The immediate impact was to
heighten nationalistic attitudes on the part of the Communist leadership, which found it both outrageous and completely unacceptable
that most of the world and the United Nations recognized the Republic of China as the legal and legitimate government of the Chinese mainland.

U.S. defense of Taiwan and the division between Taiwan and the
mainland also elicited irredentist sentiments in China. The Chinese
leadership and people have long blamed the Western powers and Japan for the deterioration of the Chinese empire during the nineteenth and twentieth centuries. Coerced into signing the infamous
"unequal treaties," Beijing has long sought to regain sovereignty
over its "lost territories." This has been an important source of legitimacy for all Chinese governments. With the establishment of a
U.S.-backed independent government on Taiwan, Taiwan joined
Hong Kong as the most prominent of China's irredentist objectives,

increasing the PRC's commitment to "liberating" it. After U.S. forces moved into northern Korea and elicited Chinese military intervention and direct U.S.-PRC hostilities, Chinese attitudes toward Taiwan and U.S.-Taiwan relations hardened.[13]

Chinese nationalism and irredentism influenced the attitudes of the Chinese elite toward regaining control over Taiwan. They also embroiled China's U.S. and Taiwan policies in Chinese domestic politics. Insofar as nationalistic and irredentist attitudes toward Taiwan were widely shared by both the elite and a politically significant sector of the Chinese people, compromise on Taiwan subjects the policy maker to potentially debilitating criticism. Under such circumstances, no leader of the People's Republic of China, regardless of his personal prestige or power, can retreat from Beijing's long-held basic position that there is only one China, that Taiwan is part of China, and that the People's Republic is the sole legal government of China.

Nonetheless, it would be a serious mistake to believe that Taiwan is merely an emotional or political issue to Chinese leaders. China has a significant strategic interest in Taiwan, and all leaders of the PRC seek to establish control over the island. During the early years of the Cold War, General Douglas MacArthur argued that Taiwan was an "unsinkable aircraft carrier." He was right. Located less than 100 miles from the Chinese mainland, Taiwan has a strategic significance for PRC leaders similar to that of Cuba for U.S. leaders. Cooperation between adversaries of China and an independent government on Taiwan can significantly aggravate the PRC's security concerns, as was the case in the 1950s and 1960s, when the United States based military forces on Taiwan. For this reason alone, Beijing seeks to control Taiwan. As Deng Xiaoping reportedly said in 1987, until Taiwan is unified with the mainland, it remains susceptible to control by another power.[14] Since June 1950, PRC leaders have wanted to "reunify" China for nationalist, irredentist, and national security reasons.

Given China's significant emotional, political, and strategic interest in Taiwan, it should not come as a surprise that Beijing is willing to use force to retain control over Taiwan. In 1954–55 and 1958, the PRC initiated use of force against Kuomintang garrisons on the offshore islands of Quemoy and, in 1958, Matsu, risking war with the United States. Although there may be some confusion over Beijing's motives, there can be no doubt that these attacks reflected the importance PRC leaders attached to ending the division between Taiwan and the mainland. Recovery of Taiwan was such an important objective that Soviet unwillingness to provide diplomatic support for the PRC's assaults on Kuomintang forces elicited significant hostility in Beijing, constituting a major source of Sino-Soviet conflict in the late 1950s and early 1960s.[15]

American interest in Taiwan since early 1950 has reflected a similar combination of emotional, political, and security considerations. When President Truman decided to defend Taiwan against a Chinese attack, he seemed to be defending a Chinese government participating in the worldwide struggle against communism; he was defending "Free China." The United States quickly developed an emotional and ideological attachment to Taiwan as a heroic defender of anticommunist values against the overwhelming power of totalitarian Communist China, and over time this attachment deepened. Many Americans came to consider "abandoning" Taiwan to "Red China" as simply immoral and inconceivable.

America's emotional attachment to Taiwan thus politicized U.S. policy toward Taiwan and the People's Republic of China. In the 1950s, when many Americans asked "who lost China," expressing dismay that the United States had failed to stop the Chinese Communist Party from defeating the Kuomintang in the late 1940s, even the suggestion that Washington might "abandon" Taiwan or improve relations with Communist China would make a policy maker vulnerable to partisan charges of being, at best, a Communist "sympathizer." Well into the 1960s, Senator Joseph McCarthy's invidious red-baiting and the influence of the "China Lobby" continued to cast a shadow over any attempt to assess U.S. intervention in the Chinese civil war dispassionately.

Finally, the United States also had a national security interest in Taiwan. In the 1950s, the United States was fully involved in the Cold War struggle against the Soviet Union. China was the Soviet Union's principal ally in Asia, and regardless of any differences between the two countries in the 1950s, Moscow would benefit from Chinese gains in Asia at U.S. expense. Defending Taiwan was thus an important element in U.S. containment policy. Moreover, the United States valued Taiwan's strategic location astride the main shipping routes connecting Japan with Southeast Asia. And the deployment of U.S. forces so close to the Chinese mainland was one element of U.S. coercive tactics designed to inflict a significant cost on Beijing's opposition to U.S. policy in Asia.[16] Finally, Washington viewed its security commitment to Taiwan as one element in its global web of commitments as a superpower and believed that failure to fulfill its pledge to the Kuomintang would undermine the confidence of other U.S. allies and cede momentum to Soviet expansionism.

These factors continued to influence U.S. policy when Washington became aware of the severity of the Sino-Soviet conflict. Throughout most of the 1960s, despite the massive superiority of Soviet capabilities and China's many significant vulnerabilities, the United States believed that China was the greater threat to world peace. Whereas Soviet General Secretary Nikita Khrushchev argued the merits of peaceful transition to socialism and the possibility of superpower détente, Chairman Mao Zedong insisted on the inevitability of international class struggle and the necessity for continued use of force to defeat U.S. imperialism and its allies. Moreover, China was intent on developing a nuclear weapons program, despite joint U.S.-Soviet efforts to curtail proliferation, and it seemed to many U.S. leaders that Beijing was using the North Vietnamese communists to extend Chinese control throughout Southeast Asia.[17]

Throughout the 1950s and 1960s, China thus emerged as the primary U.S. security concern in Asia, and Taiwan became a major U.S. ally helping to resist Chinese communist expansionism. Washington was willing to go to great extremes to defend Taiwan against mainland China, rising to its defense in response to Beijing's military initiatives in 1954–55 and 1958, including threatening to use nuclear weapons against Beijing on both occasions.[18]

The Basis for Cooperation

In the 1950s and 1960s, China's interest in controlling Taiwan clashed with Washington's interest in maintaining Taiwan's security and independence. Critical emotional and domestic political interests on both sides reinforced this conflict. The one significant asymmetry in U.S. and Chinese interests in Taiwan concerned their respective security interests. China has an intrinsic vital interest in Taiwan. Taiwan's location off the Chinese coast means that regardless of China's relations with any particular power, the mere potential that Taiwan could contribute to another state's anti-China policy is enough to make mainland leaders seek to dominate Taiwan even when there is no immediate threat. Similarly to U.S. efforts, beginning in the early nineteenth century, to minimize European influence in Latin America, regardless of the particular European country involved, Beijing seeks to deny any power the ability to establish control over countries on its periphery, particularly Taiwan.

In contrast to China's intrinsic interest in Taiwan, Washington's security interest in Taiwan has been a function of U.S. conflict with China, arising either from China's alliance with the Soviet Union or from U.S.-PRC conflict in the 1960s. Indeed, during World War II, when the United States developed cooperative relations with Chiang Kai-shek, it pledged at the Cairo and Potsdam conferences that Taiwan would be returned to China from Japanese occupation. After the war, when the Kuomintang led China, Washington reconciled itself to KMT control of Taiwan. Washington was even prepared to recognize PRC sovereignty over Taiwan during the period before the outbreak of the Korean War.[19] Without heightened U.S.-PRC conflict, as was the case prior to 1950, and subsequent to U.S.-PRC rapprochement in the early 1970s, Washington's strategic interest in Taiwan has been significantly less.

The security and political requirements of the PRC dictated that Beijing could not give up its claim to sovereignty over Taiwan. In addition, China demanded that normalization of relations require U.S. recognition that the People's Republic of China was the sole legitimate government of China, and that the United States abrogate its defense treaty with Taiwan and remove all of its troops from the island. China's ultimate strategic objective was control of Taiwan, and Beijing did not regard normalization of relations with the United States as worth undermining its ability to achieve that objective.

Nonetheless, the contrasting U.S. and PRC security perspectives on Taiwan permitted compromise. The United States was not irreversibly committed to maintaining diplomatic recognition of the Republic of China, its security treaty with Taiwan, or its military deployments on the island. Indeed, as U.S. policy toward Taiwan in the 1940s revealed, American security concerns did not necessarily prevent Washington from considering relinquishing its commitment to assure Taiwan's security and from acknowledging PRC sovereignty over Taiwan. Although U.S. policy makers preferred not to do these things, and the president's domestic situation and U.S. security in Asia would be better served by the status quo in U.S.-Taiwan relations, none of these issues, even U.S. "abandonment" of Taiwan, were set in stone, and all could be made subject to U.S.-PRC negotiations.

There was thus a degree of leeway in the two countries' positions, and hence room for cooperation. China aimed at full achievement of its objectives and could not change them, but it had a considerable range of other potential policy options. Without prejudice to its goals, it could defer negotiations on Taiwan in order to consolidate U.S.-PRC cooperation. It might also reach partial agreements, thereby preserving its ability to address its outstanding concerns at a later date. In this way, it could try to achieve its ultimate objective in a step-by-step process. Although reluctant to compromise on its Taiwan policy, the United States could nonetheless offer Chinese leaders significant incentives for cooperation, for some compromises were less disagreeable than others. The United States could be flexible in ways that could be helpful to Chinese leaders.

But for compromise to occur, Chinese and American leaders had to have the vision to look beyond the recent history of intense animosity and fear and to perceive both the necessity and the opportunity for cooperation. Richard Nixon, Henry Kissinger, Mao Zedong, and Zhou Enlai possessed such vision; historical animosities did not obscure the significance of changed circumstances. And both the necessity and the opportunity for compromise existed. The necessity was the Soviet threat experienced by each side; the opportunity lay in mutual perception of reduced threat from each other and of the mutual need for cooperation. Thus, beginning in 1969, policy makers in Washington and Beijing began the difficult job of negotiating to establish cooperation; in later years, their successors built on early successes, negotiating to maintain and consolidate cooperation despite significant ongoing conflicts of interest.

Throughout the twenty years of U.S.-PRC security cooperation, neither side could know whether or not the negotiations would succeed, or what compromises at what time would be necessary to enable cooperation. These were difficult negotiations. At times, each side had to make significant concessions in recognition of both the necessity for compromise and the importance of cooperation.

A Note on Sources

The explanations for these developments in U.S.-PRC relations are based upon a detailed examination of the international and domestic policy-making setting in each country and each country's appraisal of its counterpart's policy-making environment. They also depend on an equally detailed analysis of negotiations throughout the 1970s and 1980s.

On the U.S. side, the data are primarily drawn from public speeches and memoirs of American policy makers, contemporaneous newspapers and journals, and interviews with over 50 policy makers from various levels in the bureaucracy, from various executive and congressional offices, from both parties, and from a cross-section of the political spectrum as regards U.S.-PRC relations.

These interviews provided detailed information on both U.S. and Chinese negotiating positions.

At times, former and current U.S. officials insisted that they be cited only by their institutional affiliation. Although this is a less than fully satisfactory arrangement, the value of the information justifies the relatively ambiguous citations. Moreover, all of the interviewees agreed that their names could be identified within a list of all those officials interviewed. In addition, given the fallibility of memories, I have tried to corroborate information from participants with as many interviews as possible. The citations often reflect this effort.

On the Chinese side, the data are primarily drawn from leadership speeches, memoirs and biographies, histories of Chinese domestic politics and foreign policy, a select number of confidential interviews, contemporaneous newspaper articles, and contemporaneous analyses of U.S. security during the 1970s and 1980s in both the open literature, such as the Chinese Communist Party newspaper *Renmin ribao* (People's Daily), the Foreign Ministry–controlled weekly magazine *Shijie zhishi* (World Knowledge), and various specialized journals, and in the *neibu* (internal) literature, which is published for only the domestic audience. The most revealing analyses by China's foreign policy specialists appear in the *neibu* journals. This literature, unlike the open Chinese literature, contains Chinese assessments of the implications of immediate U.S. security circumstances for U.S. policy toward China and U.S.-PRC relations.[20]

The authors of these open and *neibu* analyses often prepare reports for the Foreign Ministry, but given the highly centralized nature of the process by which China's foreign policy is formulated, it is highly unlikely that their published analyses directly influence policy. Nevertheless, because these published analyses, including those in the authoritative journal *Shijie jingji yu zhengzhi neican* (Internal Materials on World Economics and Politics), are often based on papers prepared for senior policy makers, they frequently reflect the advice the leadership is receiving. Moreover, these analysts are all government employees, and their public role is for the most part to support and explain official policy, rather than to provide independent critiques challenging official policy. Both open and *neibu* analyses thus tend to reflect the thinking of the principal policy makers and provide valuable insights into the sources of Chinese foreign policy.

CHAPTER 2

Establishing Cooperation

FIRST CONTACTS
AND FIRST COMPROMISES

When the Nixon administration first considered developing a new relationship with the People's Republic of China, it did so in a security atmosphere that put a premium on improved U.S.-PRC relations as a counterweight to Soviet power. The two most critical issues facing the administration were the ongoing war in Vietnam and its concern for the continued development of the Soviet Union's strategic weapons program. The administration believed that both issues required an American response that Washington alone simply could not provide. Thus, the United States sought to bolster its relations with other nations in order to improve its security and to minimize Soviet abilities to capitalize on U.S. weakness. In particular, improved relations with China would reduce the U.S. defense burden in Asia and induce caution in Moscow by raising fears of enhanced U.S.-PRC cooperation vis-à-vis the Soviet Union.

Chinese leaders faced a similar strategic imperative. Since the early 1960s, Beijing had had highly conflictual relationships with both Washington and Moscow, placing China in self-imposed isolation. The cost of this policy increased in 1969 when Chinese and Soviet border forces clashed and Moscow threatened significant escalation. Moreover, China was still reeling from the political and societal chaos of the peak years of the Cultural Revolution. As China's principal makers of foreign policy, including Chairman Mao Zedong and Premier Zhou Enlai, surveyed the PRC's strategic environment, improved relations with the United States appeared to be a highly attractive option. Not only could China manipulate the superpower conflict, but the United States was becoming less of a threat as it withdrew from Indochina and prepared to retrench throughout Asia.

Initially, Beijing and Washington approached each other with common security concerns and with roughly symmetrical strategic imperatives. Toward the end of the Nixon administration's first term, however, the strategic equation shifted as Washington's situation vis-à-vis the Soviet Union improved. Breakthroughs in arms-control negotiations and in other aspects of U.S.-Soviet relations reduced U.S. security concerns. Meanwhile, Sino-Soviet relations remained frozen in distrust, and Beijing remained acutely sensitive to Soviet military pressure. There were also asymmetries in the U.S. and Chinese domestic situations. By 1972, Nixon had become increasingly popular and had gone a long way toward defusing the political implications of the Vietnam War. In November, he convincingly defeated George McGovern, the Democratic Party presidential candidate. Beijing, on the other hand, remained embroiled in elite conflict, which exacerbated the Chinese leadership's sense of its strategic vulnerability and retarded China's ability to expedite economic and military development.

Changing U.S. and Chinese security perspectives influenced U.S.-PRC negotiations. Whereas the initial negotiations were conducted on somewhat equal footing, by the time President Nixon traveled to China to meet with Chairman Mao, Washington held the upper hand. The joint Shanghai communiqué of February 27, 1972 (see Appendix A), and the later agreement on liaison offices reflected the emerging imbalance in negotiating leverage—China was compelled to wait until better times to wrest significant concessions on normalization and U.S.-Taiwan relations from the United States.

The Strategic Context of U.S.-PRC Rapprochement

U.S.-PRC rapprochement took place in a strategic context that put a premium on cooperation and encouraged revaluation of bilateral relationships. Simultaneous developments in the relations with the USSR of China and the United States gave both countries a strategic interest in cooperation. They also prompted Washington and Beijing to reevaluate the threat each posed to the other. These developments created the context for cooperation over the next twenty years. Nonetheless, within this long-term strategic context, there were more subtle changes that affected bilateral relations throughout the 1970s and 1980s. The first of these changes occurred during

President Nixon's first term, when U.S.-Soviet détente developed and U.S. security seemed to have improved significantly.

WASHINGTON'S SHIFTING STRATEGIC PERSPECTIVE

When the Nixon administration assumed office in early 1969, it faced a difficult strategic situation. Intelligence revealed that the USSR continued to deploy SS9 ICBMs at a rate of 250 launchers per year, with total deployment far exceeding earlier expectations. In 1970, the Soviet buildup quickened: over 270 ICBMs were deployed. Particularly serious was new construction in 1969 and early 1970 of over seventy-five silos for the SS9, the most threatening Soviet missile. Although deployment tapered off after mid 1970, in early 1971, Moscow started construction of a large number of silos for both the SS9 and SS11, causing renewed concern in Washington. Soviet attempts to MIRV the SS9 were an additional concern. Moreover, Moscow was modernizing its submarine forces, suggesting that it might reach quantitative parity with the United States in SLBMs much sooner than expected.[1]

Although there was extensive debate within the administration over Soviet advances, Nixon and Kissinger were genuinely concerned about the potential Soviet challenge to the survivability of U.S. land-based ballistic missiles. As early as 1970, Kissinger acknowledged that Moscow was aiming for quantitative superiority in land-based missiles, regardless of the outcome of arms-control negotiations. The U.S. Department of Defense shared this concern. Its annual reports called attention to the long-term possibility of vulnerability and discussed countermeasures designed to maintain a reliable land-based second-strike capability.[2]

It was also clear that Washington was in no position to respond to the Soviet challenge. The Defense Department's fiscal 1972 budget proposal was the first in many years to request an increase in spending for strategic systems. Nonetheless, it proposed the lowest amount of overall defense spending as a share of GNP since 1950. The nation's sentiment was best expressed the previous year, when the Senate overwhelmingly passed a resolution calling for immediate suspension of deployment of strategic nuclear weapons. Administration plans for new weapons systems, including the B-1 bomber, Trident submarines, and the MX missile, were still in the planning stage and faced congressional opposition.[3]

This strategic asymmetry was reflected in U.S.-Soviet negotiations. Throughout 1970 and into 1971, Moscow used delaying tactics in the SALT negotiations, just as its ICBM deployment was increasing and its new weapons systems were coming into production. U.S. negotiators were under pressure to conclude an agreement before their bargaining position further deteriorated. Kissinger reported that the Pentagon, fearing that severe budgetary constraints would undermine the ability of the United States to maintain its existing forces, much less match the Soviet buildup, sought rapid conclusion of a U.S.-Soviet freeze in weapons deployment.[4]

U.S. strategic dilemmas were compounded by continued regional conflicts, especially the war in Indochina. Nixon came into office expecting to end the war within the year.[5] But before long he faced a deepening conflict. Even after U.S. forces bombed North Vietnam and Cambodia, Hanoi ignored Nixon's November 1, 1969, deadline to begin serious negotiations or incur U.S. retaliation. Moreover, North Vietnam now controlled one quarter of Cambodian territory, and South Vietnamese casualties continued to mount.[6]

Not only was the administration losing the war in Indochina, it was also losing support in the United States. The 1970 U.S. incursion into Cambodia accomplished little on the battlefield, but exacerbated the administration's domestic problems, culminating in the violence at Kent State University. Kissinger reports that by mid 1970, the White House was "permeated" with fears of another round of antiwar demonstrations. Nixon was personally deeply affected by the crisis, and he was continually preoccupied with his domestic position.[7] The domestic situation further deteriorated after U.S. and South Vietnamese forces extended operations into Laos and after the release of the Pentagon Papers.

Only after Hanoi's 1972 "Easter offensive" and the subsequent U.S. mining of Haiphong Harbor did Hanoi reveal genuine interest in compromise, and by the fall, an agreement was in sight.[8] Nevertheless, the previous three and a half years of painful domestic turmoil and repeated military setbacks had been difficult to endure and created significant domestic political pressure on U.S. foreign policy.

Moreover, despite the prospects of a negotiated settlement of the war, the United States would play a reduced role in Asia. Nixon's July 1969 discussion of U.S. foreign policy, subsequently called the Nixon Doctrine, reflected this reality by calling for greater self-reliance on the part of U.S. allies. Yet, it was obvious that the non-communist Asian states could not compensate for the decline of American regional power, and that the Soviet Union would try to take advantage of the changed balance of power in Asia.

Also troubling were Soviet attempts to secure advantage elsewhere in the Third World. In 1970, conflict between Jordan and Syria challenged Washington's position in the Middle East. In the Caribbean, the United States believed, Moscow sought to deploy nuclear-armed submarines at Cienfuegos, Cuba, in 1970 and 1971. Kissinger recalled that this was a Soviet "test" and a "challenge," in which Moscow overestimated the Nixon administration's "permissiveness."[9] Only after escalated tension was the administration confident that the status quo would be maintained. And in late 1970, Salvadore Allende assumed the Chilean presidency and shortly thereafter nationalized U.S. corporate interests in Chile.

These strategic and regional challenges fostered a dark view of American security. In the context of the antiwar movement, the administration was deeply concerned that emerging American "isolationism" would be expressed by a rush to abandon U.S. security commitments and by unilateral disarmament through defense budget reductions.[10] Regarding U.S.-Soviet relations, Washington was still uncertain whether an arms-control agreement could be negotiated and whether regional conflict could be avoided. As the 1970 foreign policy report explained, the Soviet military "build-up . . . raises serious questions about where they are headed and the potential threats we and our allies face. These questions must be faced soberly and realistically."[11] Nixon's 1971 report revealed similar pessimism. The behavior of the USSR in the Middle East and its policies toward Berlin and Cuba indicated that "intransigence remains a cardinal feature of the Soviet system." And the shifting strategic balance was cause for concern, for "the enormous increase in Soviet capabilities has added a new and critical dimension" to U.S.-Soviet relations. "The growth of Soviet power . . . could tempt Soviet leaders into bolder challenges" and "to underestimate the risks of certain policies." Moreover, "the number of Soviet strategic forces now exceeds the level needed for deterrence," creating "profound questions concerning the threats we will face in the future."[12]

In the spring of 1971, however, the strategic situation began to improve. The Jordanian crisis and the Cienfuegos affairs were resolved with a return to the status quo, and there were no new Third World crises on the horizon. On May 20, 1971, Washington and Moscow announced an agreement to pursue controls on offensive and defensive weapons. The two sides also agreed to a freeze on missile launchers and a prohibition on the conversion of light missile launchers to heavy missile launchers. Important issues remained to be settled, including limits on SLBMs, the duration of the ICBM freeze, and the definition of "heavy missiles," but the administration perceived a receding Soviet challenge. Shortly thereafter, apparently in response to the July announcement of President Nixon's plan to visit Beijing, Moscow made major concessions in the negotiations over the status of Berlin, leading to the September 3, 1971, agreement. Then, at the May 1972 U.S.-Soviet summit, Nixon and Brezhnev signed the historic SALT I agreement.

These changes in U.S.-Soviet relations elicited a positive U.S. security perspective. In August, Secretary of State William Rogers, observing the progress toward an agreement on Berlin, gave an optimistic appraisal of the arms-control talks and the prospects for long-term strategic stability.[13] In October and November, the president delivered upbeat speeches on the prospects for peace, asserting that "we have a greater opportunity to build a lasting peace than at any time in this century."[14] Nixon's 1972 State of the Union Address stressed the need for increased defense spending, yet reported that Washington and Moscow had reached a "historic agreement" over Berlin, and that "we have advanced the prospects for limiting strategic armaments." Nixon recognized disappointments, but asserted that there had "also been progress we can build on."[15] Most significant, his 1972 foreign policy report to Congress stood in sharp contrast to the previous two reports. While recognizing the continued challenges to U.S. security, Nixon declared that 1971 was a "watershed year" in U.S. foreign policy, with "changes . . . of historic scope and significance." In U.S.-Soviet relations, by the fall of 1971, there had been "signal progress," creating a "new momentum" in the relationship.[16] "The foundation has been laid for a new relationship" between the superpowers, Nixon went so far as to declare on his return from the Moscow summit in May 1972. "Now it is up to us to build a new house upon that foundation, one that can be a home for the hope of mankind and a shelter against the storms of conflict." The president was confident that "this was the year when America helped to lead the world out of the lowlands of constant war and onto the high plateau of lasting peace."[17]

This optimism continued to build at the start of Nixon's second term. "As we meet here today, we stand on the threshold of a new era of peace in the world," Nixon asserted in his second inaugural address; the previous year, he said, would "be remembered as the year of the greatest progress since the end of World War II toward a lasting peace in the world."[18] A few months later, he maintained that the momentum in U.S.-Soviet relations had carried the two sides "across a new threshold" toward a "more constructive" superpower relationship. Regarding the Vietnam War, Nixon declared that in reaching a peace agreement "we completed one of the most difficult chapters in our history."[19] The president was riding a wave of foreign policy successes that he expected to continue well into his second term.

Throughout this period of increasing optimism, the Nixon administration also witnessed encouraging developments in Sino-Soviet relations. Early in the administration, the White House recognized the intensity of Sino-Soviet conflict and the collapse of "monolithic communism." The administration's 1969 defense budget preparations reflected a shift from a two-and-a-half-war strategy to a one-and-a-half-war strategy. China no longer appeared as a likely source of war with the United States, and, as the Defense Department later explained, this shift depended "to a large extent on the assumption that the USSR and the PRC could not strike more or less simultaneously in Europe and in Asia, whether separately or in renewed cooperation."[20] The March 1969 Sino-Soviet border conflict and subsequent analysis indicating that the Soviet Union was preparing its forces for a major war with China strongly accentuated this perception. At a key meeting in San Clemente in August, Kissinger learned from Allen Whiting of the RAND Corporation of the immediate possibility of a Soviet conventional attack on China and the implications for U.S.-PRC rapprochement. By early 1970, Nixon could report to the cabinet that a key element in his China policy was "the recognition that now the communist world is split."[21]

Complementing these international developments were encouraging developments in the administration's domestic situation. By mid 1972, despite the ongoing war, reduced U.S. troop presence in Vietnam had significantly diminished domestic opposition to the war, and it was clear that Nixon would easily defeat Senator George McGovern in the November election. Indeed, Nixon's victory was the largest in U.S. presidential history, giving the administration heightened confidence to deal with international adversaries and allies alike at the start of its second term. Finally, the January 1973 Paris peace agreement removed the Vietnam albatross from the administration.

CHINA'S CHANGING VIEW OF THE UNITED STATES AND THE SOVIET UNION

Sino-Soviet conflict had been escalating since the late 1950s, when the two sides developed divergent policies toward the United States. The USSR's China policy thereafter increasingly reflected Moscow's interest in coercing Beijing to rejoin the Soviet bloc and accept Soviet foreign policy leadership. Chinese threat perception increased in the 1960s as the Soviet Union enhanced its deployments on the Sino-Soviet border. When the Soviet Union invaded Czechoslovakia in 1968 and issued the "Brezhnev Doctrine," maintaining Moscow's right to use force to compel socialist states to remain within the Soviet bloc, Beijing had reason to fear that it would be the next victim of Soviet "social-imperialism." In an apparent effort to underscore its will to resist Soviet power and thus deter massive Soviet use of force against China, Beijing initiated armed clashes along the border in early 1969. Although the war remained limited, Soviet suggestions of expanded war and nuclear retaliation further exacerbated Chinese threat perception through the summer.[22]

The border crisis gradually subsided after the September meeting in Beijing between Zhou Enlai and Soviet Premier Alexei Kosygin, but through the early 1970s, it was clear that Moscow and Beijing were making little progress toward resolving any of the conflicts between them. On the contrary, the military competition between the two sides continued as the Soviet Union deployed increasing numbers of troops along the Sino-Soviet border. Between 1969 and early 1973, the Soviet forces along the border more than doubled, increasing from 21 divisions to 45. In addition, there were reports of Sino-Soviet border skirmishes and casualties during this period.[23] The immediate threat of war might have diminished, but China faced a deteriorating military balance.

Sino-Soviet border and river navigation talks underscored the distrust between the two sides. The talks began shortly after the 1969 border crisis had subsided, but the discussions went nowhere, since neither side was prepared to compromise. Whereas the Soviet Union insisted on the continued force of border treaties signed by czarist Russia and dynastic China, China rejected these treaties as "unequal" and refused to drop its claims to the large expanse of territory it had ceded to Russia in the treaties.

The Soviet Union was also expanding its influence along the Chinese border in Asia. Just as Washington faced a deteriorating situation in Indochina, so too did Beijing. Since the mid 1960s, Beijing had been advising Hanoi to eschew Soviet military assistance and rely on guerrilla warfare, which placed a premium on the kind of weaponry China could provide—low-technology rifles and ammunition. Vietnam rejected China's advice, however, and increasingly shifted to positional warfare requiring advanced weaponry. Soon Moscow became Hanoi's primary military supplier, providing the North Vietnamese army with sophisticated anti-aircraft and anti-tank weaponry. The result was increased Soviet influence in Hanoi and a cooling in Sino-Vietnamese relations.[24] By 1969, when Chinese leaders recognized that the United States was preparing to withdraw from Indochina, and that a communist victory was a distinct possibility, it also became clear that Moscow and not Beijing would be the major beneficiary. Moreover, there was little Beijing could do to alter the course of the war, because Moscow had become Hanoi's major provider and Soviet leaders were intent on helping Hanoi produce a unified Vietnam under communist rule.

China's position in South Asia was similarly poor. As the Sino-Soviet dispute unfolded in the early 1960s, Moscow increasingly supported India in the Sino-Indian conflict, and China found in Pakistan a reliable security partner in South Asia. But after Indo-Pakistani conflict escalated in 1970–71 over domestic divisions between East and West Pakistan, Moscow and New Delhi signed the Soviet-Indian Treaty of Peace, Friendship, and Cooperation, which bolstered India's security vis-à-vis China and encouraged it to intervene militarily to dismember Pakistan and create Bangladesh.[25] Moscow had thus signed a security treaty with Beijing's neighbor and enemy, India, and contributed to the dissolution and weakening of Pakistan, Beijing's strategic asset in South Asia.

Progress in U.S.-Soviet relations further aroused PRC security concerns. Whereas U.S.-Soviet détente might contribute to stability in Europe, there was no stability in Asia. On the contrary, the Nixon Doctrine in essence called for U.S. retrenchment in the region, and Washington was rapidly withdrawing its troops from Indochina. Chinese leaders witnessed this dichotomy between Europe and Asia and feared that stability in Europe would present Moscow with an irresistible opportunity to expand in Asia. Thus, by early 1973, Mao and Zhou were concerned that in the aftermath of the war in Vietnam, the United States would no longer contain Soviet power in Asia. They suspected that in order to guarantee stability in Europe, the United States would be content to "push the ill waters of the Soviet Union . . . eastward."[26]

These fears were part of blanket Chinese opposition to U.S.-Soviet détente. Not only was the United States weakening its containment of Soviet power in Asia, but it was simultaneously improving relations with the Soviet Union, China's principal adversary. Whereas Washington observed intense Sino-Soviet confrontation, Beijing witnessed improving U.S.-Soviet relations. Indeed, Washington might well sacrifice Chinese interests in order to stabilize its developing relationship with the Soviet Union. Although China was trying to capitalize on U.S.-Soviet "contention," fear of "collusion" remained an active PRC concern, insofar as China was becoming the odd man out in the era of détente.

Beijing's strategic troubles were aggravated by its domestic circumstances, for it was still experiencing the consequences of Cultural Revolution diplomacy. Beijing's self-imposed isolation, reflected in its dangerous dual-adversary policy toward the Soviet Union and the United States, severely undermined Chinese security. With the exception of Albania and North Korea, China had few supporters to help offset the growing Soviet threat. The risks of isolation were especially clear during the 1969 Sino-Soviet border conflict, when Moscow indicated that should China fail to come to its senses, it might incur the tragedy of nuclear war.

The domestic aspects of the Cultural Revolution further exacerbated the Soviet threat. The most extreme period of the Cultural Revolution ended in early 1969. Nevertheless, through the early 1970s, Chinese society remained fragmented and convulsed in a succession of destructive campaigns, and intense political conflict continued unabated. The 1970–71 Lin Biao affair was particularly divisive. After Lin failed to displace Mao and then died in a plane crash in Mongolia trying to reach the Soviet Union, Mao purged Lin's allies and staffed the leadership with members of other competing factions. He also initiated a succession of destructive political campaigns.[27]

In these circumstances, Beijing could not quickly stabilize and develop its economy to compete militarily with the Soviet Union. Indeed while China was preoccupied with domestic politics, the Soviet Union strengthened its border forces. Moreover, China's domestic convulsions might have proved irresistible to Soviet opportunism. Chinese have long believed that their adversaries take advantage of domestic divisions to go to war against China.[28]

The combination of Soviet pressure and Chinese weakness so alarmed Beijing that after the 1969 Sino-Soviet border clashes, for the second time since the mid 1960s, it mobilized the population to move Chinese factories to interior provinces to reduce their vulnerability to a Soviet attack. Labeled the "third front" of Chinese industry, the scale of the move was tremendous. Mao also thought it unwise that China's central leadership was "concentrated in Beijing," and he ordered it "dispersed" around the country. Unable to compete with Moscow militarily or economically, Beijing mobilized its only readily available resource, its people, to prepare for war.[29]

The Soviet threat was clear; yet the search for an appropriate response further divided the Chinese leadership. In contrast to the clarity of the Soviet threat, the United States posed a more ambiguous challenge to Chinese interests. Following President Lyndon Johnson's 1968 announcement that he would not seek reelection, Chinese policy makers gradually recognized that Washington seriously sought a negotiated settlement to the Vietnam War to allow it to withdraw its forces from Vietnam. Then the Nixon Doctrine emphasized the new administration's realization that the United States was overextended in Asia, and that it would have to play a less active role throughout the region. The U.S. presence in Asia and its "encirclement" of China were fading.

Nevertheless, the war in Indochina was not yet over. On the contrary, under the Nixon administration, the United States escalated its bombing of North Vietnam and extended its activities into Laos and Cambodia. And the United States continued to occupy Taiwan and deploy forces in South Korea. Given the long period of U.S.-PRC conflict and consistent post-1949 U.S. efforts to weaken mainland China through its military deployments in Asia, there remained considerable basis for continued PRC suspicion of U.S. intentions and the possibility of a reassertion of Washington's traditional anti–Communist China policy. The United States might seem to be withdrawing from the Chinese periphery, but it was much too early confidently to predict the long-term trend in U.S. China policy.

Under such circumstances, throughout the 1969–71 period, Mao's lieutenants developed different assessments of China's strategic circumstances and different policy preferences. They disagreed over the extent of the U.S. threat to China and Beijing's corresponding policy options, and they engaged in competitive efforts to influence Chairman Mao's ultimate foreign policy preferences.[30]

Lin Biao, his supporters in the military, and the radical politicians associated with Jiang Qing, Mao's wife, argued that although the United States was a declining power and would inevitably suffer defeat in Vietnam, it remained inherently dangerous, if not more dangerous than the USSR, and would continue to pose a threat to China, as well as collude with Soviet "social imperialism" against China. They proposed that Beijing maintain its across-the-board opposition to U.S. foreign policy. Even as late as July 1971, after Kissinger had visited China and Beijing and Washington had announced the forthcoming Beijing summit, Lin Biao's ally General Huang Yongsheng warned of the dangers of underestimating the U.S. threat.[31]

In opposition to Lin Biao and Jiang Qing, Premier Zhou and his colleagues in the Foreign Ministry and some of China's most influential military leaders, including Marshals Chen Yi, Ye Jianying, and Nie Rongzhen, argued that China's international circumstances were changing and the time was right to pursue improved U.S.-PRC relations. They insisted that whereas the Soviet threat was increasingly serious and immediate, the United States was a declining power. They pointed out that rapid U.S. defeat in Indochina was inevitable, and that the United States was seriously weakened by domestic and international crises outside of Asia. They also maintained that while there might be collusion between the superpowers, there was also extensive contention, implying that there were opportunities for Chinese diplomacy toward the superpowers.[32]

Towering over this debate, with unparalleled foreign policy authority, stood Chairman Mao, China's preeminent leader. And it was clear where Mao stood on these issues; he was willing to explore the prospects of an improved relationship with the United States in order to offset Soviet power. Indeed, the emerging U.S.-PRC dialogue at the Warsaw talks and through the various back channels could not have otherwise taken place. A clear and very early signal of Mao's policy preferences was the republication in late 1968 of a 1949 speech of his advocating negotiations with adversaries. Moreover, on October 1, 1970, Mao asked Zhou to invite Edgar Snow, the long-time American friend of the Chinese Communist Party, to stand on the podium to observe China's National Day parade, and Zhou then personally managed the doctoring of the photo of Mao and Snow to ensure that it gave prominence to them, and saw to it that *Renmin ribao* printed it on the front page. Shortly thereafter, Mao told Snow that he would welcome an official visit to China from President Nixon. Mao was informing both the United States and China's foreign policy moderates that he was firmly behind Zhou's argument that negotiations with the United States were both feasible and potentially beneficial.[33]

Chairman Mao and other influential Chinese leaders thus sharply distinguished between the Soviet and U.S. threats to China. By 1972, their contrasting appraisal of the superpowers was broadcast to the entire world. The joint *Renmin ribao, Red Flag,* and *Liberation Army Daily* National Day editorial held that despite its "clamors for 'peace,' " the Soviet Union was more dangerous than the United States. In his speech to the UN General Assembly in late October, Foreign Minister Qiao Guanhua warned that the superpowers were using the subterfuge of European détente in order to divide the world between themselves. But he also suggested that Moscow's real purpose in pursuing détente was to be able to occupy its allies with impunity.[34] The danger for China was clear—détente might well be the cover for a Soviet attempt to pressure China to end its opposition to Soviet foreign policy, and the U.S. interest in continued stability might deter Washington from offsetting the Soviet threat.

Despite the debate within China, senior policy makers in both the United States and China thus shared a common perception of a growing Soviet threat. Nonetheless, whereas by mid 1971, Washington had reached a preliminary arms-control agreement with Moscow, and tension between the superpowers continued to decline through 1973, China remained locked in its extreme adversarial relationship with the Soviet Union. While both "collusion" and "contention" marked relations between the United States and the USSR, there was only "contention" between the USSR and China.[35]

U.S.-PRC Bargaining: From Uncertainty to Cooperation

Chinese and American leaders faced a number of significant foreign policy problems arising from the Soviet threat, while perceiving each other as decreasingly menacing. They thus turned to each other in order to resolve their respective policy dilemmas.

But before relations could improve, suspicions had to be allayed and common expectations had to be established. Beijing and Washington therefore spent 1969–71 signaling their respective policies and intentions. Kissinger's secret July 1971 visit to Beijing confirmed the foundation for a U.S.-PRC summit, leading to the Shanghai communiqué and the establishment of liaison offices.

THE INITIAL BREAKTHROUGH

In the context of Washington's strategic circumstances, Nixon and Kissinger reconsidered America's China policy. Nixon had recognized the importance of ending the hostility between the United States and China as early as 1967. At this early date, he focused on the importance of ending Chinese isolation to promote the interests of the "world community." Almost immediately after his election victory, he stressed to Kissinger that upon assuming the presidency, he would move to change U.S. China policy, and during the first days of the administration, he instructed Kissinger to look into the possibility of rapprochement between the United States and China. Shortly thereafter, Kissinger ordered the preparation of NSSM-14, an interagency study of the policy of the United States toward China and potential alternative policy directions.[36]

Although Kissinger came to understand the importance of China later than Nixon, as early as mid 1968, he perceived a strategic benefit in easing the hostility between the United States and China. He thereupon began to develop his "triangular politics" understanding of China's strategic importance in U.S. foreign policy. By February 1969, Kissinger believed that by aligning itself with China, the United States could restrain Soviet expansionism. After the first stages of the Sino-Soviet border hostilities, the advantages of triangular diplomacy became even more apparent—improved U.S.-PRC relations would "evoke" security fears in the USSR about its eastern border and ease Soviet pressures on Western Europe. At the diplomatic level, Kissinger advised Nixon that Washington could use Soviet fears of U.S.-China cooperation to its advantage in dealing with Moscow. Improved relations between the United States and China would give Moscow a "stake in better relations" with the United States too.[37] Consequently, the Nixon administration approached China as a strategic asset that would assist it in containing Soviet power.

While the Nixon administration was reevaluating the policy of the United States toward China, the Chinese leadership was also reconsidering its U.S. policy. In early 1969, in response to suggestions of changes in U.S. policy toward China, Premier Zhou Enlai directed stepped-up study in the Chinese Foreign Ministry of the trend in U.S. policy and of the opportunities for China to make contacts with the United States.[38] Paralleling developments in Washington, Zhou's efforts to reorient Chinese policy picked up momentum after China's border clashes with the Soviet Union. Sensing that Chinese "security was subjected to direct Soviet threat," Beijing was "willing to change the situation of long-term U.S.-PRC antagonism."[39]

Indeed, Premier Zhou was not alone in suggesting that China improve relations with the United States to offset the Soviet threat.[40] In early March 1969, just as Sino-Soviet border hostilities were beginning, Mao Zedong instructed four senior Chinese marshals— Chen Yi, Ye Jianying, Xu Xiangqian, and Nie Rongzhen—to study the "intensely complicated" international situation and prepare reports for him. Through October 18, the marshals met 23 times and, in accordance with Mao's instructions, received a steady stream of documents from Premier Zhou. On July 11 they submitted their first report to Zhou. Unlike the radical-inspired April 1969 Ninth Party Congress, which in its confidential conclusions had stressed superpower collusion against China, the marshals concluded that the Soviet Union posed a far greater threat to Chinese security than the United States and they emphasized the importance of competition between the superpowers. Regarding the Soviet threat, they argued that Moscow took China as its primary enemy, created tension along the border, launched armed attacks into Chinese territory, and sought support in Asia for encirclement of China. The report concluded that these steps were part of Moscow's effort to prepare to launch a war against China.

The Sino-Soviet border conflict continued to escalate into the fall. In their September 17 report, the marshals concluded that Moscow "truly has plans to start an aggressive war against China." In the context of Soviet hints of a nuclear attack, some leaders believed that Kosygin's visit to Beijing was a mere ploy designed to mask Soviet war plans. Although the report concluded that war would probably not occur, it also argued that Moscow's decision "to a large degree depends on the posture of the United States." Fortunately, Soviet leaders were concerned about the prospects for U.S.-China cooperation and Kosygin's visit had alarmed Washington, prompting Nixon to seek contacts with the Chinese leadership. There were thus opportunities for Beijing to exploit U.S.-Soviet contention for China's "strategic benefit." Finally, at Chen Yi's insistence, the report concluded that China should resume the ambassadorial-level talks with the United States. It was sent to Mao, and its conclusions were accepted by the Party leadership.

These conclusions promoted China's first steps toward opening a dialogue with the United States. Moreover, Chen Yi held additional "unconventional" ideas. He argued that given the border situation, Chinese diplomacy simply could not "attempt nothing and accomplish nothing." Harmonizing with the thinking of U.S. policy makers, Chen suggested that the United States and China should resume the Warsaw talks and then elevate the discussions to at least the ministerial level. Only ministerial talks would be the strategic act that China required to deal with the Soviet threat. He thought that Washington would welcome the idea and that China should not pose any preconditions. As for Taiwan, the two sides should resolve this issue step by step, while consulting on strategic issues. Chen said that he would personally offer these ideas to Premier Zhou.[41]

Leaders in China and the United States were thus simultaneously revaluating U.S.-PRC relations. The first signal of an interest in better relations came from Beijing. As early as November 1968, shortly after Nixon had won the presidential election, a Chinese Foreign Ministry statement called for an "agreement on the Five Principles of Peaceful Coexistence," an extraordinary proposal for relations with the new "imperialist" American administration.[42] In the aftermath of the Soviet invasion of Czechoslovakia and before the Sino-

Soviet border clashes, China indicated an interest in ameliorated U.S.-PRC tension.

Although Nixon and Kissinger missed this early signal, they soon began their own signaling. The administration's initial policy consisted of unilateral acts not requiring the PRC to reciprocate, eliminating the necessity for endless negotiations at Warsaw, which might ultimately have bogged down in fruitless haggling and merely confirmed original PRC conceptions of U.S. animosity. Ultimately, a succession of friendly gestures might persuade Chinese policy makers that Washington's China policy had changed.[43] In the first months of 1969, the U.S. media reported that the administration was reconsidering U.S. restrictions on trade with China. The White House accompanied these signals with attempts to communicate to Beijing Washington's interest in opening a dialogue between Chinese and U.S. officials. In early 1969, Washington asked the French ambassador to Beijing to convey to Chinese leaders the administration's desire for improved relations. Similarly, the administration's relatively mild response to North Korea's shooting down of an unarmed EC-121 reconnaissance plane in April reflected Nixon's objective of signaling China that his intentions were not hostile. Then, in late May, Secretary of State Rogers visited Pakistan and asked for President Yayha Kahn's help in establishing contact with China. Chinese sources report that Yayha Kahn told Chinese leaders that Washington had asked him to relate that the United States favored neither Soviet efforts to establish an Asian collective security system nor Chinese isolation. Rather, the United States sought a dialogue with Chinese leaders.[44]

Nixon's China policy was beginning to take shape. Then, when the Sino-Soviet border conflict escalated during the summer, and Moscow sought to prevent the United States and its allies from expanding contacts with Beijing, the administration redoubled its efforts to establish contact with Chinese leaders. On July 3, Kissinger commissioned NSSM-63 on Sino-Soviet relations. And in late August, the administration learned that Soviet soldiers were training for a large-scale conventional attack on Chinese territory, adding credibility to Soviet media warnings. In this context, the State Department announced eased restrictions on trade with China.[45]

Although a Sino-Soviet war would pose great danger, the administration also recognized it as an opportunity for U.S.-China rapprochement, insofar as Beijing would be more responsive to U.S. overtures. In early August in Canberra, Rogers recalled America's "historic friendship" with the Chinese people and declared that

Washington was "seeking to open up channels of communication" with China. Then, just as the border tension was peaking in September, Under Secretary of State Elliot Richardson declared that Washington believed that improved relations with China were "in our own national interest," and that the United States "could not fail to be deeply concerned with the escalation of the quarrel into a massive breach of international peace and security," clearly signaling that Washington would not collude with Moscow against China. One month later, Kissinger used the Pakistan channel to communicate to Beijing the administration's decision to cease destroyer patrols of the Taiwan Strait. To be sure China got the message, the decision was also leaked to PRC officials through Hong Kong in November. Finally, toward the end of the year the administration lifted additional trade restrictions.[46]

Chinese leaders received and acknowledged U.S. signaling, including Rogers's Canberra speech and the statements disassociating the United States from Soviet border policy. In particular, in December, Beijing responded to the ending of U.S. patrolling of the Taiwan Strait by releasing two U.S. citizens who had strayed into Chinese waters in February and then asked Yahya Kahn to convey to Washington the importance of this gesture. Nonetheless, Beijing remained noncommittal, and Yahya Kahn suggested that the United States offer something more concrete to elicit a positive PRC response. Finally, on December 3, after nearly three months of trying, Ambassador Walter Stoessel established contact in Warsaw with PRC Ambassador Lei Yang. Less than one week later, in accordance with the recommendation of the Chinese marshals, Lei invited Stoessel to the PRC embassy.[47]

China had responded to U.S. initiatives. Nevertheless, Lei's invitation to Stoessel was relatively meaningless, for the ambassadorial-level talks had been taking place in Warsaw for over ten years. The White House, therefore, instructed Stoessel to inform Lei at the January talks that Washington was prepared to send an emissary to Beijing, overruling the State Department, which, unaware of the back-channel signaling, argued that ambassadorial-level talks would pose less risk should the initiative fail. Beyond this, however, the White House accepted State Department suggestions, including the all-important formulation regarding Taiwan, which Stoessel read to Lei, declaring that it was the hope of the United States "that as peace and stability in Asia grow, we can reduce those facilities on Taiwan that we now have." At the second Warsaw meeting in February, the administration strengthened Stoessel's statement, instructing him to report Washington's "*intention* to reduce those *military* facilities which we now have on Taiwan as tension in the area diminishes," language that later appeared almost word for word in the Shanghai communiqué.[48] This statement on U.S. troop reductions achieved three objectives. It was an early concession to China's demand for U.S. troop withdrawal from Taiwan, thus offering Beijing a tangible benefit from improved relations. It also contributed to White House efforts to redefine PRC perceptions of the United States. And it created an incentive for China to help end the war in Vietnam and thereby create the "peace and stability in Asia" that would allow the withdrawal to occur.[49]

China responded positively to the U.S. initiative. In January, it stressed its willingness to discuss "any idea or suggestion" presented by the United States "on the basis of the five principles of peaceful coexistence," reaffirming its interest in easing tension. In the February meeting, despite objections from State Department officials, Washington reaffirmed its interest in a high-level meeting, as well as strengthened its commitment to troop reductions in Asia. For its part, Beijing accepted the U.S. proposal to send an emissary to Beijing "to further probe the fundamental and principal issues" in U.S.-China relations.[50] The two sides had thus taken significant steps to assure themselves that a meeting in Beijing would be productive, and on that basis had made tentative moves to arrange such a meeting.

Shortly thereafter, the U.S. incursion into Cambodia halted progress. Thus far, unilateral U.S. concessions had reinforced the thinking of Chairman Mao and the arguments of moderate Chinese politicians, led by Premier Zhou, that U.S. policy allowed for U.S.-China cooperation against the Soviet threat. But the U.S. invasion of Cambodia in the spring of 1970 played into the hands of Lin Biao and other Chinese hard-liners who had been contending that even in decline, the United States was dangerous. The invasion thus compelled Zhou and his colleagues temporarily to mute their support for rapprochement. More important, the invasion aroused Mao's personal ire, for Washington seemed to be taking his interest in improved relations for granted and disregarding Chinese interests just when he had sanctioned sensitive negotiations with U.S. "imperialists." Under these circumstances, Beijing canceled the ambassadorial-level talks at Warsaw scheduled for May 20, and Mao wrote a blistering article condemning U.S. imperialism.[51]

Although Kissinger asserts that Washington had called China's bluff, insofar as it expanded the war into Cambodia without eliciting Chinese retaliation, the historical record suggests otherwise. True, on July 10 Beijing announced the release of Bishop James Walsh, who had been sentenced to twenty years' imprisonment in 1960. But, as Chinese historians correctly assert, Beijing had waited until the United States fully withdrew from Cambodia in June and initiated renewed contacts before it signaled its readiness to resume back-channel negotiations. Mao had put Washington on notice that U.S.-China rapprochement was premised on the winding down of U.S. fighting in Indochina.[52]

Once China released Bishop Walsh, Washington granted permission to General Motors to sell diesel engines to China and then eased restrictions on refueling of ships trading with China. Shortly thereafter, in a banquet speech honoring Romanian President Nicolae Ceauşescu, Nixon used the name People's Republic of China, the first time an American president had ever done so.[53]

Following these moves, Washington once again used the Pakistani channel in an effort to arrange a U.S.-China meeting. On October 25, Nixon asked Yahya Kahn to relay to Zhou Enlai that he considered rapprochement "essential," and that the United States was willing to send a high-level emissary to Beijing. Finally, on December 9, Washington received Zhou's mid-November reply that a presidential envoy would be "most welcomed" in Beijing. Then, in January 1971, Zhou indicated that President Nixon would also be welcomed in China.[54]

Having received these momentous Chinese messages, subsequent moves primarily reinforced the earlier signals of each side's goodwill. For its part, the United States lifted restrictions on travel to China. On China's side, Zhou put the idea of inviting a U.S. national ping-pong team to Beijing to Mao, while simultaneously recommending against doing so, thus protecting himself should Mao consider the proposal "capitulationist." But Mao liked the idea, and U.S.-PRC "ping-pong diplomacy" was thus initiated. These U.S. and Chinese steps reinforced each side's commitment to a high-level meeting and to the success of that meeting. Moreover, for China, the publicity surrounding its invitation to the U.S. ping-pong team to visit Beijing contributed to its immediate effort to use suggestions of U.S.-PRC rapprochement to curb the USSR's anti-China policy.[55]

More substantial negotiations were required to establish the focus and agenda of Kissinger's meetings in Beijing. Thus far, China's various messages emphasized that the intention of the Kissinger's visit was to discuss a U.S.-PRC summit, at which the two sides would discuss the withdrawal of U.S. troops from Taiwan so that they could resolve the Taiwan issue. The United States could not, however, allow China to dominate the agenda with demands for U.S. concessions on Taiwan. Additional negotiations were required before the two sides could reach final agreement. Thus, Nixon's May letter to Zhou, delivered through Pakistani channels, stressed that Kissinger would negotiate a presidential visit to Beijing so that each side could "raise the issue of principal concern to it."[56]

Ultimately, China compromised to move the negotiations forward. Zhou's subsequent message not only welcomed a meeting between Nixon and Mao in Beijing and a preliminary visit by Kissinger to make the "necessary arrangements," it also accepted Washington's formulation that each side could raise "the issue of principal concern to it." Equally significant, Zhou did not press for discussions on normalization; China was prepared to develop relations without focusing on the difficult issues associated with Taiwan. The two sides had reached agreement concerning the agenda of Kissinger's talks in Beijing, the last political obstacle to his secret visit.[57]

KISSINGER'S 1971 VISITS TO BEIJING

Meanwhile, by mid 1971, U.S.-Soviet relations were beginning to improve. In early spring, the Middle East and Cienfuegos crises had been resolved and the Kissinger-Gromyko back-channel arms-control talks had culminated in the May 20 agreement. By early fall, there was an agreement that there would be parallel negotiations on offensive and defensive arms, leading to simultaneous agreements. In the spring, the two sides were also coming together on the outline of a Berlin agreement, the final obstacles being overcome following Kissinger's July visit to Beijing and the announcement of the U.S.-China summit. The Berlin agreement was signed shortly thereafter in September. Similarly, Moscow first revealed an interest in an early U.S.-Soviet summit following the U.S.-China summit announcement, leading to the October 12 announcement of a May 1972 Moscow summit.[58] China was keenly aware of the progress in U.S.-Soviet relations. Kissinger had been keeping Beijing informed through secret talks in Paris with Ambassador Huang Zhen.[59]

The numerous challenges to U.S. foreign policy were thus just beginning to recede in July 1971 when Premier Zhou Enlai met with Kissinger in Beijing to open a new relationship and engage in crucial negotiations over the forthcoming Beijing summit. Indeed, as Kissinger later pointed out, the U.S.-Soviet agreement of May 20, 1971, strengthened Washington's negotiating position vis-à-vis China.[60]

Washington's diplomatic position had improved since U.S.-China signaling first began in 1969, while Beijing and Moscow had yet to move beyond media polemics.

It was in this context that the Chinese politburo met on May 26, 1971, to discuss China's policy toward the United States, preparations for Kissinger's approaching visit to Beijing, and the prospects for a U.S.-China summit. The meeting laid out China's basic policy toward the United States and normalization of relations, including various principles that would govern China's position in the negotiations. The key issue concerned U.S. troops on Taiwan. In order to agree to normalization of relations, the United States would have to commit to removing all U.S. forces from Taiwan and the Taiwan Strait region within a specified period. The politburo insisted that this was the "crux issue" of normalization, and that should Kissinger not agree to this, normalization would not be possible and the Nixon visit would "possibly" be postponed. The politburo also insisted that normalization required U.S. recognition that Taiwan was "the territory of China" and that Washington "must acknowledge that the People's Republic of China is the only legitimate government of China."[61]

While laying out China's preconditions for normalization and the Nixon visit in optimum terms, Chinese leaders were nonetheless prepared to accept partial success in order to establish a dialogue with the United States. The Nixon visit would "possibly" be delayed if the United States would not commit to full troop withdrawal from Taiwan within a specified period. Similarly, the conditions for normalization were not conditions for opening a dialogue. The politburo was prepared to wait to normalize relations with the United States. Chinese leaders understood that American leaders were constrained by domestic politics, and that Nixon might well encounter opposition to his China policy, and they wanted to move ahead.[62]

China was thus prepared to be flexible; it would not raise preconditions to opening a dialogue. Nonetheless, Beijing was aware of the strategic difficulties faced by the United States, and it saw opportunities to extract U.S. concessions. The politburo understood that Nixon needed a successful outcome of the negotiations to bolster his presidential campaign, and that this put pressure on Kissinger to reach an agreement. Similarly, just days before Kissinger's arrival in Beijing, Zhou read Nixon's July 6 speech on the decline of American power, the emergence of five power centers, and the importance of ending Chinese isolation. Zhou concluded that Washington had to reconsider its global deployments, particularly its involvement in the Vietnam War, which required ending its "passive position" and developing relations with the PRC. Washington had no choice but to "engage with China."[63]

When Kissinger secretly flew to Beijing from Pakistan in July 1971, the first order of business was to reaffirm this strategic basis for rapprochement. Zhou and Kissinger conducted a comprehensive "review of the world" discussion. Kissinger assured Zhou of common U.S.-China interests by discussing U.S. concern about Soviet foreign policy and assuring Beijing that Washington would inform Chinese leaders of any U.S.-Soviet discussions that might affect Chinese interests. Zhou emphasized the importance of resisting Soviet expansionism.[64]

With both sides assured of the strategic basis for improved relations, the discussions turned to the presidential visit to China and the Taiwan issue. The bargaining was severely constrained by the forty-eight hours available to reach an agreement. The U.S. side was acutely aware that the journalists who remained behind in Pakistan waiting for Kissinger to continue with his activities could be kept at bay only so long before they would become suspicious of Kissinger's alleged stomach flu and begin to wonder about his actual whereabouts. Equally important, Kissinger's schedule called for official meetings in Europe after his departure from Pakistan. In order to make these appointments, Kissinger's plane had to leave Pakistan sufficiently early to land at the Teheran airport before going on to Europe. Should Kissinger's departure from China be delayed, the Teheran airport would be closed, and the delegation would have to wait until the next day to leave Pakistan for Europe, forcing the cancellation of Kissinger's European appointments.

The U.S. delegation was acutely aware of the pressure the "window over Teheran" placed on the negotiations, and Kissinger was under great stress to bring home an agreement without making significant concessions. In an informal discussion in the gardens of Beijing, Kissinger and his aides discussed the influence of the deadline on Chinese and U.S. negotiating positions. The consensus was that both sides were under equal pressure; Nixon needed a successful outcome for domestic reasons, and both sides needed a presidential visit to cement the relationship and bolster their respective diplomacy toward the Soviet Union. Neither side could risk failure.[65]

Kissinger's negotiating posture reveals the importance he attached to China's strategic value in U.S. security policy; at this early stage in relations, he offered important concessions to China's position on normalization to ensure an agreement on a Beijing summit. First, he did not state that the "position of Taiwan is yet to be determined," the language of earlier administrations, which had suggested possible U.S. support for Taiwan's independence. Rather, Chinese sources report that he explicitly denied U.S. support for Taiwan's independence and expressed recognition that Taiwan belonged to China. Second, Kissinger indicated that "the issue of recognition of the PRC as China's sole legal government," and thus severance of relations between the United States and Taiwan, would be addressed within the first two years of Nixon's second term. During this very first meeting of U.S. and PRC diplomats, Kissinger held out the prospect that after Nixon's reelection, Washington would normalize relations on the basis of Beijing's "one-China" condition.[66]

Yet Kissinger also presented a key U.S. condition. He expressed U.S. interest in seeing the Taiwan issue "resolved peacefully."[67] Kissinger thus laid out early a central U.S. demand, which would remain a major tenet of the U.S. position through the Reagan administration. Zhou Enlai made equally important policy statements, laying out China's early three conditions for normalization. Following the decisions of the politburo, Zhou insisted that the United States recognize that Taiwan was a Chinese province, withdraw all of its troops from Taiwan within a specified period, and abrogate its Mutual Defense Treaty with Taiwan.[68]

But these issues concerned normalization of relations, which would only be resolved in later years. The immediate issue on the agenda was Beijing's effort to link a U.S.-PRC summit to U.S. concessions on troop withdrawal from Taiwan. At Warsaw, the United States had already agreed to withdraw its troops from Taiwan in the event of reduced tension in Asia, but China continued to demand unconditional and rapid U.S. withdrawal. Beijing, as it had in its back-channel messages, insisted that the communiqué announcing the summit state that Nixon would be visiting Beijing to discuss U.S. withdrawal from Taiwan as a prelude to normalization. When Kissinger rejected this wording, Foreign Minister Huang Hua returned with a draft communiqué that mentioned neither normalization nor earlier U.S. statements tacitly linking withdrawal from Taiwan to the course of the war in Vietnam.[69]

China also could not risk failure. It agreed to the summit without resolution of the issue of U.S. troop withdrawal, deferring the issue until the negotiations over the summit communiqué. The issue was no longer whether there would be a summit, but how successful it would be. The absence of any progress in Sino-Soviet discussions, and Beijing's interest in using the United States to offset Soviet power, persuaded it to defer the difficult issues and thus minimize the tension in relations. Beijing might eventually have to compromise, but its situation might well improve before the issue was next broached.

The one other important item on the U.S. agenda was the war in Indochina. In addition to the global basis for pursuing a better relationship with China, Kissinger also sought Beijing's help in persuading Hanoi to expedite the peace process. Indeed, the United States tried to link China's interest in resolving the Taiwan issue with American interest in ending the Vietnam War. Kissinger informed Zhou that Washington was prepared to withdraw two-thirds of its troops from Taiwan within a short period after the end of the war in Vietnam, elaborating on the U.S. statements presented at Warsaw. Although Zhou tacitly suggested his sympathy for and interest in U.S. efforts to avoid a humiliating defeat in Indochina, Chinese leaders would not pressure Vietnam to alter its negotiating position, and they turned aside Kissinger's request that they influence Hanoi to change its policy on prisoners of war.[70]

The two sides thus laid out their respective positions on Taiwan, establishing certain policies that would provide a basis for future U.S.-PRC discussion of Taiwan, and that would have to be addressed if normalization were to take place. But the Kissinger visit merely delayed the resolution of many of the tough issues that would have to be addressed in the U.S.-PRC communiqué at the conclusion of the Beijing summit.

In August, shortly after Kissinger returned to the United States, Nixon set the stage for continued tough negotiations when he insisted that there would not be "instant" U.S.-PRC détente, that neither side had any "illusions about the wide differences" between them, and that "our interests are very different." Thus, "we do not expect that these talks will settle all these differences."[71]

Kissinger next visited Beijing in October and spent fifteen hours negotiating with Zhou Enlai over the summit communiqué. The situation had changed since February, for now the important issues concerning Taiwan had to be addressed if the crucial preparations required for a successful summit were not to be left to the last moment. Once again, China initially adopted a rigid position.[72] On October 22, Kissinger presented a draft communiqué. The next day, Zhou indicated that the draft could serve as a basis for negotiations. But he was overruled by Mao. The following morning, Zhou, speaking on behalf of the Chairman, rejected the draft in its entirety and insisted that the United States renounce its ties with Taiwan. Kissinger rejected the demand and suggested that he was prepared to leave without an agreement, warning that it would be unwise to leave serious negotiations until the presidential visit.

After a short recess, Zhou returned with a proposal prepared by Xiong Xianghui under the direction of Mao and himself. The proposal allowed each side to present its respective views in separate statements. It was a novel approach, but it obviated the need for extensive negotiations between countries with radically different social systems and perspectives on Third World issues. After much protest, Kissinger accepted the approach, and the structure of the Shanghai communiqué was established. Nonetheless, compromise was still necessary; common understanding had to be established on the Taiwan issue if the summit were to be a success.

The next morning, on October 25, Kissinger and Zhou opened the negotiations using a U.S. counterproposal. The most complicated issue was the relationship between Taiwan and the mainland, and the two sides spent the next twenty-four hours focusing on this question, interrupted only by Zhou's consultations with Mao and by translation sessions. Although Kissinger had suggested in July that the United States would comply with China's "one-China" demand in Nixon's second term, Beijing now sought public U.S. recognition that Taiwan was part of China. The United States, however, sought to maximize its public options regarding U.S.-Taiwan relations and refused to commit to this position. After repeated failure to find common ground, late that night, Kissinger unearthed a State Department formula originally prepared for the canceled May 1970 Warsaw talks. On this basis, at 8:10 A.M. on October 26, after a 24-hour session, and 50 minutes before Kissinger was scheduled to leave for the airport, the two sides reached agreement on the common language that later appeared in the Shanghai communiqué:

> The United States acknowledges that all Chinese on either side of the Taiwan Straits maintain there is but one China and that Taiwan is part of China. The United States Government does not challenge that position.[73]

The success of the formula lies in its ambiguity. But it is important to recognize that the ambiguity served the United States rather than China. Not only did Washington avoid taking a public position on which government was the government of China, but the wording that the United States "acknowledges" and "does not challenge" did not imply U.S. acceptance of the Chinese position that Taiwan was part of China. Rather, despite Kissinger's confidential assurances to Zhou regarding U.S. opposition to an independent Taiwan in July 1971, in the English-language version of the communiqué, the United States did not express a position on whether or not there was but one China or whether Taiwan was part of China. In order to secure a significant communiqué, Beijing was compelled to modify its objective of gaining unqualified U.S. support for its position that Taiwan was part of China.[74]

It was also during this meeting that the United States first raised its demand for explicit linkage between U.S. troop withdrawal from Taiwan with a U.S. expression of its expectation of a peaceful resolution of the Taiwan issue. China objected to the linkage.[75] Moreover, it wanted Washington to commit to when it would complete total military withdrawal from Taiwan. Hence, these crucial issues remained unresolved when Kissinger left Beijing.

THE UNITED NATIONS AND THE INDO-PAKISTANI
WAR INTERLUDES

Just as Kissinger and Zhou were negotiating the Nixon visit to China, the U.N. General Assembly addressed the issue of Chinese representation. The U.S. position on PRC representation at the United Nations was thus intimately connected with the process of rapprochement.

The contradiction between Washington's desire for improved U.S.-PRC relations and its position that Beijing did not belong in the United Nations was readily apparent to both the State Department and other U.N. member nations by mid 1971. A State Department staff study completed in May 1971 concluded that without a change in U.S. policy, the U.N. General Assembly would simply oust Taiwan in 1971 and vote for PRC admission to the United Nations. Hence, in mid July, after Kissinger returned from Beijing, where he had learned that U.N. representation was not a major issue to Chinese leaders, the National Security Council organized a task force to press for dual Chinese representation in the United Nations.[76]

Many State Department officials believed that the time had come to accept PRC representation, but they nonetheless made intensive efforts to gain acceptance for dual representation and believed that there was a good chance of achieving passage in the General Assembly. Although there was no guarantee that dual representation would be a lasting solution, U.S. officials believed that the worst that could happen was that dual representation would be overturned in subsequent years. Moreover, after Kissinger's surprise visit to Beijing, the United States assured Taiwan that it would fight to keep it in the United Nations. For this reason alone, Secretary of State Rogers believed, it was important to push for dual representation.[77] As it turned out, the United States failed to gain dual representation by only four votes, and China replaced Taiwan both in the General Assembly and on the Security Council.

In the midst of last-minute lobbying at the United Nations in October, Kissinger visited Beijing to make preparations for the upcoming summit. Evident U.S. cooperation with Beijing undermined U.S. lobbying efforts at the United Nations, making it more difficult for U.S. diplomats to secure the votes for dual representation. Moreover, the U.S. task force at the United Nations received negotiating orders that decreased the possibility of success. It was prevented from canvassing other U.N. delegations until August 1, and from conceding PRC membership in the Security Council until approximately September 1. Had the NSC immediately given the task force the additional time to lobby wavering delegates, rather than delaying until it received Beijing's assurances that the issue would not disrupt U.S.-PRC relations, and had the NSC provided the task force with more flexible negotiating instructions, it would have been easier for the United States to win additional votes. U.S. Ambassador to the United Nations George Bush believed that the timing of Kissinger's visit changed the votes of a number of countries.[78]

In early September, Kissinger had asked for and received from the State Department an accurate estimate of when the General Assembly vote would occur; the announcement of his forthcoming visit and his visit to Beijing occurred precisely during that period, even though Secretary of State Rogers correctly and "strenuously" argued against the visit, because it would interfere with U.S. diplomacy at the United Nations. Kissinger himself acknowledges that he would have preferred to accept outright expulsion of Taiwan rather than trying for dual representation.[79]

Conceivably, despite full knowledge of developments at the United Nations and the advice of the secretary of state, Kissinger may simply have mismanaged the meshing of U.S. policy toward the PRC with U.S. efforts to achieve dual representation, as he himself suggests. More likely, however, he cleverly used the State Department to provide political protection for his maneuver to secure the PRC membership in the United Nations and the ouster of Taiwan, removing an obstacle to improved U.S.-PRC relations. Given his reputation for complex planning and his commitment to U.S.-PRC rapprochement, this explanation is at least as plausible as simple mismanagement.

No sooner had the administration put the UN issue behind it than war broke out between Pakistan and India. The external powers involved in the South Asia crisis were primarily the United States and the USSR, insofar as a U.S. ally, Pakistan, was engaged in conflict with a Soviet ally, India, and the United States suggested that it might become engaged in the war in order to maintain the integrity of western Pakistan. Nonetheless, as noted above, China had vital interests at stake in the Indo-Pakistani war. Pakistan was also an ally of China's, and it had been attacked by India, China's adversary in South Asia and the Soviet Union's ally. Moscow was significantly expanding its influence on the Chinese border.

Kissinger argues that Soviet involvement in the Indo-Pakistani war threatened to disrupt U.S.-PRC rapprochement by questioning U.S. strategic will, undermining the strategic value of détente with the United States to China, and thus China's interest in rapprochement. In this manner, Kissinger justifies the U.S. "tilt" toward Pakistan and the dispatch of a U.S. carrier task force to the Bay of Bengal, arguing that White House passivity would have led to the expansion of the war to West Pakistan and the destruction of Pakistan as an independent power. Under such circumstances, U.S.-PRC rapprochement would unravel, for Beijing's strategic interest in better relations with Washington would have vanished.[80]

Kissinger misstates the importance of U.S. involvement in the conflict to U.S.-PRC rapprochement. The most crucial stage in the rapprochement was Kissinger's July 1971 visit and the ensuing Chinese public invitation to Nixon. Regardless of the outcome of the conflict, American power would make a valuable contribution to Chinese security, and Nixon would travel to China. Moreover, given Beijing's implacable hostility toward the Soviet Union and the deep-seated conflict between the two countries, it was highly unlikely that U.S. passivity in response to the Soviet initiative in South Asia would have compelled Beijing to choose to ameliorate the Sino-Soviet conflict rather than try to contend with Soviet power on the basis of U.S.-PRC rapprochement.

Nevertheless, Washington's response to the crisis did influence bilateral U.S.-PRC relations. Soviet-Indian military cooperation against Pakistan, regardless of Pakistani provocation and the merits of Indian behavior, challenged a U.S. treaty commitment in Asia. Throughout Asia, the U.S. response would be evaluated in terms of American ability to contend with Soviet power in the context of the Nixon Doctrine and Washington's impending withdrawal from Indochina. The administration's assertion of U.S. power in Asia underscored American readiness to contend *unilaterally* with Soviet power. According to Pakistani President Zulfikar Ali Bhutto, Zhou Enlai confirmed that Chinese leaders believed India would have escalated the war in West Pakistan if Washington had not raised the stakes of the war and demanded India cease hostilities.[81] Thus, U.S. policy underscored both U.S. confidence in dealing with the Soviet Union and Chinese strategic dependence on improved U.S.-PRC relations, contributing to Washington's leverage as Nixon arrived in Beijing for the U.S.-PRC summit.

THE BEIJING SUMMIT AND THE SHANGHAI COMMUNIQUÉ

The United States and China were close to agreement on the joint communiqué, with the remaining important differences being left for the February summit. Once again, Nixon set the stage for tough bargaining. In an interview with the television journalist Dan Rather, he said there would be "tough, hard bargaining between people who have very great differences."[82] Nevertheless, he continued to signal U.S. goodwill. Prior to the summit, the administration approved the export to China of RCA receiving stations for commercial communication satellites. This equipment would be brought to China for the president's visit and remain there after he left. Washington also withdrew its nuclear-capable bombers from Taiwan just prior to Nixon's arrival in China and suspended its bombing of North Vietnam.[83]

When Nixon arrived in China, the U.S. negotiating position was bolstered not only by the outcome of the Indo-Pakistani conflict but also by recent developments in U.S.-Soviet relations. Early in 1972, the arms-control talks took an important step forward when Moscow agreed to limits on heavy missiles.[84] And following the Beijing summit, Nixon would visit Moscow and presumably announce significant progress in arms control. As before, Kissinger, using the Chinese embassy in Paris and, later, its mission to the United Nations, "took great pains" to keep Beijing informed of "all" developments in U.S.-Soviet relations. Kissinger also underscored the Soviet threat to China during his October 1971 visit, providing Beijing with sensitive intelligence on the Soviet Union, including high-resolution satellite photographs of Soviet military forces and facilities on the Sino-Soviet border.[85]

U.S. negotiating leverage was also maximized by the time constraints imposed by the president's schedule. Whereas in July 1971, the U.S. delegation believed that the "window over Teheran" imposed roughly equal pressure on China and the United States to reach agreement on the presidential visit, in February 1972, American negotiators believed that the time constraints better served the United States. From the perspective of "triangular relations," the administration's diplomacy in the intervening period had improved U.S. security, whereas Sino-Soviet relations were unchanged. Although both sides needed and actively sought an agreement on the joint communiqué, the United States was in the better bargaining position.[86]

China seemed to share Washington's appraisal of the bargaining relationship. In his meeting with Nixon, Mao downplayed the significance of the Taiwan issue as a mere domestic dispute in Chinese politics. Rather than focusing the discussion on an issue in which China would be compelled to compromise, he talked about the international situation and common U.S.-China interests. Mao observed that whereas China was weak and the United States was bringing its forces home, the Soviet Union posed a threat to world peace.[87] The common Soviet threat and Chinese strategic concerns had compelled the chairman to sidestep the Taiwan issue.

Despite Mao's cavalier attitude, the crux of the negotiations during the February summit in Beijing concerned Taiwan. Although the question of U.S. policy on Taiwan-mainland relations had been resolved in October, Beijing and Washington had yet to find common ground regarding linkage between the issues of U.S. troop withdrawal from Taiwan and peaceful unification. Washington had conceded in 1970 at the Warsaw talks that it would reduce the number of its troops on Taiwan, but as Kissinger argued in October, it wanted to establish linkage between total U.S. troop withdrawal from Taiwan and peaceful resolution of the mainland-Taiwan conflict, allowing Washington to maintain its commitment to Taiwan's defense as long as Taipei and Beijing remained at odds. In addition, Washington continued to link interim withdrawals to the reduction of tension in Asia, thereby linking U.S. policy on Taiwan to developments in Indochina and giving Beijing a powerful interest in promoting Vietnamese flexibility. The problem of U.S. troops on Taiwan had been the most important item addressed in the May 26, 1971, politburo meeting and, having already failed to establish a time limit to U.S. deployments on Taiwan, Chinese negotiators were reluctant to make any more compromises. Indeed, they raised the possibility of excluding from the communiqué a discussion of cooperation in exchanges and trade or of even forgoing a communiqué if the two sides could not reach agreement on the wording of the Taiwan section.[88]

Nonetheless, despite its earlier objections to linkage, Beijing ultimately compromised. In fact, the focus of the negotiations was not whether there would be qualifications to U.S. troop withdrawal, but rather how strong the qualifications would be. Washington's initial draft communiqué coupled its "objective" of total withdrawal with the "premise" of, and U.S. "reaffirmation" of its "interest" in, a peaceful settlement. Chinese leaders responded with wording that merely expressed U.S. "hope" for a peaceful settlement and omitted any linkage to mainland-Taiwan relations. The wording, albeit important, was now at issue, not the principle.

Chinese leaders feigned indifference to the February 26 deadline imposed by the president's scheduled departure from Beijing for Hangzhou, after which time there would be little opportunity for negotiations and for Chinese negotiators to consult with the politburo; they adopted a rigid position, attempting to pressure Washington into making the key concessions. In the end, however, the United States called China's bluff. On the afternoon of February 25, China allowed the United States to "reaffirm its interest" in a peaceful settlement and to link total troop reductions to the "prospect" of a peaceful settlement, rather than the "premise," as the U.S. side had proposed. The difference was not significant. Although Zhou told Nixon that China rejected any linkage between its Taiwan policy and U.S. troop withdrawal, and that it would determine the means of unification, China had acquiesced to the unilateral U.S. statement.[89] This precedent of mutual acceptance of contradictory statements would enable subsequent U.S. administrations to demand this same formula. Finally, later that night, at 10:30, Beijing accepted the U.S. commitment to "progressively reduce its forces and military installations" on Taiwan as the "tension in the area diminishes," thereby linking China's objective for Taiwan with peace in Indochina. Based on Mao's instructions, it also abandoned its effort to have the United States commit to "complete withdrawal" of its troops from Taiwan within a specified period.[90] Kissinger left the meeting convinced that the communiqué was complete, and at 2:30 A.M. on February 26, after Kissinger had consulted with Nixon, the two sides finished the negotiations.

Before the communiqué could be announced, however, the White House negotiators needed the assent of the State Department, which balked at approving the communiqué. Kissinger describes this episode as a case of State Department bureaucrats, incensed at being excluded from the negotiations, venting their frustrations by finding fault with inconsequential details in the communiqué. To a large extent, this may have been the case. As Kissinger concedes, that was the price the White House paid for excluding the State Department from all high-level meetings.[91]

Nevertheless, on the plane from Beijing to Hangzhou, after Rogers had actually signed off on the communiqué, State Department officials did discover a potentially serious flaw in it. In the U.S. statement, Washington reaffirmed its treaty commitments to all its treaty allies in Asia—Japan, South Korea, the Philippines, and Thailand—with the exception of Taiwan, despite the continued validity of the U.S.-ROC Mutual Defense Treaty. Assistant Secretary of State Marshall Green noted the omission of Taiwan, and the similarity to Secretary of State Dean Acheson's famous exclusion of the Korean peninsula from the U.S. defense perimeter just prior to the North Korean invasion of South Korea in 1950. Although it was unlikely that the exclusion of Taiwan would mislead PRC officials, insofar as it could be easily compensated for by subsequent unilateral U.S. statements, Green pointed out that the similarity to Acheson's 1950 mistake would undoubtedly attract the wrath of the right wing of the Republican Party. Nixon could not afford to provide his domestic adversaries with additional ammunition, he argued.[92]

At the last moment, after making extensive efforts to get beyond Nixon's advisers, and incurring Kissinger's rage at the meddling of outsiders, the State Department, with the support of John Scali, who was in charge of communications in China, finally succeeded in bringing the issue to the president's attention. Nixon concurred that changes were required, and Kissinger reopened the negotiations with Foreign Minister Qiao Guanhua after the Chinese politburo had already approved the final draft. Clearly, the communiqué could not refer to the U.S.-ROC Mutual Defense Treaty without insulting PRC officials. Thus, the White House resolved the dilemma by simply excising mention of all U.S. treaty commitments from the communiqué, thus eliminating the problem of the omission of the U.S. commitment to Taiwan.

A second glitch occurred when Kissinger tried to reopen the negotiations to change the wording of the Taiwan paragraph in the communiqué. In October, Kissinger and Zhou agreed to language asserting that "all Chinese" on Taiwan maintained that Taiwan was part of China. In Hangzhou, Kissinger proposed changing the wording to "the Chinese" in an effort to reflect the presence of non-Chinese on Taiwan who undoubtedly held different views on the international status of Taiwan. Chinese negotiators, however, refused to reopen the negotiations, particularly insofar as the proposed wording suggested additional ambiguity concerning Taiwan's status. Faced with a Chinese threat to scuttle the communiqué altogether, Kissinger withdrew the proposal.[93]

Preparations for the U.S.-PRC summit also provided another opportunity for the United States to seek PRC assistance in ending the war in Vietnam. Beijing, however, refused to become involved in the peace process. So sensitive was it to even the appearance of involvement that it rejected Ambassador David Bruce's participation in Kissinger's October 1971 delegation to China because Bruce, as U.S. ambassador to France, had been involved in the U.S.-Vietnam negotiations in Paris. Thus, more overt U.S. efforts to involve Beijing in the negotiations encountered stiff Chinese resistance. In late January, General Vernon Walters, U.S. military attaché in Paris, in the course of arranging summit matters, asked Chinese officials in Paris to use their "good offices" to moderate Vietnamese peace demands. China's response was a vitriolic no, insisting it would reject any effort to "enmesh" China in U.S. policy toward Indochina. Walters also asked if China would arrange a meeting between Nixon and the Vietnamese leader Le Duc Tho in Beijing. Once again the answer was no.[94] Similarly, in his meeting with Alexander Haig when the U.S. advance team for the summit visited Beijing in January, Zhou Enlai refused to be drawn into a discussion of the Vietnam peace process. Nevertheless, Zhou was clearly displeased by Soviet–North Vietnamese cooperation and indicated that Chinese aid to Vietnam was the minimum required to prevent a deterioration of relations between Beijing and Hanoi.[95] China had concluded that it had to support Vietnam's war effort if it even hoped to minimize Soviet influence in Hanoi, and that Chinese pressure on Hanoi to meet U.S. demands would only undermine PRC objectives. Thus, within days of Nixon's departure from China, Zhou traveled to Hanoi to brief Vietnamese leaders on his discussions with Nixon and to reassure them of Chinese support. Ultimately, Nixon had to be content with the increased isolation Vietnam experienced as Washington developed a strategic relationship with both China and the Soviet Union, Hanoi's principal backers.[96]

The Shanghai communiqué reflected Washington's ability to establish rapprochement at minimal cost to immediate U.S. policy toward Taiwan. Nevertheless, the Chinese side did not come away from the negotiations empty-handed. During discussion of future developments, Nixon had made a significant concession, offering Chinese leaders a significant quid pro quo for the compromises embedded in the Shanghai communiqué. Explaining that it was difficult for the United States to "abandon its old friends" on Taiwan, Nixon maintained that normalization would have to be delayed. At minimum, he "hoped"—and, at most, according to Chinese sources, "promised"—to realize normalization of relations during his second term. Moreover, Chinese sources report that Nixon reaffirmed Kissinger's assurances regarding U.S. policy toward Taiwan, telling Zhou Enlai that Taiwan was part of China and that the United States did not support independence for Taiwan. Although the U.S. demand for a Chinese commitment to peacefully resolve the conflict remained on the agenda, given Nixon's and Kissinger's assurances, Beijing might reasonably expect Nixon to "abandon" Taiwan and establish relations with the PRC in his second term.[97]

China also gained an important significant strategic benefit from the summit. As the Chinese Foreign Ministry explained in an internal document distributed to senior Communist Party cadres following the summit, Nixon's visit to Beijing had enabled China to make use of international "contradictions" to split its adversaries and strengthen China.[98] Strategic interests had first led Chairman Mao and his lieutenants in 1969 to reconsider China's U.S. policy, and ultimately the impact of improved U.S.-PRC relations and the Beijing summit on China's strategic situation had offset Chinese compromises on normalization of relations with United States and U.S.-Taiwan relations.

THE LIAISON OFFICE NEGOTIATIONS

The final diplomatic accomplishment of this period occurred during Kissinger's February 1973 visit to Beijing, when the two sides agreed to the establishment of liaison offices. Kissinger reports that in February 1973, he had offhandedly suggested to Zhou Enlai that the United States and the PRC establish liaison offices in each other's capitals, and that he was surprised at China's ready acceptance of the idea. In fact, the liaison-office concept had first been proposed to senior U.S. policy makers by State Department officials and then broached to the Chinese as early as Kissinger's October 1971 visit to Beijing and then during subsequent U.S.-China meetings in Beijing. In October 1971 Chinese leaders forcefully rejected the proposal. During the February 1972 Nixon visit, they were noncommittal. Subsequently, Roger Sullivan at the State Department prepared an extensive memo arguing that Chinese leaders, if properly briefed on the liaison office concept, would see its advantages. And in June 1972, when Kissinger and John Holdridge once again put forward the suggestion in Beijing and stressed its merits, the Chinese quickly jumped at the idea.[99] Indeed, Chinese sources report that the Chinese politburo had considered the idea of establishing liaison offices as early as May 1971. Recognizing that normalization might not occur immediately, Chinese leaders had reconciled themselves to intermediate steps.[100] They might have preferred normalization and may have been holding out for a better deal, but they were prepared to accept partial success rather than achieve no progress at all. Thus, when Kissinger visited Beijing in February 1973, he arrived with a fully developed proposal, and his aides, and probably he too, already knew of China's keen interest in the opening of liaison offices. For its part, the Chinese side was fully prepared to move ahead.

China's interest in establishing liaison offices reflected two concerns. The first was to consolidate the U.S.-PRC relationship. One month before Kissinger's June 1972 visit to China, Nixon had traveled to Moscow to sign the SALT I agreement. In contrast, Sino-Soviet relations remained deadlocked. As the Chinese Foreign Ministry indicated in an internal bulletin distributed shortly after the February agreement to open liaison offices, China continued to make a "distinction between the primary and the secondary threat," and that the Soviet Union "constitutes the biggest threat to China. . . . Therefore, we should focus our attack . . . on Soviet revisionism." In this context, the bulletin explained, improved U.S.-PRC relations were "conducive to our long-term struggle with Soviet revisionism." The bulletin further explained that owing to the increased threat from the Soviet Union, Chinese leaders were seeking to expedite normalization of relations with the United States. Thus, as Mao explained to Kissinger, having established "friendship," the United States and China should "work together to commonly deal with the bastard [Soviet Union]."[101]

Chinese leaders thus believed that the opening of liaison offices would expand U.S.-PRC cooperation. And, as Sullivan's memo had stressed, establishment of liaison offices would not infringe on China's absolute opposition to any semblance of legitimization of a two-China policy. Because the arrangement was unique and had never been used before in international relations, Chinese leaders could interpret its diplomatic importance in any manner they desired, thereby maintaining the fiction that Washington did not simultaneously have an official relationship with both Beijing and Taiwan. Indeed, the June 1972 U.S. delegation also assured Beijing that this concept would in no way establish a precedent for future U.S. relations with Taiwan.[102] The Chinese Foreign Ministry could accordingly argue in its internal memorandum that the liaison offices would not reduce Taiwan's international isolation, particularly given Beijing's recent success at establishing diplomatic relations with Japan and West Germany. Moreover, establishment of liaison offices would "increase [China's] influence among the American people."[103]

Second, and equally important, Beijing perceived the agreement on liaison offices as the first step toward normalization of relations. Nixon's second term had arrived, and normalization would presumably occur within the next four years. A concession on the question of liaison offices was a small price to pay if it were a mere short-term instrument that was part of the normalization process. Indeed, Chinese sources report that during this visit Kissinger said that in the first two years of his second term, Nixon would reduce U.S. troops on Taiwan and establish the liaison offices. Then, in the last two years of the term, the United States would "be ready to move in a manner similar to Japan to realize complete normalization" of U.S.-PRC relations. The United States had thus moved beyond Kissinger's July 1971 statement on Taiwan and normalization, basically accepting the Japanese formula, whereby it would sever official relations with Taiwan and establish relations with Beijing as the sole legitimate government of China. Although Kissinger insisted that the United States would protect U.S.-Taiwan nongovernmental relations, he had made significant statements that encouraged the Chinese leadership to agree to open liaison offices by heightening their expectations that the United States would accept China's conditions and establish diplomatic relations with Beijing within the next three and a half years. Thus, as one Chinese historian reported, the two sides agreed to establish liaison offices in order to "speed up the realization of normalization and to strengthen relations."[104]

But there were clear limits to Chinese cooperation with the United States. Until the United States normalized relations with China, Beijing would not engage in any activities that even suggested its acquiescence to a "two-China" policy. Thus, diplomatic exchanges would be limited to periodic visits by senior U.S. diplomats to Beijing and contacts through the liaison offices. In mid 1971 Huang Zhen forcefully rejected General Walters's suggestion that during his October visit to Beijing Kissinger discuss with Zhou Enlai exchanges of high-ranking personnel, insisting that there "is no point in talking about . . . exchanges of high-ranking officials and other exchanges until the Taiwan issue is resolved." Similarly, from mid 1972 on Beijing turned down Kissinger's frequent suggestions that Zhou Enlai or any another Chinese leader visit Washington.

Chinese officials would not visit the United States until Washington broke relations with Taipei and recognized Beijing as the sole legitimate government of China.[105]

Conclusion

During these first years of rapprochement, the United States and China sought partial solutions to contentious issues to make possible immediate cooperation against the Soviet Union. Washington and Beijing sought cooperation to offset the increasing pressure they were experiencing from Moscow. But within this context their immediate circumstances differed significantly. Although their respective negotiating strategies and the ultimate compromises reflected the mutual need for success, they also reflected the asymmetries in bargaining strength.

In the period following Henry Kissinger's first visit to Beijing, the policy of the United States in Indochina and toward the Soviet Union made what appeared to be significant progress toward ameliorating immediate U.S. security concerns. Although policy makers remained concerned that insufficient defense spending and domestic politics were undermining U.S. capabilities, the end of the Vietnam War and U.S.-Soviet détente reduced the absolute urgency of developing relations with China. Washington was thus in no hurry to make significant concessions to Chinese demands for normalization. Rather, to achieve its objectives, the Nixon administration offered China the prospect of future concessions leading to normalization of relations basically on Chinese terms. Kissinger established this trend during his first visit, and Nixon reinforced it when he indicated that he would break relations with Taiwan and normalize U.S.-PRC relations during his second term. This tactic provided the basis for rapprochement at no immediate cost, insofar as Richard Nixon could reinforce America's strategic position and reap immense domestic popularity without sacrificing any of the fundamental tenets of U.S. policy toward Taiwan. But there was a long-term cost to this strategy; it firmly established a negotiating position that severely restrained U.S. flexibility in future negotiations.

Whereas U.S. leaders could draw some optimism from the course of U.S.-Soviet relations, Chinese leaders did not observe any improvement in their strategic circumstances. On the contrary, in the aftermath of the 1969 border conflict, Sino-Soviet relations remained deadlocked. Moreover, U.S.-Soviet détente at worst suggested the potential for collusion, and at best reduced Soviet security concerns in Europe, thus giving the USSR greater flexibility in dealing with China. These circumstances and the inherent asymmetry in Sino-Soviet relations, which Washington did not experience in U.S.-Soviet relations, compelled Beijing to assume the greater burden of U.S.-PRC cooperation. Washington's ability to defer the difficult compromises meant that Beijing committed itself to U.S.-PRC cooperation notwithstanding that the United States maintained the status quo in its relations with Taipei. The sole public commitment Beijing extracted from the Nixon administration concerned U.S. troop withdrawal from Taiwan. Yet even this concession was linked to stability in Asia, which served U.S. interests in Vietnam, and was open-ended as to the time frame.

Whenever Chinese leaders encountered U.S. resistance to compromise, they bypassed the issue rather than accept a solution that entailed a commitment compromising Chinese objectives. They elected to wait until China was in a better negotiating position to secure U.S. compromises. This would remain China's negotiating style throughout the period of cooperation. China would repeatedly make the same demands on Washington, extracting concessions when the United States anxiously sought agreements and retreating when circumstances demanded patience. Throughout the 1970s and 1980s, there was no period when China was satisfied with the status quo. As for the United States, the issue throughout this period would remain whether or not it was necessary for Washington to compromise to secure its strategic objective of U.S.-PRC cooperation.

During these early years, the compromise solutions enabled Washington and Beijing to break through twenty years of mistrust to terminate costly and counterproductive hostility. This in itself was a major accomplishment of historic proportions. That they also bolstered their respective positions vis-à-vis the Soviet Union made the accomplishment all the more important.

CHAPTER 3

Domestic Politics
and Strategic Imagery

NORMALIZATION DEFERRED

The agreement to establish liaison offices was the last major development in U.S.-PRC relations through 1976. President Nixon and his successor, Gerald Ford, were soon preoccupied respectively by the Watergate crisis and the 1976 presidential campaign, undermining their ability to make the costly political decisions required to move the normalization process forward.

The Watergate crisis had a profound impact on U.S. foreign policy. The weakening of presidential power and the increasing divisiveness in U.S. society associated with the Watergate hearings and the Ford presidency led policy makers to fear a reduction in U.S. decisiveness in international affairs and raised concern that the credibility of U.S. defense commitments was in doubt, and that Moscow would take advantage of U.S. immobility to expand its influence. By 1975, international developments reinforced these concerns. The fall of Saigon, events in Africa, and the growing challenge of Eurocommunism generated concern about Soviet opportunism and the demise of détente. These changing strategic circumstances led the Ford administration to attach greater importance to U.S.-PRC relations, encouraging Washington to seek a compromise solution to normalization. Domestic politics, however, deferred the impact of international concerns on China policy until the next administration.

Developments in U.S. domestic politics and in U.S.-Soviet relations also affected China's policy toward the United States. Until late 1973, Chinese policy remained premised on the belief that consolidated U.S.-PRC relations were necessary to offset U.S.-Soviet détente and China's corresponding insecurity in the face of the Soviet threat. But after Kissinger's November 1973 visit to Beijing, Chinese leaders reappraised the PRC's strategic position. With the United States embroiled in domestic politics and increasingly defensive in the face of Soviet foreign policy successes, détente appeared on the verge of collapse, and the prospects of U.S.-Soviet collusion had diminished. China could now take greater risks in its U.S. policy, including demanding accelerated progress in the normalization of relations. But unmitigated Sino-Soviet conflict and China's relative weakness vis-à-vis the United States ultimately deterred Beijing from upsetting U.S.-PRC relations. When President Ford explained that normalization would have to wait until his second term, backing away from Nixon's assurances, China was compelled to wait. Washington essentially required Beijing to pay the foreign policy costs of U.S. domestic politics.

Although China also faced domestic instability during this period, the foreign policy ramifications were less severe than the Watergate affair was for U.S. foreign policy. For most of this period the preeminent Chinese leader was unaffected by domestic instability— Chairman Mao remained immune from the political concerns of his lieutenants. Not until Mao became incapacitated in mid 1976 did elite factionalism in China influence U.S.-PRC relations.

Watergate and the Demise of Détente:
Washington's Deteriorating Strategic Circumstances

In the aftermath of Henry Kissinger's first visit to China, Washington assumed an increasingly advantageous position in U.S.-PRC relations. But the two primary sources of this trend—superpower détente and President Nixon's domestic popularity—disappeared beginning in 1974.

U.S. domestic politics in 1974–76 revolved around the Watergate affair and its aftermath. During his March 15, 1974, press conference, Nixon first realized the "dimension of the problem we were facing with the media and with Congress regarding Watergate: *Vietnam had found its successor.*" Soon Watergate became "an almost complete preoccupation," and by mid April the administration recognized "the unpleasant fact that the whole thing was out of hand."[1] From April through Nixon's resignation on August 9, 1974, the media and the Democrat-controlled Congress had the White House on the defensive, and flexibility in foreign policy was a major casualty.

President Gerald Ford was in only a slightly better position. As the first unelected president in U.S. history and inheritor of the Watergate fiasco, he would be a vulnerable target in the 1976 election, which was just two years away. Moreover, conservative Republicans were dissatisfied with Ford's relatively moderate agenda and sought to nominate Ronald Reagan as the party's presidential candidate in 1976. Ford therefore eschewed controversial international initiatives.

These domestic divisions created considerable doubt in the administration over whether Washington could respond adequately to Soviet challenges. Kissinger expressed such fears during the September 1973 confirmation hearings for his appointment as secretary of state. After recalling the recent turmoil of assassinations, interracial violence, and the Vietnam War, he noted in a reference to Watergate that America was now "plunged into still another ordeal," potentially fostering a "loss of confidence," which would "inevitably be mirrored in our international relations" and "deal a savage blow to global stability."[2]

Moreover, Americans in general, tired by their protracted experience as a nation in the Vietnam War and the domestic strife it generated, and optimistic about the prospects of détente, sought a reduction in U.S. involvement in world affairs. In April 1973, after the signing of the Vietnam peace agreement, Secretary of State Rogers feared that "neglect and isolation are apt to flourish in the pleasant climate of détente," and he rejected proposals to reduce the U.S. military presence abroad and curtail U.S. arms transfers to the Third World.[3] Similarly, in mid 1975, just as Saigon was falling to communist forces, President Ford argued that détente had been possible "only because of U.S. strength and U.S. resolve." He warned that a "posture of deliberate weakness is most dangerous when the worldwide military balance threatens to deteriorate."[4]

Meanwhile, the Soviet Union seemed prepared to take advantage of U.S. immobility. The SALT agreement limited the number of warheads but did not constrain qualitative improvements, and in 1972 the Soviet Union began testing a new generation of ICBMs, including the SS18 and SS19 missiles. Then, in 1973, Soviet tests clearly revealed the emerging technological sophistication necessary for development of MIRVed warheads. By early 1974, the Defense Department reported that Moscow had tested four new ICBMs, including SS18s and SS19s, each with more accurate MIRVed warheads. The DOD warned that deployment of modern Soviet missiles could give Moscow significant one-sided counterforce capability, which it might try to exploit for diplomatic advantage. By the end of 1975, there was fear that Soviet ICBM modernization would render U.S. ICBMs "increasingly vulnerable during the coming decade."[5] And in mid 1976, administration officials called attention to the threat posed by Soviet deployment of SS20s in Europe.[6] Kissinger asserted that the appearance of U.S. strategic inferiority could have serious political consequences. "If we are driven to it, the United States will sustain an arms race," he warned Moscow. "Indeed, it is likely that the United States would emerge from such a competition with an edge over the Soviet Union."[7]

But at that time Kissinger's challenge was primarily a bluff, for the United States had yet to develop measures either to offset enhanced Soviet capabilities or to ensure the survivability of its land-based forces. As Nixon lamented in his 1974 State of the Union Address, the defense budget share of the annual budget had fallen continuously since 1969.[8]

Soviet momentum in the strategic balance was matched by the threat of communist participation in NATO governments. In July 1974, a coalition including communists replaced the government of General António de Spínola in Portugal. As the leftward trend progressed through 1975, Moscow provided advice and financial support to Portuguese communists.[9] In March, Kissinger warned Moscow that it "should not assume that it [had] the option . . . to influence events" in Portugal. Soviet involvement in Portuguese politics was "inconsistent with any principle of European security," Kissinger asserted. "At some point we and our European allies must ask ourselves whether major communist influence in a government is compatible with membership in an alliance dedicated to resisting Communist aggression," he went on to apprise the Portuguese people in August.[10] Italy raised similar concerns. In mid 1975, the Italian Communist Party received over one-third of the vote in subnational elections, and it did just as well a year later in national elections, leading Kissinger to warn that the alliance "could not survive" communist participation in NATO governments, and that "the foundation of our Atlantic security would . . . be eroded."[11] To compound U.S. worries, in 1974 there was political instability in Athens, and Turkey invaded Cyprus, and in November 1975, General Francisco Franco died, raising questions about the stability of the Spanish leadership. Washington was on the defensive in Europe, scrambling to minimize opportunities for Soviet foreign policy.

The situation in the Third World appeared just as bleak. In April 1975, communist forces overran the Cambodian and South Vietnamese governments. President Ford's appeals to Congress for aid to Saigon fell on deaf ears, and the United States watched as the war in Indochina came to an ignominious end. Moscow, which had provided the weaponry for the communist offensive, was the immediate beneficiary, securing greater influence in Indochina and a reduced American presence in Asia. In September, the members of the Southeast Asia Treaty Organization agreed to "phase out" that body, and in 1976, Bangkok insisted that all U.S. forces leave Thai territory.[12] "Let no potential adversary believe that our difficulties mean a slackening of our national will," Ford declared after South Vietnam fell, seeking to project an image of U.S. resolve. "As long as I am President, we will not permit détente to become a license to fish in troubled waters," he warned Moscow.[13]

Developments in Africa provided little basis for optimism. In 1974, Portugal granted independence to its African colonies, and by early 1975, there was civil war in Angola. Soon Moscow was supplying military aid to the Popular Movement for the Liberation of Angola (MPLA), and by the end of the year there were at least 7,000 Cuban troops in Angola.[14] The administration sought to offset Soviet and Cuban involvement, but Congress ultimately blocked aid to opposition forces, and the MPLA won the immediate postindependence struggle for state power, although faced with a tenacious insurgency. Regardless of the sources of the conflict and the origins of U.S. involvement, the Soviet Union was once again the beneficiary of Third World instability. For the White House, the issue was not the strategic importance of Angola but the impact of U.S. passivity on future Soviet behavior. "A stable relationship with the Soviet Union . . . will be achieved only if Soviet lack of restraint carries the risk of counteraction," Kissinger complained. "Do we want our potential adversaries to conclude that in the event of future challenges America's internal divisions are likely to deprive us of even minimal leverage over developments of global significance?" he asked.[15]

As the White House contended with American isolationism and Soviet opportunism, it also faced increasing opposition from U.S. conservatives, led by Senator Henry M. Jackson among the Democrats and Ronald Reagan among the Republicans. The Ford administration was under constant pressure to exhibit its hard-line credentials and to justify continued SALT negotiations. The Jackson-Vanik Amendment to the 1974 Trade Reform Act, linking U.S. most-favored-nation treatment of the Soviet Union with Soviet emigration policy, symbolized the strength of conservative opposition to détente. Similarly, the 1974 Vladivostok arms-control agreement was widely criticized in conservative circles as a giveaway. By 1976, the administration had ceased using the term *détente* to minimize its vulnerability to conservative criticism. Regardless of White House preferences, the domestic political basis for détente no longer existed.

Thus, beginning in mid 1973 and increasingly in 1974, the Nixon and Ford administrations perceived a growing Soviet threat emerging from the combination of developments in American society and Soviet opportunism. Although the administration tried to maintain some elements of cooperation in U.S.-Soviet relations, this was more and more difficult, given conservative pressures in an election year. Détente and superpower cooperation were quickly disintegrating.

China's Domestic Politics and Improved Security Perspective

While U.S. leaders were trying to cope with turbulence at home and scrambling to check what they perceived as Soviet strategic and regional momentum abroad, China was experiencing its own succession struggle as its elite prepared for the long-awaited death of Chairman Mao. Yet Chinese domestic divisions were in no way as severe as those in the United States. Moreover, from mid 1973 through late 1976, Beijing enjoyed a somewhat improving security environment. U.S.-Soviet détente was finally coming undone, and, just as important, with the winding down of the war in Indochina, the PRC was less isolated in Asia. Unabated Sino-Soviet tension, however, tempered these successes. China's improved strategic environment reduced the *immediate* pressure on PRC leaders, but Beijing's perception of Soviet intentions had yet to change.

FACTIONAL CONFLICT AND POLICY MAKING UNDER MAO

The period between 1973 and 1976 was an extremely turbulent time in Chinese elite politics. Beneath the Chairman, factions jockeyed for position in preparation for the post-Mao era. As the struggle intensified, the factions polarized into two competing groups—the radicals, clustered around the so-called Gang of Four, and the more moderate leaders, led first by Zhou Enlai and later by Deng Xiaoping. This polarization led to the politicization of all policy decisions, as Mao's potential successors considered the implications of their policy positions, including those concerning U.S.-PRC relations, on their prospects for survival both during and after the Mao-ist era.

Nevertheless, heightened elite contention among Mao's lieuten-ants only marginally influenced China's U.S. policy. This is a crucial point, requiring detailed and lengthy analysis. If, as is often argued, political instability in the United States and China persuaded policy makers in both countries to prolong the normalization negotiations until they were prepared to incur the inevitable political costs, then the lack of progress toward normalization during this period re-flected tacit mutual consent and did not result in any substantial dissatisfaction on either side.[16] But if only the United States sought to delay the negotiations, while China's senior policy makers, free of political constraints, were prepared to normalize relations, there was conflict, and negotiations were needed to determine which side would compromise.

During the period covered in this chapter, Chinese domestic poli-tics did not affect China's willingness to normalize relations. De-spite the existence of intensified factional conflict, Chinese radicals were for a number of reasons unable to alter China's fundamental U.S. policy. First, they had no responsibility whatsoever for making foreign policy. The radicals' primary responsibilities concerned the media and cultural affairs. The Foreign Ministry and policy-making responsibility remained firmly in the hands of Zhou Enlai and later Deng Xiaoping. When Jiang Qing complained to Mao that she was a mere "idler," Mao responded that she was merely to "research do-mestic and foreign trends. This is already a large [enough] assign-ment. I have told you this many times. Do not say that you do not have any work."[17] When she specifically requested responsibility for foreign policy matters, Mao insisted that "daily reading of the two large [issues of] *Reference News* was large enough [responsibility]"[18] Jiang Qing and her colleagues lacked the access to the policy-making process necessary to influence foreign policy choices directly.

Second, the radicals possessed insufficient political authority to dissuade their moderate adversaries from making controversial for-eign policy decisions. A careful reading of the political history of the mid 1970s reveals that from late 1973 through late 1975, Jiang Qing and her allies enjoyed only minimal support from Chairman Mao and experienced diminishing power, while Mao protected Zhou En-lai and gave increasing support and authority to Deng Xiaoping.[19]

Mao's disillusionment with Jiang Qing and the other radicals in the post–Lin Biao era first surfaced in a politburo meeting on November 17, 1973, when they tried to use Mao's unhappiness with Zhou's management of foreign policy to launch the "11th line struggle" against Zhou, charging that he planned to seize power from the Chairman. Mao was clearly troubled by Jiang's overreaching herself and the attack on Zhou. Jiang was wrong, he told both the radicals and Zhou; she, not Zhou, was the one who was impatient to seize power. Then, in January, the radicals tried to use a campaign to criticize Lin Biao and Confucius against Zhou and his allies. Although Mao had approved the radicals' suggestion for the campaign, he quickly criticized Jiang's effort to use it to attack Zhou and Ye Jianying. the At a politburo meeting on February 15, 1974, Mao criticized Jiang's "unilateralism"—she had not consulted Mao or anyone else on the politburo before holding a mass rally, and he forbade her to distribute transcripts of the speech she had delivered at the rally. Ye Jianying also criticized her for trying to "grab power." Mao instructed her to perform a "self-criticism."[20] Similarly, in a July politburo meeting, he criticized Jiang for her arrogant personality and her unwillingness to listen to him. "She does not represent me, she represents herself. With her, one divides into two. One part is good, one part is not very good," he declared. "She plans a Shanghai group," he told the others, admonishing them to "pay attention." Mao warned Jiang not to form a "four-person small faction."[21]

While Mao was protecting Zhou and restraining Jiang, he was promoting Deng Xiaoping. In early March 1973, Mao restored Deng's Party activities and appointed him vice premier. As Zhou became increasingly ill, Mao turned to Deng to manage government and military affairs. In December, Mao announced that Deng would join the politburo and serve as its informal secretary; he would be its "chief of staff."[22] The next year, he ignored Jiang's objections and agreed with Zhou that Deng should represent China at the U.N. special session in April and he approved of Deng's speech. He wrote to Jiang Qing: "That Comrade Deng Xiaoping should leave the country is my idea. . . . Take care to be prudent. Do not oppose my suggestions."[23] Then, in October 1974, as he planned for the fourth session of the National People's Congress, he decided that Deng would become first vice premier and assume Wang Hongwen's responsibilities in government work and Zhou's for foreign affairs.

Mao had decided that after eight years of the Cultural Revolution, stability was now most important, and that Deng was the leader most able to implement stability. Although Wang Hongwen and other radical leaders tried to persuade Mao to change his plans, Mao appointed Deng Party vice chairman, first vice premier, and vice chairman (second only to Mao) and chief of staff of the Central Military Commission, commenting to Zhou that he is "a person of extraordinary ability."[24] Meanwhile, Mao continued to criticize the radicals. Deng's "political thinking is strong," he told Wang Hongwen. "Politics is stronger than you," he added. "You are not as strong as Deng Xiaoping." He warned Wang and Jiang Qing not to "make a gang of four" and told Jiang: "Don't show your face so much; don't comment on documents, don't form a cabinet. . . . You have incurred widespread resentment; you must unite with the majority."[25]

Deng reached the height of his authority under Mao in the spring of 1975. When Jiang Qing and Yao Wenyuan tried to use the campaign to study proletarian dictatorship to attack the moderate leadership, Mao accused them of ignoring the danger of "dogmatism" and charged that they had only a limited understanding of Marxism-Leninism. He distributed his comments to the politburo and then, in a politburo meeting, insisted to the radicals that "there must be stability, there must be unity" no matter what the problems were in Chinese politics. Mao reiterated his demand that they not form a gang of four, and he insisted that they adhere to Party discipline, clearing all decisions with the politburo. He told them to write self-criticisms and instructed Deng Xiaoping to chair politburo meetings focusing on the radicals' errors.[26]

These politburo meetings occurred on May 27 and June 3. Deng, Ye Jianying, and Li Xiannian all severely criticized the four radical leaders, reading Mao's criticism to them and insisting that they practice unity, go through channels, and avoid becoming dogmatic in criticizing revisionism. In response, Wang Hongwen and Jiang Qing performed self-criticisms. Jiang then wrote a self-criticism for Mao, in which she acknowledged the "existence of a gang of four" and the resultant danger of factionalism. She also agreed that Mao had been correct in criticizing her four times in 1974 and 1975. Mao told Deng that he supported his handling of Jiang and her allies, and that he would tell Wang Hong wen to seek instructions from Deng.[27]

Deng continued to enjoy Mao's support at least through mid September, when Mao criticized the anti-Deng slant of a speech Jiang Qing delivered at the September 15 opening of the "Learn from Dazhai" conference. Mao said Jiang's statements were "wide of the mark" and told Hua Guofeng, "Do not distribute the manuscript, do not play back the recording, and do not print the speech."

But beginning in late September, Jiang turned to Mao's nephew, Mao Yuanxin, to influence Mao's thinking. By late October, Mao Yuanxin had persuaded the increasingly isolated and physically weakened Chairman that Deng paid mere lip-service to Mao's policy preferences, and that he was repudiating the Cultural Revolution. After several previous meetings that focused on Deng's mistakes, on November 2, the politburo stopped the majority of his work, so that he could "specialize on managing foreign matters." The next day the radicals launched a "criticize Deng" campaign at Qinghua University, and in late January 1976, Mao chose Hua Guofeng to take over the daily work of the government and Hua soon replaced the deceased Zhou Enlai as premier.[28] Deng had once again fallen from power, and his moderate colleagues were now on the defensive.

Nevertheless, Mao's choice of Hua Guofeng is instructive. Even after the radicals had succeeded in ousting Deng, they were unable to assume leadership of the state. Mao remained doubtful of their intentions and abilities, and he continued to restrain their power. Moreover, Mao's initial decision to leave the making of foreign policy in Deng's hands underscores that he did not trust the radical leadership to manage foreign affairs in China's national interest. From late 1973 through the end of 1975, the radicals were simply not an independent political coalition capable of influencing, either directly or indirectly, the foreign policy preferences of the moderate leadership responsible for making foreign policy, including Zhou Enlai and Deng Xiaoping.

Third, when Zhou and Deng got into political difficulties, the source of the trouble was Chairman Mao himself rather than the rival radical faction. This was clearly the case in late 1975. Mao's decision to remove Deng did not directly reflect resurgent radicalism; rather, it showed the Chairman's awesome personal power and his personal reevaluation of Deng's leadership qualifications, however much of his thinking was influenced by Mao Yuanxin. Thus, to the extent that Mao's moderate lieutenants encountered opposition to their foreign policy and were compelled to act with caution, the source of opposition was the powerful preeminent leader, Chairman Mao, who had both the authority and the legitimacy to assess China's national interest personally and select policy accordingly. Caution in Chinese foreign policy thus did not have its source in the parochial political concerns of a policy maker seeking to ensure his political survival in the face of the attacks of a rival faction.

This was also clearly the case in 1973, when Zhou Enlai encountered serious criticism of his U.S. policy. In December 1972, Mao overruled Zhou's dictum that ultraleftism and anarchism were the major difficulties in managing foreign affairs. He told Wang Hongwen and Zhang Chunqiao that the major issue was rightism, and that focus on ultraleftism was revisionist. Soon the anti–Lin Biao campaign adopted a clear anti-rightist focus.[29]

Zhou's troubles deepened in mid 1973. In July, Mao received Wang Hongwen and Zhang Chunqiao in his home office. He expressed numerous complaints about Zhou's foreign policy and his handling of the Foreign Ministry. He criticized Foreign Ministry documents that, in the aftermath of 1973 SALT II agreement and the subsequent visit by Soviet Party Secretary Leonid Brezhnev to Washington in June, expressed considerable concern about the implications of U.S.-Soviet détente for China. Mao insisted that despite improved superpower relations, the major trend was superpower tension, and that China need not be overly concerned.[30] Mao also criticized the Foreign Ministry's mistakenly pessimistic analysis of Japanese politics and Sino-Japanese relations. Equally important, Mao was unhappy with what he perceived as the Foreign Ministry's lack of respect for him. He charged that whereas his ideas were infrequently mentioned, the ideas of European communists received much unwarranted praise. He said that he could not bear to read the ministry's speeches and documents, including those prepared by Zhou. Moreover, in recent years, China's policy makers had not sought his opinion on policy matters. Perhaps, he suggested, they thought he was wrong and that they were right. He warned Wang and Zhang that the Foreign Ministry harbored treacherous "pirates" and that they should "avoid the tricks" of its "old masters." Summing up, Mao said: "The big issues are not discussed, but . . . the small issues are always sent [to me]. If this tune does not change, it will inevitably become revisionism. Do not say that I did not say so in advance." He instructed Wang and Zhang to read about international affairs so that they would not be "cheated" by Foreign Ministry "intellectuals."[31]

Mao continued his attack in the fall. Based on the translator's report of Zhou's November 1973 meeting with Kissinger, Mao concluded that Zhou was too weak and guilty of right capitulationism. Soon afterward, he criticized Zhou's stand that there were two possibilities for the liberation of Taiwan—peaceful liberation or armed liberation. "It can only be attacked," he insisted. Then, in late November, he convened a politburo meeting to criticize Zhou's "rightist error" in China's U.S. policy. He invited a number of radicals who were not members of the politburo to participate in the meeting, and encouraged them to attack whoever committed "capitulationism."[32]

These were serious charges. Mao verged on accusing Zhou of "re-

visionism," and previous "revisionists" had been violently ousted
from the Party and government. Zhou clearly had to exercise caution. Apparently, Mao was more hawkish than Zhou. The charges of
"revisionism" and "capitulationism" reflected his personal unhappiness with Zhou's foreign policy management. Zhou's troubles
were with his superior, not with a rival faction, and to the extent
that he implemented a tougher policy line than he might have
wished in 1973, or even afterward, when Mao reversed course and
protected Zhou against radical attacks, he was reflecting Mao's
policy preferences.

For most of the period covered in this chapter, particularly from
late 1973 to late 1975, the factional battles among Mao's lieutenants
did not affect China's fundamental U.S. policy. Mao was clearly the
arbiter among his lieutenants, and he had the final voice in matters
of policy. This was the case despite his failing health. His personal
physician reported that in January 1972 Mao suffered a near-fatal
attack of congestive heart failure and pulmonary edema. His doctors
were barely able to restore his strength so that he could meet with
Nixon in late February. By 1974, advanced amyotrophic lateral scle-
rosis (Lou Gehrig's disease) had severely weakened Mao's physical
condition; he had also lost nearly all of his eyesight and needed special translators who could interpret his garbled speech and personal
assistants to support him when he walked. Nonetheless, as the preceding discussion as well as a wealth of other materials reveal, Mao's
deteriorated physical condition undermined neither his political authority nor his ability to establish the political pecking order among
his lieutenants.[33] Mao remained firmly in command of Chinese elite
politics until the last months of his life in 1976, and China's U.S.
policy reflected his personal policy preferences.

This is not to say that the radicals had no influence whatsoever
on China's foreign policy during the mid 1970s. However, their main
efforts were directed at cultural issues, over which they had authority. One of Jiang's first initiatives aimed at fomenting tension in
U.S.-PRC relations over the Nixon visit. Jiang tried to use her supporters in the Ministry of Culture to block live television transmis-
sions of Nixon's doings in China back to the United States, but Zhou
overruled her. In early 1973, Zhou was compelled to defend China's
practice of sending experts abroad to study the "strong points" of
foreign systems against radical attacks. In November 1973, when
Zhou was coming under severe criticism from the Chairman, Jiang
attacked China's program of inviting foreign art and music groups

to China, charging that the Foreign Ministry had "opened the door to robbers." After Zhou defended the practice, Jiang launched a number of campaigns aimed at discrediting China's participation in international cultural exchanges. Similarly, she tried to disrupt commercial ties with the United States by charging that Corning Inc. had insulted the Chinese people by offering a set of glass snails as a gift. Zhou, however, blocked her attempt to return the gift to the company.[34]

Jiang acknowledged that Chinese diplomats required greater autonomy from ideology, and that launching ideological attacks on foreign leaders was not possible. She therefore confined her efforts to ensuring a suitably ideological work environment in Chinese embassies by requiring that study classes be held for embassy personnel and encouraging diplomatic staff to report on the ideological deviations of their superiors.[35] These efforts influenced the work of Chinese diplomats in Washington. In late 1975 the head of the liaison office, Huang Zhen, was compelled to organize the embassy staff to participate in the campaigns to criticize Deng Xiaoping and to "counterattack the wind of reversals." Huang himself encountered substantial criticism from embassy leftists and was unable to control a junior subordinate who "dared to rebel" and insisted on defying orders from the "old guard." Huang was forced to complain to Mao personally in order to resolve the issue. More serious, Huang had to return to China several times during the 1973–75 period to report to Premier Zhou in order to rebut charges of "capitulationism" and excessive expenditures in Washington. Huang's reports seem to have cleared things up, however, and each time he returned to Washington to continue his duties.[36]

Thus, as long as Mao was in command, the influence of the radicals on Chinese foreign policy was limited to relatively uninfluential criticism of peripheral aspects of Chinese policy or serving as Mao's personal attack dogs. But between June 1976, when Mao became critically ill and stopped receiving foreign dignitaries, and September 9, when he died, the policy-making environment changed fundamentally. With Deng politically inactive and Hua dependent on a weak coalition, the radicals had greater political flexibility, and both the domestic and foreign policy agendas of the PRC shifted to the left. Nonetheless, as argued below, although these three months witnessed subtle changes in China's U.S. policy, they were relatively marginal, inasmuch as China's strategic environment continued to determine the parameters of policy making in Beijing.

CHINA'S IMPROVED SECURITY PERSPECTIVE

China's foremost strategic concern during this period remained the Soviet Union. In the summer of 1973, there were indications of a thaw in Sino-Soviet relations. Regular air service reopened between Moscow and Beijing, and Beijing reportedly agreed to purchase eleven Soviet transport planes.[37] Before long, however, relations assumed the familiar pattern. In January 1974, China expelled five Soviet diplomats on espionage charges. Moscow retaliated by expelling PRC diplomats. In March, PRC border forces arrested three Soviet pilots after their helicopter entered Chinese territory. After trading protests with Moscow, Beijing announced in October that it would try the crew for espionage. Amid these incidents, Beijing refused a Soviet offer regarding navigation cooperation on the border rivers because the proposed agreement called for respect of territorial integrity, suggesting Chinese recognition of Soviet territorial claims. And in October, Deng Xiaoping reported that there had been "absolutely no progress" in Sino-Soviet border talks.[38] The suggestion of a thaw developed in December, when Beijing released the helicopter crew, stating that the authorities found "credible" their claim that their intrusion on Chinese territory had been unintentional.[39] Nevertheless, there were no further overtures, and China's Soviet policy resumed its rigid position. Beijing remained wary of Soviet coercion and feared that a conciliatory posture would merely encourage Soviet efforts to pressure China to succumb. Indeed, although China might seek to clarify the motives behind Soviet probes, Chairman Mao concurred with Zhou's suggestion that Beijing should not take the initiative in Sino-Soviet contacts.[40]

Sino-Soviet competition in the Third World also exhibited unrelenting hostility. The most significant developments occurred in Indochina. In the aftermath of North Vietnam's victory, Moscow quickly moved to establish a predominant position in Hanoi. Through 1975, the Soviet Union repeatedly reminded Hanoi of the significance of Soviet support for Vietnam during the war against the United States and assured it that Moscow would now support Hanoi against the intrigues of Chinese "hegemony." Moscow also agreed to provide Hanoi with a generous aid package for the 1976–80 period, and the two sides agreed to "coordinate" their five-year plans. In 1976, the Soviet Union used the delivery of aid to pressure Hanoi to distance itself from China. Moscow was now directing its encirclement strategy at China's southern periphery, and China was concerned. Thus, in September 1975, Deng Xiaoping, speaking for Chairman Mao, warned the Vietnamese Communist Party leader Le Duan that resisting "superpower hegemonism" was a "vital task" facing all countries.[41]

The USSR and the PRC supported opposing armies in the Angolan civil war. Beginning in May 1974, seeking to prevent the Soviet-backed MPLA from coming to power, China began providing military assistance and training to approximately 5,000 soldiers of the Front for the National Liberation of Angola (FNLA), and it also provided limited financial assistance to a third Angolan force, UNITA. By June 1975, however, it was clear that Washington would not be able to contribute to the anti-Soviet effort in Angola, and China informed FNLA leaders that it would end its financial aid, and that its military training mission would soon be withdrawn. As a parting gesture, in July, Beijing authorized Zaire to hand over Chinese military equipment originally provided to the Zairean military to the FNLA. Then, in October, it withdrew the Chinese military instructors who had been training FNLA forces in Zaire.[42] Although the Chinese commitment had been small, Moscow had thus achieved a foreign policy success in Africa not only against Washington but against Beijing as well.

Ongoing Chinese perception of a significant Soviet threat was reflected in PRC analyses of Soviet global behavior. Whereas Qiao Guanhua treated the superpowers with some degree of balance in his late 1973 report to the UN General Assembly, by September 1975, he charged that "the danger of war comes mainly from the wildly ambitious social-imperialism."[43] Similarly, in his review of developments in 1974, Ren Guping charged in *Renmin ribao* that "the Soviet revisionists further exposed themselves as the most cunning and insidious social imperialists." Ren argued that "Soviet revisionist social imperialism . . . [has] strong ambitions to replace U.S. imperialism by aggression and expansion." A year later, Ren's *Renmin ribao* article expressed even greater alarm, insisting that the Soviet Union was the "most dangerous source of war."[44] For Chinese strategists, the Soviet threat remained real and very serious.

In these circumstances, China continued to rail against Washington's ongoing efforts to maintain elements of U.S.-Soviet détente. Kissinger himself came under criticism for his attachment to détente, and China made very clear its preference for Secretary of Defense James Schlesinger and its opposition to his dismissal. *Renmin ribao* reported that Moscow would use the Helsinki agreement to "produce a psychological influence . . . aimed at politically obstructing the defense efforts of the Western countries." It criticized the so-called "Sonnenfeldt Doctrine," whereby the United States would acknowledge the "organic" relationship between the Soviet Union and Eastern Europe, charging that from the signing of the Helsinki agreement to "the appearance of the Sonnenfeldt Doctrine, we can clearly see that an appeasing sentiment similar to that of the 1930s exists in the West." Chinese leaders argued that U.S. leaders pursued appeasement to "urge social-imperialism eastward and divert this peril toward China."[45] A major Chinese theme during Kissinger's frequent visits to China was the dangers of détente and the need for greater U.S. resistance to Soviet expansionism. In 1975, Deng Xiaoping sternly lectured Kissinger that détente was the equivalent of British appeasement of Germany during the 1930s.[46]

Nevertheless, China took note of the significant hardening in U.S. policy toward the Soviet Union in 1974–75. In particular, China increasingly focused on growing conservative opposition to détente. As noted, Secretary of Defense Schlesinger was a Chinese favorite; his calls for a strengthened U.S. defense posture were frequently cited in the media. Indeed, despite the absence of normal diplomatic relations, Beijing frequently proposed that Schlesinger visit China. But Kissinger neither accepted the suggestions nor informed Schlesinger of the invitations.[47] China did, however, welcome Senator Henry M. Jackson, an outspoken opponent of détente, to Beijing. By May 1976, a *Renmin ribao* commentary reported that "more and more politicians" in the United States were insisting on a "reappraisal" of U.S. Soviet policy and demanding that Washington eschew any indication of a "retreating attitude toward Soviet expansion." The author was also pleased that increasing U.S. domestic opposition to détente had aroused Soviet concern.[48]

Chinese leaders also found evidence of increasing White House resistance to Soviet "hegemonism." President Ford received praise for his harsh critique of Soviet policy during his two visits to Europe in the summer of 1975. Also in 1975, the PRC media praised Kissinger's effort to counter Soviet-Cuban intervention in the Angolan civil war. In the aftermath of the fall of Saigon, the U.S. administration seemed to wake up to the perils of détente and the necessity for active opposition to Soviet foreign policy.[49] As Mao instructed his subordinates in the second half of 1973, the major trend in superpower relations was not détente, but heightened tension and preparation for war.[50]

Chinese foreign policy also scored some successes in Southeast Asia. Following the 1973 Paris agreement on the war in Vietnam and the emerging U.S. retrenchment in Asia, the countries of the Association of Southeast Asian Nations (ASEAN), concerned that the Soviet Union would seek to capitalize on U.S. weakness, reached out to China to balance Soviet power. In 1974, Malaysia established diplomatic relations with the PRC. Thailand and the Philippines did the same in 1975, and in 1976, Singapore's President Lee Kuan Yew visited the PRC, tacitly recognizing the Beijing regime as the government of China. Beijing had feared that after "repelling the wolf [the United States] through the front gate," Asia would let "the tiger [the Soviet Union] in through the back door." Instead, the isolation of the PRC in the region ended. The ASEAN countries preferred friendship with China to increased vulnerability to Soviet power.[51]

Overall, then, during the 1973–76 period, China's strategic situation had at least stabilized, and in some respects, it had marginally improved. Although the Soviet threat continued to plague Chinese security, the United States was increasingly concerned with Soviet "hegemonism," and U.S. enthusiasm for détente was quickly eroding. These changes in U.S. policy combined with developments in Southeast Asia to reduce China's isolation vis-à-vis the Soviet threat and to lessen its immediate dependence on the United States.

U.S. Domestic Politics and Chinese Leverage: The Ford Visit to China

The differing domestic political conditions and security perspectives of the United States and China created the context in which the two sides negotiated over normalization of diplomatic relations and the resolution of the Taiwan issue. U.S. domestic disarray and heightened U.S.-Soviet tension enhanced the administration's evaluation of China's strategic contribution to U.S. security. As perceptions of the Soviet threat increased, Washington sought to improve U.S.-PRC relations. This was especially the case after Nixon resigned and Gerald Ford became president. Ford had visited China in 1972, and he personally shared the strategic calculus that had motivated the Nixon administration to open relations with China. He believed that improved relations with China enhanced Washington's position vis-à-vis the Soviet Union. Moreover, given the host of international problems he had inherited from the Nixon administration, China's strategic importance had increased. This was particularly the case after the fall of Saigon; Ford believed that China was a "critical" aspect of the administration's efforts to offset American setbacks in Asia. China was a "vital" and "major link" in these circumstances.[52]

But the Ford administration was not prepared to normalize relations. The domestic political cost was simply too high. Hence, it sought the strategic benefit of improved relations without paying the price of normalization on PRC terms.

Beijing, on the other hand, had a diminishing strategic incentive to seek immediate improvement in U.S.-PRC relations. Although the Soviet Union remained a substantial threat, emerging U.S. misgivings about détente and growing U.S.-Soviet tension were an improvement over prior U.S. dependence on Soviet interest in détente. Moreover, China was winning new friends among the noncommunist countries of Asia. During this period, Beijing could press the United States for concrete progress toward normalization, taking advantage of U.S. strategic concerns, and evaluate U.S. normalization overtures on the merits of a particular offer rather than focusing only on the strategic benefits to China of improved U.S.-PRC relations. At the same time, however, given continued U.S.-Soviet détente and steady Sino-Soviet conflict, China had to protect its stake in U.S.-PRC relations, and thus could not allow the relationship to deteriorate. China's leverage had improved, but not to the extent that it could endanger cooperation with the United States.

Kissinger's visits to China in the fall of 1973, in 1974, and in 1975, and the Ford visit to Beijing in December 1975, were the diplomatic focus of U.S.-PRC relations during this period. The negotiations during and between these visits reveal the impact of each country's strategic and domestic conditions on the negotiating process.

Following the agreement to establish liaison offices, Chinese leaders expected that Nixon would fulfill his 1972 commitment to seek U.S.-PRC diplomatic relations in his second term, and they were prepared to enter into serious negotiations over the terms of a normalization agreement. In the aftermath of the March 1973 Vietnam settlement, Premier Zhou explicitly conveyed to U.S. negotiators his understanding of a mutual U.S.-PRC agreement to accelerate the normalization process. And in April, Beijing stopped shelling the Taiwanese-occupied offshore islands of Quemoy and Matsu. Nixon seemed to encourage optimism when he met with Huang Zhen, head of China's liaison office, in May 1973 and said that he would like to visit Beijing a second time. Although there was no indication of when he would like to travel, Huang seemed to attach significance to the statement, noting, "This was very good news indeed. I will speedily report this to our government." Shortly thereafter,

Huang Hua conveyed through Kissinger an invitation from Mao for Nixon to visit Beijing again at the "appropriate time." Chinese leaders, including Mao, were preparing for the final stages of U.S.-China normalization.[53]

Developments in U.S.-PRC trade in 1973 provided further optimism regarding the trend in relations. In January 1973, Mao and Zhou approved a State Planning Commission proposal calling for expanded imports, including the import of complete sets of equipment costing U.S. $4.3 billion from advanced Western countries.[54] Also in early 1973, Washington permitted U.S. corporations to open discussions with Beijing regarding exploration for oil in China. In this context, the two nations took their first tentative, but significant, steps toward developing trade relations. In May, China agreed to buy substantial amounts of cotton from the United States, and in July it placed orders for tobacco and increased its purchases of soybeans. In November, negotiations between the M. W. Kellog Corporation and China resulted in an agreement calling for the American corporation to build five complete fertilizer plants in China. This was the first time that the PRC had contracted with an American corporation to conduct work in China. Previous deals had involved a mere swap of Chinese capital for American products.[55]

Equally important, as noted above, through 1973, the Chinese Foreign Ministry was increasingly concerned about the implications of ongoing improvement in superpower relations for China's strategic position in the "delicate triangle" of China and the superpowers. The June 1973 Washington summit between Brezhnev and Nixon and the conclusion of the U.S.-Soviet Agreement on the Prevention of Nuclear War worried Chinese policy makers. Although this agreement was the last hurrah of U.S.-Soviet détente and was mostly symbolic, Moscow clearly sought such an agreement in order to suggest U.S.-Soviet collaboration against China. The final agreement stipulated that the two countries would "immediately enter into consultations" should there appear to be a "risk of a nuclear conflict" between either of them and a third party, and that they would "make every effort to avert this risk." Given Beijing's fear of superpower collusion and its concern about Soviet power, Chinese leaders undoubtedly read this clause as directed against China, and Moscow certainly tried to give this impression. Thus, as the deputy head of the Chinese liaison office Han Xu recalled, "such a situation had to cause concern to the Chinese government." Indeed, during the six weeks surrounding the June superpower summit, Huang Zhen met as many as six times with Nixon and Kissinger to discuss U.S.-

Soviet relations, and he frequently reported to Beijing on trends in the international situation. For its part, the Chinese Foreign Ministry observed heightened and consolidated U.S.-Soviet cooperation and was similarly concerned about the triangular implications for China.[56]

Thus, when Kissinger and his team visited Beijing in November 1973, they received an extremely warm reception by Chinese officials expecting a significant U.S. initiative that would also bolster Chinese security. Kissinger further encouraged such optimism in his banquet speech, reporting that the United States wanted to "complete the process" of normalization "as rapidly as possible." He had come to Beijing "with an open heart to speed up progress toward normalization with China," he said.[57]

The two sides appeared ready to take the final plunge. Zhou Enlai even seemed ready to compromise on the terms of U.S.-Taiwan relations after normalization and on Chinese policy on achieving unification of Taiwan with the mainland (in consequence, as we have seen, Zhou was subsequently charged by Mao with "capitulationism"). Zhou was eager to settle the outstanding issues blocking an agreement establishing diplomatic relations, and to expedite the normalization process.[58] Now that the Vietnam War was over and the liaison offices had been opened, and in a strategic context recommending improved relations with the United States, China was prepared to move ahead in accordance with the second-term scenario of normalization that Nixon and Kissinger had been suggesting since July 1971.

One issue blocking normalization was the claims-assets issue. After the communists seized U.S. investments in China in 1949, Washington froze Chinese assets in the United States. Normalization required settlement of this issue so that each side would not be subject to lawsuits from claimants on the other. In the belief that normalization was on the agenda, China participated in serious negotiations over the claims-assets issue. Although it is unlikely Beijing would have signed an agreement, insofar as this would have implied the existence of official U.S.-PRC relations while Washington still maintained official relations with Taiwan, successful negotiations would have removed a potential obstacle to normalization and provided the basis for a postnormalization claims-assets settlement.

The claims-assets issue was first discussed during Kissinger's February 1973 visit to Beijing—the same visit that finalized the agreement on liaison offices. In meetings between John Holdridge of the

U.S. National Security Council and a Chinese Foreign Ministry official, Zhang Wenjin, the two sides agreed on the principle of a simple swap of U.S. claims for seized Chinese assets in the United States, which would clear the accounts. Then, in March, when Secretary of State Rogers was in Paris for the signing of the Vietnam peace agreement, he met with Chinese Foreign Minister Ji Pengfei to discuss the issue. The two statesmen agreed on the principles reached in February and decided that lower-level officials should work out the details of a formal agreement.[59] Nonetheless, such an agreement remained elusive, and negotiations continued in Beijing through the U.S. liaison office. Despite the earlier agreements, these were sensitive negotiations, because from the perspective of the PRC, the U.S. position was essentially that China had to compensate the United States because Chinese communists had reversed over a century of humiliation by ousting "imperialist" corporations from Chinese territory. This was difficult for Chinese leaders to accept. Nonetheless, the negotiating teams made substantial progress, and during Kissinger's November 1973 visit to Beijing, PRC officials seemed quite flexible. At one point in the negotiations, the U.S. side thought they were close to an agreement.[60]

Nevertheless, the talks fell apart, and in June 1974 Beijing withdrew its agreement to the package settlement. This occurred for three reasons. First, the Chinese negotiators repeatedly reopened the negotiations, seeking to reduce the PRC's obligations and thus minimize both the cost and the shame of having to pay for China's victory over imperialism. Second, as noted above, a signed agreement would have been difficult to achieve prior to normalization.[61] Third, and most important, the Chinese leaders finally understood that Watergate prevented the Nixon administration from normalizing relations. An agreement on claims-assets would thus give a false impression of progress toward normalization, for real progress would be impossible until U.S. leaders were prepared to incur the domestic political costs. By early 1974, Chinese leaders understood that Kissinger was not, in fact, prepared to make the difficult compromises necessary to meet China's minimal demands for normalization, including U.S. derecognition of Taiwan.

When Huang Zhen and his colleagues arrived in the United States in May 1973 to open the Chinese liaison offices, their first and most pressing task was to analyze and report back to Beijing on the Watergate affair. This was a daunting task, and they were at a total loss in trying to comprehend this episode in U.S. elite conflict. Searching for explanations and applying the logic of Chinese regional politics to the American system, Chinese diplomats were clearly bewildered. They asked U.S. officials if Nixon's troubles arose from the fact that he and many of his associates were from California and had thus incurred the opposition of the eastern elite.[62]

Throughout 1973, Chinese diplomats in Washington failed to understand the bilateral ramifications of Nixon's troubles fully. When Kissinger met with Mao in November 1973, the Chairman's principal concern was whether U.S. domestic politics and the Watergate affair would weaken U.S. containment of Soviet Union.[63] Only in 1974 did Chinese leaders fully realize that Watergate would interfere with their plans to normalize relations during Nixon's second term.[64]

Coinciding with Beijing's reevaluation of Washington's interest in normalization was the increasingly apparent collapse of U.S.-Soviet détente. The November 1973 meeting in Beijing between Zhou and Kissinger was the last time during the Nixon and Ford administrations that Chinese concern about U.S.-Soviet détente would influence Beijing's negotiating strategy on normalization of relations. By 1974, it was clear to Chinese leaders that U.S. policy makers were no longer confident that détente would suffice to constrain Soviet behavior. On the contrary, U.S. policy makers had become disillusioned with détente. Chinese policy makers, including Chairman Mao, therefore discounted détente and formulated the PRC's policy toward the United States based on deteriorating superpower relations and rising U.S. concern about the growth of Soviet power.

As U.S. policy toward China and U.S.-Soviet relations changed, China's attitude toward U.S.-PRC relations changed dramatically. Whereas the United States would derive strategic benefit vis-à-vis the Soviet Union from progress in U.S.-PRC relations, China would not secure any tangible benefits in the form of recognition. Although strategic benefits also accrued to China from the relationship, its security situation had improved, so that the imperative of further U.S. cooperation had been reduced, while the U.S. imperative had increased. Unlike the situation in 1969–72, this situation demanded that Washington pay for its strategic benefits with real progress toward normalization, instead of simply "standing on China's shoulders" in order to improve relations with the Soviet Union, as Beijing alleged had been the case. China was seeking to redistribute the costs of anti-Soviet cooperation by eliciting the U.S. compromises necessary for normalization.[65]

China's reassessment of U.S.-China relations began in the second half of 1973, when Chinese leaders adopted an increasingly disinterested attitude toward continued U.S. efforts to engage in strategic dialogues and visit diplomacy. In late September at the United Nations, Foreign Minister Qiao Guanhua responded unenthusiastically to Kissinger's suggestion that he visit Beijing in October. A week later Qiao told Kissinger that China was dissatisfied with the pace of normalization. Kissinger accepted Beijing's suggestion that he visit in November, when Chairman Mao and other Chinese leaders would focus on the impact of Watergate on U.S. foreign policy. Then, in April 1974, Kissinger explained to Deng that his thinking on normalization remained inconclusive and that Washington was still studying the problem of carrying out the "one-China" policy. He even solicited Chinese suggestions for resolving the issue. Deng, who had already expressed China's unhappiness over Watergate, countered that normalization could only be achieved in accordance with the Japan formula and that China hoped the problem would be "relatively quickly resolved." Although Deng indicated that China was prepared to wait until the United States was ready to normalize relations on Chinese terms, as the United States continued to hesitate through the year and into 1975, Chinese leaders became increasingly frustrated and went on the diplomatic offensive.[66]

In August, after his assumption of the presidency, President Ford wrote to Chairman Mao that his administration had no higher priority than "accelerating" the normalization process and that Kissinger should visit Beijing to talk about the details of normalization. Ford's letter was welcomed in Beijing as an indication that the new American president, apparently free from the domestic constraints of his predecessor, would seek rapid normalization of relations. Nonetheless, preparations for this visit indicated to Beijing that Kissinger's agenda would not be rapid normalization but merely piecemeal steps designed to demonstrate progress toward normalization while actually delaying the final result until U.S. domestic politics permitted the White House to sever relations with Taipei. Under such circumstances, Chinese leaders adopted an ambivalent attitude toward another Kissinger visit to Beijing and questioned U.S. commitment to normalization, asking if Kissinger's tactic of "gaining time" was not his actual objective.[67]

For China, the primary issue was not piecemeal progress toward normalization but the act of normalization. Having made substantial compromises in the interest of realizing normalization, Chinese leaders were ready for the final step. Moreover, Mao had been granting Deng increasing authority since Kissinger had visited in April, and Deng wanted to deliver normalization on the basis of the "Japan formula" to Mao. On the other hand, given Mao's reaction to Zhou's conciliatory posture in November 1973, Deng could not even suggest Chinese flexibility or tolerance of U.S. ambivalence. These conflicting U.S. and Chinese objectives created increased tension between the two sides.

Prior to his arrival in Beijing, Kissinger had been in Vladivostok for the Ford-Brezhnev summit. Kissinger apparently agreed to hold the U.S.-Soviet summit on the Sino-Soviet border and then travel to Beijing in order to accentuate the implications of U.S.-Soviet détente for Chinese interests and thereby pressure China into accommodating U.S. policy objectives. Nevertheless, the effect was to harden China's opposition to the mere appearance of improved U.S.-PRC relations, which would improve U.S. security, and possibly further superpower détente, without obtaining substantive progress toward U.S. recognition of the PRC.[68]

When the American side arrived in Beijing, Chinese leaders were in no mood to cooperate. China's new attitude was reflected in Deng Xiaoping's response to Kissinger's stalling tactics on normalization. During this period, Kissinger tried out a number of formulas designed to achieve normalization while preserving U.S. interests with respect to Taiwan. China, however, was only interested in the Japan formula, which the United States had basically offered during Kissinger's February 1973 visit to Beijing. Thus, when Kissinger explained to Deng in November 1974 that because of Washington's unique relationship with Taiwan, including its Mutual Defense Treaty, the United States would need a "liaison office" in Taiwan after normalization, as well as a statement by Beijing of the PRC's plans for "peaceful unification" with Taiwan, in order to facilitate U.S. abandonment of its defense relationship with Taiwan, Deng charged that Washington had "retreated" from its earlier proposals. This was not the Japan formula; it was "nothing more than a proposal for 'reversing liaison offices' which China cannot accept." Moreover, in 1972 and 1973, U.S. officials had assured Chinese negotiators that the establishment of liaison offices in Beijing and Washington would not set a precedent for postnormalization U.S.-Taiwan relations. As for a Chinese statement on peaceful unification, Deng rejected this proposal and insisted that China would use "whatever means necessary" to resolve the Taiwan issue, thus retreating from Zhou Enlai's relatively conciliatory 1973 position.[69]

Chinese patience was wearing thin. Despite Kissinger's clear expression of interest in one, he was offered no meeting with Mao (who had been receiving other foreign guests in Changsha) and reluctantly visited Suzhou instead. Kissinger had met with Mao in previous visits, and then in November 1975, but he was pointedly denied this "privilege" in October 1974. Still, Beijing agreed to Kissinger's proposal that Ford visit Beijing in 1975. Although the prospect of a U.S.-PRC summit might give the impression of continued progress in relations, as was the case in the aftermath of Kissinger's July 1971 visit to Beijing, this time China could use Washington's relatively greater interest in a "successful" summit to try to pressure it to accept Chinese conditions and normalize relations. Beijing had not even deigned "to invite" Ford to Beijing, and it remained unclear whether President Ford would have the "honor" of meeting Chairman Mao.[70]

Having conceded to a summit, but having received no tangible benefits in return, China was in no hurry to make additional concessions. It was prepared to allow relations to stagnate until the United States made the necessary compromises permitting normalization of relations rather than allow Washington to use China to bolster U.S. security vis-à-vis the Soviet Union. This was the context in which Kissinger had to negotiate the outcome of the forthcoming summit; these negotiations proved even more difficult than those in December 1974.

Chinese leaders had agreed to a Ford visit. But now they started questioning the purpose of the summit, suggesting a cavalier attitude toward possible cancellation. Throughout much of 1975 they asked what the point of a summit would be if there were no normalization agreement to sign. And even if the summit occurred, it was difficult to understand what the two sides would be celebrating. The probable result would be an anticlimactic meeting underscoring the tension in relations. On the other hand, Chinese leaders intimated that if the United States was prepared to normalize, then it was possible to imagine a grand meeting celebrating consolidated U.S.-PRC diplomatic and political relations. Piecemeal agreements or symbolic communiqués were, however, out of the question; China sought concrete benefits in exchange for cooperation with Washington against the Soviet Union.[71]

China's negotiating position and its intimations to the media that it was dissatisfied with the pace of the normalization process were perfectly tuned to raise U.S. anxieties. Washington's objective was to accentuate U.S.-PRC cooperation so as to offset U.S. passivity in the wake of Vietnam and Watergate. A summit that was less than completely successful would reveal the bankruptcy of that strategy, further laying bare U.S. vulnerability to Soviet opportunism. Indeed, as the year progressed, U.S. vulnerability to Chinese maneuvering increased as communist forces triumphed in Vietnam and Angola, and as Eurocommunism attracted increased support in Portugal and Italy. U.S.-Soviet détente was crumbling and the United States was on the strategic defensive.

In these circumstances, despite developments in U.S. domestic politics, Kissinger had not given up hope of normalizing relations during 1975 and consolidating cooperation between the United States and China. The Ford administration prepared for normalization by withdrawing U.S. military forces from Taiwan. Not only did these measures show good faith by meeting the terms of Kissinger's 1973 normalization schedule and the Shanghai communiqué, insofar as tension in Asia had diminished since the end of the Vietnam War, but they also prepared for full U.S. military withdrawal from Taiwan without causing unnecessary surprise or alarm in Taipei. In September 1973, the United States announced that it would begin to withdraw its C-130 transport planes and approximately 3,000 tactical airlift troops from Taiwan. This was the first U.S. military withdrawal from Taiwan since Nixon's February 1972 visit to China. By the end of the year, all the aircraft and the 3,000 soldiers had departed.[72] In May 1974, Washington announced it would withdraw combat aircraft from Taiwan, and by June 1975, all such planes had been withdrawn. Moreover, over 1,600 U.S. personnel were scheduled to leave in June, bringing the total force presence down to approximately 2,800.[73] American diplomats on Taiwan and Taiwan government officials both recognized that Washington was preparing for normalization of relations with the PRC by meeting one of Beijing's key conditions.[74]

Nevertheless, U.S. presidential politics interfered with Kissinger's efforts to normalize relations with China. As the presidential election approached, Ford's political requirements became more demanding. The right wing of the Republican Party, led by Senator Barry Goldwater and including Senators Strom Thurmond and Jesse Helms, threatened to back Ronald Reagan for the Republican nomination. Moreover, they were particularly opposed to the Ford administration's China policy. Reagan's first foreign policy speech in June 1975 criticized détente with China, and he agreed with Goldwater that if Ford were to visit Beijing, he should visit Taipei as well. In October, just before Kissinger left for China, Goldwater insisted that the president "switch the interests of the United States . . . away from Communism and toward freedom in the Far East," and that he should cancel his visit to Beijing and visit Taiwan instead. On the day Ford left for China, Reagan criticized the president's decision to visit Beijing, arguing that Washington should not normalize relations with "Red China" at the expense of U.S. diplomatic ties with Taiwan. Conservative congressional leaders were also pleased to flaunt the results of a number of Gallup polls reporting that at least 70 percent of Americans opposed establishing diplomatic relations with China at the expense of U.S. diplomatic relations with Taiwan.[75]

Clearly, the president was in no position to make the difficult decision to break diplomatic relations with Taiwan; U.S.-PRC normalization would have to wait. Indeed, at various times during 1975, Ford turned down Kissinger's suggestions that Nixon's original schedule for normalization of relations after the 1972 presidential election be implemented. Ford explained that breaking relations with Taiwan would entail excessive political costs.[76]

Thus, despite the ongoing U.S. military withdrawal from Taiwan, the United States would continue to prolong the normalization process. Kissinger, however, had yet to give up hope for a successful summit. Trying to reenact the diplomacy of the Shanghai communiqué, he planned to complete the negotiations for a second summit communiqué during his October 1975 visit to Beijing. During the summer he proposed to Huang Zhen the possibility of a summit communiqué announcing halfway measures toward normalization. China, however, continued to resist such maneuvers. Then, on September 28, Kissinger explicitly informed Foreign Minister Qiao in New York that U.S. domestic politics prohibited normalization of relations during Ford's visit to Beijing. Qiao responded: "We understand you have problems. We have no problems." The Chinese leadership, free of the kind of domestic political constraints experienced by Ford and Kissinger, wanted to normalize relations. Nonetheless, Kissinger still said that he would be bringing to Beijing a draft of a summit communiqué. The stage was thus set for a confrontation, for Chinese leaders were in no mood to cooperate with Kissinger's tactics aimed at obtaining the strategic benefits of normalization without meeting Chinese normalization conditions, and Kissinger arrived in China still unsure whether or not Chairman Mao would greet President Ford during the upcoming Beijing summit.[77]

Kissinger informed Beijing in advance that he would be bringing a draft communiqué that could serve as the basis for negotiation. During his first meeting in China, he presented this document, which consisted chiefly of flowery phrases suggesting progress toward nor-

malization and made no substantial U.S. policy commitments. Beijing dragged its feet in presenting a response, feigning various problems, such as translation difficulties or the need for more time to
study the document. The U.S. side continued to spend hours seeking
Chinese acceptance of an interesting formulation for the communiqué or some other diplomatic instrument that would suggest progress. Still, PRC leaders continued to delay, turning away every U.S.
suggestion and repeatedly alluding to Nixon's indication that he
would normalize relations in his second term. Deng was particularly
derisive of Kissinger's probing on the Taiwan issue. Not only was he
tired of Kissinger's machinations, but now that Mao was beginning
to doubt his loyalty, Deng could not appear more "dovish" than Mao
and risk the charge of "capitulationism." He forcefully demanded
that Kissinger stop tinkering and that he grasp the importance of the
global strategic necessity for normalization. He also rejected Kissinger's various proposals for bilateral agreements covering air transport and commercial and navigation issues, reiterating China's position that such arrangements would not be possible until the
establishment of diplomatic relations. Moreover, Deng and other
Chinese leaders continued to question the point of a summit if there
would not be a significant breakthrough on normalization.[78]

Nothing better reflected the changed negotiating dynamics than
the impact of the deadline on the two sides. In the past, deadlines
had either affected both sides equally or worked to the U.S. advantage. Moreover, since 1973, the United States had been content to
string out the normalization process, as it was better positioned
than China vis-à-vis the Soviet Union. But in the fall of 1975, the
situation had changed. Washington now wanted an immediate partial agreement to improve its rapidly deteriorating strategic situation, and Beijing was more willing than Washington to incur a less-
than-glorious summit. Thus, the deadline of Kissinger's return to
Washington worked to Beijing's advantage. China, rather than the
United States, strung out the negotiations, attempting to pressure
the United States into making compromises. Chinese leaders undoubtedly enjoyed seeing Kissinger fume over a magnificent banquet
in Beijing's Western Hills while he waited for their response to his
proposed joint statement. The U.S. side were so upset at China's
attitude that at one point they seriously considered abruptly return-
ing to Washington. But Kissinger did not dare to risk a setback in
relations.

By undermining the image of U.S.-China cooperation, they were
trying to reduce China's strategic value to the United States and,

thus, push the United States to make concrete normalization concessions. As Mao told Kissinger, the United States was trying to use China's shoulders to get at Moscow, "but these shoulders are now useless." Indeed, one American participant recalled that China's position was that the United States needed China more than China needed the United States, so Beijing could take the offensive. Indeed, U.S. negotiators believed that strategic factors and Watergate made the United States particularly vulnerable to Chinese pressure, and they considered themselves in a weak bargaining position.[79]

Finally, after midnight on the day the U.S. participants were to depart Beijing, the Chinese side called a meeting to discuss the U.S. draft statement. In a very tense discussion, Qiao Guanhua subjected Kissinger to a barrage of blistering criticisms, provoking Kissinger to respond with a strident defense of the United States and of himself as the representative of the president. Qiao completely rejected Kissinger's proposed communiqué and presented a confrontational draft communiqué that sharply delineated the various U.S.-China differences over global issues, the Soviet Union, and Taiwan. The Chinese proposal was obviously unacceptable to the U.S. side, for it would have laid bare the tensions in U.S.-China relations and exposed the United States to increased pressure from the Soviet Union. When Kissinger rejected the proposal, Qiao responded that China was prepared to have a summit without a communiqué. Kissinger responded that a summit had to have a communiqué, but the meeting broke off early in the morning without an agreement, and he returned to Washington empty-handed.[80]

Nevertheless, despite Kissinger's fears that he would be snubbed, in contrast to the treatment he had received in Beijing the previous fall, he was greeted by Mao on his last day in Beijing. That Mao met with Kissinger for an hour and a half reaffirmed the chairman's personal commitment to the relationship, despite the lack of progress in bilateral relations and the reemergence of radicalism in domestic politics. And although it was clear that Ford would not normalize relations during his visit, Mao conceded that there was no great hurry, and that the Taiwan issue would be resolved in a hundred years or even "several hundred years."[81]

Ford could come to China, and he would meet with Mao. Nonetheless, Qiao Guanhua had also made it very clear that the administration could not assume that Ford would receive a warm welcome, or that China would help Kissinger create the impression of a successful visit. The U.S. administration therefore quickly moved to shorten the length of the Beijing summit and scheduled visits by the president to Indonesia and the Philippines following his visit to China, reducing the diplomatic significance of the Beijing summit.[82] Although dissatisfied with Chinese behavior and concerned that the president might be embarrassed by his reception in Beijing, Washington decided to proceed with the summit.

But, even after he returned to Washington, Kissinger refused to reconcile himself to a lackluster summit. Advised by his aides that the summit would be a fiasco, and concerned that he was sending the president into an untenable situation, he tried for the last time to persuade Ford to move ahead with normalization, only to be told that the campaign pressures from Ronald Reagan and the Republican right wing prohibited such a move. Kissinger therefore continued to press for an interim U.S.-PRC joint statement by way of ultimately fruitless negotiations with Chinese leaders through George Bush at the liaison office in Beijing. The State Department was instructed to develop proposals to contribute to the appearance of a successful summit. There were even suggestions of having Chinese join a U.S. space mission—anything to avoid the appearance of an unsuccessful summit.[83]

While Kissinger scrambled to wring something successful out of the forthcoming summit, Beijing remained aloof and continued to reject Kissinger's various draft communiqués. In early November the U.S. advance team had to change its travel plans at the very last minute because Beijing was not ready to welcome it. Even after Kissinger returned to Washington, Beijing delayed setting a precise date for the summit.[84] Although they had relented on holding a summit, Chinese leaders were intent on signaling Washington that the United States could not take Chinese cooperation for granted, and that Beijing would not cooperate in Kissinger's attempt to bolster U.S. Soviet policy by manipulating a U.S.-PRC summit.

But for all of China's threats and bluster, Mao was unwilling to undermine the status quo. Beijing's objective was not to damage the relationship but to compel the United States to consolidate it. Whereas the PRC's leaders felt sufficiently secure to tolerate significant tension in the relationship, and to pressure the United States to expedite the normalization process by threatening to widen the "cracks" in the relationship, they did not carry out their threat and allow the relationship to deteriorate, for they could not jeopardize the relationship without also jeopardizing Chinese security.

Just when it appeared that the relationship might actually unravel owing to U.S. domestic politics, China retreated and became compliant and forthcoming. On November 3, President Ford announced the dismissal of James Schlesinger as secretary of defense, the withdrawal of George Bush (who was known to be an advocate of normalization) from Beijing to become director of the CIA, and Kissinger's loss of his position as national security adviser, which he had held concurrently with his position as secretary of state. Practically overnight, the signals from Beijing changed and the pressure on the United States disappeared. Chinese leaders now indicated that Ford would be treated with respect, and that he would not be embarrassed by his treatment in Beijing.[85]

Although China would not bend on the issuance of a communiqué, its entire attitude had changed. The political changes in the Ford administration suggested that China's allies in the administration had lost ground, and thus that the U.S.-PRC relationship might suffer should there be continued tension. As had been the case since 1974, China preferred the status quo to the mere appearance of improved relations. But just like the United States, it could not tolerate a setback in relations—Chinese security considerations demanded stability.

Ford's visit to Beijing proceeded as scheduled, and Chinese leaders preserved the facade of cooperation. Nonetheless, there was nothing for the two sides to discuss, because there would be no communiqué and the two sides' divergent perspectives on the Soviet Union made extensive discussions on strategic affairs awkward and conflictual. Nevertheless, in his meeting with Deng Xiaoping, Ford tried one more time to implement Kissinger's strategy of expanding U.S.-PRC cooperation in the absence of normalization of relations. The president suggested that the two sides should expand trade, cultural, and scientific exchanges. But Deng once again refused, continuing to insist that no further improvement in relations would be possible until Washington was prepared to meet Chinese conditions for full normalization of relations.[86]

Ford's meetings in Beijing were thus friendly but uneventful. One participant recalled that the summit was one of the dullest meetings he had ever attended. Yet appearances were everything. When Ford and Mao found nothing more to say with more than a half hour remaining in their meeting, they kept to schedule rather than suggest to the world less than harmonious relations.[87] But for all their efforts to portray stability, the absence of a communiqué underscored that friction between the United States and China over normalization was an unsurmountable obstacle to further improvement in relations.[88] As one Chinese account explained, at the time of the Ford visit, "compared to the promise made by the previous

Nixon administration, the U.S. government's position on the Taiwan issue was a retreat. Because the U.S. government could not decide to correctly manage [the Taiwan issue], U.S.-China normalization was delayed."[89]

Nonetheless, the two sides held important discussions on the terms and schedule of normalization. According to Chinese sources, Ford retreated from Kissinger's suggestion that the United States would need a liaison office in Taipei after normalization. The United States would normalize relations in accordance with the Japan formula. As for the issue of peaceful unification, Ford did not insist on a Chinese statement but returned to the formula in the Shanghai communiqué. He conveyed his "expectation" that Beijing would "peacefully resolve the Taiwan issue." Equally important, Ford privately "assured" Chinese leaders that if he were elected president, normalization of relations would be one of his most important priorities during his first term.[90] Thus, although Washington had retreated to its more conciliatory position, it again told the Chinese leadership that it would have to wait until after a U.S. election before it could expect normalization of relations. Prior to then, Ford said, the United States would cut an additional 1,400 troops from the 2,800 remaining on Taiwan.[91]

Unable to normalize relations with China in 1975, the best Ford and Kissinger could do was plan for normalization in the hope that Ford would win the 1976 election. Indeed, Ford and Kissinger developed "specific plans to proceed with normalization," and Ford planned to move as "rapidly as possible" to reach an agreement after reelection. By the end of the Ford administration, Kissinger had already prepared a draft normalization communiqué. The administration was ready to move; only the appropriate domestic circumstances were now required.[92]

In the interim, however, U.S. inability to normalize relations with China, and Beijing's corresponding impatience, produced a chill in U.S.-PRC relations. In the summer of 1976, the PRC held amphibious military exercises off the coast of Fujian, directly opposite Taiwan. These exercises were the largest of their kind since 1962, when Beijing had feared that the United States might support a landing on the mainland by Taiwanese forces. But unlike the earlier troop movements, the 1976 exercises were clearly offensive maneuvers, involving both the air force and the army. They included amphibious operations simulating an assault on Taiwan. An interagency study conducted by the Central Intelligence Agency concluded that the exercises were not threatening. Rather, the study concluded, the maneuvers possibly reflected strong PRC exasperation at U.S. delays in moving toward normalization.[93]

Heightened Chinese succession politics added to the chill in U.S.-PRC relations. In April, Deng Xiaoping was officially stripped of his official positions, and in June 1976, Mao's health seriously deteriorated and he stopped receiving foreign visitors. Mao's failing health, which undermined his authority over his lieutenants and his ability to protect his preferred foreign policy; the decline of the moderate faction; and Hua Guofeng's tenuous hold on his position as premier and first deputy chairman of the Communist Party combined to enhance the power of the radicals and their ability to affect China's U.S. policy. In this context, the divisions between radicals and moderates grew more distinct as the sides jockeyed for position.

On the one hand, the established policy makers seemed to go out of their way to signal interest in U.S.-PRC cooperation. In contrast to past patterns, in mid May 1976, Foreign Minister Qiao Guanhua agreed to meet with the new U.S. liaison office chief, Thomas Gates, within two weeks of Gates's request for an appointment. It was a friendly meeting, and Qiao said he looked forward to a productive relationship with Gates. In contrast, one week later, Gates met with Wang Hairong, a Foreign Ministry official who was a close associate of Jiang Qing's, who took the initiative to express Chinese dissatisfaction with U.S. policy toward China and suggested that should Washington not satisfy Chinese demands, Beijing would be compelled to use force to detach Taiwan from the United States.[94]

In early June, China's new premier, Hua Guofeng, agreed to meet with Gates. This would be the first one-on-one meeting between the U.S. liaison office chief and a Chinese premier. President Nixon was the only other American to have met Hua. Rather than following the example of Wang Hairong, Hua associated himself with the policy line established by the Zhou Enlai and recently reaffirmed by Qiao Guanhua. At this early date, Hua was aligning himself with the moderates on foreign policy issues. Similarly, when Senator Hugh Scott led a congressional delegation to Beijing in July 1976, Qiao Guanhua was more accommodating than Vice Premier Zhang Chunqiao, a member of the "Gang of Four." Although Scott's discussions with Qiao were characterized as "frank and friendly," Qiao was prepared to move the discussion away from Taiwan and toward less difficult issues. Zhang, on the other hand, initiated discussion of Taiwan and, with most unusual "vehemence," asserted that there was still civil war, and that Taiwan was unconditionally China's domestic business. Like Wang Hairong, Zhang warned that China was

prepared to settle the Taiwan issue "with bayonets." American officials considered the meeting discouraging and worrisome.[95]

Even former Secretary of Defense James Schlesinger became part
of the succession struggle. After his resignation, he was invited to
China to signify Beijing's support for American politicians intent on
adopting a harder line toward the Soviet Union. But when Chairman
Mao died during Schlesinger's visit, Schlesinger became a symbol of
China's and Hua Guofeng's interest in ongoing cooperation with the
United States. Hua was in charge of the funeral services and con-
spicuously placed Schlesinger within the first group of mourners
and invited him to lay a wreath at Mao's bier. Schlesinger was the
only foreigner permitted to make this gesture.[96]

The contrast between the exchanges between U.S. and Chinese
leaders in 1976 and previous U.S.-PRC diplomatic exchanges, including Kissinger's October 1975 visit to Beijing, was striking. For
the first time since Kissinger had visited Beijing in July 1971, domestic politics were influencing China's relationship with the
United States; China's radicals were participating in diplomatic exchanges and expressing policy preferences contrary to the pattern
established by Chairman Mao in 1969. Given the possibility that
they might inherit the leadership of China from Mao, these developments contributed to a distinct frostiness in relations. Nevertheless, the radical-influenced PRC media did not attack U.S. policy
toward Taiwan or even U.S. society, as they had done in 1974. The
upsurge in left-wing influence did not significantly disrupt China's
relationship with the United States, for despite threats in their private conversations with American leaders, even the Chinese radicals were compelled to refrain from actions that would upset U.S.-
PRC relations.

Finally, even U.S.-PRC trade, which in 1973 had been cause for
optimism, reversed course during this period. In 1975, China cancelled over 75 percent of its orders for wheat and a contract to purchase 200,000 bales of cotton. Compared to 1975, Chinese imports
from the United States dropped by over 50 percent in 1976. Although these developments primarily reflected changes in Chinese
economic circumstances, the trade downturn added to the gloom in
U.S.-PRC relations.[97]

The Illusion of Military Relations

Although Kissinger had managed to arrange a meeting between
President Ford and Chairman Mao, the Beijing summit did not give

the impression that China and the United States were consolidating relations in the face of ongoing Soviet advances. On the contrary, Beijing resisted Kissinger's efforts to use summitry to enhance Washington's position vis-à-vis Moscow. The U.S. media were becoming increasingly aware of the friction in relations, leading Kissinger to deny reports of differences and to insist that Beijing remained patient about normalization.[98]

In these circumstances, Kissinger took unilateral measures to foster the impression that China and the United States were establishing security ties. He used transfers of military-related technology to China for this purpose. In tactics reminiscent of his approach to the UN vote on PRC representation in 1971, Kissinger publicly and internally denied knowledge of British and French intentions to transfer military technology to China and instructed State Department officials to try to block the sales, thus protecting himself from domestic criticism. But he secretly told British leaders to ignore U.S. attempts to block sales, and that Washington would look the other way should their exports to China bypass COCOM (the coordinating committee of NATO nations, plus Japan, supervising the export of strategic goods to communist states). Indeed, Sino-British negotiations over the sale of Rolls Royce Spey aircraft engines to China, which began in 1973, were closely monitored by the U.S. liaison office in Beijing. Thus, although the December 1975 Sino-British agreement calling for London to sell Rolls Royce Spey aircraft engines to China shocked U.S. military officials, it was not a surprise to Kissinger. On the contrary, the British informed senior U.S. officials that the United Kingdom would proceed with the sales, and that the United States could either insist that the COCOM regulations be followed, challenging British policy and risking Britain ignoring COCOM and thus undermining its integrity, or it could acquiesce to British bypassing of COCOM.[99] Kissinger quickly opted for the second option. He thus not only avoided Anglo-American conflict but also used Britain to suggest consolidated NATO ties with China, warning Moscow that imprudent behavior would have its cost, and perhaps soothing Beijing's dissatisfaction with the administration's delay of normalization.

The administration's late 1976 decision to license the export to China of Cyber 172 computers reflected similar calculations. Since 1973, China had expressed to U.S. corporations its interest in buying military-related high technology, including satellite cameras, radar and communication equipment, and military helicopters and transport aircraft. In 1973 and 1974, the CIA and the Defense Department each conducted studies of the prospects for and potential benefits of U.S.-PRC military relations. Cabinet-level officials, including Secretary of Defense Schlesinger, had discussed and were briefed on the strategic merits of such transfers and of military aid to China. In this context, in 1974, the administration began evaluating Control Data Corporation's request for a license to sell China a Cyber computer.[100]

In early October 1976, despite the objections of the Energy Research and Development Administration and despite stringent safeguard requirements, the National Security Council approved the sale to China of the Cyber 172 computer on the basis of Kissinger's conclusion that it was in the interests of U.S. foreign policy.[101] By licensing the computer sale, Kissinger once again gave the impression that U.S.-PRC ties were improving. Like Kissinger's interest in a Ford-Mao summit, to his colleagues this and similar security measures were ploys designed to compensate for U.S. strategic vulnerability vis-à-vis the Soviet Union and for the stagnation in U.S.-PRC relations, and to placate Chinese leaders until normalization became politically feasible in the United States.[102]

Kissinger used foreign policy statements in the spring and fall of 1976 for similar purposes. In mid October 1976, for example, in a news conference at Harvard University, Kissinger declared: "We believe that the territorial integrity and sovereignty of China is very important to the world equilibrium, and we would consider it a grave matter if this were threatened by an outside power." When the media failed to attach sufficient importance to the statement, the State Department went out of its way to call it to the attention of journalists, and Kissinger repeated and dramatized the commitment on network television.[103] Although there was nothing particularly new in these statements, there was no apparent reason for Kissinger to reiterate them when he did or for the State Department to emphasize his Harvard comments to the media. Rather, the statements served Kissinger's objective of creating the impression of developing U.S.-PRC ties. Without the domestic consensus required to contain Soviet power, bolster U.S. security, and conciliate Chinese normalization demands, Kissinger was forced to rely on imagery.

Conclusion

U.S.-PRC bargaining from 1973–76 on reveals the influence of mutual security dependence. Their common security perspective on the Soviet Union gave Beijing and Washington the foreign policy incentive to normalize relations. But the bargaining also showed that U.S. domestic politics prevented the Ford administration from following through on normalization. The result was that each side was dissatisfied with the treatment it received from the other. The United States wanted a significant communiqué to emerge from the 1975 summit, and China wanted normalization of relations, not a public-relations summit. Nevertheless, in the end, both sides worked to preserve the relationship. Strategic concerns compelled each side to overlook secondary grievances in the interest of dealing with their respective security problems.

China paid the higher price for the disruptions of U.S. domestic politics. The issue was which national leadership would pay the price for the political problems of the Ford administration. Would it be the Ford administration, by normalizing relations and thus jeopardizing its reelection? Or would it be the Chinese leadership, by deferring normalization until the United States was ready to move? Ultimately, Beijing was forced to yield. Despite the common security perspective and the increasing bilateral strategic symmetry, China accepted U.S. conditions for stability—summitry without normalization. Indeed, during the Ford visit it declined to publicize its dissatisfaction with U.S. normalization policy and did not refute Kissinger's public insistence that Chinese leaders, concerned with the Soviet threat, were patient about the pace of normalization. The United States was simply more powerful than China, and thus less threatened by the Soviet Union. And, unlike Beijing, Washington continued to negotiate with Moscow, which left China the most isolated of the three countries. This disparity in each nation's ability to deal with the Soviet Union ultimately dictated that Ford's domestic interests would determine the course of U.S.-PRC relations.

The future, however, held out greater promise for Beijing. President Ford had assured Chinese leaders that he would normalize relations in his second term. Even if Ford lost the November 1976 election, the election would resolve American political instability. Chinese leaders were confident that America's president in 1977, whoever he might be, would have both the strategic perspective and the political will to make the difficult choices necessary for normalization. But Beijing had failed to take into account the new Carter administration's relatively benign view of the Soviet Union and its initial equanimity regarding normalization.

CHAPTER 4

America's New Strategic Perspective

NORMALIZATION STILL DEFERRED

When the Carter administration entered office, the United States and the People's Republic of China had already gone a long way toward reaching agreement on normalization. Based on the concessions of the Nixon and Ford administrations, the United States would adopt the "Japan formula," whereby it would sever diplomatic relations with Taiwan and recognize the PRC as the sole government of China. Nevertheless, a number of important issues remained outstanding. Beijing and Washington had yet to agree on the nature of U.S.-Taiwan relations after normalization, particularly defense relations. In order for the United States to be able to sever diplomatic relations with Taiwan, it needed assurances that it would be able to maintain Taiwan's security during the postnormalization period.

But before the two sides could even address this issue, the United States had to be ready to normalize relations. Unlike its predecessor, the Carter administration entered office with a relatively disinterested attitude toward normalization. Although normalization was listed as one of the administration's primary goals for its first term,[1] it was not an immediate objective. On the contrary, it was pushed to the "back burner" as President Carter and Secretary of State Cyrus Vance pursued more pressing concerns, particularly U.S.-Soviet détente.

This shift in the policy of the United States toward China in the early Carter years reflected the new president's personal view of the Soviet threat and its implications for U.S. security. In contrast to the reevaluation that took place during the Ford administration,

Carter and Vance subscribed to a view of the Soviet Union more reminiscent of the Nixon and Kissinger perspective of the early 1970s. Soviet behavior caused them little apprehension, and they were optimistic about the prospects for reinvigorating détente between the superpowers. Having a relatively sanguine view of U.S. security, the administration attached less strategic importance to China, and it therefore retreated from its predecessor's interest in making the compromises necessary for rapid completion of the normalization process.

Chinese leaders found the U.S. presidential transition frustrating. Since 1974, U.S. security perspectives had enhanced Washington's interest in improved U.S.-PRC relations, but American domestic politics had obstructed normalization. The 1976 election finally eliminated domestic obstacles to normalization, but the new administration adopted the optimistic security perspective characteristic of the détente policies of the Nixon administration, which meant that China would have to wait still longer to secure U.S. diplomatic recognition.

But while China may have been frustrated at the shift in U.S. policy, it still lacked the ability to coerce Washington to adopt a more compliant China policy. Despite the leadership turmoil in Beijing in 1977 and 1978, China maintained a consistent view of the Soviet Union. If anything, the Soviet menace was increasing, for Chinese leaders believed that the Carter administration failed to understand the severity of the threat, and that Moscow's influence was growing in the Third World, including Indochina. As was the case during the Ford administration, Beijing was in no position to "rock the boat" of U.S.-PRC relations, and its U.S. policy reflected this continuity. Indeed, because of the new president's relatively complacent view of the Soviet Union, it had even less leverage over the Carter administration than over the Ford administration.

U.S. Strategic Complacency
and Chinese Strategic Apprehensions

The Carter administration entered office with a radically different interpretation of the strategic balance from the Ford administration. Although Soviet foreign policy had not changed, the president and his secretary of state perceived opportunities for expanded superpower cooperation. In this context, they attached relatively less strategic importance to U.S.-PRC relations than their predecessors. Chinese leaders, on the other hand, not only witnessed renewed U.S. "appeasement" of the Soviet Union, but also increased Soviet activities in Indochina. Owing entirely to the change in U.S. leadership, the balance of leverage reverted to the pattern of the early Nixon administration.

JIMMY CARTER, CYRUS VANCE, AND THE REEMERGENCE OF U.S. STRATEGIC OPTIMISM

The political context of foreign policy making during the Carter administration was vastly different from that of the Ford administration. Whereas Ford had faced the political exigencies of reelection, Carter, during his first years in office, was free from the demands of campaign politics. But within the administration, foreign policy making was subject to greater conflict. Unlike the Ford and Nixon administrations, in which Kissinger was the dominant foreign policy actor, the Carter administration, through Secretary of State Cyrus Vance and the national security adviser, Zbigniew Brzezinski, engaged in constant struggle over the direction of U.S. foreign policy. Whereas Brzezinski pressed for a tougher Soviet policy, Vance was considerably less alarmed than Brzezinski over Soviet weapons modernization and Third World activities and he sought to preserve détente and maximize the prospects for arms control. This was true not only in Soviet policy but also, as we shall see, in the development of policy toward China.

During the administration's first fifteen months, Carter and Vance shared an optimistic view of the Soviet Union and U.S. security. This U.S. reassessment of the Soviet threat was not based on any observable changes in Soviet behavior since the election. The president simply believed that the previous administration had overreacted to the USSR's strategic arms development and behavior in the Third World. Moreover, Carter had more confidence than Ford in American capabilities and the strategic balance of power. When questioned by reporters, he affirmed U.S. strategic superiority and expressed no concern over ongoing Soviet ICBM deployment. Although Carter voiced some unease over continued Soviet testing of mobile SS20 IRBMs, he not did seem especially concerned about the implications for NATO security of the new weapons system. Soviet deployment of both the SS20 and the Backfire Bomber in October 1977 did not alter the president's position.[2]

Carter's sanguine attitude toward both the nuclear balance and Soviet intentions was clearly expressed in his decisions on key U.S. weapons systems. Although Moscow continued to deploy the increasingly sophisticated SS18 and SS19 ICBMs and to develop MIRV technology, suggesting that it was not prepared to exercise any restraint in developing its counterforce capabilities, Carter reversed the strategic trend of his predecessors by canceling the development of the B-1 bomber and closing down production of the Minuteman III. Moreover, he had not yet made a decision on production of the MX missile and whether or not to deploy a mobile missile.[3] Similarly, Carter announced strict guidelines on transfers of U.S. conventional arms to the Third World. The production of weapons solely designed for export was prohibited, and a ceiling was placed on the dollar amount of exports for fiscal year 1978.[4]

American optimism was also reflected in the arms-control proposals that Vance brought to Moscow in March 1977. Vance proposed a SALT II agreement calling for disproportionately large Soviet ICBM reductions. Essentially, Washington sought substantial Soviet concessions, while its own limited defense program simultaneously undermined Soviet incentives to compromise. It was not surprising that Moscow rejected Vance's proposal and even failed to offer a counterproposal.

Carter's strategic optimism was also evident in his various foreign policy speeches during this period. In May 1977, at Notre Dame University, in his first significant foreign policy speech, Carter emphasized that U.S. policy could no longer be based on containment of Soviet expansion and "almost exclusive reliance" on an alliance composed of the noncommunist states of Europe and the Western hemisphere. In the place of traditional U.S. foreign policy principles, Carter called for a new policy to meet the demands of a new world—a policy "based on constant decency in its values and on optimism in our historical vision." Part of this vision called for a reaffirmation of the prospects for U.S.-Soviet détente. "I believe in détente. . . . it means progress towards peace," Carter declared.[5] The contrast with the trend during the Ford administration could not have been clearer. Carter stressed similar themes in late July. He rejected past definitions of U.S. security, which were "often defined almost exclusively in terms of military competition with the Soviet Union." Given the changing nature of the world, U.S. policy toward the Soviet Union must be guided "by a vision of a gentler, freer, and more bountiful world." Ultimately, Carter sought to establish "a relationship of cooperation" with Moscow.[6] Equally significant is that throughout his speeches, Carter expressed little concern over Soviet weapons production and the trend in the strategic balance.

Carter held onto these themes a full year into his term. In his first State of the Union Address, while stressing his commitment to maintaining U.S. strength, Carter emphasized his administration's commitment to enhancing U.S. security via agreements with potential adversaries and to promoting international "harmony." And he failed to express concern about Soviet military policy.[7]

Carter's sanguine attitude toward the Soviet Union was also expressed in the administration's Third World policy. Whereas Kissinger had repeatedly tried to rouse American resistance to Soviet intervention in Third World conflicts and warned that Soviet Third World policy was undermining détente, the Carter administration stressed that the source of superpower contention in the Third World was neither great power politics nor Soviet expansionism, but the conflicts among Third World countries themselves. Rather than trying to contain Soviet expansionism through superpower competition in the Third World, Carter preferred to eliminate the opportunities for Soviet involvement by helping resolve local conflicts and improving relations between the United States and its Third World adversaries. Carter's many speeches on Third World issues thus neglected mention of Soviet policy and aspirations but stressed indigenous sources of regional conflict. Secretary Vance best expressed this view in an early speech setting forth the administration's Africa policy: "We proceed from a basic proposition that our policies must recognize the unique identity of Africa. We can be neither right nor effective if we treat Africa simply as . . . a testing ground of East-West competition." Vance further insisted that a "negative . . . policy that seeks only to oppose Soviet or Cuban involvement in Africa would be both dangerous and futile. Our best course is to help resolve the problems which create opportunities for external intervention."[8]

This perspective on Third World conflict was reflected in policy. Despite ongoing Cuban involvement in Angola and an increasing Cuban presence in Ethiopia, Carter sought improved U.S.-Cuba relations. Although he noted that "it would be better if . . . other nations would not send . . . military forces into Africa," and that "we would like very much for Cuba to refrain from intrusion into African affairs," he was nonetheless hopeful that there would be strengthened U.S.-Cuba relations in the near future.[9] Carter's decision to renegotiate the Panama Canal treaty revealed similar concerns. A U.S. guarantee of Panamanian sovereignty over the Canal Zone would reduce Soviet opportunities in the region, "increase" U.S. "influence in this hemisphere, . . . help to reduce any mistrust and disagreement and . . . remove a major source of anti-American feeling."[10]

Washington's Vietnam policy reflected a similar attempt to reduce U.S. conflict with Third World countries. Whereas the Ford administration refused to discuss aid to Vietnam and demanded Vietnamese accounting of Americans missing in action, one of Carter's first acts was to send a goodwill mission to Hanoi composed of opponents of U.S. involvement in the Vietnam War. In discussions with Vietnamese officials, the delegation downplayed the MIA issue as an obstacle to improved U.S.-Vietnam relations. Carter also gave serious consideration to providing economic assistance to Vietnam.[11]

The most serious and divisive Third World issue that faced the Carter administration during this period was its response to the conflict between Somalia and Ethiopia. In February 1977, a coup in Ethiopia led to a realignment in Ethiopian foreign policy toward the Soviet bloc. U.S. influence soon dwindled, and the USSR sent tanks to Ethiopia. After a visit to Moscow in May by Mengistu Haile-Mariam, the Ethiopian leader, Cuban military advisers arrived in Ethiopia. In July, planeloads of Soviet arms began arriving each week.[12]

In this atmosphere, border conflict between Somalia and Ethiopia in the Ogaden region intensified. In late July, Somali forces crossed into the Ogaden and full-scale war developed. In September, Moscow shipped MiG-21s to Ethiopia and Cuban troops joined in the fighting. During November and December, Moscow carried out an airlift to Ethiopia of large amounts of weaponry and of Cuban troops.[13] Moscow was taking advantage of the conflict to expand its influence in the region.

Brzezinski lobbied hard for the administration to respond actively to Soviet and Cuban involvement in the Ogaden conflict. Soviet policy, he argued, was a challenge to U.S. interests and credibility in the Middle East and an attempt to carry out expansion without risking détente. But Vance successfully argued that Soviet policy was a "textbook case of . . . exploitation of a local conflict," and that the administration should seek a local solution that would minimize the opportunity for Soviet meddling. In early 1978, Brzezinski pressed for a military response to the conflict, including sending a carrier task force to the Horn of Africa and encouraging other states to send arms to Somalia. But he stood alone among Carter's advisers, and the president decided to refrain from involving the United States in the conflict.[14]

Once again, the contrast to the Nixon-Ford era was striking. Whereas Ford and Kissinger had been trying to arouse domestic support for U.S. opposition to Soviet policy, Carter and Vance did not perceive a significant challenge. The parallel to the 1971 Indo-Pakistani conflict was also striking. In 1971, Nixon responded to the threat of escalation by sending a carrier task force to the Bay of Bengal. Carter rejected this option during the Ogaden conflict.

Thus, through the end of the Ogaden conflict in early 1978, Carter held to an optimistic view of the Soviet Union and of the prospects for consolidating U.S.-Soviet détente. During this period, not only did Secretary of State Vance enjoy the president's support in developing Soviet policy, he also maintained control over China policy. As a result, China policy was dominated by a concern for maintaining U.S.-Soviet stability, rather than by an effort to compensate for perceived U.S. vulnerability to Soviet opportunism.

INCREASED CHINESE ISOLATION AND SOVIET POLICY IN ASIA

Whereas the 1976 U.S. election resolved Washington's political instability, Chinese succession politics continued through 1977 as Chinese leaders continued to struggle for political leadership in the post-Mao era. Moreover, in contrast to the 1973–76 period, China's security situation deteriorated. The Carter administration had rediscovered détente, with all its connotations for Chinese security, and the Soviet Union was making inroads into Indochina, China's strategic "backyard."

In mid 1976, Chairman Mao's deteriorating health had led to increased radical authority. But his death on September 9, 1976, transformed the policy-making environment. There no longer existed a leader with sufficient preeminence to establish unchallenged policy-making authority in Chinese politics. Premier Hua hoped to assume Mao's mantle. Nearly one month after Mao died, with the assistance of moderate politicians and military leaders, he ousted the radical leadership and assumed the leadership of the Chinese Communist Party. But this did not end the succession struggle, for Hua was anything but secure in his position. He and Deng Xiaoping, who exercised far greater authority in Chinese politics now that Mao had died, struggled for dominance. By March 1977, Deng had already criticized Hua's policy line, and senior politicians were calling for Deng's rehabilitation. By May, the pressure on Hua was irresistible and Deng was back at work. By August, Deng had assumed control of foreign policy.[15] Nevertheless, the struggle for preeminence continued well into 1978.

The absence of a preeminent leader and the ensuing power

struggle in 1977 compelled Hua and Deng to consider the domestic political ramifications of their respective foreign policies. To expand his political base, Hua had to overcome his career history as a beneficiary of the Cultural Revolution and Mao's chosen successor by establishing a reputation for moderation in foreign policy. In other words, he had to evince a readiness to work with the United States. On the other hand, both he and Deng Xiaoping had to avoid any suggestion of weakness on the Taiwan issue. Taiwan is the most sensitive nationalist issue in Chinese politics, and any sign of softness on the part of a politician might expose him to very damaging criticism.

Domestic politics further impinged on Chinese foreign policy by enhancing Beijing's sense of vulnerability to Soviet power. Following Mao's death, Moscow initiated an effort to reduce Sino-Soviet tension. It softened its anti-China polemics, and Soviet leaders personally stressed their interest in better relations. Chinese leaders recognized these and other Soviet signals, but they concluded that Moscow expected China to make all the concessions. They believed that Moscow hoped that China's "complex domestic political process" during the post-Mao succession and its "extreme difficulties in domestic affairs" would compel Beijing to seek improved relations with Moscow. Moreover, Chinese leaders believed that "fake" Soviet overtures sought to convey the image of Soviet reasonableness to other communist parties and to the Soviet people, so that Moscow could blame Beijing for ongoing Sino-Soviet tension. Moscow also hoped that an atmosphere of improved Sino-Soviet relations would thwart improved relations between the United States and the PRC. China could expect ongoing Soviet attempts to probe Chinese intentions, but it believed that Moscow's "basic anti-China policy" would not change.[16]

Thus, although Beijing initially reciprocated Soviet gestures by quieting its polemics against Moscow, this respite quickly passed, and the two sides returned to their familiar pattern of polemical exchanges and rigid hostility. Hua Guofeng was soon railing against Soviet hopes for reduced conflict, while *Renmin ribao* attacked Soviet "nuclear intimidation" and stressed the need for vigilance.[17] Despite the death of Mao and the purge of radical politicians, Sino-Soviet conflict failed to relax through 1977. The tension ran far deeper than mere leadership policy preferences. Moreover, as the Chinese analysis of Soviet probes reveals, Chinese political instability had heightened Beijing's sensitivity to Soviet pressure and aggravated the PRC's suspicion of Soviet intentions.

U.S. Soviet policy further aroused Chinese concern about Soviet foreign policy. The Carter administration's stress on Soviet human rights violations and initial U.S.-Soviet conflict over arms control suggested that Washington might eschew détente in favor of a tough containment policy.[18] Before long, however, it was clear to Chinese leaders that the United States was prepared to forsake a tough line in order to protect détente. By September, Beijing was issuing China's harshest criticism of U.S. "appeasement" of the Soviet Union since 1971. In his September speech at the United Nations, Foreign Minister Huang Hua declared that "the United States is on the defensive," and that "there is still a strong trend toward appeasement in the West. Some people hope that temporary ease can be gained by making compromises and concession." Huang criticized leaders who believed they could "restrain" the Soviet Union "by signing agreements and expanding economic exchanges with it and by giving it loans." The danger for China was clear, for these Western leaders were trying to "divert [the Soviet] peril toward the east." Concerning arms control, *Xinhua* insisted that the United States made "most of the concessions," while the Soviet Union made "no meaningful concessions in return." In November, an authoritative article in *Renmin ribao* accused "some political figures" and "certain leading figures of the U.S. monopoly bourgeoisie" of forgetting the lessons of the 1938 Munich Pact with Hitler and "repeating [British Prime Minister Neville] Chamberlain's old ploy."[19]

U.S. policy on the war in the Ogaden reinforced PRC attitudes. China viewed the conflict in light of its anti-Soviet struggle and offered Somalia military hardware.[20] The United States, on the other hand, declined to intervene. Whereas President Ford had tried to resist Soviet-Cuban involvement in Angola in 1975, Carter failed to perceive a challenge in Soviet-Cuban involvement in the Horn of Africa. The U.S. contribution to the anti-Soviet united front had reached its nadir.

Thus, while China experienced debilitating domestic divisions, the United States seemed to be encouraging further Soviet expansion by pursuing an appeasement policy. Moreover, the danger of expansion was the greatest on China's periphery, for stability in Europe would encourage Moscow to pursue its expansionist tendencies in Asia.

Indeed, whereas Vietnam had adopted an independent stance in 1976, by May 1977, it had abandoned its efforts to seek significant Western economic assistance and reconciled itself to greater dependency on the Soviet Union, joining the International Bank for Economic Construction of the Council on Mutual Economic Assistance (CMEA) and the Soviet-sponsored International Investment Bank. As an apparent reward for Hanoi's decision to move closer toward the Soviet economic bloc, Moscow promised to expedite its industrial shipments to Vietnam and to provide Hanoi with "big easyterm credits."[21] By early 1978, the Soviet Union was playing a crucial role in Vietnamese development. Moreover, Moscow and Hanoi were also improving military ties. The Vietnamese defense minister, Vo Nguyen Giap, visited Moscow in March and May 1977. In July, a Soviet military delegation visited Da Nang and Cam Ranh Bay, giving substance to Giap's and Soviet Defense Minister Dmitry Ustinov's "readiness to promote the expansion and deepening of the friendly ties" between their respective armed forces.[22]

In the midst of these developments, Sino-Vietnamese border conflict developed, and tension over Vietnam's treatment of its overseas Chinese population and disputed offshore islands intensified. Then in June 1977, Li Xiannian turned down Vietnam's request for additional economic assistance, criticized Hanoi's border and overseas Chinese policies, and warned Pham Van Dong that China was disturbed by the trend in Vietnam's Soviet policy.[23] When Le Duan visited Beijing in late November, the gulf between the two sides was clear, and China could only hope to minimize the damage rather than prevent it.[24]

Meanwhile, Vietnam was pressing ahead in its effort to establish a "special relationship" with its smaller Indochinese neighbors. In June, Vietnamese Party Secretary Le Duan and Premier Pham Van Dong visited Laos and signed a defense treaty. With full Soviet support, Hanoi had established dominance over Laos.[25]

Hanoi experienced greater difficulty in relations with Phnom Penh. Following the victory of the Khmer Rouge leader Pol Pot over his factional opponents in early 1977, Vietnamese-Cambodian border hostilities escalated. In the late summer, Hanoi shelled Cambodia heavily and deployed artillery, aircraft, and tanks along the border, while the two sides exchanged incursions into each other's territory. Meanwhile, Phnom Penh had broken off border negotiations and rejected Hanoi's offer to negotiate the conflict. In late December, Vietnam launched an attack on Cambodian border forces and penetrated 65 miles into Cambodian territory.

Chinese leaders met with Vietnamese and Cambodian diplomats in an attempt to mediate the conflict and moderate Phnom Penh's Vietnam policy. But Phnom Penh rejected Beijing's efforts and Vietnamese-Cambodian conflict continued, leading Beijing to back

Phnom Penh rather than accede to expanded Vietnamese, and hence Soviet, influence in Indochina. As an authoritative commentary explained, Moscow aimed to "establish its hegemony in Southeast Asia" and was "playing an old trick in the conflict between Cambodia and Vietnam. Obviously it is the one who is doing the agitation and is anxious to stir up trouble." Moscow was "adding fuel over the Cambodia-Vietnam conflict in order to fish in troubled waters," *Xinhua* declared.[26]

Thus, in 1977 China faced a deteriorating strategic position on its southern periphery in the context of ongoing domestic instability. It was in no position to create bilateral tension to pressure Washington to normalize relations. On the contrary, given U.S. strategic complacency, patience was its sole recourse.

A Step Backward in U.S.-PRC Relations

President Carter's complacent view of U.S. security allowed the administration to take a relaxed attitude toward normalization. In contrast to the Nixon/Kissinger stress on China's global importance, the Carter administration's early views expressed indifference to China's strategic role and the pace of normalization. Vance believed that regardless of Sino-Soviet relations, as far as economic development and military strength were concerned, China was not a "major strategic power." Accordingly, he was in no hurry to normalize relations. Early in the administration, he repeatedly stressed that normalization was the administration's "ultimate goal," and that "ultimately" the two sides would achieve it. He insisted, however, that there should be no "artificial deadlines" compelling the administration to seek rapid normalization at the expense of its original objectives.[27]

In contrast to the Carter administration's lack of interest, China's first foreign policy signals following the death of Mao and the purge of the radicals indicated an interest in lifting the chill in U.S.-PRC relations and a readiness to consider early normalization. Beijing may have hoped that now that the United States had resolved its own "succession crisis," the time was ripe to normalize relations. When a U.S. congressional delegation visited China in November 1976, it encountered none of the belligerency Hugh Scott had faced in July. Rather, it held "friendly" talks with Li Xiannian, and China did not raise the Taiwan issue, preferring to stress the Soviet threat.[28] Hua Guofeng's personal statements seemed to imply heightened Chinese interest in U.S.-PRC cooperation against the Soviet

Union. Similarly, in January 1977, an important analysis of Zhou Enlai's contribution to Chinese diplomacy offered unprecedented praise for U.S.-PRC rapprochement and made the conciliatory assertion that Beijing had "consistently held" that the Taiwan issue "be solved through negotiations and not by resort to armed force."[29] Mao had criticized Zhou Enlai in 1973 for suggesting a similar approach to restoring mainland control over Taiwan.

The United States did not grasp China's offer. It was content to defer normalization until both its domestic agenda and U.S.-Soviet relations provided the appropriate opportunity. But whereas Beijing had tried to press the Ford administration to normalize relations quickly, its leverage over the United States diminished with Carter's victory. As long as the United States was unconcerned about the Soviet threat, regardless of Beijing's understanding of the misguided nature of U.S. policy, the threat of increased U.S.-PRC tension would have little impact on U.S. China policy. On the contrary, increased tension would merely exacerbate the isolation of the PRC in the face of the growing Soviet threat. Beijing was thus compelled to accept in near silence the Carter's administration's rejection of the Ford administration's agenda of rapid normalization.

Moreover, domestic politics soon encouraged the immediate post-Mao leadership to retreat from its conciliatory posture. Albeit avoiding the belligerency of the radicals, Hua Guofeng ceased making unconventional statements, and the media adopted a less conciliatory posture.[30] At the height of the post-Mao political succession, Hua was in no position to suggest compromise. And Deng Xiaoping faced similar constraints. Although he might be China's most dominant politician, he, too, had to avoid criticism on the Taiwan issue. By the spring, Chinese normalization policy had returned to that of 1975—Beijing wanted and expected complete normalization and awaited U.S. compromise, and it would not accept preliminary agreements. But its policy exhibited greater patience, reflecting its vulnerability to isolation in a period of increased Soviet expansion in Asia and the White House's renewed interest in superpower détente.

THE CLAIMS-ASSETS EPISODE

Chinese policy was clearly reflected in Beijing's response to the administration's first China initiative. When David Rockefeller returned from China in January 1977, he reported to his good friend Secretary of State Cyrus Vance that China was prepared to recommence negotiations and reach an early agreement on the claims-assets dispute. Relying on Rockefeller's advice, even before the new administration had completed its study of China policy, Secretary Vance overruled his China specialists in the State Department and decided to move ahead with a claims-assets initiative.[31]

The China specialists, particularly those who had been in the Ford administration, argued that raising the claims-asset issue would be a counterproductive start for the new administration. Without first laying the groundwork with Beijing for normalization, a U.S. initiative on claims-assets would merely reinforce PRC perceptions that the United States aimed to reap additional advantages from the U.S.-PRC dialogue without having to compromise on Taiwan.

The China specialists were right. When William Gleysteen approached Chinese officials in Washington in April 1977 with a proposal to open negotiations, Han Xu, the deputy head of the liaison office, responded with a stern, hard-line refusal, causing the administration to make an embarrassing retreat. Gleysteen concluded that the proposal was a "non-starter." China had refused such gambits in 1975, and it turned down the Carter administration's 1977 initiative as well. Moreover, Chinese officials were now suspicious that the United States was not taking normalization seriously.[32] Consequently, as in 1975, Beijing rejected partial agreements, seeking full normalization of relations.

THE VANCE VISIT TO CHINA

In truth, the Carter administration did not even have a China policy. Nor did it seem much interested in developing one. When the president's national security team first met in January 1977 to consider the most important issues requiring analysis, it omitted U.S.-PRC relations. The omission of China is particularly noteworthy, because the team ordered Presidential Review Memorandums (PRM) for fifteen issues, including various regional matters and the Panama Canal, North-South relations, and U.S. bases in the Philippines. That the analysis for China was PRM 24 reflected the administration's inattention to China policy; the study was launched in April and would not be completed until well into the summer.[33]

PRM 24 reached the conclusion that the administration should seek normalization of relations with China in accordance with the commitments of its predecessors. It conceded that the administration would abrogate the U.S.-ROC Mutual Defense Treaty, withdraw all U.S. troops from Taiwan, and break diplomatic relations with Taipei.[34] But the study did not lay out a timetable for normal-

ization. When the United States would make the concessions required for normalization remained to be determined. And it was
clear that Carter was in no hurry to conciliate PRC interests. He
believed that the previous administration had been too accommodating to the Chinese, and he instructed Brzezinski that the Carter
administration "should not ass-kiss them the way Nixon and Kissinger did."[35] Nor did PRM 24 resolve the issue of how the United
States would maintain ties with Taipei in the postnormalization era.
Although the United States would accept important Chinese conditions, the administration still had to find a mutually acceptable
formula for maintaining ties between Washington and Taipei. Moreover, the issue of linkage remained on the agenda. PRM 24 reportedly concluded that the administration would seek an explicit commitment from China not to use force against Taiwan in exchange
for U.S. compliance with Chinese demands that the United States
abrogate its defense treaty with Taiwan.[36]

Thus began a debate in the administration over the timing and
terms of normalization that developed during the summer of 1977
in preparation for Vance's upcoming August trip to China. As was
the case in other aspects of administration security policy, Brzezinski adopted the position most geared to resisting Soviet expansion.
From day one, in fact, Brzezinski sought to develop a security relationship with China to "discourage Soviet expansion."[37] During discussions over PRM 24 in June, he argued that during his visit to
Beijing, Vance should make a commitment to normalization, and
that the administration should adopt measures aimed at deempha-
sizing U.S. ties to Taiwan. Brzezinski, however, was fairly isolated
among the administration's senior policy advisers and China specialists, who argued that the pace he suggested was too fast. But
Brzezinski continued to raise the issue with Carter, and on July 30,
in a preparatory meeting for the Vance trip, Carter suddenly announced that Vance should move ahead on normalization as quickly
as possible.[38] The stage seemed set for normalization.

But the second unresolved issue still had to be addressed. How
would the United States maintain ties with Taiwan after normalization? Analysts in the State Department's Policy Planning Office argued that Vance should propose to Beijing that although Washington
would break diplomatic relations with Taiwan, it would nonetheless
maintain an official presence in Taipei—either a consular office or
something similar. Paul Kreisberg, Policy Planning's chief China
specialist, strongly argued this position against the opposition of As-

sistant Secretary of State Richard Holbrooke and the China specialists in the State Department's Office of East Asia and Pacific Affairs.
Kreisberg argued that it would be embarrassing for the United States
to jury-rig a relationship with Taiwan, and that it was worthwhile
to try to obtain Chinese agreement to the U.S. optimal position before having to fall back to a compromise stance.[39] Once again, the
China specialists elsewhere in the State Department argued that
this would be unacceptable to Beijing and would set back the relationship. Indeed, Kissinger had made a similar proposal to Beijing in
1974, only to have Deng reject it.

But the real issue in the dispute was how quickly to move toward
normalization. Those officials who argued for official U.S. representation on Taiwan were also in no hurry to normalize and were unprepared to make the necessary compromises. The China specialists
and the NSC were now ready for normalization, and they promoted
a position that would exclude official U.S. representation from Taiwan and expedite normalization. Vance ultimately agreed with his
Policy Planning advisers and prepared to propose to Beijing that
there be official U.S. representation on Taiwan after normalization.[40]

Much has been made about the role of U.S. domestic politics in
delaying normalization. Certainly, Carter's first priority was to obtain passage of the Panama Canal treaty by Congress and he could
not afford to alienate wavering congressmen with a controversial
China initiative. Thus, despite Brzezinski's urging, Carter decided
that while in Beijing, Vance should leave the draft normalization
communiqué in his pocket.[41]

Although this account is accurate, it does not fully explain the
delay in normalization. Had he presented Beijing with the communiqué, Vance recalls, he expected the leadership of the PRC to refuse
to normalize relations because of his insistence on stationing U.S.
officials in Taiwan. Regardless of the domestic politics of the congressional vote on the Panama Canal treaty, Vance was not prepared
to abandon the Carter administration's position on official representation in Taipei in the postnormalization period. The United States
was not ready to normalize relations, and Vance was content to use
a maximum negotiating position, aware that it would most likely
be rejected by Beijing, in order to extend the negotiations until he
was confident that U.S.-PRC normalization would not interfere with
U.S. arms-control negotiations with the Soviet Union. When the final U.S. advance team came to Beijing just prior to Vance's arrival
and informed the U.S. liaison office that Vance's presentation would
include the demand for an official U.S. presence in Taipei after nor

malization, U.S. officials in Beijing quickly concluded that Vance's visit would not advance the normalization process.[42]

The secondary influence of domestic politics on U.S. policy at this time is also revealed by comparing the Carter administration's reaction to its domestic difficulties to that of the Ford administration. Whereas Kissinger chafed under the domestic political constraints of the upcoming presidential election and sought to advance U.S.-PRC relations despite the domestic obstacles, Vance was content with the status quo and was prepared to string out normalization negotiations, unperturbed by delays imposed by U.S. domestic politics. Indeed, there was little expectation in the administration that Vance was going to China to advance any aspect of the relationship. For example, despite obvious Chinese interest in purchasing advanced technology and in developing science and technology exchange agreements with Western countries, during the preparation for the Vance visit, U.S. officials gave no consideration whatsoever to holding discussions on technology transfer or science and technology issues.[43] Given a context of similar domestic restraints, the contrast in the attitudes of the Ford and Carter administrations toward developing U.S.-PRC relations reflected their different strategic perspectives on the Soviet Union.

Vance expressed his tough position toward normalization before leaving for Beijing. His late June speech at the Asia Society advised China that "mutual and reciprocal" efforts were required for normalization, indicating that Washington expected China to compromise on key issues. Just prior to his departure for Beijing, administration officials called the press's attention to this part of the speech, once again signaling China its expectations.[44]

For Beijing's part, when Huang Zhen, the head of the Chinese liaison office, met with President Carter in February, he underscored China's expectation that the Carter administration would pick up where the Ford administration had left off—a commitment to pursue normalization actively after the 1976 election and U.S. acceptance at least of the Japan formula. Then, in early July, Li Xiannian publicly insisted that China had the right to decide whether or not to use force to unify Taiwan.[45] Although this statement may have served Li's domestic political objectives by establishing his hard-line credentials, it also put the United States on notice that China would not compromise on the Taiwan issue and suggested limits to Chinese patience.

Chinese leaders thus hoped that Vance would come to Beijing prepared to normalize relations in accordance with past U.S. commitments. Although China remained engulfed in succession politics, this was not an insurmountable obstacle to normalization. Deng was still struggling for control of economic policy making, but he had assumed responsibility for Chinese foreign policy. If he could deliver U.S.-PRC normalization without compromising on Beijing's most important conditions, this diplomatic success would bolster his overall prestige and assist him in his battle with Hua for the preeminent voice in Chinese politics.

But when the Vance mission arrived in China in late August with Washington's maximum position on postnormalization U.S.-Taiwan relations, PRC politicians were in no mood to listen to proposals they had rejected during the previous administration. Vance laid out the U.S. position on normalization in an early meeting with Foreign Minister Huang Hua. Vance explained to Huang that in order to guarantee ongoing exchanges between the United States and Taiwan in such areas as trade, investment, and travel and scientific exchanges, after normalization of relations it would be necessary for U.S. "officials" to remain in Taiwan "under unofficial arrangements." Adding greater specificity to the Nixon/Ford statements on "peaceful resolution of the Taiwan issue," he also said that after normalization the United States would need to make an announcement declaring its concern for and interest in having the Chinese people themselves peacefully resolve the Taiwan issue. Vance also insisted that China not issue an announcement opposing this statement or advocating use of force to resolve the Taiwan issue. Vance said that if China accepted these U.S. conditions, then the United States would withdraw all of its troops and military equipment from Taiwan and recognize the People's Republic of China as the sole legal government of China.[46]

American officials believed that Vance's presentation was a momentous act. Despite the caveat about postnormalization official U.S. representation of Taiwan, this was the first time an American official had declared U.S. readiness to normalize relations. U.S. domestic political issues were clearly manageable, and it was now simply a matter of reaching agreement on U.S.-Taiwan relations after normalization. Indeed, members of the U.S. delegation left this first meeting with Huang convinced that there had been significant progress toward normalization of relations.[47]

Nevertheless, China firmly rejected Vance's proposal. Vice Premier Deng Xiaoping, having recently returned to his posts, and clearly speaking with greater authority than Party Chairman and

Premier Hua Guofeng, delivered China's reaction. Deng told Vance that the U.S. position that American officials would remain in Taiwan after normalization was "a step backward." The Ford administration had offered the Japan formula, Deng correctly noted, and the Vance proposal was thus a retreat. Deng also put forth China's three conditions for resolving the Taiwan issue and establishing diplomatic relations: the United States must "abrogate the treaty, withdraw troops, and break relations." Not only did Vance suggest a continued U.S. official presence on Taiwan, but his presentation failed to mention the abrogation of the U.S.-ROC Mutual Defense Treaty.[48]

Deng's harsh response was nonetheless not a retreat from the PRC's previous negotiating positions. Although Deng rejected continued presence of U.S. officials on Taiwan in accordance with the Japan formula, he "made allowance for reality" and conceded that after normalization, people-to-people, unofficial exchanges could be maintained. Most important, he did not challenge Vance's insistence that the United States would issue a postnormalization statement concerning its interest in peaceful unification, and that China not contradict this statement. Insofar as Vance's demand elaborated on the Shanghai communiqué and on the majority of subsequent statements by Kissinger and Ford in their meetings in Beijing, rather than seeking explicit Chinese acceptance of this position, as Kissinger had unsuccessfully tried to do in 1974, China did not object. It thus appeared that the two sides would have little difficulty reaching agreement on this significant issue.[49]

Moreover, Deng had also formally and explicitly reformulated the PRC's three conditions. Whereas the politburo and Zhou Enlai had insisted in 1971 that the United States accept that Taiwan was a Chinese province, Deng did not include this condition among the three conditions that he presented to Vance. Since 1971, it had apparently become clear to Beijing that China simply lacked the leverage to compel Washington to make this concession. Given the importance of normalization in Chinese foreign and domestic policy, Beijing would have to content itself with the ambiguous language of the Shanghai communiqué—Washington might acknowledge the PRC position that Taiwan was part of China, but it could not be compelled to state its own position.

Many of the obstacles to normalization had been resolved. Nevertheless, the issue of postnormalization U.S.-Taiwan relations remained on the agenda and, in this respect, the two sides were no closer to agreement than they had been in 1975. Beijing was not persuaded by Vance's presentation that the United States was ready to move forward. On the contrary, whereas PRC leaders undoubtedly expected that Carter would fulfill Ford's commitments, the new administration, as Deng noted, had actually retreated from the position of the Nixon and Ford administrations. To the Chinese, Vance's presentation seemed one more useless meeting with indecisive U.S. diplomats.[50]

Yet the United States seemed to have a different understanding of the results of the Vance mission. An article written for the *Boston Herald American*, based on a leak by Samuel Huntington from the NSC, reported that the White House believed that the Vance mission had found Chinese leaders flexible on the terms of normalization, and that there had been "progress" toward normalization. The NSC assessment was based on cables from Beijing reporting the U.S. mission's early optimism after Vance's initial meeting with Huang Hua. But the administration also suggested optimism even after Vance returned from Beijing. The president praised Vance for having achieved a "major step forward" toward normalization, and he reported that Vance had discussed normalization conditions that would allow the people of Taiwan to "live in freedom," suggesting that the U.S. position on subsequent U.S.-Taiwan relations was not an obstacle to normalization.[51]

Not only did the administration's optimism reflect Washington's misreading of China's reaction to Vance's presentation, but it was also sure to arouse a harsh response from the leadership of the PRC. In a meeting with the board of the Associated Press, Deng charged that the Vance mission represented a setback in U.S.-PRC relations, and that Vance had retreated from the position of his predecessors.[52]

Deng's public rebuke of the Carter administration was a response not only to the inaccuracy of the media report but also to its diplomatic and domestic political importance. The incorrect newspaper report and Carter's later statement, no matter how innocent they may have been, suggested a crude revival of Kissingerian tactics of seeking to use the mere image of improved U.S.-PRC relations to strengthen U.S. Soviet policy, when the reality was just the opposite. Given the fiasco over the claims-assets negotiations, the Vance proposal must have reinforced Chinese suspicions that the Carter administration was not committed to normalization, despite Vance's assurances. These reports also played back into Chinese politics. Deng Xiaoping could not afford a reputation for flexibility on the Taiwan issue. Thus, by firing off a public salvo setting the record straight and adding a hint of tension to U.S.-PRC relations, he

quickly protected his domestic position and undermined any benefits to U.S. Soviet policy that Washington might have hoped to derive from the misleading report.[53]

U.S. STALLING ON NORMALIZATION

The Carter administration was in no hurry to either mend fences
or to resume the negotiations. On the contrary, following Vance's
return from Beijing, normalization was placed on the "back burner,"
inasmuch as the president was preoccupied with securing Senate
ratification of the Panama Canal treaty, and the State Department,
under Vance's guidance, tried to delay the normalization process until U.S.-Soviet relations were back on track. Vance remained the administration's principal formulator of foreign policy, and he and Carter were in no rush to accommodate Chinese demands. Carter told
reporters that he did not feel compelled to "act precipitously" on
normalization. "I feel like I've got time," he said. He insisted that
"if" the administration decided to recognize the PRC, the decision
was "undoubtedly going to be well in the future." Vance later recalled that he thought the negotiations were proceeding at the right
pace, and that an agreement would eventually emerge.[54]

The administration's reluctance to move ahead with normalization was reflected in the difficulty it had in abandoning its demand
for an official U.S. presence on Taiwan after normalization. It was
clear from both the negotiating record of the Nixon and Ford administrations and from Vance's own experience in Beijing that Washington would have to accept the "Japan formula" in full and completely
sever official relations with Taipei in order to establish diplomatic
relations with Beijing. And it should have been a fairly easy step
simply to retract this demand and return to the position Kissinger
and Ford had presented to Beijing in 1975. Nevertheless, the State
Department dragged its feet on this issue, trying to string out the
normalization process until it believed that normalization of U.S.-
PRC relations would not interfere with Vance's efforts to secure an
arms-control treaty with the Soviet Union.

When the head of the U.S. liaison office in Beijing, Leonard Woodcock, returned to the United States in late September to attend a
meeting of foreign ministers at the United Nations, he and Secretary
Vance met with Foreign Minister Huang Hua in New York. This was
Vance's first opportunity to inform the Chinese that Washington had
reconsidered its position. Deng Xiaoping's presentation in September had been most helpful in explaining Chinese policy, and the
United States would respond, he told Huang. But since the response

had not yet been prepared, Vance explained, Ambassador Woodcock would present it to Huang when he returned to China. Vance also said that all future normalization negotiations should be held in Beijing, and that Woodcock would conduct the negotiations on behalf of the United States.[55] Vance thus suggested that upon Woodcock's return to China, the United States would recommence the negotiations and retract its demand for an official presence in Taiwan after normalization.

The next day, in a meeting with Vance and his aides, Woodcock was told that he would receive new written instructions within three or four days. But when Woodcock later called for the instructions, State Department officials replied that they were not ready. For six weeks Woodcock pressed for his new instructions, and for six weeks the State Department failed to respond, despite another meeting between Vance and Woodcock on October 14, in which Vance confirmed that there were no problems in issuing new instructions. Finally, in November, Assistant Secretary of State for East Asia Richard Holbrooke suggested that Woodcock should return to China and wait there for new instructions.

The delay was caused by discussions within the State Department as to whether Woodcock should be instucted to initiate normalization negotiations or merely to temporize. But because Woodcock did not look forward to meeting his Chinese counterparts without a new negotiating position, he insisted that he would not return to Beijing without new instructions until he had met with the president and determined that these were his wishes. Given Woodcock's personal relationship with Carter, he could easily bypass Vance and make a direct appeal to the president.[56]

Woodcock's threat prompted the State Department to arrange another meeting between Vance and Woodcock, and this time Vance had the new instructions. Yet the policy makers favoring further delay had carefully constrained Woodcock's negotiating flexibility. Rather than accentuating the positive aspects of a new round of negotiations and laying out a new position permitting Woodcock to engage in substantive discussions, the instructions simply allowed him to inform the Chinese leadership that Washington no longer sought an official presence on Taiwan after normalization. Woodcock could return to Beijing as the administration's chief negotiator, but he could not resume the negotiations. He was personally unhappy with this outcome, for normalization remained on the "back burner."[57]

Given Vance's assurances in September at the United Nations and the six-week delay, not only Woodcock but also the leadership of the PRC believed that Woodcock's return to China would permit serious negotiations to begin. Foreign Minister Huang Hua had expected Woodcock to make a substantive presentation, and he expressed some disbelief and disappointment at the brevity of the U.S. response to Deng's September comments.[58] Washington was clearly still not ready to normalize relations, and China would have to wait.

Like Woodcock, Brzezinski was not prepared to allow China policy to stagnate. As Vance tried to maintain a slow pace for normalization, Brzezinski tried to develop momentum toward closer relations. One way he did this was to develop a dialogue with Chinese leaders that might provide the basis for a strategic relationship. He and Han Xu, the acting head of the Chinese liaison office in Washington, held regular discussions of foreign policy, which kept China up to date on the U.S. administration's assessment of the Soviet threat. Brzezinski also reached into the State Department to develop support for normalization. He held policy review meetings with Michel Oksenberg, his National Security Council specialist on Chinese affairs, and Assistant Secretary of State Richard Holbrooke, who shared the NSC's enthusiasm for developing closer relations with China.[59]

Brzezinski's most important initiative to develop U.S.-PRC relations was to promote a personal visit to Beijing. He understood that a visit to China would not only allow him to shape the agenda of his own visit but would also yield him greater voice in making China policy and allow him to influence the course of the normalization process. Oksenberg accordingly suggested to Chinese officials in Washington that Brzezinski would welcome an invitation to visit China. Because Brzezinski was the Carter administration's leading "hawk," and the U.S. official most likely to appreciate the strategic significance of normalization, Chinese leaders quickly responded to Oksenberg's suggestion, and by early November, Brzezinski had received his invitation.[60]

Yet for the very reason that Brzezinski had arranged for a visit to China, Vance opposed such a visit. Vance had been trying to manage China policy in the context of U.S.-Soviet relations and suspected that Brzezinski would use such a visit to try to promote U.S.-PRC cooperation against the Soviet Union, and that, at a minimum, Brzezinski's mere reputation as an anti-Soviet hawk would foster the impression of U.S.-PRC strategic cooperation. Moreover, Vance was not confident that Brzezinski would adhere to established policy, fearing that he would make policy on his own. Finally, Vance must

have been concerned that Brzezinski would use the visit to capture
U.S. China policy for the NSC and expedite normalization at the
risk of jeopardizing superpower détente. Thus far, Brzezinski had
unsuccessfully tried to change China policy. But should he go to
China, he would acquire greater authority in the policy debate and
might well undermine State Department influence over the course
of normalization. Clearly, to delay normalization, as he had done
with his instructions to Woodcock, Vance had to block a Brzezinski
visit to Beijing.[61]

There thus ensued a struggle over whether any administration official should go to China and, if so, who. Vance's preferred candidate
was Vice President Walter Mondale, who, unlike Brzezinski, would
not make foreign policy, and thus could not challenge Vance's control over China policy. Vance also trusted Mondale more to stick
with established policy rather than try to reorient administration
priorities. The president, however, deferred a decision both on who
should go to China and on normalization of relations. In a February
1978 meeting with Ambassador Woodcock, Carter reaffirmed his interest in establishing relations with China, but indicated that the
appropriate opportunity would be sometime between the congressional elections in November 1978 and the start of the presidential
campaign season, presumably in late 1979. As for the relationship
between SALT and normalization, Carter believed they could move
on parallel tracks. Having thus sided with Vance on both Soviet
policy and China policy, the president neither initiated the normalization process nor sent an emissary to Beijing.[62]

The only normalization initiative during this period was an informal effort by Woodcock to probe Beijing's attitude to Washington's insistence on postnormalization U.S. weapons sales to Taiwan. On his return to Beijing in February, he raised this demand in
open statements in the U.S. embassy in Beijing and in meetings
with diplomats with close ties to the Chinese Foreign Ministry. He
knew that Chinese leaders would be briefed on his statements, and
that they would have similarly indirect opportunities to respond.
Through May, however, Beijing remained silent, suggesting that
the issue would not be an obstacle to normalization. Nevertheless,
China would have to be formally presented with this policy before
the United States could be sure that there was no misunderstanding.[63] This, however, required direct negotiations, and Washington
was not yet ready for that step.

Through 1977, the Carter administration had not moved the
United States any closer toward normalization. It seemed that Wash-

ington would once again fail to meet Chinese expectation of "second-term" normalization. Indeed, by early 1978, the Chinese leadership understood that the Carter administration was not serious about normalization, and Deng personally complained that the momentum toward normalization had slowed.[64] Still, Chinese leaders did not respond with either the aloofness or the pressure tactics that they had employed during the Ford administration. Such a posture might have worked when the United States wanted better relations to offset its own international immobility, and when Beijing could leverage U.S. fear of Soviet expansionism to its advantage. But the strategic perspective of the Carter administration in 1977 undermined the value of such tactics. As long as President Carter and Secretary of State Vance, the president's principal foreign policy adviser, held sanguine views of the U.S.-Soviet balance and of the prospects for détente and an arms-control treaty, the threat of public "cracks" in U.S.-PRC relations would not energize Washington to expedite normalization. Rather, cracks in the relationship would merely undermine Chinese security vis-à-vis the Soviet Union without yielding any payoff on the Taiwan issue. Thus, while the Carter administration apparently remained oblivious to the Soviet threat and fought bureaucratic battles over China policy, Beijing was compelled to back away from its surly and petulant posture and return to its 1972–73 tactics of soft-pedaling the Taiwan issue while trying to raise American consciousness about the Soviet threat. The most Chinese diplomats could do was to hold meetings with Brzezinski in Washington and invite him to Beijing, thus helping to bolster the position of their ally in the administration.

Thus, Deng Xiaoping's September 1977 public salvo against the Carter administration did not usher in a Chinese policy reminiscent of the 1974–76 period. Although Li Xiannian responded to President Carter's equanimity toward normalization by saying he was "quite unhappy" with the president's reluctance to part with "his old friend" Taiwan, Beijing was compelled to wait until the president recognized the necessity for cooperation against the Soviet Union, and, thus, the corresponding importance of compromise on Taiwan. When Foreign Minister Huang Hua met with Vance in New York in September, he was most friendly and revealed no lingering discontent from the August discussions in Beijing. Moreover, he assured Vance that China was in no hurry to hear U.S. views on normalization and that it would not press the issue. Similarly, in November, when Woodcock presented Huang with Washington's relatively brief reply to Deng's presentation, Huang was surprised and expressed dismay, but there was no evidence of frustration or impatience. As the months went on, Chinese diplomats would needle Woodcock regarding U.S. procrastination, but there was no Chinese suggestion of pressure or hostility.[65]

U.S.-PRC Military and Trade Relations

The Carter administration's early retreat from its predecessor's interest in consolidating U.S.-PRC relations through rapid normalization of relations was also reflected in its policy toward U.S.-PRC military relations and U.S. export to China of high-technology items.

Concerned about Soviet efforts to take advantage of U.S. domestic divisions and American withdrawal from activism in Third World politics, the Ford administration had emphasized U.S.-PRC strategic ties. Kissinger's frequent assertions in 1976 of U.S. interest in Chinese security was one component of this strategy. Under the new administration, there were no such statements. President Carter and Secretary of State Vance, less wary of Soviet intentions and more concerned with maximizing Moscow's positive interest in arms control, rejected such theatrics. As long as they believed that the USSR was exercising restraint, they saw little benefit in antagonizing Moscow with unnecessary statements suggesting U.S.-PRC strategic cooperation.

The Carter administration adopted a similar attitude toward the transfer of military technology to China. As far as Vance was concerned, as long as relations with Moscow were manageable, there was no imperative to consolidate relations with China, and thus no reason to risk provoking Soviet hostility. Although Brzezinski argued for closer military ties with China in order to consolidate the security relationship, as with his other differences with Vance during this first year, he lost this argument.

The issue first arose during the preparation of PRM 24. The third item addressed in PRM 24 concerned technology transfer to China. Brzezinski and, to a lesser extent, Harold Brown argued for early development of a strategic relationship with China and supported developing technology transfer with China. They maintained that such steps toward a U.S.-PRC strategic relationship would encourage Moscow to exercise caution with respect to U.S. interests. Consistent with other aspects of his preferred China policy, Vance argued to the president that development of U.S.-PRC security ties would be "quite dangerous," because "nothing would be regarded as more hostile" by the Soviet Union, and it would lead Moscow to reevaluate the benefits of diminished U.S.-Soviet tension. Vance was so concerned that he feared that a mere leak indicating that the administration was even considering transfer of defense-related technology to China would have a considerable effect on superpower relations. Ultimately, Vance's position prevailed, and the analysis of technology transfer in PRM 24 excluded discussion of defense-related technology transfer, reportedly concluding that such transfers would lead to a "fundamental reassessment" by Moscow of its U.S. policy and to increased tension between the superpowers. Thus, not only did the Carter administration not engage in dual-use technology transfer to China, it also retreated from the Ford administration's policy of encouraging other countries to develop an arms-sales relationship with China.[66]

Nevertheless, Brzezinski continued to press for the development of a security relationship. When retired Admiral Elmo Zumwalt visited Beijing in July, Brzezinski asked him to "make clear" to Chinese leaders that the United States had not decided to block weapons sales to China.[67] When the issue of sales of dual-use equipment next arose in early 1978 in the context of PRM 31 discussions, Brzezinski, with greater support from Brown, again pushed for enhanced security relations and Vance again resisted, insisting that Washington must have a balanced policy toward the Soviet Union and China regarding military technology, for a tilt toward China would damage U.S.-Soviet relations.[68]

For the most part, Vance continued to prevail over Brzezinski. The exception was the administration's policy on military-related technology transfer to China by U.S. allies. So concerned was Vance over this issue that he blocked even the discussion of it within the State Department and in his presence. Ultimately, Carter split the difference between Vance on one side and Brzezinski and Brown on the other, who had proposed that Washington explicitly welcome such transfers. He decided not to oppose arms sales to China by other countries. Thus, in January 1978, nearly a year since the administration first received reports of Chinese interest in purchasing West European military equipment, Carter informed French President Valéry Giscard d'Estaing that it was up to France to decide whether or not it should sell weaponry to China.[69]

Carter's decision cleared the way for the development of security ties between Washington's NATO allies and China, and it was the first step toward restoring U.S. interest in developing a security relationship with China. Nevertheless, it was not part of an established and well-thought-out policy aimed at promoting a security relationship with China, and it did not reestablish Ford administration policy, which promoted European defense-technology transfer to China to compensate for America's inability to contain Soviet power. The Carter administration's decision was the exception to a policy that remained premised on the manageability of U.S.-Soviet relations. It consequently gave less importance to China's role in U.S. security, and thus to U.S.-PRC security ties.

Meanwhile, U.S.-PRC economic cooperation continued to stagnate.[70] The volume of 1977 U.S.-PRC trade had yet to return to pre-1975 levels. There was only a marginal increase in two-way trade in 1977, and it was below the increase in total Chinese foreign trade for the year. Moreover, the increase that did occur (11 percent) was mostly because of Chinese imports of selected U.S. agricultural products. Overall, Beijing had yet fully to resume purchases of U.S. grain, and the volume of imports of manufactured goods remained low. As in the 1975–76 period, the low level of trade was not significantly related to Beijing's dissatisfaction with U.S. China policy, but to domestic policy decisions about the extent of the PRC's exposure to the international economy. Nonetheless, minimal trade relations contributed to the overall sense of inertia in U.S.-PRC relations.

Conclusion

In 1977 President Carter entered office with radically different perspectives from his predecessor on America's global capabilities and responsibilities, Soviet foreign policy, and the prospects for U.S.-Soviet détente. He believed that the trend in U.S.-Soviet relations was compatible with U.S. security, and that American foreign policy should strive to make the world more orderly and secure. In collaboration with Secretary of State Vance, Carter developed a corresponding China policy. Not only did Carter and Vance see China as less important than their predecessors, but they also viewed normalization of U.S.-PRC relations as a potentially disruptive influence on world order, insofar as it would frustrate U.S. efforts to develop stable relations and an arms-control treaty with the Soviet Union.

Thus, unlike Kissinger and Ford, who believed that normalization was in the U.S. strategic interest and who might have normalized relations in 1975 if Ford had not had to contend with serious domestic political challenges, Carter and Vance were content with the status quo in 1977 and did not want to normalize U.S.-PRC diplomatic relations. Similarly, they did not want to develop U.S.-PRC security relations, in contrast to the Ford administration, which viewed strategic relations as a substitute for developing political relations. Thus, during the early period of the Carter administration, the United States was simply uninterested in consolidating U.S.-PRC relations.

Beijing, on the other hand, did not possess a sanguine security perspective. It witnessed renewed U.S.-Soviet détente, U.S. "appeasement" of the Soviet Union, and renewed and increasing Soviet pressure on China. As a result, during this period, Beijing's ability to maneuver declined. Thus, Washington's lack of interest in improved relations, including normalization, was the critical factor shaping U.S.-PRC negotiations. Without White House interest in China's strategic role, Beijing had no ability to affect U.S. policy toward China. In particular, it could not compel a quid pro quo that would produce normalization of relations based on China's three conditions. In contrast to its behavior from 1974 to 1976, in 1977 it had little choice but to wait patiently on the sidelines for the international changes that would encourage the United States to seek consolidated relations with China.

Developments in 1977 underscore the extent to which Beijing was the most reactive state among the Soviet Union, the United States, and China. Whereas U.S. policy toward the Soviet Union and China was a function of President Carter's personal strategic perspective, China's limited strategic weight undermined the ability of Chinese policy makers independently to shape, not only the China policy of other countries, but also their own policy toward a vital Chinese interest—the future of Taiwan. The international influence and leverage of the PRC was not primarily a function of its policy makers' creativity and diplomatic ingenuity. It was dependent on the diplomatic opportunities created by changing international circumstances.

CHAPTER 5

Normalization of Relations
THE NECESSITY FOR COMPROMISE

On December 15, 1978, the United States and China agreed to normalize diplomatic relations on January 1, 1979. To reach agreement, both sides had to make significant compromises in their long-standing positions on U.S.-Taiwan relations. The impetus for these changes reflected the changing security perspective of both states. The Carter administration's effort to ease America's preoccupation with Cold War concerns eroded when Soviet activities in the Third World prompted President Carter to reevaluate his personal commitment to U.S.-Soviet détente and his reliance on Secretary of State Vance as his principal foreign policy adviser. As the president's view of the Soviet Union changed, U.S. policy toward China no longer reflected an effort to encourage voluntary Soviet restraint in the Third World and interest in superpower arms control. Meanwhile, Chinese leaders found Moscow's interventions in the Third World particularly alarming, especially insofar as Soviet-Vietnamese cooperation extended the Soviet Union's military influence to China's southern border and into Cambodia, exacerbating Beijing's anxiety over Soviet "encirclement."

In many respects, then, normalization of relations was a strategic response to changing American and Chinese views of the international environment. But it had far broader implications for U.S.-PRC relations. Once Washington and Beijing overcame the diplomatic hurdle of establishing official relations, bilateral relations developed beyond a mere security dialogue. Washington and Beijing established military relations, trade relations, and educational and scientific programs, responding to a wide range of strategic and nonstrategic interests and establishing domestic institutional foundations for a more enduring relationship.

Washington and Beijing and the Common Soviet Threat

Beginning in 1978, the United States and China developed a common perception of the Soviet threat. Since the late 1960s, the United States and China had agreed that the Soviet Union was the greatest threat to their respective security. But this was the first time since the early Nixon administration that both sides had agreed that the threat was significantly growing. This development was crucial to the negotiations over normalization of diplomatic relations.

CARTER'S REASSESSMENT OF THE SOVIET THREAT

Although President Carter declined to send a carrier task force to the Horn of Africa during the war in the Ogaden, Cuban involvement in the war led him to begin to reassess his evaluation of the Soviet threat. Most revealing was Carter's speech—prepared by NSC officials who believed that it was time for the administration to take a harder line toward the Soviet Union—at Wake Forest University on March 17, 1978. In contrast to his earlier homilies on the importance of international cooperation, Carter called attention to an "ominous inclination on the part of the Soviet Union . . . to intervene in local conflicts . . . with mercenaries, as we can observe in Africa today." Soviet foreign policy demanded that the United States "maintain adequate responses—diplomatic, military, and economic—and we will."[1]

This pivotal speech initiated a hardening in U.S. foreign policy. Through the year, a succession of developments in U.S.-Soviet relations reinforced the trend. In April, a military coup in Afghanistan overthrew the increasingly pro-Western government of Lt. Gen. Mohammad Daoud Khan. Under the new leadership of Hafizullah Amin, Afghanistan pursued more radical and unpopular economic and social policies and invited in an expanding Soviet presence. By June 1978, the number of Soviet advisers in Afghanistan had doubled, and it continued to grow. At the end of the year, the Soviet Union and Afghanistan signed a security treaty, consolidating Kabul's pro-Soviet orientation.[2]

In May 1978, Katangan rebels based in Angola occupied the Kolwezi region of Zaire. Whereas in 1977 the White House might have treated such an issue as separate from superpower rivalry, now Carter took a hard line. He charged that Moscow had "no reticence about becoming involved militarily" in Africa. "It's a joke to call Cuba non-aligned," he said. "They act at the Soviet Union's direction, . . . as a surrogate for the Soviet Union." He accused Cuba of training and equipping the Katangan rebels and insisted that Cuba shared "a burden and a responsibility" for the conflict in Zaire.[3] Carter also warned Moscow that its Africa policy would undermine the prospects for a SALT II agreement. Despite Vance's best efforts, Carter was suggesting "linkage" between SALT and Soviet Third World policy. In a meeting with Soviet Foreign Minister Gromyko two days after his public statements, Carter sharply criticized Soviet African policy and was furious at what he believed to be Gromyko's attempt to deceive him.[4]

In his June 7 speech at the U.S. Naval Academy, despite Vance's counsel to avoid increasing U.S.-Soviet tension, Carter expressed further hostility. Although he offered Moscow a choice between conflict or cooperation and underscored the potential benefits of détente, he argued that for Moscow, détente seemed to mean "a continuing aggressive struggle for . . . advantage and increased influence." The USSR saw "military power and military assistance as the best means of expanding," but preferred to use "proxy forces" to achieve its objective, which was to "export a totalitarian and repressive form of government."[5]

In late June, Soviet policy confirmed Carter's worst suspicions. South Yemenese troops backed by Cuban and East German forces bombed, shelled, and occupied the South Yemen Presidential Palace. The troops seized and executed President Salim Rubaya Ali, who had tended to favor Chinese interests in the socialist world, and created a pro-Soviet government. Moscow had once again relied on armed force to expand its influence.[6]

Soviet policy in Africa and the Middle East transformed Carter's view of the Soviet threat. In September, Carter confided to Egyptian President Anwar Sadat that he was "becoming increasing concerned about the entire Middle East and Persian Gulf region, with the threat of the Soviet Union in South Yemen, Afghanistan, Libya, Iraq, Syria, and possibly Sudan."[7]

Carter's changing view of Soviet intentions was also influenced by Soviet defense policy. Since the first days of the administration, Soviet force modernization had been a hotly debated issue. Once again, Brzezinski was the hard-liner. He argued that Soviet deployment of a new generation of strategic missiles would pose a significant and meaningful threat to the retaliatory capability of Washington's land-based strategic missiles. But, as noted in the previous chapter, Carter maintained a sanguine attitude toward the trend in the U.S.-Soviet strategic balance.

As new Soviet deployments took place, however, Carter became increasingly concerned. In October 1977, the USSR deployed the SS20 missile and the Backfire bomber in Europe. By the end of the year, eighteen SS20s had been deployed, and the pace showed no sign of slackening. The SS20 in particular posed a threat to NATO, for it was designed to cause great destruction in Western Europe. The danger was greatest in the political sphere, for Washington lacked a regional response to Soviet use of the SS20. Soviet deployment of the missile undermined the credibility of the U.S. commitment to Western Europe, and thus NATO solidarity.[8]

Ongoing Soviet deployments ultimately influenced the president's perception of Soviet intentions. Whereas Carter had stressed the prospects for peace and reduction of tension in Europe in January 1978, by May, he was much less sanguine and his primary focus was on the military challenge to NATO. "We have a serious problem in . . . Europe," he warned. "The Soviet Union has built up a tremendous quantity of tank force, military force of all kinds, nuclear weapons like the SS20, which is 30 times more destructive than any neutron weapon that we've ever considered."[9] Similarly, in a May 30 speech to the leaders of the NATO countries, Carter charged:

> The Soviet Union and other Warsaw Pact countries pose a military threat to our alliance which far exceeds their legitimate security needs. For more than a decade, the military power of the Soviet Union has steadily expanded. . . . In significant areas, the military lead we once possessed has been reduced.
>
> Today, we can meet that military challenge. But we cannot be sure of countering the future military threat, unless our alliance modernizes its forces and adds additional military power.[10]

Although Carter subsequently decided to forgo production of the neutron bomb, during this period he moved ahead with development and production of the Pershing II missile as a counter to the Soviet SS20. In August 1979, the administration announced that it was prepared to deploy a total of 572 ground-launched cruise missiles and Pershing II missiles in Western Europe should Moscow decline to engage in serious arms-control negotiations over theater nuclear forces.[11]

Carter's view of the strategic balance underwent a similar evolution. The immediate concern was Soviet development of SS18 and SS19 ICBMs. By April 1978, tests of the SS18 and SS19 missiles revealed major improvement in the accuracy of their MIRVed warheads, sufficient to make credible successful strikes against U.S. ICBMs. In contrast to his earlier confidence, in late 1978, Secretary of Defense Harold Brown briefed the president on the growing vulnerability of the U.S. land-based ICBMs to the SS18 and SS19, and in October he predicted that the new generation of Soviet ICBMs might "pose a substantial threat in the 1980s" to U.S. land-based strategic forces.[12]

Whereas Carter was confident in 1977 of U.S. superiority, his Wake Forest speech criticized the pace of Soviet defense spending and warned that the Soviet nuclear arsenal might be used for "political blackmail, and they could threaten our vital interests." His Annapolis speech argued that the Soviet military buildup appeared to be "excessive, far beyond any legitimate requirement to defend themselves or to defend their allies."[13]

By mid 1979, there was a consensus in the White House that the strategic balance "was deteriorating faster than we had expected . . . and would continue to do so into the early 1980s."[14] Studies on a new U.S. ICBM were taking shape, and Carter decided in June to develop a mobile ICBM. Although the announcement may have been timed to win conservative support for the controversial SALT II treaty, which Carter would soon present to the Senate, there is little doubt that he believed strongly in the growing Soviet strategic threat, and that this contributed to his decision to seek funding for the mobile missile.[15]

Moscow's December 25, 1979, invasion of Afghanistan completed the evolution of Carter's view of the Soviet Union. As the president explained after the invasion, "My opinion of the Russians has changed most [*sic*] drastically in the last week than even the previous two and one-half years before that."[16] The subsequent declaration of the so-called Carter Doctrine, asserting that "any attempt by any outside force to gain control of the Persian Gulf region will be regarded as an assault on the vital interests of the United States . . . and will be repelled by any means necessary, including military force," reflected the White House's acute fear that Iran and Saudi Arabia were now extremely vulnerable to Soviet power, and that Moscow might try to expand its domination into areas adjacent to Afghanistan.[17]

Thus, beginning in 1978, President Carter grew increasingly apprehensive about Soviet foreign policy. This influenced not only American defense policy, but also U.S. policy toward China. Now that the Soviet Union appeared more threatening, it was time for Washington to consolidate relations with its strategic partners. This meant that Washington was prepared to expedite normalization of U.S.-PRC relations in the spring of 1978, and subsequently, as the president's view of the Soviet threat further developed in 1979 and 1980, to pursue U.S.-PRC military relations. In the changed security environment, the White House was prepared to deal.

CHINA'S DETERIORATING SECURITY ENVIRONMENT

In 1978, Soviet policy toward China appeared especially ominous to Beijing. In military relations, Moscow was deploying an increasing share of its most modern weaponry along the Sino-Soviet border, including its advanced fighter aircraft and assault helicopters. Moreover, in 1978, Moscow deployed the SS20 IRBM for the first time in the Soviet Far East. In April, Soviet Party General Secretary Leonid Brezhnev and Defense Minister Dmitry Ustinov traveled to the border region to witness maneuvers simulating Sino-Soviet hostilities. At the same time, the Soviet Navy, Marines, and Air Force conducted an unusually large joint exercise in the coastal waters in Northeast Asia.[18]

Chinese Minister of Defense Xu Xiangqian warned that Soviet deployments and exercises were part of Moscow's "objective of invading China." He charged that the Soviet Union posed a "direct military threat to China" and was elevating its preparation for "an aggressive war against China."[19]

Soviet Third World policy compounded Chinese fears. Policy makers in the PRC echoed Zbigniew Brzezinski's alarm over Soviet Africa policy. *Red Flag* warned that developments in the Horn of Africa revealed Moscow's "expansionist tactics," and that "tomorrow wars such as those in Angola and the Horn of Africa will occur in other areas of the world." In August, Defense Minister Xu noted Moscow's use of Cuban "mercenaries" and asked whether there was "any region where . . . a disturbance is going on that the evil shadow of Soviet social-imperialism does not loom?"[20]

The next region on Moscow's expansionist agenda appeared to be Indochina.[21] In the spring of 1978, Moscow fully supported Vietnam's "anti-China" policies. After Hanoi ended private markets in the south in March and confiscated personal savings in April, ethnic Chinese in Vietnam started leaving northern and southern Vietnam in droves. Vietnam's economic policies had focused on its Chinese community, and Hanoi encouraged the Chinese to leave the country. By July, despite Beijing's warnings of retaliation, over 170,000 ethnic Chinese had crossed the Sino-Vietnamese border into southern China. Moreover, Moscow was encouraging Hanoi to "develop the socialist sector" and to ignore the opposition posed by the ethnic Chinese.[22]

Beijing was sensitive to Soviet involvement in Sino-Vietnamese conflict. In May, when Moscow moved a portion of its Pacific fleet southward along the coast of China, Beijing associated the movement with Sino-Vietnamese tension. Liao Chengzhi, director of the State Council's Office of Overseas Chinese Affairs, charged that "it is the Soviet Union which is encouraging the Vietnamese authorities to behave like this." As the conflict over the overseas Chinese worsened, Deng Xiaoping observed that Vietnam was "leaning toward the Soviet Union, which is the arch-enemy of China" and affirmed that there was a "third country" instigating the conflict.[23] A commentator's article in *Renmin ribao* explained that Moscow was "anxiously seeking a base it can count on in Southeast Asia. It backs up . . . Vietnam with a view to bringing that country into its strategic framework. . . . It is a move to oppose China and to edge out U.S. influence, gain control over Southeast Asia and improve its strategic position in the world."[24]

Vietnam maintained its ethnic Chinese policy, and after Beijing ended its aid program, Hanoi joined CMEA. China and Vietnam were now adversaries, and Vietnam had joined Moscow's anti-China coalition. Then, in early November, Moscow and Hanoi signed a Treaty of Friendship and Cooperation, which Deng charged was a "military alliance." He alleged that a "big power and a small power are cooperating. . . . to encircle China." *Red Flag* argued that Vietnam was the "Cuba of the East," serving Soviet objectives in Asia.[25] Despite repeated PRC warnings, on December 25, Vietnamese forces invaded Cambodia, ousted the Pol Pot government, and installed a pro-Vietnamese leadership. Soviet encirclement had become reality, and now China sought to "teach Vietnam a lesson."

China was experiencing the greatest Soviet threat since the 1969 Sino-Soviet border clashes, and it needed a strong United States to offset Soviet power. Fortunately for PRC interests, Chinese leaders perceived growing U.S. resistance to Soviet policy. Beijing viewed Carter's May 1978 speech to NATO leaders favorably and was pleased with the tough stance Vance adopted in his meeting with Gromyko in late May. *Renmin ribao* reported that "the quarrel between the Soviet Union and the United States [had] resumed" and would "continue to occur on and off . . . in the future. This is inevitable."[26] In October, a *Red Flag* commentator asserted that the "anti-appeasement forces in the West are growing." Shortly thereafter, Beijing reported that Vance's mission to Moscow had failed to resolve important differences in the SALT negotiations, and it praised Carter for not making "concessions simply to make an agreement easier." It was also encouraged when Paul Warnke, whom it had portrayed as an advocate of "appeasement," stepped down as head of the U.S. Arms Control and Disarmament Agency.[27]

Beijing could also draw satisfaction from the trend in U.S.-Vietnam relations. Beijing might have welcomed improved U.S.-Vietnam relations in the immediate postwar era as maximizing Hanoi's ability to avoid dependency on Moscow. But by 1978, after cooperation between the USSR and Vietnam had expanded significantly, Beijing sought to isolate Vietnam, and it therefore objected to U.S. efforts to improve relations with Vietnam.[28]

U.S. policy conformed to PRC interests. In September 1978, Hanoi finally dropped all demands for U.S. aid as a precondition to normalization of U.S.-Vietnam relations. But developments in Indochina, including the boat-people crisis and intelligence reports of Vietnamese preparations for war in Cambodia, indicated that this was not the time for the United States to improve relations with Vietnam. In addition, Brzezinski and Leonard Woodcock argued that given the progress in the U.S.-PRC normalization negotiations and the greater importance of China to U.S. security, Washington should delay normalization of relations with Hanoi rather than endanger U.S.-PRC negotiations. These two factors deterred the administration from establishing diplomatic relations with Hanoi.[29]

Although developments in U.S. Soviet policy contributed to PRC security, they could not compensate for Soviet momentum in Asia. In the aftermath of the 1975 fall of Saigon, Washington had washed its hands of Indochina, leaving Beijing to contend with Soviet power in its strategic backyard. In this context, improved U.S.-PRC bilateral relations would make a difference in China's ability to resist Soviet pressure. But to improve relations, China had to make the difficult compromises required for normalization. International circumstances encouraged Chinese willingness to compromise.

Moreover, by the end of 1978, China had resolved its leadership succession. Although Deng Xiaoping had assumed control over foreign policy the previous year, through most of 1978, he and Chairman Hua remained at odds over economic policy. Hua pushed a grandiose economic plan that promised rapid and significant growth for all sectors of the economy—a policy promising all things for all people. Insofar as China had just emerged from ten years of chaos, he soon encountered skepticism and opposition from within the Party and government, and Deng was the beneficiary. At the Third

Plenum of the Eleventh Central Committee in December 1978, the Communist Party turned to Deng for leadership and endorsed his policy line of "seeking truth from facts." Although policy debates would inevitably continue, the succession to Mao had been resolved with the emergence of a strong and decisive leader.

Thus, at the end of 1978, domestic stability in China converged with the international pressures encouraging Beijing to seek closer U.S.-PRC relations. Like the United States, China was ready to deal in 1978.

The Brzezinski Visit to China

In 1978, both China and the United States believed that normalization would serve to offset their respective deteriorating strategic situations. Both sides were consequently prepared to make the tough compromises necessary to make normalization possible. A close look at the normalization process reveals this interplay of strategic circumstances with negotiations over significant conflicts of interests.

The normalization process received its first boost when President Carter decided that Brzezinski should visit China, despite Secretary of State Vance's objections. The struggle between Brzezinski and Vance over who should go to China had continued into March. Vance remained apprehensive that a Brzezinski visit to China would undermine his ongoing efforts to make U.S. policy toward China policy with a view to maximizing the prospects for U.S.-Soviet détente. Indeed, Brzezinski did hope to use his visit to China to develop improved U.S.-PRC relations as a response to what he perceived as ongoing Soviet exploitation of détente.[30]

In March, the president finally sided with Brzezinski, whose memoirs give significant credit for his victory to the bureaucratic "alliance" he forged with Vice President Walter Mondale and Secretary of Defense Brown. In contrast to his earlier ambivalence toward developing relations with China, Brown had come to believe that Washington should have a more explicit relationship with China. Given Vance's reluctance to develop relations, Brown thought it would be best that the State Department not manage the visit, and that Brzezinski should go to China.[31]

But Carter's decision also reflected his growing alarm over Soviet foreign policy and the corresponding recognition of the benefit of using relations with China as a strategic response. Given the less-than-satisfactory results of Vance's 1977 visit to Beijing, and China's respect for Brzezinski's Soviet policy, by sending Brzezinski rather than Vance to China, Carter chose the man most likely to succeed in promoting improved U.S.-PRC relations. Carter was also aware of the strategic importance of a Brzezinski visit. He was using Brzezinski to signal Moscow Washington's decision to improve relations with China as a strategic response to Soviet foreign policy. Given Brzezinski's reputation as the hard-liner in the administration, he served this purpose better than Vance.[32]

Carter made clear the strategic value he attached to improved U.S.-PRC relations in the negotiating instructions he gave Brzezinski prior to his departure for Beijing. Carter instructed Brzezinski to "share with the Chinese my view of the Soviet threat." He wanted Chinese leaders to understand

> my concern . . . that increasing Soviet military power and political short-sightedness fed by big-power ambitions might tempt the Soviet Union both to exploit local turbulence and to intimidate our friends in order to seek political advantage and eventually political preponderance.
>
> That is why I do take seriously Soviet action in Africa and this is why I am concerned about the Soviet buildup in Central Europe. I also see some Soviet designs pointing toward the Indian Ocean through South Asia, and perhaps to the encirclement of China through Vietnam.[33]

Most important, Carter told Brzezinski to explain to Chinese leaders that the United States would respond to the increasing Soviet threat by pursuing "wider cooperation with our key allies and also with *new regional influentials* [read China]." Thus, when Vance tried to undercut the strategic significance of the Brzezinski mission by inviting Soviet Foreign Minister Gromyko to visit the White House when Brzezinski would be in Beijing, Carter supported Brzezinski and forced postponement of the Gromyko visit.[34]

Having overruled Secretary of State Vance and chosen Brzezinski to go to China, Carter expanded the mission's objective. Brzezinski had initially proposed that he limit his talks with Chinese officials to a strategic dialogue and not discuss normalization. But later Carter again overruled Vance and agreed with Brzezinski and Brown that Brzezinski should commence the normalization process.[35] Carter instructed Brzezinski to convey to Chinese leaders that he had "made up his mind"—that he had accepted China's three conditions for normalization and wanted to begin serious negotiations aimed at rapid normalization.[36]

Responding to the shifting trends in U.S. policy, the State Department supported the president's decision and prepared a paper calling for normalization after the fall 1978 elections and before the 1979 start of the presidential campaign. It concluded that normalization might actually facilitate Senate support for a SALT II treaty. But at this point, Vance remained convinced that he had to manage the normalization schedule so as not to undermine the prospects for an arms-control agreement. If U.S.-Soviet negotiations dragged on, he might have to delay normalization into 1979.[37]

The Brzezinski visit to China reflected Brzezinski's increasing influence on U.S. China policy and the president's growing interest in consolidating U.S.-PRC relations. At the same time, China was beginning to soften its attitude toward the United States; improved U.S.-PRC relations would help China offset the rapid Soviet expansion in Indochina. In 1978, for the first time since 1975, China revealed renewed interest in expanding U.S.-PRC trade relations. In April, it purchased U.S. grain, the first such purchase since the cancellation of grain contracts in 1975. Also, early in the year, a Chinese delegation came to the United States as *official* representatives of the Chinese government. Prior to this time, PRC representatives had visited America under the fiction that they were not officials.[38] Beijing was not allowing the absence of diplomatic relations to interfere with improved relations. For the first time since the early 1970s, China, rather than just Washington, needed the appearance of improving U.S.-PRC relations in order to caution Moscow against disregarding PRC interests.

Brzezinski thus arrived in China in May 1978 with the appropriate message at the perfect time. The United States was gearing up to challenge Soviet expansion, and, as part of this effort, it wanted to consolidate relations with China, including normalization of diplomatic relations. Brzezinski held wide-ranging strategic discussions with Chinese leaders, sharing with them his impression of Soviet designs in the Third World. He delivered an extraordinarily detailed briefing on the SALT negotiations and shared with Chinese leaders various U.S. documents on U.S.-Soviet relations. Brzezinski also stressed China's strategic importance to the United States, conveying President Carter's desire to focus on "China's central role in maintaining the world balance." He emphasized the "central importance" of U.S.-PRC relations in "U.S. global policy," and that President Carter "is determined to normalize relations with China."[39] The delegation also conveyed Washington's willingness to transfer various technologies to China that it had previously withheld, and that the United States would not sell the Soviet Union. These included the Landsat airborne infrared scanning equipment, which had not been licensed for export when Vance visited Beijing in 1977.[40] Brzezinski likewise proposed exchanges of military delegations and expressed willingness to modify COCOM restrictions on technology transfer to China, indicating that the United States would license the export of previously proscribed technology.

Brzezinski also staffed his delegation with officials sure to satisfy Chinese demands for a hard-line U.S. Soviet policy and to signal Washington's interest in consolidated U.S.-PRC relations to the USSR. Morton Abramowitz, the first Department of Defense official to visit China, briefed his PRC counterparts on the Soviet military. Brzezinski also included Samuel Huntington, reputedly the most hard-line official on the NSC, who briefed his Chinese counterparts on PRM 10, the administration's basic document on U.S.-Soviet relations. Ben Huberman, director of science and technology issues on the NSC and deputy science adviser for space and defense, accompanied the mission on Carter's instructions to let both Moscow and Beijing know that Washington was ready to liberalize technology transfer to China.[41] Not surprisingly, Chinese leaders referred to Brzezinski as the "polar bear tamer," a reputation he encouraged during his visit to the Great Wall by joking that the last to reach the top would oppose the Soviets in Ethiopia.[42]

Regarding normalization, Brzezinski repeatedly assured Chinese leaders that the United States had "made up its mind." President Carter understood that it was his responsibility, and not Beijing's, to bear the domestic political costs associated with normalization. Hence, the United States was prepared to assume the burden of accepting China's three normalization conditions—it would sever diplomatic relations with Taipei, abrogate the bilateral defense treaty, and withdraw all of its troops from Taiwan.

Brzezinski also probed Chinese attitudes on the important issue of peaceful resolution of the Taiwan issue. The White House expected that when it put forward its "expectation that the Taiwan issue [would] have a peaceful resolution, it [would] clearly not encounter a Chinese refutation," he said. "This will make it easier to resolve U.S. domestic difficulties," he explained. Once again, China did not make an issue of this U.S. demand.

Finally, Carter instructed Brzezinski to inform China that the United States would reserve to itself the right to sell weaponry to Taiwan after normalization. This was the first time that the United States directly presented Chinese leaders with the condition that Woodcock had been indirectly communicating to them since February. Deng heard Brzezinski's presentation and did not respond.

Thus, by May 1978, postnormalization U.S. arms sales to Taiwan were the only normalization issue that had not been adequately discussed during the seven years since Henry Kissinger first visited Beijing. The Brzezinski-Deng discussion of the issue was a first step, but it was insufficient to assure U.S. policy makers that China understood the U.S. position. There would have to be additional discussions to clarify each side's position on this issue. Of Washington's three normalization conditions—ongoing economic, cultural, and other relations with Taiwan; no public refutation by China of a U.S. statement expecting peaceful resolution of the Taiwan issue; and U.S. arms sales to Taiwan after normalization—it would prove the most sensitive.[43]

Brzezinski suggested that the negotiations to start the normalization process begin the following month in Beijing. The United States had "bit the bullet" and was prepared to establish diplomatic relations with Beijing.

The Normalization Negotiations

President Carter met with Vance and Brzezinski after the latter's return to Washington and decided to try to obtain a normalization agreement by December 15. Washington now had a tentative target date. Ambassador Woodcock was instructed to meet with his Chinese counterparts roughly every two weeks and to address each outstanding issue separately, deferring the most difficult issues to the end of the process. In this manner, the administration sought early successes in order to ease agreement on the tough issues of arms sales to Taiwan and the unilateral U.S. statement. But as Woodcock later explained, this was an untenable negotiating strategy, because it is impossible to extract concessions or agreements from one's counterpart until the entire package is presented. Hence, Woodcock's first five sessions with the Chinese, from July through September, were unproductive. He was obliged simply to recite the U.S. position, without being able to elicit a Chinese reply, and never had the opportunity to address the more difficult issues.[44]

Nevertheless, these meetings gave the administration an opportunity to communicate its position, so that there would be no misunderstandings either during the final stages of normalization or afterward. During the second meeting, for example, the United States laid out its expectation of full cultural, economic, and other relations with Taiwan after normalization, and in the third meeting, Woodcock explained that there would have to be postnormalization congressional involvement in creating domestic legal substitutes for the existing bilateral agreements between Washington and Taipei. This suggested that something akin to the Taiwan Relations Act would be required.[45]

But the meetings were one-sided. Woodcock presented the U.S. point of view, and Foreign Minister Huang Hua merely restated China's formal position. The United States still needed explicit Chinese acquiescence to its normalization conditions. President Carter tried to jump-start the process in a September 19 meeting with the head of the PRC liaison office, Chai Zemin. Carter insisted on Washington's right to continue to sell defensive arms to Taiwan after normalization, explaining that no U.S. president could agree to termination of arms sales to Taiwan. Yet Carter also conveyed his understanding of Chinese sensitivity on this issue by indicating that Washington would avoid provocative arms transfers to Taiwan. He also stressed the importance of an uncontradicted U.S. statement on the peaceful resolution of the Taiwan issue.[46]

The president had forcefully presented the U.S. position, and it was up to China to move the negotiations forward. Thus far, however, Huang Hua had been content merely to recite China's long-held position. It was unclear whether China was prepared to accept the U.S. conditions and normalize relations.

MANAGING U.S.-TAIWAN RELATIONS

Just as the United States was trying to push ahead with serious normalization negotiations, the administration faced the issue of which military equipment to transfer to Taiwan in 1978. The U.S.-Taiwan agreement on co-production of the F-5E fighter jet was due to expire in 1978, and new agreements were necessary. In this context, the State Department's Taiwan Desk prepared a paper proposing that Washington sell a more advanced aircraft to Taiwan.[47]

Taiwan had not signed any new contracts for U.S. weapons since the early part for the Ford administration. The State Department had quickly rejected a Taiwanese request for the F4 in view of its offensive capabilities. After consultation with officials in the Department of Defense, the Taiwan Desk proposed a version of the F-5E equipped with improved avionics and sophisticated air-to-air missiles. This more advanced aircraft was labeled the F-5G. Assistant Secretary of State for East Asian Affairs Richard Holbrooke accepted the proposal and, with the support of the DOD, pushed within the administration for approval of the F-5G sale.[48]

The National Security Council, however, opposed the sale. Brzezinski and Michel Oksenberg, the NSC staff member responsible for China policy, argued that the sale of a more advanced fighter to Taiwan posed an unacceptable risk of upsetting the normalization negotiations. Oksenberg recalls the importance of calling to the president's attention the sensitive stage the negotiations were in—the president would decide whether or not to sell the F-5G to Taiwan well after Woodcock had begun negotiating with Chinese leaders over normalization.[49]

The priority given to normalization might have been enough to scuttle the F-5G deal. But the proposal provoked additional opposition within the administration because the F-5G would have been produced solely for export, thereby contravening President Carter's policy of prohibiting production of weaponry only for export. Before the State Department memo reached the Oval Office, an NSC staff member, Jessica Tuchman Matthews, therefore attached a memo objecting to the proposal because it violated the president's arms-export policy. Given the sensitive stage of U.S.-PRC normalization negotiations and the president's opposition to productions of arms for export, the president decided against the F-5G proposal and settled on extending the U.S.-Taiwan agreement on the co-production of the F-5E.[50]

REACHING AGREEMENT ON NORMALIZATION

The United States had accepted China's conditions for normalization, and President Carter had presented Beijing with Washington's own conditions. Having resolved the Panama Canal issue, the president's changing view of the Soviet threat had set the pace of U.S. interest in normalization of relations. As Brzezinski later recalled, for the United States, "the timing of normalization . . . was definitely influenced by the Soviet dimension."[51] But it takes two sides to reach agreement, and it was now up to China to decide whether or not to accept the U.S. conditions for normalization.

It was difficult for Chinese leaders to tolerate Washington's insistence that it would continue to sell weapons to Taiwan after normalization. Beijing insisted that Taiwan was part of China, and Chinese leaders believed that recognition by the United States of the People's Republic of China as the government of China committed Washington to this principle. Yet ongoing U.S. arms sales to Taiwan would challenge Beijing's sovereignty claim in a crucial area. Continued U.S. arms sales to Taiwan would also maintain Taipei's defense capability and symbolize a continued U.S. defense commitment to Taiwan, thus undermining the PRC's ability to isolate Taiwan and pressure it to acquiesce to Beijing's demands.

Through early October, the PRC failed to respond positively to the

U.S. offer to normalize relations. On the contrary, China's first response to the presentations by President Carter and Woodcock suggested that Beijing had rejected U.S. conditions for normalization. When Huang Hua traveled to New York in early October for the foreign ministers' meeting at the United Nations, he met with Secretary of State Vance. For four hours, Huang railed against U.S. policy, particularly the prospect of continued U.S. arms sales to Taiwan after normalization, which he said China would never allow, suggesting that the U.S. demand would lead Chinese leaders to discontinue the normalization negotiations.[52]

Still, the door to normalization was not fully closed. As this meeting in New York concluded, an aide to the foreign minister suggested to Woodcock that additional meetings were needed in Beijing to address these issues. Huang Hua seemed to have been posturing, and China might actually be ready to conduct serious negotiations. Indeed, a few weeks later, Deng Xiaoping signaled that if the United States were ready to move, China would follow. During his October visit to Tokyo, he said that normalization depended on the decisiveness of President Carter, and that if the United States were willing to follow the Japan formula, it could maintain economic, trade, and cultural ties with Taiwan after normalization. Now that Deng had personally and publicly committed himself to early normalization of relations, China was ready to move into the final stage of the negotiations.[53]

The two sides were moving in tandem, because back in Washington, on October 11, President Carter met with Brzezinski and Woodcock and stressed January 1 as the target date for completing the normalization negotiations. Carter instructed Brzezinski to prepare a draft communiqué for Woodcock to bring back to Beijing. At this same meeting, Woodcock advised the president against early normalization of relations with Vietnam, because he feared that it would derail U.S.-PRC normalization. Carter accepted his advice.

But the communiqué was not ready when Woodcock returned to Beijing. Before it was cabled to him, additional discussions occurred in Washington concerning the normalization date. Whereas Brzezinski favored placing a January 15 normalization date on the communiqué, Vance opposed setting any date whatsoever. He clearly preferred that U.S.-Soviet arms-control talks set the schedule for U.S.-PRC normalization. The president decided the issue. Carter not only wanted the date on the communiqué but favored January 1, accelerating the process beyond Brzezinski's expectations.[54]

President Carter had decided to make the final push to normalization. To underscore the seriousness of the opportunity, before Woodcock left for Beijing, Brzezinski met with Chai Zemin in Washington and advised him that unless China grabbed this opportunity for normalization, it would have to wait until late 1979. Then, on November 2 in Beijing, Woodcock presented Huang Hua with a succinct one-page draft normalization communiqué calling for a January 1 announcement. Besides conveying to the Beijing leadership that Washington was in earnest this time—an important step considering prolonged U.S. delays on the issue in the past, and the resulting Chinese skepticism about U.S. seriousness—inserting the announcement date in the draft communiqué suggested a deadline, putting pressure on Chinese leaders to "either fish or cut bait." Washington presently announced the continuation of the F-5E co-production agreement with Taiwan, clearly signaling both the U.S. intention to continue to sell weapons to Taiwan after normalization and Washington's sensitivity to PRC concerns, insofar as it was declining to sell Taiwan more advanced aircraft.[55] The PRC's leaders were now fully aware of both the deadline and U.S. insistence on continuing to sell weaponry to Taiwan after normalization.

For over a month, China failed to respond. In late November, there remained a great deal of skepticism among State Department and White House officials, including Vance and Brzezinski, that a normalization agreement would be concluded by the end of the year. The Chinese had yet to engage with the United States seriously on the outstanding issues, and it seemed that an agreement would require much more difficult bargaining, over an extended period.[56]

Finally, in a meeting on December 4, China signaled its readiness to move. The Cultural Revolution holdovers Nancy Tang and Wang Hairong had been removed from the negotiating team, and Han Nianlong, substituting for Foreign Minister Huang, presented a Chinese draft communiqué that also called for a January 1 normalization date. Both sides were now operating under the same deadline. Han further conceded that Beijing would not contradict a U.S. statement expressing American interest in a peaceful resolution of the Taiwan issue. Although other issues remained unsettled, Han told Woodcock that Deng Xiaoping wanted to meet with him on December 12. Deng was now fully engaged in the negotiations, the sine qua non of an agreement, which was now in sight.[57]

The day before the Woodcock-Deng meeting, Brzezinski met with Chai Zemin to emphasize the narrowing window of opportunity for normalization. Now was the time to move, Brzezinski stressed. A U.S.-Soviet arms-control agreement was near completion, and Brezhnev was likely to visit the United States in January. Brzezinski said that he hoped that normalization and a visit by Premier Hua Guofeng or Deng Xiaoping to the United States would precede the U.S.-Soviet summit, but that depended on normalization. Brzezinski was confident that Chai would relay these remarks back to Beijing.[58]

When Deng and Woodcock met on December 12, Deng personally accepted the U.S. demand that China not counter a unilateral U.S. statement expressing interest in a peaceful resolution of the Taiwan issue, agreed to a January 1 announcement, and accepted the U.S. position that the normalization communiqué establish Washington's intention to maintain economic and cultural ties with Taiwan. He also reluctantly acquiesced to the U.S. demand that the U.S.-ROC Mutual Defense Treaty be terminated in accordance with the terms of the treaty—one-year notice would have to be given to Taipei. Washington would not "abrogate" the treaty, as China had demanded; it would "terminate" it in accordance with the language in the agreement. In return, however, Deng insisted that during that one year, the United States not make any new commitments to sell arms to Taiwan. He also accepted the U.S. invitation to visit the United States after normalization of relations. After consulting with Washington, Woodcock agreed on December 14 to a one-year moratorium on new U.S. commitments to sell weaponry to Taiwan.[59]

During these final days, the president decided to announce the January 1 normalization on December 15, and Woodcock notified Deng Xiaoping of the president's preference during their December 14 meeting. When the president made this decision, Vance was in the Middle East and excluded from the deliberations. Vance had still hoped to conclude the major issues of the SALT II negotiations in a late December meeting with Soviet Foreign Minister Gromyko and hold a U.S.-Soviet summit in early 1979. In this way, the negotiations for SALT would basically be completed before the January 1 normalization, but normalization would precede White House presentation of the SALT treaty to the Senate for ratification, which would undermine some of the political opposition to the SALT agreement. In Vance's absence, however, the president revised the normalization schedule, deciding on the December 15 announcement in order to eliminate the possibility of politically damaging leaks during the two weeks before January 1. Vance failed to persuade the president to return to the original schedule. He continues to argue that mismanagement of U.S. China policy significantly disrupted the arms-control negotiations and seriously contributed to the administration's inability to achieve Senate approval of the SALT II treaty.[60]

Despite Vance's misgivings, the United States and China had

agreed that the January 1 establishment of diplomatic relations be announced on December 15. China had agreed to normalize relations with full knowledge of U.S. policy, having been briefed by Woodcock, Brzezinski, and Carter. Deng's insistence on a one-year moratorium acknowledged the U.S. position on arms sales to Taiwan—he did not insist on an indefinite ban of U.S. arms sales to Taiwan. As Woodcock argued in cables to Washington, the deal was done, and there was no need for further negotiations.[61]

But the White House was apprehensive that without a clear and focused discussion on the arms-sales issue, PRC leaders might misunderstand Washington as having agreed to terminate its arms-sales relationship with Taipei; China had yet to acquiesce directly to Washington's insistence that it would continue to sell defensive weapons to Taiwan after normalization, albeit now subject to the one-year moratorium. Moreover, Chai Zemin seemed to think that the United States had agreed to terminate arms sales to Taiwan. Therefore, the night before normalization was to be announced, the president instructed Woodcock to request one more meeting with Deng Xiaoping to address this issue.[62]

An agreement on normalization had been reached, and the arms-sales issue had been resolved without China having had to accept the embarrassment of overt compromise. The United States, moreover, had already obliged Deng to agree to the "termination" rather than the "abrogation" of the U.S.-ROC defense treaty and to acquiesce to a one-year "moratorium" on U.S. arms sales to Taiwan rather than an end to sales. Indeed, Woodcock believed that there was no need for further negotiations, and he was reluctant to reopen the issue with Deng.

As might have been expected, Deng was outraged at being forced to respond to what he saw as a humiliating demand. He launched an extended vitriolic attack on the United States for insisting on violating Chinese sovereignty by selling arms to Taiwan. U.S. policy was completely unacceptable. Taiwan was Chinese territory, and Chinese leaders would never agree to U.S. interference in internal Chinese affairs, particularly U.S. arms sales to Taiwan. Finally, Deng asked Woodcock what should be done. Woodcock quietly suggested that the two sides simply proceed with the original normalization agreement and announce on December 15 that diplomatic relations would be established on January 1. Deng agreed.[63]

The timing of Deng's decision to normalize relations without satisfactorily resolving the arms-sales issue reveals the relative importance of domestic and international factors in Chinese decision making. When Deng met with Woodcock, the Chinese Communist Party was concluding a Central Workshop Conference in preparation for the Third Plenum of the Eleventh Central Committee, which would begin two days later. On the day he met with Woodcock, Deng delivered the speech that would provide the basis for the Third Plenum's reform program. Indeed, the Workshop agreed on a number of far-reaching decisions implementing Deng's basic political and economic policy preferences.[64] The post-Mao succession crisis had finally ended, and Deng had emerged with preeminent authority on all significant political issues.

This coincidence suggests that the normalization agreement was dependent on Deng's new authority, which enabled him to face the opposition of his colleagues to a controversial compromise. Yet the true relationship was probably the reverse. Deng was able to make the necessary compromises because he had the support of the Chinese elite, not in spite of its opposition. The compromise agreement was undoubtedly discussed at the Central Workshop Conference, and Deng could not have secured both a normalization agreement and political preeminence had there been significant opposition to his willingness to compromise on the arms-sales issue. An elite consensus had developed that normalization was a strategic necessity, and that China had to compromise on the arms-sales issue.

Indeed, both in the draft normalization communiqué that Woodcock delivered to Huang Hua on November 2 and in frequent oral statements, the United States presented China with a negotiating deadline. Failure to reach agreement before January 1 threatened to postpone normalization into the indefinite future. Under different circumstances, Chinese leaders might have postponed normalization for additional negotiations seeking restrictions on U.S. arms sales to Taiwan. But the prospect of consolidated U.S.-Soviet détente and the likelihood of a Vietnamese invasion of Cambodia during the rapidly approaching dry season made normalization strategically invaluable and the necessary compromises thus became more acceptable. As early as August, Chai Zemin explained to Brzezinski that "judging from the current international situation, the earlier that normalization would be realized, the better."[65]

By the fall, in fact, normalization had become imperative for China. In September, the Soviet Union transferred large amounts of military equipment to Vietnam, and under the protection of extensive Vietnamese air attacks on Cambodian territory, a Cambodian insurgent movement was expanding in eastern Cambodia along the Vietnamese-Cambodian border.[66] By October, Chinese newspapers were warning that Vietnam would launch a large-scale invasion of Cambodia during the coming dry season. The signing of the Soviet-Vietnamese treaty on November 3 removed any lingering doubt about Hanoi's intentions. It merely remained for Beijing to determine its response.

Should Vietnam invade Cambodia, China would have to give serious consideration to a military response. Although Beijing would not send troops to Cambodia, a Chinese incursion into Vietnam would underscore to Hanoi and Moscow the risks of transgressing on Chinese interests. It would also help to restore the credibility of the PRC in Asia, which would be undermined by Vietnamese disregard of Chinese warnings not to invade Cambodia. But Chinese use of force against Vietnam risked war with the Soviet Union. Chinese leaders believed it likely that Moscow would retaliate militarily against a Chinese invasion of Vietnam with limited incursions across the Sino-Soviet border, and they did not rule out a large-scale attack.[67] Moreover, Beijing would feel particularly insecure should the invasion take place on the heels of a U.S.-Soviet SALT agreement.

Normalization of U.S.-PRC relations therefore reduced the risk of Soviet military retaliation by reducing Beijing's isolation and diminishing Moscow's confidence that the United States would be a mere spectator to Sino-Soviet hostilities. Indeed, China's insistence that the normalization communiqué reaffirm U.S. and PRC opposition to hegemony contributed to PRC security vis-à-vis the Soviet Union. The anti-hegemonism statement in the normalization communiqué, Hua Guofeng pointed out after normalization (in terms reminiscent of China's justification for opening liaison offices in 1973), "would contribute to the struggle in Asia . . . against both big and small hegemony." *Renmin ribao* said the statement aided "opposition to major hegemonism and minor hegemonism, global hegemonism as well as regional hegemonism [read Vietnam]."[68]

In addition, now that the United States recognized the People's Republic of China as the government of China, a PRC leader could participate in a meeting in the United States. Deng Xiaoping thus accepted President Carter's invitation to visit America, the importance of which was enhanced by developments in Indochina. Deng fully used his visit to Washington to give the impression of U.S.-PRC security cooperation. "We must further develop the relationship in a deepening way," he declared preparatory to his visit; "the only realistic thing for us is to unite" against the Soviet Union.[69] This and similar statements, his meeting with members of Congress who encouraged China to teach Vietnam a lesson, his visit to U.S. defense industry corporations, and his generally masterful public relations campaign all suggested enhanced U.S.-PRC security cooperation vis-à-vis the Soviet Union and Vietnam. None of this would have been possible without normalization of U.S.-PRC relations, which required the PRC to compromise on U.S. arms sales to Taiwan.

Since 1971, China had preferred to wait until the United States was prepared to meet Chinese conditions before normalizing relations rather than accept less than satisfactory conditions. This had been a productive strategy, and Chinese leaders seemed prepared to wait indefinitely. Yet in 1978, despite the objections of the Chinese leadership, including Deng Xiaoping, Beijing acquiesced to postnormalization U.S. arms sales to Taiwan, which undermined China's condition that the United States recognize that there was only one China, and that Taiwan was part of China. Strategic circumstances compelled Deng to compromise rather than wait until the PRC achieved all of its demands.

But Beijing did not agree that Washington could continue to sell arms to Taiwan. Rather, Beijing's pressing security requirements encouraged it to normalize despite its disagreement with Washington over this issue. Chinese leaders reserved the right to raise this issue in the future when their security environment was not so pressing and their leverage over the United States had improved. That time would come during the Reagan administration.

DOMESTIC POLITICS AND THE TAIWAN RELATIONS ACT

Just as the Carter administration was enjoying the success of its China policy, it became embroiled in the domestic politics of foreign policy making. The White House had recognized that legislation would be required to maintain relations with Taiwan in the postnormalization period. Insofar as the system of treaties covering a wide range of economic and cultural relations would become void in the absence of diplomatic relations, congressional action would be required to give force of law and the associated predictability to bilateral commitments after U.S. recognition of the PRC. But what the White House had not foreseen was that its failure to consult adequately with congressional leaders during the final stages of normalization would lead to congressional efforts to impose legislation that would severely undercut the administration's China policy.

In late 1977, congressional leaders with responsibility for Asia had warned the Carter administration that failure to consult with Congress on U.S.-PRC relations would likely lead to a "divisive debate" over China policy. Just a few months prior to recognition, a sense of the Congress resolution approved by a 94 to 0 vote advised the White House that Congress expected "prior consultation" before the administration implemented any changes "affecting the continuation in force of the Mutual Defense Treaty of 1954." The State Department announced that it recognized and accepted the need for such consultation.[70] Yet a few months later, the White House announced to a surprised country, including Congress, that it had normalized relations with China, and that it would terminate the Mutual Defense Treaty at the end of one year.

The State Department had argued that the congressional leadership could be trusted not to leak the normalization agreement, and that failure to brief Congress would provoke a backlash that would undermine support for the president's policy. But White House foreign policy specialists insisted that absolute secrecy was required to avoid leaks that would enable conservative politicians to mobilize sentiment against normalization prior to January 1, thus undermining the popularity of the breakthrough. Ultimately, the president agreed with the White House staff and limited consultation to an insufficient number of Democratic leaders to avoid a congressional backlash.[71]

The administration's failure to seek prior consultation with Congress, and congressional suspicion that the administration's focus on the strategic importance of the PRC undermined its commitment to Taiwan, created a bipartisan consensus that congressional involvement was legitimate and necessary in the shaping of U.S. policy toward China. Democrats such as John Glenn, Richard Stone, Clement Zablocki, and Edward Kennedy joined with Republicans in opposition, reflecting their concern for the future of Taiwan.[72]

The focus was legislation proposed by the White House that would give legal standing to future U.S.-Taiwan relations. Whereas the White House had expected a passive Congress simply to concur with the proposed legislation and accept the president's unilateral statement concerning U.S. interest in the security of Taiwan, Congress took the lead in drafting legislation that it believed better provided for U.S.-Taiwan relations and Taiwan's security. Yet this legislation might also set back U.S.-PRC relations. Congressman Zablocki, for example, repeatedly insisted that the legislation refer to Taiwan as the "Republic of China," language that would certainly have damaged the nascent U.S.-PRC diplomatic relationship significantly. The most difficult issue to resolve was the proposed wording of the section regarding the U.S. security commitment to Taiwan. Members of Congress sought to replicate the language of the U.S. commitment in the Mutual Defense Treaty in the proposed legislation, which also would have surely disrupted U.S.-PRC diplomatic relations.[73]

The White House objective in its negotiations with Congress was to persuade Congress to produce legislation that Carter would not have to veto. Administration representatives, led by Roger Sullivan, had frequently to use the threat of the veto to persuade members of Congress to drop potentially disruptive language. Ultimately, the White House and Congress found acceptable wording that both expressed congressional concerns and was sufficiently ambiguous to be consistent with the normalization agreement and leave the administration sufficient flexibility to manage U.S.-PRC relations. On the crucial issue of the U.S. security commitment to Taiwan, the Taiwan Relations Act declared that the United States would "consider any effort to determine the future of Taiwan by other than peaceful means, including by boycotts and embargoes, a threat to the peace of the Western Pacific area and of grave concern to the United States," and it called for the United States to provide Taiwan with "such defense articles and defense services in such quantity as may be necessary to enable Taiwan to maintain a sufficient self-defense capability" (see Appendix B).[74]

The ambiguity in these two statements provided the president with sufficient flexibility to conduct policy as he saw fit. Most important, however, was the phrase that all arms sales to Taiwan would be "in accordance with procedures established by law." Insofar as Congress does not have the authority to require arms sales, but only to veto presidential decisions, Sullivan understood that the legislation did not require anything of the president, but merely authorized him to carry out the legislation. Thus, after signing the Taiwan Relations Act, Carter observed that the act "authorize[d]" the president to maintain relations with Taiwan and that it granted "discretion" to the president, which he would "exercise . . . in a manner consistent with our interest in the well-being of the people on Taiwan and with the understandings we reached . . . with the People's Republic of China."[75]

Despite initial PRC complaints that the Taiwan Relations Act violated the normalization agreement and constituted interference in Chinese domestic affairs, congressional involvement in U.S.-PRC relations did not elicit a significantly counterproductive reaction from Beijing. The president just managed to avoid a foreign policy blun-

der. Moreover, congressional involvement provided a useful correc-
tive to the administration's haste in dealing with the complexities
on postnormalization U.S.-Taiwan relations. Without the legislation, the administration would have proceeded with its plans to allow numerous bilateral accords to lapse.[76]

But the passage of the Taiwan Relations Acts also instilled into
PRC leaders a degree of suspicion that the American leadership
could not be trusted to accommodate Beijing's concerns on the sensitive issue of postnormalization U.S.-Taiwan relations, particularly
concerning U.S. arms sales to Taiwan. Beijing thus developed a hy-
persensitive attitude toward even the suggestion that a U.S. politician would not balance the expectations of the Taiwan Relations
Act with White House commitments to unofficial U.S.-Taiwan relations. Chinese suspicions contributed to heightened bilateral tension when Ronald Reagan became president.

Institutionalizing Cooperative Relations: Military, Economic, and Educational Ties

Normalization was only the most immediate issue on the agenda
of U.S.-PRC relations in 1978. Now that it had taken place, cooperation could occur on other fronts. Most important was the development of new governmental and societal institutions that would provide a foundation for stable U.S.-PRC relations as Washington and
Beijing faced the inevitable challenges to developing cooperative relations. Twenty years of Cold War conflict and ten years of limited
strategic cooperation had enabled institutions to develop in the
United States and China with an interest in ongoing U.S.-PRC conflict. The government bureaucracies and the most influential sectors of society with an interest in U.S.-PRC relations were focused
on maintaining each nation's Cold War policies. In the aftermath of
the normalization of relations, the opportunity existed to promote
cooperation, not just between the two leaderships, but also between
their respective government bureaucracies and societies. During the
remaining years of the Carter administration, the two countries
took important steps in this direction.[77]

THE POLITICS OF DEVELOPING U.S.-PRC MILITARY RELATIONS

Although U.S.-PRC military relations would contribute most significantly to the overall relationship, the initial impetus for their
establishment arose on both sides from immediate security consid-

erations. For China, the context was the unrelenting Soviet pressure on Chinese security and the uncertainty about U.S. interest in cooperating with Beijing against the Soviet Union. In this situation, the development of military relations with the United States added substance to the American diplomatic contribution to Chinese security vis-à-vis the Soviet Union. Moscow would now hesitate further before challenging Chinese interests. Moreover, access to Western technology and weaponry would contribute to Chinese defense capabilities and enhance the technological sophistication of the People's Liberation Army.

China had been interested in developing military relations with the United States since the Ford administration, and its interest had deepened under Deng Xiaoping, who favored developing a modernized and reformed military with Western technology and had the authority to pursue such a policy. In the absence of countervailing conflict in bilateral relations, the only constraint on Chinese interest in Western military equipment was Beijing's lack of foreign reserves to purchase large quantities of weaponry.

The primary obstacle to consolidated U.S.-PRC military relations thus lay in Washington. Whereas in China the strategic imperative was clear and decision making was highly centralized, U.S. policy on military relations with China was considered in the context of administration differences over Soviet policy, and there was no consensus on developing military ties with the PRC. Not until President Carter agreed with his more hawkish advisers did Washington decide to pursue military ties with China.

Military relations with China remained a hotly debated issue well into 1980. The issue remained what it had been since the start of the Carter administration—differing views over how best to integrate U.S. policy toward China into U.S. Soviet policy. Secretary of State Vance, primarily concerned with consolidating U.S.-Soviet cooperation and, in the aftermath of the Soviet invasion of Afghanistan, salvaging the remnants of détente, advised against developing U.S.-PRC military relations. He counseled the president to avoid provoking the Soviet Union into adopting policies that would aggravate superpower relations. Brzezinski and Secretary of Defense Brown, on the other hand, expressed greater interest in resisting Soviet expansion through confrontation and advocated enhanced military relations with China in order to consolidate Beijing's participation in the U.S.-led anti-Soviet coalition.

Ultimately, Vance lost the battle, and the administration expanded military relations with China. As in the case of normalization, the deciding factor was not bureaucratic politics. Rather, developments in U.S.-Soviet relations persuaded the president that the development of U.S.-PRC military relations was required to develop an adequate response to Soviet foreign policy.

U.S.-PRC security relations moved along a number of tracks. At the most basic level were direct administration warnings to Moscow that Soviet impingement on U.S. interests would result in enhanced U.S.-PRC cooperation. Kissinger issued many such warnings, including those in 1976. During the Carter administration, the Vietnamese invasion of Cambodia elicited similar warnings. A few months after the invasion, the president went so far as to include in a letter to Brezhnev a warning that continued Soviet support for Vietnamese policy would influence the course of U.S.-PRC relations. Similarly, the administration warned the Soviet Union that an increased Soviet naval presence at Cam Ranh Bay would lead Washington to reevaluate its security position in Asia, implying that Soviet policy would affect the course of U.S.-PRC relations.[78]

After normalization of relations, the United States also sought greater exchanges between the two sides' senior policy makers on the current international situation and on the prospects for strategic cooperation. This process had begun as early as 1977. After the Vance visit to Beijing, Brzezinski had initiated it in informal discussions with Chai Zemin. An important step forward was taken in the aftermath of the war in the Ogaden. As has been noted, during the Brzezinski mission to China in May 1978, Morton Abramowitz became the first U.S. Defense Department official to visit China since the 1940s. Abramowitz briefed Chinese Defense Ministry officials on DOD analysis of Soviet military developments. Shortly thereafter, Frank Press, the president's science adviser, led a science and technology delegation to Beijing that included representatives of U.S. agencies dealing with militarily sensitive high technology, including the head of the U.S. space program.[79]

The process accelerated after normalization. In January 1979, the president took a personal role in developing U.S.-PRC strategic consultations. He authorized Brzezinski to begin "special negotiations" with Chinese officials on U.S.-PRC security cooperation. Then, in early May, Carter held a lengthy "important meeting" with Chinese Ambassador Chai Zemin to discuss enhanced U.S.-PRC security ties. "It is not bad for the Soviets to think there is an embryonic U.S.-China military relationship," Carter explained to Secretary of Defense Brown the next day.[80] Then, in June 1979, Brzezinski proposed to Chai that the U.S. Navy visit Chinese ports. That same month, at Peking University, Vice President Mondale declared that a "strong and secure and modernizing China" was in the U.S. interest, and that "any nation which seeks to weaken or isolate you in world affairs assumes a stance counter to American interests." Deng personally encouraged these efforts in April when he expressed interest to a U.S. Senate delegation led by Frank Church in purchasing U.S. military aircraft, U.S. naval visits to Chinese ports, and Chinese use of U.S. electronic equipment to gather information on Soviet nuclear testing and share it with Washington.[81]

It was in this atmosphere that Carter administration officials offered the president conflicting advice over the merits of a visit to China by Secretary of Defense Brown. Mondale had proposed the Brown visit to Chinese officials during his June visit to Beijing. In September, however, Vance advised Carter that he opposed the visit and argued for a delay until U.S.-Soviet tension over the discovery of a Soviet brigade in Cuba had subsided, so as to reduce the likelihood that the visit would be perceived in Moscow as an anti-Soviet move. Carter rejected Vance's advice, instead agreeing with Brown, who argued that an early visit would be timely given Washington's difficulties in dealing with the Soviet Union. Thus, in January 1980, America's highest military official visited China. Then, in May, Chinese Minister of Defense Geng Biao visited Washington. The diplomacy of military relations had been finalized.[82]

Closely paralleling these diplomatic moves were equally significant developments in U.S. policy regarding technology transfer to China. In early 1978, Brown and Brzezinski gained increased authority in this area when, despite Vance's objections, the administration established an interagency committee to oversee technology transfer to China. Nonetheless, Vance continued to oppose transfers of military-related technology to China, and the administration failed to follow through on Brzezinski's May 1978 commitment to Beijing to sell to China advanced Landsat infrared airborne geological scanning equipment that it would not sell to Moscow. In July 1979, Brzezinski and Brown tried again, proposing the transfer to China of five items that the United States would not sell to the Soviet Union. When Vance objected, the two sides compromised and some of the items were approved for sale to China.[83] The Carter administration was gradually catching up to the technology-transfer policy of the Ford administration.

This was also the situation regarding policy on sales of high-technology equipment and military matériel to China by other NATO countries. Carter had passed word to France in November

1978 that the United States would not oppose the sale of a French nuclear reactor to China, and during a January 1979 meeting of the leaders of the United States, France, West Germany, and Britain, he said that he "would not be unhappy with a more relaxed Western attitude regarding Chinese arms purchases." Even Vance was falling into line. Brzezinski reports that in late April, in the context of increased Soviet use of Vietnamese naval and air facilities, he persuaded Vance to tell the British that Washington "had no objection" to Britain selling weapons to China and, following Kissinger's lead, that it would "prefer them not to submit such a sale to [COCOM], where it would become a matter of dispute."[84]

Nevertheless, differences in the administration continued over whether Washington should permit U.S. sales of equipment with possible military end-use to China. In May, DOD analysts presented Brown with a study concluding that it was in the U.S. interest to bolster Chinese military capabilities vis-à-vis the Soviet Union. In December, as Brown prepared for his January visit to China, he pressed for further liberalization of export controls on high technology with possible military uses. He further argued that the administration should not exclude the possibility of arms sales. Vance, on the other hand, who was concerned about the potential for "destabilizing consequences," opposed further liberalization of technology transfer. On December 17, Carter decided against developing an arms sales relationship with China. He did, however, instruct Vance to develop an initiative on liberalized export regulations before Brown left for China. One such issue concerned the sale to China of the airborne geological scanning equipment. Debate on this issue continued even after the July decision to expand exports of military-related technology to China. "I don't give a shit what the Soviets think," Carter said when some officials continued to express concern about the Soviet reaction.[85] Vance's influence on U.S.-PRC relations had clearly deteriorated.

President Carter had thus far refrained from permitting sales to Beijing of equipment that might be used by the People's Liberation Army, but the Soviet invasion of Afghanistan changed his policy on the sale of military-related goods to China. Despite Vance's objections, the day before Brown left for China, Carter instructed him to inform the Chinese of his decision to permit the sale to China of technology that it would not sell to the Soviet Union, including nonlethal military equipment and over-the-horizon radar. After his meeting with Deng Xiaoping, Brown finally announced that the United States was prepared to export to China the Landsat Earth

Resources Satellite, which had possible military uses and which Brzezinski had committed to sell as early as May 1978. Brown's visit also promoted intelligence cooperation. Morton Abramowitz gave Chinese military officers classified information on Soviet deployments on the Sino-Soviet border, including reconnaissance photos.[86]

Not only had the Soviet Union altered U.S. China policy, but it also fundamentally changed the relationship among the key policy makers in the administration. Since spring 1978, as the president's view of Soviet policy hardened, he increasingly turned to Brzezinski for policy advice. The emerging China policy reflected this trend. The Soviet invasion of Afghanistan completed the process, and Vance's influence in the administration quickly declined. His advice on a wide range of issues, including China policy, was no longer appropriate, given the president's profound distrust of Soviet intentions.[87] Thus, in 1980, China policy reflected Brzezinski's role as the president's dominant foreign policy adviser.

In March, following Brown's return to Washington, the Department of State issued Munitions Control Newsletter no. 81, which listed items the United States would consider for export to China on a "case-by-case basis." The list included approximately 30 different categories of nonlethal military equipment, including air-defense radar and communications and transportation equipment. According to Assistant Secretary of State Holbrooke, for an item on the list to receive an export license, it had to be available for purchase by "all of our friends," which placed considerable restrictions on the review process.[88] The administration then officially formalized its new trade policy toward China in April 1980. In 1979, Deng Xiaoping had personally complained that China was still put in the same export category as the Soviet Union, and made the simple request that the United States simply choose another letter for China among the 26 in the English alphabet. Ben Huberman relayed the request to Brzezinski, who secured President Carter's approval. But Vance stalled the process, and only after Brzezinski insisted that he would have Carter personally call Vance did the secretary of state reluctantly authorize the change, formalizing the administration's pro-China "tilt" on technology transfer. Thus, in April the United States moved China from export category "Y," comprised of Soviet-bloc countries, to its own category, "P," formally permitting enhanced Chinese access to nonlethal military equipment.[89]

The next month, the Pentagon announced further easing of export regulations, granting permission for the sale of 212 civilian Bell helicopters and liberalizing control over the export of computers and communications equipment. Then, in September, Under Secretary of Defense for Research and Engineering William Perry led a delegation to China to discuss China's ability to absorb advanced technology with PRC officials. So successful were these discussions that Perry's report on his visit proposed the U.S. sale to China of U.S. military hardware, including ground-to-air missiles and anti-submarine-warfare equipment. Soviet foreign policy had propelled the United States into a security relationship with China. As President Carter explained to Premier Hua Guofeng in Tokyo in July, consolidated U.S.-PRC relations would "minimize the threat of the Soviet military buildup."[90]

The first concrete step in the security relationship was intelligence sharing and the placement in China of U.S. intelligence equipment to monitor Soviet compliance with arms-control agreements. The idea was likely raised in early May 1979, when Carter held his "important meeting" with Ambassador Chai Zemin to discuss the expansion of U.S.-China security ties. Carter made "some proposals," and "an important threshold was crossed" in security cooperation. The issue was first publicly raised by Senator Joseph Biden in April 1979 after his meeting with Deng Xiaoping as part of the Senate delegation led by Frank Church. As noted above, Deng welcomed the idea, as long as there would not be a U.S. "base" on Chinese territory, U.S.-trained Chinese technicians managed the equipment, and China had access to the intelligence. Intelligence cooperation deepened when Stansfield Turner, director of the Central Intelligence Agency in the Carter administration, visited China, reportedly to address some final issues regarding the deployment of the listening stations. Sometime in 1980, the monitoring equipment was installed in western China.[91]

U.S. arms sales to China were the only missing piece in U.S.-PRC security relations. They would come at the height of the escalation of U.S.-Soviet tension during the Reagan administration.

THE DIPLOMACY OF ESTABLISHING ECONOMIC RELATIONS

Just as normalization opened the door to U.S.-PRC strategic cooperation, it also enabled rapid expansion of trade relations. Indeed, in 1977, Deng had personally explained that China preferred to buy from countries with which it had diplomatic relations, and in 1978, the PRC's minister of the petroleum industry indicated that China would purchase U.S. oil technology only after normalization of relations.[92] Thus, acceding to a dynamic unlike that of strategic cooperation, after normalization the two sides entered into economic relations for their intrinsic value and with an understanding of the long-term political benefits of economic cooperation. It was also different from the establishment of strategic cooperation, in that there was little conflict within the Carter administration over the value of such a policy. Rather, conflict occurred between China and the United States because the two sides came to the negotiating table with different conceptions of the rules governing trade.

Trade conflict was exacerbated because economic relations on both sides were handled by specialists. Whereas political and strategic relations were managed in both Beijing and Washington in the context of security considerations by the preeminent leaders and their respective foreign policy advisers, these officials ceded management of economic relations to the departments responsible for international economic affairs. In the absence of high-level intervention and overriding strategic factors, economic conflict proceeded for the most part unaffected by extraneous considerations.

In this context, the course of negotiations was determined by the balance of interests in establishing economic relations. China clearly had the most to gain from expanded economic relations. Economic relations with the United States would give China access to advanced technology and to the U.S. market, which was essential if China were to acquire the foreign currency needed to buy that technology. Economic relations would also contribute to technology transfer, because Chinese workers would develop "on-the-job training" in joint ventures and Western investment projects.

For the United States, economic relations were primarily an instrument to promote stable political relations and continued economic and political reform in China. The latter would contribute to better political relations as the differences between the two countries' economic and social systems diminished. Although specific U.S. industries might ultimately benefit from U.S.-PRC economic relations, the political implications of such benefits were the immediate consideration, rather than the overall impact on the U.S. economy, which for the foreseeable future would be negligible. The potential economic benefits to the United States would not be insignificant, but in the context of U.S.-PRC negotiations, they weighed less on U.S. negotiators than Chinese economic interests weighed on Chinese negotiators. Indeed, in some respects, the United States had more to lose economically than China. Whereas the Chinese economy would develop more jobs by acquiring Western investment and exporting to the United States, the United States would experience a net loss of jobs as inexpensive Chinese imports affected the low-technology, labor-intensive sectors of the U.S. economy. These asymmetries in the costs and benefits of economic relations shaped the course of the conflict over trade relations.

In particular, the asymmetries permitted the pace and content of U.S.-PRC relations to be determined by U.S. domestic politics. Just as an asymmetrical strategic relationship had permitted President Ford to place the burden of U.S. election politics on China, Washington imposed the cost of placating Congress and various domestic economic groups on China in trade negotiations.

The two sides conducted negotiations in three areas: The claims-assets dispute; a trade agreement, which included provision for U.S. most-favored-nation (MFN) trade treatment of China; and a textile agreement.

The claims-assets dispute had been under negotiation since 1973. An agreement had been held up by the absence of diplomatic relations. China would not sign an "official" document with a country that did not recognize it. There was also Chinese concern that a claims-assets agreement might assist U.S. policy toward the Soviet Union, thus encouraging Washington to delay the difficult decisions required for normalization. For these reasons, China deflected U.S. efforts to reach an agreement.

After normalization, Chinese leaders showed heightened interest in resolving the dispute. But because Chinese economic officials, rather than the political leadership, managed the negotiations in Beijing, there was further delay. When Secretary of the Treasury Michael Blumenthal visited China in February 1979, he and Minister of Finance Zhang Jingfu appeared to reach a final agreement. But after Blumenthal left Beijing, Chinese officials continued to insist on minor changes, holding up a settlement. Chinese bureaucrats fell into line only after Secretary of Commerce Juanita Kreps informed Deng Xiaoping of the delay. Expressing exasperation, Deng instructed his subordinates to present him with an agreement before Kreps left China, and she initialed it before her departure.[93]

U.S. policy toward the U.S.-PRC trade agreement reflected similar nonstrategic dynamics. The core issue here was U.S. granting of most-favored-nation treatment to China. When Kreps was in China, she initialed a trade agreement calling for China to received MFN status. But the administration delayed full signature of the agreement and its presentation to Congress. Two issues delayed the agreement. First, as part of its effort to maintain balanced treatment of the Soviet Union and China, the State Department wanted to withhold MFN status from China until it could be offered to the

Soviet Union. Thus, the stumbling bloc was Soviet compliance with the Jackson-Vanik amendment, which required free emigration from communist states as the precondition of the granting of MFN treatment. Whereas the Soviet Union refused to suggest compliance with this regulation, Beijing satisfied administration concerns during Deng's visit to Washington. When Carter raised the issue of emigration, Deng asked how many immigrants the United States would like and said that he would be pleased to allow ten million Chinese to emigrate to the United States. The president considered this statement, other personal Chinese assurances, and various other aspects of PRC emigration policy sufficient to allow him to waive the provisions of the Jackson-Vanik amendment.[94]

If the United States nevertheless maintained a balanced trade policy toward the Soviet Union and China, it would mean that Soviet emigration laws dictated U.S. China policy and denied China the benefits of MFN treatment. When U.S.-Soviet relations deteriorated in 1979, undermining the president's predilection for caution in U.S.-Soviet relations, Carter favored offering MFN status to China before offering it to the Soviet Union. Moreover, during the negotiations over the claim-assets dispute, U.S. negotiators had committed the United States to granting MFN treatment to China in return for a claims-assets agreement favorable to the United States.[95] Finally, in the aftermath of normalization, there was an overall atmosphere favoring steps that would consolidate U.S.-PRC relations in a wide variety of issue areas. Thus, on July 7, the two sides formally signed the trade agreement. Shortly thereafter, Vice President Mondale informed Chinese leaders that Washington would abandon "evenhandedness" on a wide-range of economic issues.[96]

Nonetheless, in contrast to the dynamics of political and security relations, change in U.S.-Soviet relations and the inherit benefit of improved U.S.-PRC relations were not the determining forces in the making of U.S. trade policy toward China. Deteriorating U.S.-Soviet relations may have removed an obstacle to the granting of MFN status to China, but security concerns and bilateral considerations were insufficient to move the process forward. Rather, the primary determinant of the timing of the administration's decision to seek MFN status for China was U.S. domestic politics.

After the July 7 signing of the trade agreement, Carter still had to decide when to present the Senate with the agreement. The primary obstacle to passage was the opposition of senators from textile-producing states, which would lose jobs to imports of Chinese textiles. The administration decided that it would not send the bill to

Congress without first obtaining an agreement that would protect these states from excessive imports of PRC textiles.[97] But the administration was facing difficulties in obtaining a textile agreement. Beijing refused to acquiesce to U.S. quotas, and the negotiations, which had started in December 1978, thus carried on through the end of May 1979 without success. At that time, Special Trade Representative Robert Strauss unilaterally imposed quotas on a number of categories of textiles.

Ironically, the breakdown of the textile negotiations and the unilateral imposition of quotas improved the prospects for a U.S.-PRC trade agreement. With the quotas in place, senators from textile-producing states, assured of protection for their states' workers, could more easily vote for the trade agreement. When Carter imposed quotas on two additional categories in late October 1979, he persuaded the remaining reluctant congressmen that he was committed to protecting U.S. textile jobs, and thus finally removed congressional opposition to MFN status for China.[98]

The textile negotiations were similarly guided by domestic economic considerations in both Washington and Beijing. Whereas the emergence of common views of the Soviet threat promoted greater bargaining symmetry in the normalization negotiations, Washington still possessed far superior leverage in trade negotiations, as reflected in the fact that Beijing was obliged to incur the costs of protecting the Carter administration's domestic political interests.

The Carter administration's special concern for China was reflected in its willingness to grant Beijing immediate entry into the U.S. textile market at a level comparable to that enjoyed by Hong Kong, Taiwan, Korea, and the other large exporters of textiles. China's strategic importance, U.S. interest in the success of China's reform program, which depended on textile exports to accumulate foreign reserves, and the fact that China would inevitably become the largest exporter of textiles to the United States, necessitated sacrifice by the U.S. textile industry. There would thus be an immediate and noticeable impact on the U.S. textile industry.[99]

On the other hand, Beijing could not be allowed unimpeded access to the U.S. market. Thus, Washington also sought an agreement that would provide some protection for jobs in the U.S. textile industry, and to the president from political attacks. In pursuing this objective, U.S. negotiators experienced no interference from the foreign policy bureaucracies. The fate of the trade agreement in Congress or of the general state of the bilateral relationship did not affect their negotiating demands. Instead, domestic political considerations focusing on the interest of politicians from textile-producing states shaped their position.[100]

On the Chinese side, domestic considerations were equally important. Textile exports to the United States could become a major source of foreign exchange, and Chinese leaders, including Deng Xiaoping, had a large stake in, and great expectations of, access to the U.S. market. This made it politically difficult for Chinese leaders to compromise on this issue, and thus difficult for Chinese trade negotiators to recommend an agreement that ran counter to the expectations of their leaders. This was particularly the case in 1979, when China experienced a large budget deficit in the aftermath of its February invasion of Vietnam, and when its foreign exchange reserves were relatively low. Under such circumstances, it was politically safer for both the reform-minded elite and their negotiating subordinates to adopt a hard line and defer the difficult compromises until compromise was recognized on all sides as necessary.

These two differing sets of political priorities clashed in Beijing in May 1979. After months of fruitless negotiations, Special Trade Representative Robert Strauss presented Deng Xiaoping with an ultimatum. Either Beijing compromised in three days or the United States would break off the negotiations and unilaterally impose quotas in accordance with article 3 of the U.S. trade law, which would hold annual Chinese textile imports to the level of the first twelve of the previous fourteen months. This would actually reduce imports of Chinese textiles compared to the previous year. Moreover, this was an absolutely small quota, because Beijing had yet to develop its textile export program. Indeed, China would have much greater access if it accepted the U.S. offer, because its exports would be based on Washington's decision to allow it high quotas on a par with the major exporters of textiles to the United States. But Chinese leaders, fully understanding the ramifications of the breakdown of negotiations, refused to bend, and after allowing the White House an opportunity to object, Strauss followed through on his threat and imposed quotas on five categories of Chinese textiles.[101]

The breakdown of the negotiations reflected the conflicting domestic interests of the two sides. But China would have to compromise eventually, because the absence of an agreement was costing it valuable foreign exchange, whereas the United States would not miss Chinese textiles. But before an agreement could be signed, the two sides conducted another round of fruitless negotiations. As had his predecessor, the new special trade representative, Governor Rubin Askew, allowed his negotiators great leeway. The domestic political ramifications of a textile agreement were his primary concern. Neither he nor his negotiators conducted negotiations in the context of the larger bilateral relationship. Moreover, despite the deadlocked negotiations, neither the White House nor the State Department interfered.[102] Hence, the textile negotiators continued to press for an agreement that protected U.S. jobs.

But in China, the situation was still not conducive to compromise. The political costs of admitting that textile exports would be less than expected remained too great to allow for compromise. Hence, when negotiations picked up in mid October 1979, the two sides remained at a stalemate. After China flatly rejected every U.S. proposal, the U.S. side decided to end the negotiations and inform their Chinese counterparts that it was up to them to request the next round of negotiations. Shortly thereafter, Washington imposed quotas on two additional categories of Chinese textiles, which had the effect of preventing any additional imports in these categories through the end of May 1980. Indeed, a considerable quantity of Chinese products were locked in U.S. Customs warehouses.[103]

Finally, in April 1980, China invited U.S. negotiators to Beijing for negotiations. The delegation met with a new Chinese negotiating team led by Vice Minister of Foreign Trade Wang Mingjun, who was also general manager of the China Textile Import and Export Corporation. This was the first time the U.S. side had negotiated with such a senior trade leader. As was the case with the change in the Chinese negotiators just prior to U.S.-PRC agreement on establishing diplomatic relations, the emergence of a new Chinese negotiating team indicated that Beijing was ready to deal.

Wang asked the U.S. negotiators why there had been no negotiations. Ambassador H. Reiter Webb replied that the negotiations had ended because China had rejected the U.S. proposals and had not made any counteroffers. He added that the United States was not prepared to continue the negotiations until China offered a response to the U.S. proposals. After excusing himself and his colleagues for a few minutes, Wang returned and embarked on serious negotiations. An agreement was in sight.[104]

When Wang traveled to Washington in May, the two sides were operating under the deadline of Wang's return flight. It had been one year since Washington had imposed annual quotas, and an agreement was required for China to avoid their reimposition. Nonetheless, although 99 percent of the details were settled, Wang returned to China empty-handed. Apparently, the final U.S. offer exceeded his instructions, and he had to return home. Five days after his departure, Washington reimposed the quotas.

Vice Premier Bo Yibo's visit to Washington triggered the final compromises. With the visit approaching, Chinese foreign trade officials and U.S. embassy officials in Beijing completed and initialed the agreement. Shortly thereafter, in Washington, Vice Premier Bo and President Carter signed the agreement. Although the final quotas reflected mutual give-and-take, Beijing had reconciled itself to working within the parameters initially offered by Washington. Ironically, now that Beijing had formally acquiesced to the quotas, it could take advantage of Washington's decision to allow China immediate high-level access to the U.S. market. The agreement called for a 40 percent average increase in Chinese quotas.[105]

Chinese leaders finally made the politically difficult concessions required to establish access to the U.S. textile market. These concessions would not only provide China with the foreign reserves necessary to support its technology import program, but also removed a significant obstacle to the expansion and consolidation of U.S.-PRC economic relations in later years.

ESTABLISHING EDUCATIONAL AND SCIENTIFIC EXCHANGES

Strategic considerations and U.S. domestic politics determined the pace of military cooperation and domestic politics in both countries, and various international economic asymmetries determined the pace of economic relations. But in the development of educational and scientific exchanges, there were neither domestic conflicts nor international asymmetries to disrupt expanded ties, which were accordingly established and already contributing to long-term U.S.-PRC cooperation by the end of the Carter administration.

Once again, each side derived distinct benefits from this functional relationship. The United States would benefit by training members of China's future intellectual and political elite. Exposure to U.S. society and political institutions might foster a favorable elite attitude toward U.S.-PRC relations. Moreover, such exchanges might provide these future leaders with an interest in stable relations, insofar as their career prospects would be directly related to the state of U.S.-PRC relations.

For Beijing, developed educational and scientific ties would be another source of Chinese modernization. China's post-Mao leadership understood that China's technological level could not begin to provide China with the expertise required to develop China's economy; China would have to learn from the technologically advanced countries. China's future leaders in physics, chemistry, biology, computer science, and engineering would need to receive important advanced training in the United States and learn from visiting U.S. specialists in China, thus promoting the technological development of various aspects of Chinese society. University-level educational exchanges would also make a valuable contribution to Chinese economic development. Beijing would send its best students abroad, where they could receive the advanced training required to elevate China's economic and educational institutions to world-class levels.

While both sides could benefit from such exchanges, neither side would experience any appreciable immediate cost.[106] These negotiations thus reflected a true case of "positive-sum" politics. Rather than cooperation, there was "harmony."

The transformation of Chinese thinking regarding U.S.-PRC educational and scientific programs was evident during the Brzezinski visit to China. State Department officials had predicted that Chinese opposition to leadership exchanges and official agreements prior to normalization would lead Beijing to rebuff efforts to establish such programs, just as they had rejected U.S. efforts to negotiate the claim and assets issue in early 1977. Moreover, since 1971 Beijing had rejected every U.S. attempt to develop diplomatic and technical exchanges peripheral to the normalization process. But Chinese leaders were in fact keenly interested in the U.S. delegation's presentation of the prospects for science and technology exchanges. Indeed, under the leadership of Deng Xiaoping and in the context of China's post-Mao economic modernization agenda, they were prepared to abandon the Chinese policy of opposition to such exchanges prior to normalization and responded positively to the U.S. suggestions. Thus, the NSC subsequently advised Carter to approve concrete discussions with Chinese leaders aimed at initiating exchanges. The president agreed, and the NSC started preparation for the first U.S. science and technology delegation to visit China. The Chinese leadership welcomed the idea, and in July 1978, the president's science adviser, Frank Press, led a delegation to China. Shortly thereafter, Chinese leaders welcomed a delegation led by Secretary of Energy James Schlesinger. Beijing was prepared to move ahead on U.S.-China exchanges.[107]

The July mission led by Frank Press had very modest hopes for the visit, expecting merely to establish a basis for the long-term development of educational ties. State Department officials continued to believe that Beijing would reject all U.S. efforts to reach agreement. But to the delegation's surprise, Chinese leaders were prepared to begin immediate and wide-ranging exchanges. This was clearly the case with university-level student exchanges. When Press ventured that China might want to send 50 students to the United States, Chinese leaders responded that they wanted to send 500 students. Fang Yi, head of the State Scientific and Technical Commission, even volunteered that China would pay all of the expenses for the 500 students, clearly unaware of how much the program would cost. Deng Xiaoping fully supported the program. He gave a warm reception to Press and for the first time broached the prospect of joint economic ventures in China with a U.S. official. *Renmin ribao* published Press's banquet speech, which stressed the virtues of global interdependence and the necessity for international cooperation, in full. It was the warmest reception that a U.S. delegation had ever received in China since 1949.[108]

In the context of their domestic modernization agenda, Deng and his colleagues were prepared to move forward on an international exchange program that would have been heretical during Mao's reign. American and Chinese working groups continued to hold meetings on educational exchanges, and in October, the United States and China signed an "Understanding on Educational Exchanges," which was later subsumed under the "Agreement on Cooperation in Science and Technology" that Deng and Carter signed during Deng's January 1979 visit to Washington. The program quickly flourished. In 1979, 1,330 Chinese, and in 1980, 4,324 Chinese, came to the United States on education-specific visas. By 1983, approximately 19,000 Chinese had visited the United States for educational purposes.[109]

These educational programs clearly served China's interest in modernization and the U.S. interest in building bridges throughout Chinese society. But it would be a mistake to assume that there was no educational benefit for the United States. Although sufficient access to Chinese society to permit adequate research opportunities for American social scientists was slow to develop, it would be difficult to overestimate the benefit of the exchanges to U.S. graduate programs in the natural sciences. Chinese graduate students compensated for the declining enrollment of American students in physics programs, for example, and they proved to be among the very best graduate students in the field, helping raise the standards of doctoral work.[110]

But the significance of the 1978 Press mission extended beyond student exchanges. China's warm welcome reflected its recognition that the United States was also interested in developing science and technology exchanges. The mission included the heads of all the U.S. technical agencies, including the heads of the National Science

Foundation, the National Institutes of Health, the National Aeronautics and Space Administration, the Bureau of Standards, and the U.S. Geological Survey. This was the highest-level science and technology delegation the United States had ever sent abroad. It was also the highest-level delegation the United States had sent to China, with the exception of presidential and foreign policy delegations. The delegation brought dozens of proposals for scientific exchanges, including proposals for cooperation in hydropower, space and aeronautics, agriculture, pest control, energy, and geological survey using satellite technology.[111]

This was no ordinary delegation, and Chinese leaders grabbed this opportunity to establish a full-range of scientific exchanges with the United States. Indeed, reminding the U.S. delegation of Benjamin Huberman's proposal during the Brzezinski visit that a Chinese astronaut participate in a U.S. space-shuttle mission, Chinese leaders accepted the offer, making a highly symbolic commitment to scientific and technology exchanges. The two sides also established working groups to discuss details of various exchange programs. In addition to the 1978 agreement on scholar and student exchanges, between 1978 and 1980, China and the United States signed thirteen cooperation agreements, covering such areas as high-energy physics, space technology, medicine and public health, environmental protection, and earthquake studies. One of the most innovative and successful of these early programs was the establishment in Dalian of the National Center for Industrial Science and Technology Management Development, which was first proposed by Commerce Department officials during the Frank Press visit. In eight years, it trained over 1,500 mid-level Chinese managers in managerial skills and practices. Overall, by 1987, the two sides had signed 29 agreements and developed over 500 cooperative projects involving more than 5,000 scientists. This was the largest exchange program for both countries.[112]

Conclusion

The Carter administration made the difficult political decisions required for normalization of relations. Although its handling of the interplay between the Taiwan issue and U.S. politics was less than exemplary, normalization would have had severe domestic repercussions even had there been greater sensitivity to domestic considerations. The administration maintained the most essential elements of U.S. policy toward Taiwan, including the public commitments to provide Taiwan with defensive weaponry and to peaceful resolution of the Taiwan issue. It also maintained U.S. ambiguity regarding the international status of Taiwan. Despite the stronger language regarding Taiwan's status in the Chinese version of the normalization communiqué, as compared to the Shanghai communiqué, the English version of the normalization communiqué holds that the United States "acknowledges the Chinese position that there is but one China and Taiwan is part of China" (see Appendix A). Thus, the Carter administration, like its predecessors, avoided stating the U.S. position on the status of Taiwan.[113] Although Washington terminated the U.S.-ROC Mutual Defense Treaty, it clearly established its interest in Taiwan's security. The administration's compromises were the minimum necessary to secure an agreement.

Nevertheless, the United States had made significant compromises, including breaking diplomatic relations with Taiwan, abrogating its defense treaty with Taipei, and abandoning its objective of securing an explicit Chinese commitment not to use force against Taiwan, which PRM 24 had decided would be an important part of the normalization agreement. The administration's willingness to make these compromises and the timing of the administration's crucial decisions leading to the agreement were the result of President Carter's growing perception of the Soviet challenge to American security and of the evolution of his understanding of the value of consolidated U.S.-PRC relations in resisting Soviet foreign policy. The president's personal perception of American security was the key determinant of the shift in U.S. China policy and of Washington's readiness to incur the costs of compromise.

Similarly, it was not easy for Chinese leaders to agree to normalize relations, given the insistence of the United States that it would continue to sell weaponry to Taiwan, but China's deteriorating situation vis-à-vis the Soviet Union persuaded Deng Xiaoping and his colleagues to compromise. Soviet encirclement of China was increasing both along the Sino-Soviet border and through the extension of Soviet influence into Indochina via the Soviet-Vietnamese alliance. Under such circumstances, the immediate strategic merits of normalization, as well as its long-term benefits to Chinese modernization, far outweighed the discomfort of compromising over arms sales to Taiwan. Moreover, Deng clearly maintained the right to challenge U.S. arms-sales policy at a later date.

The irony of the normalization process is that a crucial determinant of the development and consolidation of U.S.-PRC relations—reemerging U.S.-Soviet tension—would ultimately contribute to

PRC willingness to confront the United States with its dissatisfaction with the status quo in U.S.-Taiwan relations. Within a year of normalization, it was clear that U.S.-PRC relations were entering a more turbulent and tension-ridden era. Chinese leaders decided to renegotiate the arms-sales issue, which the Carter administration had finessed, essentially leaving it to be addressed during the Reagan administration.

Chinese leaders also had to reconcile themselves to U.S. ambiguity regarding the status of the island of Taiwan. Although Henry Kissinger and Richard Nixon had reportedly accepted China's position that Taiwan was part of China in 1971 and during the 1972 summit, Beijing never succeeded in pressing the United States to make this its formal, declared policy. On the contrary, after Deng reformulated China's three normalization conditions during Vance's August 1977 visit to Beijing, China never again pressed the issue in the course of the normalization negotiations. Chinese leaders understood and accommodated themselves to the limits to Chinese leverage and to the reality that the best China could do was to maintain its own position that Taiwan is a Chinese province.

After normalization of relations, U.S. and Chinese officials addressed various nonstrategic issues that had been deferred while the two countries negotiated the Taiwan issue. Through various channels, and at times difficult negotiations, U.S. and Chinese negotiators laid the basis for the long-term development of governmental and societal institutions supportive of stable cooperation. Although this process would be briefly interrupted during the Reagan administration while China and the United States renegotiated the rules governing U.S.-Taiwan relations, these initial developments in nonstrategic cooperation provided the framework for the expansion of relations.

CHAPTER 6

Renegotiating Cooperation

RENEWED COLD WAR TENSION
AND U.S. ARMS SALES TO TAIWAN

Negotiations over the Taiwan issue resumed during the first two years of the Reagan administration. In retrospect, both sides were clearly dissatisfied with the normalization agreement. China wanted greater restrictions on U.S. arms sales to Taiwan, and Ronald Reagan sought to establish closer diplomatic and military relations with Taiwan. Thus, despite normalization of relations, conflict between the United States and the PRC over Taiwan continued.

Moreover, the very process that had led the United States to expedite normalization of U.S.-PRC relations and expand security relations laid the basis for escalated bilateral tension. The Carter administration's growing apprehension over the Soviet threat and the collapse of détente in the aftermath of the Soviet invasion of Afghanistan contributed to China's positive reevaluation of its strategic circumstances, and Chinese leaders gradually adopted a more assertive posture toward U.S.-PRC conflicts of interests.

The downward trend in superpower relations accelerated with the election of Ronald Reagan and the full emergence of the "new" Cold War in U.S.-Soviet relations. President Reagan and his advisers focused on the Soviet global challenge to U.S. interests and the necessity for mobilizing a full array of domestic and international resources to respond to the Soviet threat. For Secretary of State Alexander Haig, the president's chief adviser on U.S.-PRC relations, China was a major component of the anti-Soviet global coalition, and the need for compromise with China loomed larger than ever before.

In contrast to Haig's preoccupation with the Soviet threat, China experienced an increasingly favorable strategic situation and correspondingly heightened confidence in U.S.-PRC relations. The Reagan administration's decision to renew the Cold War and challenge Soviet power offset Soviet pressure on China. Moreover, Sino-Soviet relations began to improve significantly for the first time since the late 1950s. Chinese leaders had also resolved the post-Mao succession struggle, and Deng Xiaoping possessed increased authority in stable political conditions. These developments combined with heightened tension between the superpowers and the Reagan administration's perception of U.S. strategic vulnerability to increase Beijing's estimate of its value to U.S. security. China was therefore no longer content to abide by the status quo in U.S. policy toward Taiwan.

American perceptions that U.S. security was deteriorating and China's simultaneously improved strategic circumstances largely explain the heightened tension between the two countries and the course of U.S.-PRC negotiations in 1981–82. These contrasting strategic trends notwithstanding, however, just as during the Ford administration, the ultimate outcome of the negotiations also reflected the inherent disparity in U.S.-PRC relations. When China actually faced the prospect of worsening relations, it made significant compromises rather than call Washington's bluff and possibly confront the Soviet Union with reduced U.S. support. The contrasting trends in strategic circumstances combined with the disparities in national power to produce the compromises on each side that characterized the outcome of the negotiations and the content of the joint communiqué of August 17, 1982. Nevertheless, although China elicited significant compromises from the United States, Washington preserved the essential elements of its Taiwan policy.

Finally, too, personality influenced the outcome of the negotiations. President Reagan differed with Secretary of State Haig over U.S. policy toward Taiwan and resisted his efforts to distance the United States from Taiwan.[1] Haig was clearly more willing than Reagan to adjust U.S. policy toward Taiwan to consolidate U.S.-PRC cooperation. The ultimate outcome of U.S.-PRC negotiations reflected both Haig's greater desire to ameliorate U.S.-PRC conflict and President Reagan's decision to restrain Haig's more conciliatory inclinations.

Diverging Assessments of the Soviet Threat

In the aftermath of the Soviet invasion of Afghanistan, U.S. and Chinese views of the Soviet threat significantly diverged. The contrasting trends that had first appeared during the Ford administration reemerged in the early 1980s, but with far greater depth and intensity in both Washington and Beijing. Whereas White House perceptions of the Soviet threat became as great as at any time since the 1950s, China's fear of Soviet power diminished. These contrasting perceptions carried significant implications for each country's assessment of the strategic importance of the other and were reflected in contrasting appraisals of the value of stable relations. They also significantly affected U.S.-PRC negotiations and the terms of the joint communiqué of August 17, 1982.

GROWING U.S. THREAT PERCEPTION

The Soviet invasion of Afghanistan had drastically altered President Carter's view of the Soviet threat, leading him to change course and risk greater U.S.-Soviet tension in order to resist further Soviet advances. Carter 1980 defense budget request was accordingly much larger than that of the previous year, and the president withdrew the SALT II treaty from the Senate, where it was being considered for ratification. After U.S. imposition of trade and cultural sanctions and Soviet retaliation, there was nothing left of détente.

But whereas President Carter simply abandoned détente, President Reagan engaged the United States in a "new" Cold War. The new administration's perspective was not based on any additional Soviet moves, but on greater concern about American political and military weakness vis-à-vis the Soviet threat. Soviet leaders, Reagan said, assumed "the right to commit any crime, to lie, to cheat," in order to promote "world revolution and a one-world socialist or communist state." Détente had been a "one-way street," and America now faced a relentless Soviet challenge without the ability to respond.[2]

The Reagan administration took steps to reverse the perceived challenge by engaging the Soviet Union on all fronts. This had the short-term effect of further aggravating U.S. relations before any appreciable change in the strategic balance was observable. The administration's early efforts to confront the Soviet threat thus contributed to greater insecurity. Moreover, the United States was experiencing its worst inflation since World War II, which undermined its ability to restore its global power and national confidence.

Of foremost concern was the Soviet military challenge. Reagan believed that having outspent the United States since 1970, the Soviet Union had gained a "significant numerical advantage in strategic nuclear delivery systems, tactical aircraft, submarines, artillery, and anti-aircraft defense." Moscow's strategic missile buildup had given the USSR a "definite margin of superiority"; as a result, there was now a "window of vulnerability" to a Soviet first strike.[3] Secretary of State Haig shared the president's concern and repeatedly emphasized the danger, arguing that the shift in the strategic balance undermined the "margin of safety" for the West and affected both U.S. deterrence and crisis-management capability and the overall effectiveness of U.S. diplomacy. The nuclear balance of power influenced "every geopolitical decision of significance." The United States faced the prospect of "vulnerability to nuclear blackmail" and the "susceptibility of our friends to political intimidation" was threatened.[4]

The situation in Europe was no better. Soviet deployment of the SS20 missile challenged America's commitment to the defense of Europe, thereby eroding the political solidarity of the NATO alliance. The administration believed that in response, it had to deploy the Pershing II ballistic missile in Western Europe. By threatening Soviet territory from European bases, the U.S. Pershing II would reestablish the linkage between European territorial security and the U.S. defense commitment. Thus, in its first weeks in office the administration affirmed its commitment to the Carter policy of production and deployment of the Pershing II and insisted that only if the Soviet Union removed all its SS20s from positions within reach of Western Europe would the United States abandon plans for deployment. There was, however, no guarantee that the NATO allies would accept the Pershing II on their territories. The Western European peace movement had developed significant political influence in recent years and might well prevent even conservative politicians from permitting Pershing II deployment on their nations' territory. The Soviet Union would be the beneficiary.[5]

In the meantime, Soviet activities in Eastern Europe aroused concern. Moscow remained inflexible on political developments in Poland, including the emergence of the Polish labor movement under the leadership of Lech Wałesa and Solidarity. In April 1981, Moscow seemed to be preparing for a military occupation, and in December 1981, after continued anticommunist activities on the part of Solidarity and its supporters, the Polish government declared martial law, outlawed Solidarity, and imprisoned Wałesa. Prior to the imposition of martial law, Moscow had deployed its troops to support martial law and to prepare for possible intervention. Although Soviet military intervention did not occur, the Soviet Union revealed little willingness to accept anything but complete control over its Eastern European allies, and to use military force if necessary.[6]

The trend in the Third World was equally alarming to the new administration. Soviet forces and their allies had already succeeded in numerous parts of the world, most recently in Afghanistan. Moreover, Soviet and Cuban support for the Sandinista government in Nicaragua and Cuban arms shipments to the communist insurgents in El Salvador threatened further Soviet successes in Central America. The president was determined to resist Soviet expansion, and the administration provided large-scale military and economic assistance to El Salvador to help it defeat the insurgency. The White House also demanded greater Soviet restraint in the Third World as a condition for better superpower relations. President Reagan complained of "totalitarian forces in the world who seek subversion and conflict around the globe to further their barbarous assault on the human spirit," and he personally complained to Soviet Party Secretary Leonid Brezhnev in 1981 about Moscow's "pursuit of unilateral advantage in various parts of the world through direct and indirect use of force in regional conflicts," calling the role of Cuba in Africa and Latin America "particularly disturbing."[7]

The administration believed that a crisis in confidence, domestic divisions, and a severely troubled economy had left U.S. foreign policy unable to respond to an unrelenting Soviet threat. Indeed, the United States was much to blame for the shift in the balance of power. Secretary of State Haig argued that while the Soviet military program developed, the "cohesion" of U.S. foreign policy had "disintegrated"; while the United States was "debating the utility of military power," it "watched a vigorous Soviet military modernization program take shape without pursuing compensating actions" and "allowed the military balance to shift toward the Soviets." Domestic convulsions had shaken "America's confidence in itself . . . and American leadership faltered." The United States had "earned a reputation for 'strategic passivity' and that reputation still weighs heavily on us," Haig said. Only "through a steady accumulation of prudent and successful action" could Washington reestablish confidence in American power. Similarly, Secretary of Defense Caspar Weinberger maintained that America's failure to respond to the Soviet buildup created a "diminution of confidence" in the United States among its allies and a perception of U.S. "inability to respond adequately and promptly," which encouraged Soviet "exploitation of . . . instability."[8]

The administration had yet to mobilize an adequate response to this situation. Moreover, it had inherited an economy that was in a shambles, and that would get worse before it would get better. Inflation was running at over 10 percent annually, and interest rates were over 20 percent. There was little economic growth and high unemployment. The economy was suffering from the symptoms of "stagflation." Not only had the United States failed to keep pace with the Soviet arms buildup, but its weakened economy further undermined its international power and its ability to reverse the trend in the global balance.[9]

Seeking to correct the alleged imbalance in U.S.-Soviet relations, the Reagan administration significantly increased the defense budget and pushed for the development of new weapons systems. The administration's proposed five-year defense program called for the largest military buildup since the Korean War and 8 percent real growth in the defense budget. Given Reagan's convincing electoral victory and his personal popularity, most of his defense-spending requests received congressional support. Between 1981 and 1985, actual spending on defense increased by 7 percent a year, its share of the federal budget increased from 23 to 27 percent, and authority for defense procurement doubled.[10]

Not only did the Reagan White House increase defense spending far beyond the limits of the Carter administration, but it also reversed many of President Carter's decisions regarding particular weapons systems. President Reagan called for the development of the B-2 bomber and continued to promote the B-1 bomber and the MX missile programs. The president was also concerned about developments in Europe. Reversing the decision of the Carter administration, Reagan ordered production of the neutron bomb. Most important, the administration reaffirmed the U.S. commitment to the deployment of the Pershing II missile in Western Europe.

While the United States faced a serious Soviet threat and a weakened economy, it was in no hurry to hold a summit or pursue any other aspect of détente. "Rarely in history have we or any great nation pursued such noble goals, risked so much, and yet gained so little," Secretary Weinberger said, summing up the new U.S. administration's attitude to arms-control negotiations.[11] The administration believed that to negotiate from weakness would merely increase the confidence of the USSR in its ability to infringe on U.S. interests and lead to an inequitable agreement reflecting the imbalance in military power. As Secretary Haig emphasized, because the United States had not maintained its strategic and conventional forces, the USSR was not "compelled to agree to major limitations." Not only could the Soviet Union not be trusted, but American strategic weakness undermined Washington's negotiating position.[12]

The president's attack on Soviet human rights violations and his engagement in ideological polemics further inflamed relations. Reagan insisted that the Soviet Union was the "greatest violator of human rights in all the world" and proclaimed that it was the U.S. objective to develop a program to eliminate the Soviet system of government and "leave Marxism-Leninism on the ash-heap of history."[13] The president used every opportunity to remind the world of the ongoing repression in the Soviet Union.

But the administration's Soviet policy did not produce a consensus on China policy. In many respects, Haig shared many of the strategic views of Henry Kissinger, whose aide he had been during the Nixon and Ford administrations. Haig had adopted Kissinger's triangular view of the global balance and his focus on developing U.S.-PRC strategic cooperation, which, in the context of heightened U.S.-Soviet tension, he took to an extreme. He believed that Chinese participation in the anti-Soviet strategic consensus was imperative; in terms of U.S. strategic interests, he thought, China might be "the most important country in the world." Moreover, he was not reluctant to broadcast his view of China's strategic importance, thus undermining any potential caution in China's U.S. policy.[14]

Haig was so concerned with the Soviet threat that he was prepared to subordinate other U.S. foreign policy objectives to creating a global anti-Soviet "strategic consensus." This strategic preoccupation affected U.S. policy toward Taiwan. Haig saw U.S.-Taiwan relations as an obstacle to consolidated U.S.-PRC strategic cooperation. He viewed U.S.-PRC conflict over Taiwan as a problem to be solved rather than a conflict involving legitimate U.S. interests in stable U.S.-Taiwan relations. Haig and his advisers in the State Department were therefore prepared to bend over backward to accommodate Beijing's demands in order to solve the "Taiwan problem" and consolidate anti-Soviet cooperation.

The president and other officials of his administration—including Richard Allen, Reagan's national security adviser; Paul Wolfowitz, director of policy planning at the State Department; and Gaston Sigur, the Asian affairs specialist at the NSC—recognized the importance of U.S.-PRC relations in U.S. policy toward the Soviet Union, but they also insisted that reversing the trend in U.S. policy on Taiwan should be a major focus of the administration's foreign policy. Reagan, Allen, and these other administration officials believed that in its handling of normalization, the Carter administration had mistreated Taiwan, a longtime U.S. friend and ally in Asia. Although they did not advocate restoring official relations with Taiwan, they argued that the United States should treat it with greater dignity by, among other things, bolstering U.S.-Taiwan diplomatic and defense relations. In particular, Richard Allen believed that the United States should sell Taiwan an advanced-technology jet fighter. These officials did not see improved U.S.-Taiwan relations as an obstacle to cooperative U.S.-PRC relations. Rather, they argued that the State Department underestimated Washington's negotiating leverage with China. They agreed that Washington needed to cooperate with Beijing, but they also argued that Beijing faced an even greater imperative of cooperation, and that China's strategic position would compel it to make significant compromises on U.S.-Taiwan relations. Finally, they were prepared to risk increased U.S.-PRC tension in order to maintain U.S. commitments to Taiwan. Sharing Cyrus Vance's skeptical view of China's strategic importance, they were less concerned than Secretary Haig about assuaging Chinese dissatisfaction.[15]

This conflict in the administration did not reflect major differences over U.S.-PRC relations, but rather differences over the importance of U.S.-Taiwan relations and the risk the United States should take in challenging Chinese policy toward U.S.-Taiwan relations. President Reagan and his more conservative advisers wanted both to develop U.S.-PRC strategic cooperation and to have a relatively free hand to improve diplomatic and military relations with Taiwan. Haig and his advisers in the State Department preferred to adjust U.S. policy toward Taiwan to avoid Chinese retaliation and further damage to U.S. security vis-à-vis the Soviet Union.

Between January 1981 and July 1982, U.S. China policy primarily reflected Haig's exaggerated appraisal of Chinese power and fear of Chinese retaliation. But toward the end of the negotiations, in the summer of 1982, the president intervened to constrain Haig's inclination to conciliate China by placing limits on U.S. willingness to sacrifice the future of U.S.-Taiwan relations for the prospect of consolidated U.S.-PRC strategic cooperation. Reagan's intervention played a key role in determining the outcome of the negotiations.

RECEDING CHINESE THREAT PERCEPTION

While the United States perceived an increasing threat from the Soviet Union under Carter and Reagan, because of Washington's increasing resistance to Soviet power and reduced Sino-Soviet tensions, Chinese leaders conversely perceived a reduced Soviet threat and an improved security position. In 1979, for the first time since the late 1960s, China's security situation began to improve significantly.

Following normalization of diplomatic relations, China depicted the Carter administration as having abandoned Washington's passive international posture vis-à-vis the USSR. The U.S. "trend of taking the 'offensive while being on the defensive' is gradually increasing," Zeng Qing asserted in *Shijie zhishi*.[16] Zhuang Qubing, a senior America watcher at the Foreign Ministry's Institute of International Studies, argued that "more and more people" were advocating that to deal realistically with Soviet global expansionism, the U.S. administration should "'seek peace through strength,' [and] increase the military budget." Nevertheless, the United States had yet to commit itself to a new foreign policy direction. There remained considerable ambiguity in U.S. policy, for "there is still so much debate in the U.S. that no consensus can be reached."[17]

But all Chinese doubts about the direction of U.S. Soviet policy fell away after the Soviet invasion of Afghanistan. Zhuang Qubing observed that Washington had "adopted several measures to resist the Soviet Union that it had not previously adopted," including promoting a strategic relationship with China. He predicted that the superpowers would now "unavoidably open a new round of the arms race, and [their] global rivalry will further sharpen."[18] *Renmin ribao* reported that the increased U.S. defense budget signaled "a major change in U.S. defense policy." Washington now held a "realistic appraisal" of the Soviet Union. Most significant, after Afghanistan, détente was inconceivable: "it is quite impossible to return to the bygone situation of East-West relations." In the future, "antagonism will be the main feature in the relations between the two countries. . . . the tendency toward intensive competition . . . is irreversible."[19]

Not only did Beijing observe the reemergence of U.S. containment policy, but, as Zhuang pointed out, Washington was improving relations with China to improve its security. China was now a more valuable strategic partner to the United States. As Deng Xiaoping observed in 1980, Washington "alone is not in a position to deal with Soviet hegemonism. The Soviet challenge can only be coped with if the United States strengthens unity with its allies and unites its strength with all the forces [e.g., China] that are resisting the Soviet challenge."[20]

Beginning in 1979, the Chinese leadership also perceived a diminished threat to the PRC from the Soviet Union. Now that Washington was meeting the Soviet challenge, the likelihood of continued Soviet expansionism in the Far East was reduced. Moreover, normalization of relations and the development of U.S.-PRC strategic relations helped to offset Soviet pressure on China. And in the aftermath of its invasion of Afghanistan, Moscow was on the diplomatic defensive, experiencing "unprecedented isolation."[21]

Beijing took advantage of its improved position to engage in its first serious discussions with Moscow in over fifteen years. In April 1979, shortly after normalization of U.S.-PRC relations, Beijing proposed normalization discussions with Moscow. Through October 17, there were five preliminary meetings and six meetings between deputy foreign ministers. Even the Soviet invasion of Afghanistan could not reverse the trend. Beijing waited three weeks after the invasion before announcing that it would "apparently" be inappropriate to continue the negotiations.[22] For the first time since Nixon and Kissinger had begun secret negotiations with Zhou Enlai, China was improving relations with the Soviet Union.

These were significant developments affecting Chinese security, and the situation further improved when Ronald Reagan became president. Jimmy Carter had turned U.S. Soviet policy around, and President Reagan intensified the trend toward heightened superpower tension. Chinese leaders observed his record of hostility toward the Soviet Union and believed that his arms-control position and proposed defense budget challenged, rather than "appeased," Moscow's alleged ambitions. In a book entitled *Cong Haolaiwu dao Baigong* (From Hollywood to the White House), Yi Bianzhu observed that Reagan had criticized previous administrations, "emphasizing that détente is only a 'fantasy,' that the Cold War never ended, and that peace cannot be achieved through concession and compromise." Reagan treated "practically every problem as part of the U.S.-Soviet struggle for hegemony" and believed that East-West competition was "unavoidable" and "continually intensifie[d]."[23] Zhuang Qubing observed in *Shijie zhishi* that the new administration had "explicitly" made resistance to Soviet expansion *"the central link of its foreign policy."* Although the Carter administration had responded to the Soviet invasion of Afghanistan with a "new policy of containment, . . . it did not put forward a set of new strategic concepts." In contrast, Reagan and his associates "stress[ed] that the Soviet Union [was] 'the root cause of all troubles.'" In all, "an important change" had taken place.[24] In 1981, *Xiandai guoji guanxi* (Contemporary International Relations), the journal of the State Council's international relations think tank, maintained that "compared to Carter," Reagan "paid greater attention to increasing . . . military strength to engage in global struggle with the Soviet Union." He believed that the United States "must speed up military preparation" to deal with increased Soviet power.[25]

By the middle of 1981, Chinese leaders were convinced that there was no possibility that U.S.-Soviet relations would improve. When Reagan expressed a desire to open discussions with Moscow on theater nuclear forces in Europe, *Renmin ribao* saw it as a mere propaganda ploy, saying it made "no difference" whether or not the two sides held talks, since the struggle was "in any case going to continue."[26] In November, on the eve of the talks, a *Renmin ribao* news analysis noted that the Reagan administration "ha[d] not acted with weakness" in response to Soviet deployments of the SS20 missile. Rather, its plan to deploy the Pershing II missile in Europe "dealt a heavy blow" to the Soviet Union.[27] China's confidence in continued U.S.-Soviet hostility and its skepticism of Reagan's calls for negotiations continued throughout 1982. By June of that year, a *Renmin ribao* special commentary declared that an arms race was well under way, and that it could not be stopped "even if both sides wished to" stop it. The superpowers' arms race and their "tit-for-tat war preparation activities" had become "increasingly more intense and dangerous."[28] Chinese leaders, who had once been preoccupied with détente and with an alleged U.S. plan to divert the Soviet threat eastward, were now confident that heightened Soviet-U.S. tension would continue.

Moreover, a second component of Washington's strategic posture further suited Chinese policy objectives. Although Washington recognized the need to cope with Soviet power, the United States was perceived as still relatively weak and unprepared. A leading U.S. watcher at the Foreign Ministry's Institute of International Studies wrote that the Reagan victory was the U.S. reaction to the "new low" in its international position and to the prospect that it was becoming a "second-class power, militarily inferior to the Soviet Union." Americans hoped that Reagan would stop the "trend of their country's declining position in the world."[29] Writing in late 1981 in China's leading *neibu* journal of international affairs, *Shijie jingji yu chengzhi neican*, Wang Baoqin of the Institute for Contemporary International Relations argued that although the Reagan administration was "eager to turn around its disadvantageous position . . . it suffer[ed] from an unfavorable situation, beset by difficulties at home and abroad . . . and its ability [fell] short of its ambitions." The major problem was that the domestic economic situation had worsened, so that the administration had "no choice but to reduce the defense budget and call off the grain embargo against the Soviet Union."[30] Wang Shuzhong of the Institute of International Economics and Politics of the Chinese Academy of Social Sciences concurred with this outlook. Writing in *Shijie jingji yu zhengzhi neican*, he explained that because the U.S. "economy continue[d] to deteriorate," restoring the U.S. military was a "slow process" and Washington sought to make compromises with Moscow.[31]

Washington's objectives were clear, but China doubted its ability to secure them. In late July 1982, just prior to the signing of the August 17 communiqué, Zhang Yebai, a senior analyst at the Institute of American Studies of the Chinese Academy of Social Sciences, offered an especially disdainful view of U.S. policy. In a comprehensive "special commentary" in *Renmin ribao*, Zhang insisted that despite the Reagan administration's "ambitious" objectives, its foreign policy was "divorced from complex reality" and "progressing with difficulty," placing the United States in a "passive position." Whereas "Soviet expansion policy had not changed at all," Washington's "'position of strength' had not fundamentally improved," and its military strength was insufficient "to check Soviet expansion." Such weakness was caused primarily by U.S. political and economic difficulties, exacerbated by conflict with Western European countries over economic policy and over policy toward Moscow, including defense spending and the construction of the natural gas pipeline from Western Europe to the Soviet Union. Zhang concluded that "under pressure and constraints from all sides," the Reagan administration's foreign policy could "hardly avoid falling into a passive position."[32]

Chinese analysts concluded from this assessment that the Reagan administration needed stable U.S.-PRC relations to resist Soviet expansion and would thus compromise on U.S.-Taiwan relations. As Zhuang Qubing had pointed out, the Reagan administration took "resistance to the Soviet expansion as the key link in its foreign policy." Similarly, Wang Shuzhong argued that a key factor determining the success of Reagan's foreign policy was whether the administration abandoned "its unrealistic stand toward Taiwan." Wang Baoqin believed that because of the weaknesses in U.S. policy toward the Soviet Union, Washington did not dare "act rashly or hastily" on U.S.-PRC relations and affect "the entire strategic position."[33]

Moreover, in the context of revitalized U.S. containment of the Soviet Union, Beijing was better positioned to negotiate with Moscow than during the late Carter administration. Although the Reagan administration was not fully prepared to contend with Soviet power, its commitment to the containment of the Soviet Union far exceeded that of any other U.S. administration since 1969. And in contrast to Washington's perception of its weak position in superpower negotiations, by 1982, Beijing believed that the cost of the

Soviet Union's occupation of Afghanistan and of its military and economic support for Cuba and Vietnam, the instability in Eastern Europe, and domestic economic troubles had weakened Soviet expansionist capability. Although the struggle against hegemonism could not be abandoned, the threat was less immediate.[34]

Thus, in 1981, following the interruption caused by the Soviet invasion of Afghanistan, Sino-Soviet rapprochement recommenced when Beijing suggested a resumption of border talks, and in April 1982, Moscow and Beijing agreed to recommence border trade and increase the value of two-way trade by 45 percent, attaining the highest level since 1967.[35] Moreover, by this time China had stopped labeling the Soviet leadership "revisionist." As Chinese leaders pursued domestic economic reform, even the ideological basis for Sino-Soviet conflict eroded.[36]

China's domestic situation also dramatically improved. By the early 1980s, the reformist coalition had ousted the remnants of the Maoist era and consolidated its political power. The succession to Mao was clearly resolved, and Deng Xiaoping had emerged as China's preeminent leader. Whereas in previous years, Chinese politics had been riddled by factional politics and elite instability, by 1981, China experienced considerable stability: the domestic policy debate narrowed, economic reforms proved highly successful, and Deng consolidated his political power. A united Chinese leadership was better prepared to cope with the challenges of Soviet "hegemonism."

Thus, as the United States began to develop strategic policy based on a pessimistic appraisal of U.S. capabilities and of the U.S.-Soviet balance, and in the context of heightened superpower tension, Beijing perceived Washington as reluctant to challenge Chinese interests on Taiwan. Chinese leaders also felt greater international security and the necessary confidence to seek decreased tension in Sino-Soviet relations. These contrasting strategic circumstances fundamentally affected the character of U.S.-PRC relations, promoting a significant transformation of the bargaining dynamics.

Emerging Chinese Initiative in the Carter Administration

China's new foreign policy activism first emerged during the later stages of the Carter administration, when Chinese leaders perceived the initial breakdown of détente and Washington's increasing suspicion of Soviet intentions. China capitalized on its heightened importance in U.S. security by taking the initiative against a number of U.S. policies.

The first issue to arouse PRC concern was the Taiwan Relations Act. The Carter administration insisted that there was no contradiction between the Taiwan Relations Act and the normalization communiqué. China argued otherwise. Most offensive was the act's stipulation that the United States would "provide Taiwan with enough defensive arms to maintain a sufficient self-defense capability." Although the Taiwan Relations Act did not violate the communiqué, insofar as the United States undertook no new commitments in the communiqué regarding arms sales, it embodied in U.S. law a policy China was on record as opposing, and which it planned to challenge at a later date. The United States seemed to be taking immediate advantage of China's compromise over the arms-sales issue and using the Taiwan Relations Act to consolidate U.S. arms-sales policy in anticipation of future problems with China.

China offered a muted, yet significant, protest to the passage of the Taiwan Relations Act. Beijing summoned Ambassador Woodcock to the Chinese Foreign Ministry to receive a Chinese protest, and the Foreign Ministry warned that the act did "great harm" to U.S.-PRC relations. Deng Xiaoping personally complained about the act's arms-sales stipulations and warned that Washington would carefully consider the implications of its arms-sales policy.[37]

Nevertheless, the arms-sales issue had yet to interfere with the development of U.S.-PRC relations. Although Deng criticized U.S. Taiwan policy, he also welcomed the prospect of developing military relations and the suggestion that the United States place monitoring equipment on Chinese territory to verify Soviet compliance with arms-control agreements.[38] Moreover, as noted in Chapter 5, trade and cultural relations commenced in 1979.

Not until U.S.-Soviet relations further deteriorated in the aftermath of the Soviet invasion of Afghanistan, and Washington actively sought a military relationship with China, did Beijing suggest a more vigorous challenge to U.S. Taiwan policy. China viewed President Carter's June 1980 decision to allow Northrop and General Dynamics to discuss the sale of an advanced jet fighter known as the FX to Taiwan as a direct challenge to Chinese policy—the United States was now taking the first steps toward postnormalization arms sales to Taiwan—and it issued a strong warning. A *Xinhua* commentary criticized the decision, as well as the transfer of large amounts of military equipment to Taiwan in 1979 and 1980. The commentary insisted that U.S. arms sales to Taiwan were "harmful" to U.S.-PRC relations and were "bound to aggravate tension in the Taiwan Strait." It made a "strong demand" that the United States "stop forthwith its arms sales to Taiwan." Such forceful language concerning Taiwan had not been heard since rapprochement. More important, China was now on record as opposing future U.S. arms sales to Taiwan, and it warned that ongoing arms sales would affect the entire relationship.[39]

Beijing reacted with similar threats in late 1980, when the Carter administration granted diplomatic immunities and privileges to representatives of the Taiwan government. U.S. Ambassador Woodcock was summoned to China's Foreign Ministry, where he received a "protest note" expressing China's "unhappiness and concern" about U.S.-Taiwan relations. An article by an authoritative *Renmin ribao* commentator insisted that this policy was "completely unacceptable," because it reflected a "two-China" policy. The newspaper suggested that U.S. failure to accept Beijing's demands might lead to greater U.S.-PRC conflict and would be harmful to cooperation against Moscow. The decision to pursue continued development of U.S.-PRC relations or to "reverse them" was said to be of "major strategic importance" to U.S. leaders.[40] For the first time since rapprochement, China was threatening the United States with a reversal of relations if Washington did not alter its policy.

U.S.-PRC relations had begun to undergo a significant transformation. The changes in U.S. security circumstances during the Carter administration had encouraged China to issue preliminary challenges to the status quo in U.S.-Taiwan relations. Indeed, Michel Oksenberg, the Carter administration's National Security Council staff member responsible for China, recalled that beginning in summer 1980, U.S.-PRC relations "experienced a troubled and tense period."[41] But this trend in relations developed further as Beijing watched the Reagan administration pursue the new Cold War with the Soviet Union, and as its own relationship with Moscow gradually eased. Beijing's confidence that Washington would conciliate China's interests in order to protect U.S.-PRC cooperation increased, and it directly challenged Washington's insistence on continued U.S. arms sales to Taiwan, risking both diplomatic and military relations.

The Reagan Administration and the August 17 Communiqué

Chinese leaders were understandably concerned about the new U.S. administration's intentions toward China. Even before the administration entered office, it suggested a policy guaranteed to arouse Chinese apprehension and opposition. The president's campaign statements revealed his contempt for the Carter administration's treatment of Taiwan. He said he "would not pretend, as Carter does," that the relationship "we now have with Taiwan . . . is unofficial." Reagan characterized U.S.-Taiwan relations as "official relations" and suggested that the U.S. government would treat Taiwanese statesmen as official representatives of Taiwan, a practice the Carter administration had consistently avoided.[42] After the election, members of the congressional inauguration committee invited numerous representatives of Taiwan's leadership to attend the inauguration in an official capacity. After the president assumed office, a White House aide, Michael Deaver, met with Taiwanese officials in his White House office, breaching the restrictions on such meetings established by the Carter administration and suggesting U.S.-Taiwan official relations. The president also chose advisers who shared his perspective on U.S.-Taiwan relations. Richard Allen, Reagan's national security adviser, favored the U.S. sale of advanced military aircraft to Taiwan and greater diplomatic attention to U.S.-Taiwan relations. Treasury Secretary Donald Regan argued that Taiwan should be readmitted to the World Bank as a "special country." And Edwin Meese, counselor to the president, reaffirmed the administration's intention to receive representatives of Taiwan in government offices.[43]

In contrast to these sentiments, Secretary of State Haig and Assistant Secretary of State Holdridge were preoccupied with China's strategic importance and with developing U.S.-PRC security cooperation. Holdridge considered the entire FX issue a "complicating factor" in U.S. policy. It made "life miserable" for policy makers, insofar as it interfered with stable U.S.-PRC relations. In March, Haig recommended to the president that the United States give priority to reassuring Beijing of the U.S. commitment to stable relations, because U.S.-PRC relations played a crucial role in U.S. security. In an interview with *Time* magazine, Haig said that the president viewed continued development of U.S.-PRC relations as a "strategic imperative," and that it was of "overriding importance to international stability." Similarly, in the context of increased Soviet pressure on Poland and the growing possibility of Soviet military intervention, even Secretary of Defense Weinberger, who sympathized with the president's concern for Taiwan, suggested the possibility of linkage between Soviet policy toward Poland and U.S. China policy. Weinberger warned that Soviet intervention might cause the United States to sell weaponry to China.[44]

Despite the Reagan administration's unanimous concern about the Soviet military challenge, Chinese leaders feared that the president's ideological anticommunist sentiments and the influence of "diehard elements" of the "Taiwan lobby" in the administration would lead Washington to "reverse the wheel of history" and pursue policy contrary to Chinese interests. They protested the administration's various "pro-Taiwan" initiatives, asserting that they violated the terms of the normalization communiqué, and suggested that relations would deteriorate if these "die-hard" elements continued to influence U.S. policy toward China.[45]

But it was clear that China was not merely seeking to restore the status quo in U.S.-PRC relations. Rather, it was discontented with ongoing U.S.-Taiwan military relations and was seeking to compel the United States to make new concessions on this issue. At the time of normalization of relations, Beijing had declared its opposition to U.S. arms sales to Taiwan and suggested that it was only deferring discussion of the issue. At the start of the Reagan administration, it returned to the issue. In so doing, it took advantage of the administration's assessment of the Soviet threat and Secretary of State Haig's preoccupation with China's strategic importance.[46] This outlook would presumably encourage Washington to compromise on Taiwan in order to consolidate strategic cooperation between the United States and China.

In January, as the president prepared to take office, Beijing warned that the sale of weapons to Taipei would incur a diplomatic cost. When the Netherlands announced that it would sell submarines to Taiwan, Beijing warned that if the deal went through, it would downgrade relations, and that the United States would be subject to similar retaliation if it sold weapons to Taiwan. When the Netherlands signed the agreement in February, China withdrew its ambassador from the Netherlands, downgrading relations to the chargé d'affaires level. Beijing had clearly signaled that it would not tolerate U.S. arms sales to Taiwan, and it would be difficult for it to retreat from that stance.[47]

Secretary of State Haig quickly moved to limit the damage to U.S.-PRC relations, expecting to maintain the status quo of the Carter period by reassuring Beijing of U.S. good intentions. Although various members of the administration explained to the Chinese embassy that the presidential inauguration was not an official U.S. government function, and that the invitations to Taiwan's officials had not been issued by the White House, Chinese officials were not sympathetic. On the instructions of Deng Xiaoping, the Chinese embassy in Washington issued a strong protest and demanded that the invitations be rescinded.[48] Haig complied, seeing to it that the invitations to representatives of Taiwan to attend the inauguration in their official capacity were withdrawn, and the administration advised Taipei that it would not welcome Taiwan's participation in the inauguration. Haig also criticized Deaver's meeting with officials from Taiwan. Haig and Holdridge then prepared and issued guidelines stipulating that meetings between U.S. and Taiwanese officials would closely follow the practice of the Carter administration. White House and State Department officials were not to meet with Taiwanese government representatives in U.S. government offices. Other executive agencies could make exceptions only for officials below the level of assistant secretary who were involved in strictly commercial matters. Haig won the initial administration skirmishes over U.S.-Taiwan relations, and when Taiwan's officials tried to meet with the assistant secretary of state for East Asia, they were refused.[49]

Haig also adopted a number of other measures designed to assure Beijing that Washington valued stable U.S.-PRC relations. In January, he announced that the United States was considering selling weapons to China, and he approved the sale of search-and-rescue helicopters to China. He also moved to reassure Beijing that the administration would adhere to the commitments undertaken by the Carter administration. In February, the State Department announced the U.S. intention to adhere to the normalization communiqué. Then, in March, Haig arranged for a meeting between Reagan and Ambassador Chai Zemin, in which Reagan expressed his interest in good relations with China and his personal intention to abide by the normalization communiqué, despite his commitment to maintain his long-standing friendship for Taiwan. The administration also arranged for former President Ford to convey Ronald Reagan's understanding of the importance of U.S.-PRC relations and commitment to developing the relationship to Deng Xiaoping.[50]

In May, in response to a request from Deng, the administration announced that Secretary Haig would visit Beijing the following month. In preparation for the visit, Washington took a number of initiatives seeking to calm PRC apprehensions. It agreed to classify China as a "friendly, non-allied" country, liberalizing its access to U.S. technology. Prior to Haig's departure, the administration also formally licensed computer equipment for export to China that the Carter administration had decided to approve for licensing, but Harold Brown had been unable to push through the Pentagon approval process. Encouraged by Richard Allen and James Lilley, the NSC specialist on Asia, as well as by Haig, Reagan had informed Ambassador Chai Zemin of the decision during their meeting in March.[51]

Most important, the president agreed to make China eligible to purchase U.S. weaponry, which would presumably persuade China that Washington valued its strategic contribution, and that it was intent on developing a strategic relationship to counter the Soviet threat, thus helping finesse conflict over U.S. arms sales to Taiwan. Reporters on Haig's flight to Beijing were told that Haig and Richard Burt, director of politico-military affairs at the State Department, planned to persuade Chinese leaders that Washington would adopt an assertive policy toward the Soviet Union, and that the growing Soviet military threat to both China and the United States created a "strategic imperative" to establish closer U.S.-PRC relations. In his Beijing banquet toast, Haig insisted that now "cooperation was all the more important."[52]

But Haig's efforts were based on the mistaken belief that China was irritated merely by Reagan's unpolitic suggestions that he would challenge Chinese interests vis-à-vis Taiwan. They thus failed to quell PRC criticism, because Beijing was less concerned about the rhetoric and trappings of U.S. diplomacy than about the reality of U.S. military assistance to Taipei; it insisted that it would not focus on strategic cooperation while there was ongoing U.S.-Taiwan military cooperation. Moreover, in the context of Haig's public focus on the Soviet threat, Chinese leaders were less inclined to be conciliatory. A March commentary asserted that it was a fallacy to assume that as long as Washington took a hard line on the Soviet Union, China would "be tolerant over Taiwan," and it expressed China's hope that Washington would not do anything that caused a "retrogression" in relations.[53] Just prior to Haig's arrival in Beijing in June, the Chinese Foreign Ministry insisted that China would not buy U.S. weapons if it meant agreeing to U.S. arms sales to Taiwan. A *Xinhua* commentary published the day before his arrival insisted that a policy seeking such a trade-off was "doomed to failure," and that "any arms sales to Taiwan" would "certainly draw strong reactions from China." As for enhancing U.S.-PRC security ties, it insisted that U.S. arms sales to Taiwan were "the outstanding issue" to developing relations, and it was irrelevant whether the weaponry was offensive or defensive. This was a clear challenge to the Carter administration's commitment to continue sales of defensive arms to Taiwan after normalization.[54]

In Beijing, Haig conveyed President Reagan's invitation to Premier

Zhao Ziyang to visit the United States and reported the administration's decisions to consider arms sales to China and liberalize trade restrictions. He also arranged for PLA Deputy Chief of Staff Liu Huaqing to visit the United States in August to discuss U.S. arms sales to China. At the end of his visit, Haig declared that he could report to the president that U.S.-PRC relations were "strong and improving" and that "our common resolve" to restrain Moscow's "opportunities for exploiting its military power ha[d] . . . grown stronger."[55]

Haig was wrong. Relations were not improving, because China held developing U.S.-PRC relations, including military cooperation and a U.S.-PRC summit in Washington, hostage to U.S. concessions on arms sales to Taiwan. China was using the U.S. interest in expanded cooperation as leverage on the Taiwan issue and, as during the Ford and early Carter administrations, unless Washington made concessions regarding U.S.-Taiwan relations, it would not allow the United States to use the image of improved relations, such as a summit or bilateral military cooperation, to suggest expanded anti-Soviet cooperation.

Haig tried to finesse the arms-sales issue by saying that Washington would merely continue providing defensive weaponry to Taiwan at the rate of the Carter administration, and that it saw no urgent necessity to respond to Taiwan's request for advanced aircraft. But Chinese leaders were not satisfied. When relations were normalized, Deng Xiaoping told Haig unequivocally, Beijing had announced that it opposed U.S. arms sales to Taiwan, expecting that the issue would soon be resolved. But the United States had yet to take any steps to end arms sales to Taiwan.[56] China was after more than preventing the sale of the advanced FX fighter jet to Taipei; it wanted a U.S. commitment to retreat from the policy of the Carter administration and curtail *all* weapons sales to Taiwan. Deng told Haig that there were limits to Chinese tolerance, and he and Foreign Minister Huang Hua warned of the possibility of a break in relations if the United States failed to satisfy Chinese demands.[57]

Haig responded by reiterating the assurances of the Carter administration. He expressed understanding for Chinese sensitivity on the arms-sales issue and assured Deng that Washington would use unusual caution and restraint in making new arms sales to Taiwan. Haig explained that "for the foreseeable future," the United States would continue to sell Taiwan "carefully selected, defensive weapons."[58]

When Haig returned from China, he went to work to formulate a policy decision stating that the Taiwan did not need the FX. At the suggestion of James Lilley at the National Security Council, and with Haig's full support, the Pentagon was ordered to manage an interagency analysis of Taiwan's security requirements and the necessity for an advanced fighter aircraft. The study was organized within the office of the Joint Chiefs of Staff and conducted by military specialists in the Defense Intelligence Agency.[59] Haig hoped that a formal finding that Taiwan did not need the FX would allow Washington to mollify Chinese leaders by making a commitment not to sell advanced aircraft to Taiwan, while allowing it to continue to sell Taiwan defensive weapons at the existing level of technology.

At the same time, Haig used the interagency process to develop a list of weapons that China would be eligible to purchase. After Haig's visit to Beijing, China had presented Washington with a "wish list" of weaponry it wanted. Haig believed that Beijing's reluctance to commit to a date for the Liu Huaqing visit reflected its unhappiness with the arms package Washington had offered, and he hoped that a more attractive U.S. offer would appease Chinese leaders and permit military cooperation to develop. He thus pushed the interagency group to expand Chinese access to U.S. weaponry.[60] At the same time, State Department officials tried to devise a jet that would give Taiwan an improved version of the F-5E but that would not arouse Beijing's ire. One serious suggestion was to install FX technology on the dual-engine F-5E, in contrast to providing Taiwan with a distinctly different single-engine aircraft, such as the F-5G.[61]

China, on the other hand, was making it clear that it sought a fundamental change in U.S. policy and that it expected the United States, rather than China, to make the necessary compromises to promote cooperation. Whereas Haig argued in Beijing that "the strategic realities" that had fostered U.S.-PRC reconciliation in the early 1970s were "more pressing than ever" and that U.S.-PRC "common resolve . . . to limit" Soviet opportunism had "grown stronger," a *Xinhua* commentary released shortly after he left China stated that the United States should assume the burden of strategic cooperation. It recognized that some U.S. officials believed that China "would consider the overall strategic interests . . . and swallow the bitter pill of U.S. arms sales to Taiwan." But it asserted that "this is completely illogical. In fact, if the American side had proceeded from . . . strategic interests . . . , it should have . . . put a firm stop to the arms sales to Taiwan." Chinese diplomacy carried a similar message. In early July, Beijing handed Ambassador Arthur Hummel a démarche insisting that if the United States continued to sell any weapons to Taiwan, there would be a "very strong" Chinese response "with grave consequence for the strategic situation." Beijing also began to suggest to U.S. embassy officials that there was linkage between U.S. policy toward Taiwan and the planned Liu Huaqing visit to Washington. Then, in late August, a Hong Kong newspaper published an interview with Deng Xiaoping in which Deng insisted that while China desired strategic cooperation with the United States, if Washington forced China "to act according to the will of the United States," Beijing was prepared to see "relations retrogress." Shortly afterward, Beijing informed Washington that Liu Huaqing's visit to Washington would be deferred.[62] China had suspended U.S.-PRC military cooperation until it achieved U.S. concessions.

China raised the issue to the highest level in October when Zhao Ziyang met with President Reagan in Cancun at the North-South summit meeting. Haig had advised Reagan to sidestep the Taiwan issue, apparently hoping that the issue could be deferred until the Pentagon released its study of the importance of the FX for Taiwan's defense. But Zhao took the initiative and explained to the president that while China wanted strategic cooperation, the issue of Taiwan remained an obstacle. Later, in Cancun, Huang Hua explained to Haig that the FX was only a small part of the larger issue of all U.S. arms sales to Taiwan. In order to resolve the conflict, he insisted that the United States must "give clear assurances that within a specified period of time the level of arms sales to Taiwan will not exceed that of the Carter administration in both quality and quantity" and that within this finite period "arms sales will be reduced year-by-year and completely stop at the end." A week later, in Washington, Huang reiterated his demands, proposed that the two sides open negotiations, and, adhering to the specific negotiating position ordered by Deng Xiaoping, warned that the United States must not conclude any agreements for U.S. weapons sales to Taiwan while the U.S.-PRC negotiations were under way. As far as Chinese policy makers were concerned, there was no point to the negotiations if Washington used them simply to mask an open-ended policy of arms sales to Taiwan. Huang warned that President Reagan would bear the responsibility for the resultant downgrading of relations should Washington not respect this demand. China had adopted a threatening posture aimed at pressuring Washington to concede to its demands, and relations were clearly on hold pending the outcome of the negotiations over Taiwan. At Cancun, Reagan had personally reiterated the invitation to Premier Zhao to visit Washington originally extended by Haig in June that year, but Zhao temporized, saying that the diplomats should confer on the timing.[63]

Haig's response to Huang Hua was that the United States could not agree to a cut-off date for U.S. arms sales to Taiwan, and that the United States would continue to carry out "a policy of sensitive, restrained and selective arms sales to Taiwan." He did, however, make Washington's first concession to Beijing, pledging that U.S. arms sales to Taiwan would not exceed the level under the Carter administration. He further maintained that the replacement of Taiwan's military aircraft would be handled in this manner, suggesting that the United States would not sell Taiwan the FX, even though the administration had yet to decide the issue. Finally, Haig said that Washington was willing to negotiate this issue, and that during the negotiations it would act cautiously, implying that it would try to accede to Hua's demand that it not reach any new arms-sales agreements with Taiwan while the negotiations were under way. Nonetheless, he also said that the United States would "still have to do things that must be done," suggesting that Washington could not suspend arms sales to Taiwan indefinitely.[64] Washington could not allow Beijing to use the negotiations to create an indefinite suspension of U.S. arms sales to Taiwan.

Haig had made important concessions regarding the FX and the level of future U.S. arms sales to Taiwan, but the United States had rejected China's demand for a cut-off date. This issue and the recurring issue of linkage between U.S. Taiwan policy and Chinese policy on peaceful unification would be the most difficult issues to resolve. In the meantime, however, given Beijing's reaction to the Dutch submarine deal with Taiwan, China could be expected to take similar action should the United States reach a new arms-sales agreement with Taiwan before reaching a new accord with Beijing. The United States, on the other hand, as Haig pointed out, could not defer arms sales to Taiwan indefinitely. Within the next year or so, either Washington would conclude a new arms-sales agreement with Taiwan, despite ongoing U.S.-PRC tension, which would elicit a harsh PRC response, or it would first reach an agreement with Beijing that would satisfy Chinese demands for a revision of the status quo and allow the United States to sell arms to Taiwan, thus permitting renewed U.S.-PRC cooperation. Either way, by late October, it was clear that U.S.-PRC negotiations had an implicit deadline.

THE DECISION NOT TO SELL THE FX
AND THE HOLDRIDGE MISSION

Despite China's forceful posture, Haig and his team of China specialists at the State Department continued to believe that it would be possible to defuse the tension and restore the cooperative relations that had existed prior to the Reagan presidency without placating China with new commitments. Haig was still working on the assumption that strategic cooperation was China's paramount objective; Beijing simply needed assurances of the administration's friendly intentions in order to resume its participation in the anti-Soviet coalition and purchase U.S. weaponry.

But Beijing continued to disparage the need to compromise for the sake of strategic cooperation and remained committed to redefining U.S. policy toward Taiwan. Indeed, U.S. policy in early 1982 underscored the extent to which Washington valued Chinese strategic cooperation. In the context of continued Soviet pressure on Poland and the imposition of martial law there, administration officials stressed the importance of U.S.-PRC cooperation. In January 1982, the State Department sent the chief of its East European Office to China with Assistant Secretary of State Holdridge to hold a dialogue on Soviet policy in Poland. But Chinese leaders merely rejected U.S. efforts to elicit their support for U.S. Soviet policy. They almost refused even to discuss the situation in Poland.[65]

In response to Foreign Minister Huang Hua's "ultimatum," Haig had conceded that U.S. arms sales to Taiwan would not exceed the level of arms transfers to Taiwan during the Carter years.[66] Although defining the level of that period had not been addressed, it was clear that to fulfill his commitment to Huang, Haig needed an administration decision not to sell the FX to Taiwan in order to adhere to the 1978 Carter administration decision merely to continue coproduction of the F-5E. But there was a great deal of support in both the White House and the Pentagon for selling Taiwan an advanced fighter jet. Notwithstanding concerns about the Soviet threat and interest in developing U.S.-PRC military cooperation, both Secretary of Defense Weinberger and Richard Allen, Reagan's national security adviser, thought it important to sell Taiwan the FX.[67]

The key to winning an administrative consensus on the FX was the forthcoming Pentagon analysis of Taiwan's defense requirements. In accordance with the language of the Taiwan Relations Act, the terms of the analysis were based on Taiwan's ability to maintain its self-defense capability. Hence, the focus of the study was on the trend in the military balance between Taiwan and the PRC, and the likelihood that Taiwan's security situation would deteriorate. Defense Department analysts observed that the PRC's armed forces were in terrible condition, and that it was unlikely that the PRC would acquire more advanced weaponry enhancing its ability to launch a successful invasion of Taiwan during the next ten years. Thus, the F-104 and F-5E aircraft were sufficient to provide for defense of Taiwan. On this basis, despite the contrary policy preferences of the secretary of defense, the report concluded that the United States did not need to sell Taiwan the FX.[68]

The Pentagon reached its decision in December 1981, permitting Haig to establish policy that the United States would simply continue co-production of the F-5E. Nevertheless, throughout the fall, while the Pentagon conducted its study, Beijing made clear that it sought more than merely a decision not to sell the FX to Taiwan, and that it remained prepared to set back relations over all U.S. arms sales to Taiwan. As Huang Hua told Haig, Beijing wanted explicit U.S. concessions on the level and duration of all U.S. arms sales to Taiwan. Beginning in November, when the Western media reported that the Pentagon was likely to conclude that the F-5E was sufficient for Taiwan's defense, Beijing made it clear that continued sale of *any* arms to Taiwan by Washington would set back relations.

When Under Secretary of State Walter Stoessel met in Beijing with Chinese Foreign Ministry officials in early November, *Xinhua* warned that the arms-sales issue was the "litmus test" of U.S. intentions and warned that China was following U.S. policy with "great concern." Later in the month, just after Deng Xiaoping met with former Vice President Walter Mondale, *Xinhua* explained that even if Washington decided not to sell the FX and chose simply to sell an updated F-5E, China would retaliate. "Sales of any weapons, whatever type they might be" violated China's sovereignty and intervened in its internal affairs, it insisted. "Insistence on military sales to Taiwan" by the United States was "irreconcilable with the desire to develop U.S.-China relations."[69] When Deng met with Mondale, he explained that relations should be shaped by "global strategy," and that he hoped that they would not experience any setbacks. The implication was clear—the United States, and not China, should change its policy to consolidate the anti-Soviet coalition. At the same time, Beijing recalled its response to the January 1981 Dutch sale of submarines to Taiwan, warning that it would downgrade diplomatic relations to the chargé d'affaires level if Washington sold weaponry to Taiwan. "Any arms sales to Taiwan" would not only lead to "a setback in relations," but would also "possibly" reverse the trend in relations between the mainland and Taiwan, which might "become tense again," PRC Ambassador Chai Zemin asserted,[70] suggesting that ongoing stability across the Taiwan Strait would be determined by U.S. arms-sales policy.

The United States and China had not come any closer to resolving the arms-sales issue. Whereas Washington sought to finesse it, Beijing insisted on explicit U.S. concessions on the level and duration of all U.S. arms sales to Taiwan—Huang Hua's October demands remained on the negotiating table—and absent such concessions, it was prepared to downgrade relations in response to the next weapons sales, regardless of the item. In the meantime, Beijing continued to spurn Washington's attempts to move relations forward.

In December, the Reagan administration lifted the ban on U.S. munitions sales to China and approved the first Export-Import Bank loans for U.S. investment in China. It also renewed President Reagan's invitation to Premier Zhao to visit Washington, suggesting that the summit coincide with the tenth anniversary of the February 1972 Shanghai communiqué. When Chinese leaders failed to reply to the invitation, Ambassador Hummel drew their attention to the importance the United States attached to the tenth anniversary of the communiqué.[71] Beijing still did not respond. It continued to hold a Washington summit hostage to U.S. concessions on the arms-sales issue.

During this same period, the White House notified Congress of its intention to sell military spare parts to Taiwan. Taiwan had needed these for some time, but the State Department had delayed the decision to avoid arousing Chinese hostility. Ultimately, Taiwan's legitimate and pressing need for the spare parts and the fear of pressure from pro-Taiwan Republican Party members of Congress forced the issue.[72] Chinese leaders were enraged; the United States had failed to take seriously Huang Hua's October warning to President Reagan regarding new U.S.-Taiwan arms-sales agreements, and they strongly protested the announcement. On December 14, Deputy Foreign Minister Zhang Wenjin, presenting an "urgent" notification to the United States government, told Ambassador Hummel that if the United States proceeded with the sale of spare parts to Taiwan, Beijing would have "no alternative but to react strongly." In Washington, Ambassador Chai Zemin delivered an equally strong message to Deputy Secretary of State William Clark and Assistant Secretary of State Holdridge. But the administration responded that the sale did not involve weaponry, and that the agreement with Taiwan had been concluded prior to Reagan's meeting with Zhao. China should not therefore think that the United States was bargaining in bad faith. The administration also said that for the foreseeable future, transfers of "small-scale defensive equipment" would continue as during the previous nine years since the Shanghai communiqué,[73] implicitly assuring Beijing that it would make no decision on major weaponry or large-scale transfers while the negotiations continued.

Then, on January 11, 1982, the State Department formally announced that while it anticipated ongoing U.S. sales to Taiwan of defensive military equipment, and that President Reagan had concluded that such steps would include the extension of co-production of the F-5E, the United States would not sell Taiwan an advanced-technology jet fighter. Although this was a U.S. concession, because Washington would only maintain the existing level of Taiwan's self-defense capability, the announcement failed to address China's demand for a cut-off date to all U.S. arms sales to Taiwan.[74]

Assistant Secretary of State John Holdridge arrived in Beijing on January 11 to communicate this important decision to Chinese leaders. Haig and Holdridge believed that, the battle within the administration over the jet fighter having been won, the way had been cleared for resolving U.S.-PRC conflict. They thought China would welcome the decision on the FX, and that it would now be prepared to improve relations. Holdridge also submitted a draft statement comprised of a number of principles, which the United States hoped would celebrate the tenth anniversary of the Shanghai communiqué and also resolve the arms-sales issue. The statement expressed a U.S. commitment to sell only defensive weapons to Taiwan and not to exceed the level of arms sales to Taiwan of the Carter years, and a reaffirmation by Beijing of its policy of peaceful unification with Taiwan. The State Department thought that with the FX issue behind it, the tension in relations could be easily resolved by simply proclaiming the assurances Haig had made to Huang Hua in October 1981.[75]

Chinese leaders were not impressed. As Holdridge recalled, they certainly did not regard the decision merely to continue co-production of the F-5E as a "great gift." On the contrary, they remained "quite upset" about the entire arms-sales issue, and they were angry with U.S. tactics. Not only had Washington merely agreed not to sell Taiwan an advanced jet fighter, rather than agreeing to a cut-off date, but it had announced its intention to sell Taiwan additional

F-5E's, once again defying China's warning not to sell weaponry to Taiwan while the negotiations were under way. Given their unhappiness with the December announcement of the spare-parts transfer, and the fact that Deng had personally insisted on this position, Chinese diplomats were outraged, and they rejected all of Holdridge's attempts to reach a compromise solution. The Foreign Ministry spokesman issued a strong protest, and Foreign Minister Huang Hua delivered a blistering criticism of U.S. arms-sales policy. Beijing once again insisted that the United States not sell Taiwan any weaponry while Beijing and Washington negotiated. Moreover, Huang suggested there was no room for compromise, insisting that Washington agree to a cut-off date. Deputy Foreign Minister Zhang Wenjin's reworking of the proposed U.S.-PRC statement included this demand,[76] and an authoritative *Xinhua* commentary, issued just after Holdridge left China, publicly reinforced it, arguing that the U.S. decision on the advanced-technology jet fighter was not a concession and warning that continued arms sales were "menacing" the development of relations. The arms-sales issue had "reached a point calling for an immediate solution and the Sino-American relationship is facing a rigorous test. We do not want to see any retrogression . . . , but this depends on whether or not . . . Washington will . . . make a wise choice. . . . This people will wait and see," *Xinhua* declared ominously.[77] Similarly, Li Xiannian, in a thinly veiled reference to U.S. arms-sales policy, said in his first public statement on U.S.-PRC relations since Reagan had assumed office that Chinese leaders "firmly oppose expansionists who invade and occupy the territory of other countries. We are willing to actively develop diplomatic relations with all countries. . . . [But we] will never barter away principle. . . . It is absolutely intolerable that anyone should try to encroach on China's national sovereignty, interfere in our internal affairs and obstruct the reunification of our country. We can never tolerate this."[78]

The State Department responded to China's demands with additional compromises. While still in Beijing, Holdridge tried to assuage Chinese anger by reaffirming the administration's pledge not to sell weaponry to Taiwan while negotiations were in progress, which he said Washington would make public. He also backpedaled on the F-5E decision, explaining that the United States had not made a decision to "sell" the F-5E to Taiwan, but only to "not sell" it the FX.[79]

Given Chinese leaders' view of Washington's strategic plight and the importance of China in U.S. security policy, the State Department's efforts appeared as concessions to Chinese pressure. Beijing interpreted Washington's conciliatory response to its complaints over the December spare-parts announcement as the result of its firm protests. Similarly, Beijing believed that the U.S. decision not to sell Taiwan an advanced fighter jet was a response to Chinese threats to retaliate. One well-informed analyst argued in the authorative internal publication *Shijie jingji yu zhengzhi neican* that Reagan's decision not to sell Taiwan an advanced fighter jet was owing to the combination of China's "resolute and forceful struggle against the United States" and Washington's need for a "united front which included China to contend with the Soviet Union" in response to the crisis in Poland.[80]

This pattern of Washington striving to reach a compromise solution and China using diplomatic coercion to elicit additional U.S. concessions continued after Holdridge's visit to China. Developments within the Reagan administration were an important factor promoting this trend. Throughout 1981, Haig's efforts to reach a compromise on the U.S. position encountered stiff resistance from Reagan advisers who were less inclined to sacrifice U.S. policy on Taiwan to assuage Chinese hostility. The most important figure in this battle was Richard Allen, the national security adviser, who strongly advocated improved U.S.-Taiwan relations. Allen had pushed for the sale of an advanced fighter jet to Taiwan and was disappointed at his inability to forge a coalition within the administration in favor of the sale.

Despite Allen's opposition, by the end of 1981, Haig was the dominant force in China policy. The NSC did not even regularly receive the cable traffic from the U.S. embassy in Beijing. Allen's role was thus limited to reminding the president of his original intentions regarding China and Taiwan. But Haig's authority further increased in early 1982 when Allen left the administration and was replaced by William Clark. Clark was a close friend of the president's, but he was a novice on foreign policy issues, particularly concerning U.S.-PRC relations. With Allen gone and Clark serving as the president's only alternative to Haig as a foreign policy adviser, the State Department was relatively free to pursue a conciliatory policy regarding Taiwan in order to develop the U.S.-PRC strategic relationship.[81]

Just as important as these changes within the administration was Chinese understanding of their significance. Beijing understood that Allen's departure meant that the "pro-Taiwan" forces had lost their most influential figure in the administration, and that the "power of the pro-Taiwan faction" was "greatly reduced." Thus, in addition to recognizing the importance of Chinese pressure and U.S. security policy in shaping Washington's decision not to sell Taiwan the FX jet fighter, Beijing thought Allen's departure also contributed to the decision. One Chinese analyst emphasized that there was not a single objection raised in the NSC meeting that decided the issue.[82]

The combination of the State Department's increased willingness to forge a compromise solution and Washington's view of its strategic and political circumstances encouraged Chinese leaders to maintain their stance. China continued to insist that Washington agree to a cut-off date for U.S. arms sales to Taiwan, and that during the interim the level of arms sales would diminish. It also continued to threaten that it would downgrade relations if arms sales took place before the two sides reached agreement.

After Holdridge left Beijing, Ambassador Arthur Hummel continued the negotiations in Beijing, first with Deputy Foreign Minister Zhang Wenjin and then with Deputy Foreign Minister Han Xu. The negotiations remained focused on the State Department's objective of a U.S.-PRC statement that would commemorate both the tenth anniversary of the Shanghai communiqué and resolve the arms-sales issue. To secure an agreement, the U.S. side offered a significant concession. In February, it presented China with a new set of principles, which added significant specificity to the earlier U.S. commitment that arms sales to Taiwan would not exceed the level of the Carter administration. The new U.S. proposal said that the quality of U.S. arms sold to Taiwan would not exceed the level under the Carter administration, and that the quantity of arms sold would gradually decrease.[83]

Haig and his advisers hoped that this formula would enable the two sides to reach agreement before February 28, in time to issue the tenth anniversary statement commemorating the Shanghai communiqué. But in mid February, Chinese leaders completely rejected the U.S. proposal. They continued to demand that the U.S. agree to a cut-off date for all arms sales to Taiwan. The negotiations thus broke down, and the State Department had to settle for a mere exchange of letters between President Reagan and Premier Zhao Ziyang to commemorate the tenth anniversary.[84]

During the next few months, U.S.-PRC tension increased, inasmuch as there was no progress whatsoever and the possibility existed that the United States would formally sell the improved F-5E to Taiwan despite PRC objections. As for Liu Huaqing's plan to visit Washington to discuss U.S. arms sales to Taiwan, Haig acknowledged that the U.S.-PRC military relationship was "hostage . . . to a resolution of the arms sales to Taiwan issue." Similarly, there was no progress toward a U.S.-PRC summit in Washington. Chinese diplomacy had placed the entire relationship on hold pending the outcome of the negotiations over U.S.-Taiwan relations.[85]

As the stalemate continued, each side threatened the other with failed negotiations. In early February, Haig told a reporter that negotiations were at a "delicate stage," and that "I will be . . . frank when I tell you that I am not in a position to predict the outcome." Deng Xiaoping personally responded, staking his considerable prestige on the outcome of the negotiations. China "held no room for maneuver. If nothing can be done, then relations will retrogress," Deng declared in a mid-February interview published by *Liaowang* in March. "What is so extraordinary about that?" he asked cavalierly. "I think the Chinese nation will still exist." In conclusion, Deng warned: "Now we will wait and see. We are prepared for any situation that can happen." A *Xinhua* commentator underscored Deng's complacency, insisting that China was "in a better position than anyone else to survive" a retrogression, and that far from it having to depend on the United States to resist Soviet expansionism, the PRC's policy of "anti-hegemonism" would not change. A "special commentator" in the April 1 issue of the Foreign Ministry's *Guoji wenti yanjiu* (Journal of International Studies) insisted that "China absolutely cannot tolerate . . . U.S. arms sales to Taiwan to continue for an indefinite period," and that Chinese tolerance had a "definite limit." It further warned, "The Chinese side strives for a good future, but it is also prepared for a bad outcome." A senior State Department official later recalled that from February through April, relations were "terribly tense," and Haig recalled that the U.S. side perceived no opportunity for a breakthrough. Chinese negotiators had become so intransigent that at one point Holdridge wondered whether the negotiations were even worth continuing.[86]

In early April, President Reagan sent personal letters to Deng Xiaoping and Zhao Ziyang. Reagan's letter to Deng emphasized his personal commitment to developing U.S.-PRC relations in an era of "growing threat from the Soviet Union." Reagan proposed that Vice President Bush visit Beijing in May to discuss the outstanding issues in person in order to overcome differences and promote strategic cooperation. The president thus underscored the strategic importance he attached to relations. But his letter to Zhao merely reiterated the proposal the United States had presented in February. "In the context of progress toward a peaceful solution, there would naturally be a decrease in the need for arms by Taiwan,"

Reagan wrote. "Our position over the last two months reflected this view. We are prepared, indeed welcome, further exchanges of view during the months to come."[87] The president personally reaffirmed U.S. policy, hoping his personal commitment might encourage PRC flexibility. Yet he also suggested that if China were dissatisfied with the U.S. position, it should not expect new U.S. initiatives. Rather, Washington would "welcome" China's suggestions.

Nonetheless, China remained rigid, expecting that U.S. interest in anti-Soviet cooperation would compel Washington to make additional compromises. Beijing continued to insist on a U.S. commitment to end all arms sales to Taiwan during a precise time period, as well as on no linkage between U.S. arms sales to Taiwan and China's Taiwan policy. "China will in no case tolerate a long continuation of U.S. arms sales to Taiwan," a *Renmin ribao* commentary warned in early May, just prior to Vice President Bush's arrival in Beijing. In a reference to the U.S. threat to recommence arms sales in a "few months" should the negotiations not produce an agreement, the commentary warned that the arms-sales issue was a "time bomb" that could "only be defused by Washington."[88]

Nevertheless, as the president indicated in his April letter to Premier Zhao, when Vice President Bush visited Beijing in early May, he did not bear with him any major new initiatives. Rather, the purpose of the visit was to communicate directly at the highest level both the limits of U.S. flexibility and the interest of the United States in cooperative relations. U.S. diplomats hoped that the insistence of the vice president, the president's "personal emissary," that the United States would not agree to a definite end to arms sales to Taiwan would compel Chinese leaders to recognize the limits to PRC leverage. Bush thus underscored U.S. unwillingness to agree to a cut-off date. The most he would offer was the conciliatory suggestion that the refusal of the United States to agree to a cut-off date did not imply that it foresaw U.S. arms sales to Taiwan continuing indefinitely. This would be Washington's final concession. Nonetheless, Bush encountered persistent criticism from Foreign Minister Huang Hua, and Deng Xiaoping reiterated China's demand for an end to all U.S. arms sales to Taiwan within a specified period.[89]

But Bush's visit did persuade Chinese leaders to adjust their negotiating position. The vice president and Deng Xiaoping had scheduled a private meeting that would last for ten minutes, after which time negotiations would be conducted by Foreign Ministry and State Department negotiators. But the meeting between Bush and Deng lasted two hours, and when they emerged from the meeting room, they cancelled the larger meeting. The two men held a productive discussion of both the immediate issues and the larger global context. Most important, after a prolonged deadlock in the negotiations, Deng freed Chinese diplomats to search for a compromise solution. Although he had reiterated China's demand for a cut-off date, he said that there should be consultations regarding the form and the wording of the U.S. commitment.[90]

Despite Deng Xiaoping's effort to advance the negotiations, the ensuing talks remained difficult. Even after Beijing finally dropped its demand for an explicit cut-off date, it sought a communiqué that committed the United States to "phase out" its arms sales to Taiwan. Nonetheless, this formulation failed to break the stalemate. American negotiators insisted that the United States could not agree to any language that suggested an end to arms sales to Taiwan under any circumstances.[91] Thus, despite the important developments in the Chinese position, relations continued to stagnate, and tension remained high. Moreover, the deadline was quickly approaching. When Congress returned from summer recess in September, the administration would have to provide it with formal notification of its decision to sell Taiwan the F-5E. This would challenge China's demand that Washington not sell Taiwan any weaponry while the two sides negotiated. Unless Beijing and Washington first reached agreement, China might have to fulfill its threat to retaliate by downgrading relations.

In the midst of this growing tension, President Reagan accepted Alexander Haig's resignation. But before Haig left office, he decided to send a final policy recommendation to the president. On June 29, he offered Reagan two options. One option recommended that the United States stipulate that it looked forward to ending all arms sales to Taiwan, thus reconciling itself to China's new position. The second option recommended that the U.S. maintain its current position and risk Chinese retaliation. Haig advised Reagan to adopt the first option, warning that failure to compromise would lead to a rupture in relations, severely damaging America's strategic position. If Reagan rejected this advice and precipitated a crisis in U.S.-PRC relations, Haig further warned, he would personally participate in the public condemnation of the president's policy that would undoubtedly ensue. Reagan rejected Haig's advice, however, and approved the second option. He was willing to risk Chinese retaliation rather than fundamentally alter U.S. policy toward Taiwan.[92]

Shortly after Reagan's decision, the text of Haig's less conciliatory draft communiqué setting forth his second option was circulated among White House officials and State Department officials who had not been part of the drafting process. White House officials were disturbed at how far Haig had already gone to conciliate Beijing and hardened some of the language. George Shultz, Haig's successor as secretary of state, did not support the draft communiqué, but decided not to stand in the way of reaching final agreement so late in the game. Finally, on July 14, Ambassador Hummel presented Chinese leaders with President Reagan's final offer on the arms-sales issue, as well as the president's suggestion that the two sides put the issue behind them, and that Premier Zhao accept his standing invitation to visit the United States.[93]

Then, within three days after China received Washington's final offer, Ambassador Hummel notified the Foreign Ministry that in early September, the White House would have to apprise Congress formally of its intention to continue U.S.-Taiwan co-production of the F-5E. In addition to the return of Congress, which would compel the administration to announce a decision, the ambassador explained, if the agreement were not concluded in the near future, the production line would have to be shut down, imposing enormous additional costs to future production.

In the absence of a prior U.S.-PRC agreement on arms sales, Beijing might well be compelled to retaliate. Holdridge feared that there might well be a Chinese "explosion."[94] But faced with the combination of the approaching deadline, President's Reagan's final offer on the arms-sales issue, and the resignation of Alexander Haig, China's bureaucratic ally in the Reagan administration, and the appointment of George Shultz as his successor, who was, at best, an unknown on U.S.-PRC relations, Chinese leaders understood that they had exhausted their negotiating leverage, and that they had to compromise. On July 17, within one day of receiving Hummel's warning about the approaching deadline on the F-5E, Beijing dropped its demand that the United States agree to a termination of arms sales. The best Beijing could achieve was the vague U.S. commitment to "reduce gradually its sales of arms to Taiwan, leading over a period of time to a final resolution." (See Appendix A.)[95] The only remaining obstacles concerned the details of U.S. arms-sales policy and the language linking peaceful unification with U.S. policy. Thus far, Holdridge said, prying a compromise from China on linkage had been like "opening an oyster with your bare hands."[96] But just as was the case in the negotiations over a cut-off date, Beijing had lost the initiative and was compelled to compromise.

Having backed off of its demand for a "phase out" of U.S. arms sales to Taiwan, China now tried various ploys to pin down other aspects of U.S. policy. It came up with the phrase "progressively decline" to characterize the future trend of U.S. arms sales to Taiwan. Washington rejected this for the English-language version of the communiqué, which calls for the United States to "reduce gradually" arms sales to Taiwan, thus leaving Washington free to increase sales in any one year as long as the long-term trend revealed declining sales. Beijing also tried to specify how the United States would determine the amount of sales, but Washington refused to discuss definitions or numbers with Beijing and indicated that it would have to consider inflation when calculating the quantity of arms sales to Taiwan, insofar as inflation had considerably diminished the monetary value of arms sales to Taiwan during the Carter administration. Beijing also wanted to establish the technological level that would be the basis for determining the qualitative limit of U.S. arms sales to Taiwan. Washington refused and insisted that if an existing technology went out of production owing to obsolescence, it could sell the more advanced version of the weaponry that was closest to the original technology.[97] Having made the quantity and quality concessions to Beijing, Washington maximized its flexibility within those parameters.

The remaining issues concerned Chinese policy on peaceful unification and the linkage between that and U.S. policy on arms sales to Taiwan. The August 17 communiqué included Beijing's conciliatory statement that China had developed "a fundamental policy [*fangzhen*] of striving for peaceful unification," suggesting that it was a relatively enduring and long-term aspect of its general foreign policy. The United States had sought stronger language. In September 1981, Zhang Wenjin privately insisted not only that peaceful unification was China's fundamental policy but also that it would not be reversed. U.S. negotiators tried to incorporate this stronger language in the communiqué but ultimately backed off in the face of Chinese resistance.[98] Nevertheless, *fangzhen* was a "crucial word" for the Chinese negotiators.[99] This wording provided the strongest commitment to peaceful unification that Beijing had made in any U.S.-PRC joint communiqué.

The last issue concerned linkage between China's commitment to a peaceful unification and U.S. arms-sales policy. Beijing had been rejecting linkage since the first days of U.S.-PRC rapprochement, and it rejected it in January 1982 when Holdridge presented Chinese leaders with the first set of principles for a joint statement. It continued to reject it even after agreeing to the language committing it to a "fundamental policy" of peaceful unification. The turning point came when Secretary of State Shultz cabled Ambassador Hummel a memo insisting that linkage was absolutely imperative in order for the two sides to reach agreement. When Hummel revealed the memo to Chinese leaders, they compromised. The final language of the communiqué prefaces U.S. commitments on arms sales to Taiwan with "Having in mind the foregoing statements of both sides," referring to Beijing's statement on peaceful unification. Although it continued to reject linkage, the PRC thus acquiesced to U.S. linkage of U.S. policy on arms sales to Taiwan and Chinese policy on peaceful resolution of the Taiwan issue.[100]

Conclusion

Between 1981 and 1982, U.S.-PRC relations experienced a reversal in the post-1969 trend of improving relations. Not only did the diplomatic relationship suffer amid threats and counterthreats of downgraded relations, but military relations suffered as well. The reason is clear. China was holding the development of all aspects of U.S.-PRC relations hostage to an agreement on arms sales. China withheld from the United States the benefit of expanded U.S.-PRC relations to increase Washington's incentive to compromise. And in so doing, it established the credibility of its threat to retaliate. China was willing to forgo the benefits of U.S. military technology if they meant sacrificing its interests vis-à-vis Taiwan.

In these circumstances, military relations deteriorated. Whereas during the Carter administration, the two sides had exchanged visits by U.S. Secretary of Defense Harold Brown and Chinese Minister of Defense Geng Biao, and Chinese leaders welcomed William Perry, head of development and research in the Department of Defense, to Beijing, all such exchanges ceased during 1981–82. Liu Huaqing's promised visit to Washington never took place. Moreover, despite Secretary of State Haig's announcement that the United States would consider selling weaponry to China, Chinese purchases from the United States of goods on the U.S. munitions control list declined from $2.8 million in 1981 to $151,000 in 1982.[101] Despite its interest in Western technology, China was not prepared to purchase U.S. military-related technology as long as the dispute over arms sales continued.

Both this downward trend in relations and the eventual resolution of U.S.-PRC conflict over Taiwan reflected the relative bargaining strength of the two sides. Initially, Chinese leaders, sensitive to U.S. alarm at the Soviet threat and to Haig's role in the Reagan administration, took the diplomatic offensive and demanded a revision of the status quo in U.S.-Taiwan relations. To a large extent they were successful. Nevertheless, the outcome of the negotiations and the nature of the August 17 communiqué also revealed China's inherent strategic weakness. Beijing had clearly benefited from a shift in the strategic balance and had greater negotiating leverage over the United States, but it never acquired sufficient leverage to extract complete U.S. compliance with Chinese demands. By any measure of power, the United States was in a superior position to China vis-à-vis the Soviet Union. The breakdown of cooperation would expose China more to Soviet pressure than it would the United States. Washington could count on Beijing's greater need for strategic cooperation to elicit Chinese flexibility.

But this perspective on the balance of relations should not obscure the role of individuals in policy making. Alexander Haig was a significant source of U.S. conciliation. His apprehension about the Soviet threat, and the correspondingly great significance he attached to U.S.-PRC relations, fundamentally affected the negotiating dynamics. U.S. willingness to compromise reflected a combination of the change in the strategic balance and Haig's perception of that change. Among senior administration figures, only Haig believed in the importance of making significant concessions to assuage Chinese anger. Similarly, the limits to American willingness to compromise reflected President Reagan's personal view of the importance of U.S.-Taiwan relations and his willingness to risk Chinese retaliation. The president balked at approving Haig's proposal that the United States explicitly commit to ending arms sales to Taiwan.

Thus, in 1981–82, the combination of the immediate strategic trend and the role of Alexander Haig in U.S. policy making offset the enduring asymmetries in relations between the United States and China and created a semblance of balance in negotiating strength. This was the best China could expect in negotiations with a superpower, and it was the most favorable position China experienced at any time during the entire period of U.S. strategic cooperation from Nixon to Reagan.

China had used its diplomatic "window of opportunity" well. It elicited from Washington a commitment that the United States did not "seek to carry out a long-term policy of arms sales to Taiwan," which suggested that it might eventually end arms sales to Taiwan; that the United States would not enhance the relative quality of U.S. arms sales to Taiwan; and that the United States would over time gradually reduce the quantity of arms sales to Taiwan. It had to pay for these U.S. concessions by compromising on the issue of linkage between U.S. arms-sales policy and a statement of China's policy of peaceful unification. It also abandoned its objective of compelling the United States to agree to a definite cut-off date for arms sales to Taiwan. Nevertheless, it had negotiated a true compromise solution rather than having to accept the status quo. This was a significant achievement. It would be China's last significant achievement in U.S.-PRC negotiations through the end of the Cold War.

CHAPTER 7

Consolidation of Cooperation

U.S. STRATEGIC CONFIDENCE AND
CHINESE POLICY ADJUSTMENT

The joint communiqué of August 17, 1982, established a new set of rules governing both U.S. and Chinese policies toward Taiwan. The United States agreed to limit its arms sales to Taiwan, and Beijing proclaimed its "fundamental policy" of peaceful unification. Nonetheless, there was also significant ambiguity in the communiqué, both as regards the linkage between these two points of agreement and, most serious, the pace of the reduction of U.S. arms sales to Taiwan. Moreover, in the context of ongoing conflict over these fundamental issues, new, but seemingly minor, conflicts assumed enhanced importance in China's U.S. policy. Thus, for more than a year after the United States and China agreed to the August 17 communiqué, they negotiated over whose interpretation of it would prevail and over a host of new issues in U.S.-PRC relations.

As had been the case since the early 1970s, the course of the negotiations was determined by a combination of strategic circumstances and domestic developments. In the aftermath of the August 17 communiqué, developments in both arenas benefited U.S. diplomacy. In the strategic realm, the United States developed enhanced strategic confidence, and the Soviet threat lessened. Beijing noted these changes, while its perception of the Soviet threat to China diminished only slightly. Beijing's negotiating position thus gradually deteriorated as it again adopted a conciliatory posture in U.S.-PRC relations.

There were also significant changes in the United States. The resignation of Secretary of State Alexander Haig and the appointment

of George Shultz as his successor coincided with the relative improvement in U.S. security. In these circumstances, Shultz and his
senior aides agreed that China was not the global strategic actor that
previous administrations had believed it to be. Despite efforts on the
part of some State Department officials to maintain the conciliatory
trend of the previous two years, the administration would thus be
less willing to conciliate China for the sake of a cohesive anti-Soviet
coalition. Similar to the dynamics of the early years of the Carter
administration, this combination of a sanguine view of U.S. security
and the corresponding view of China's secondary strategic importance influenced the trend of the bilateral negotiations.

In the context of these two developments, China was compelled
to reevaluate its U.S. policy. Because China lacked both the strategic
leverage of the previous period and the support of U.S. policy makers
who attached great strategic importance to U.S.-PRC cooperation, it
could either accommodate itself to U.S. interests or maintain disruptive, but unproductive, pressure on Washington to change its Taiwan policy. Given its ongoing need for U.S.-PRC cooperation, it
chose conciliation and ultimately agreed to a U.S.-PRC summit in
Washington, despite its inability to extract additional concessions
from the Reagan administration.

The Transformation of the Global Balance

Crucial to the establishment of stable U.S.-PRC relations was the
reevaluation in both Beijing and Washington of China's strategic importance to the United States. This development required that
Washington reappraise its Soviet policy and the value of U.S.-PRC
cooperation, and that China recognize the changes in U.S. thinking.
But there was a definite lag between the shift in Washington's assessment of the strategic challenge posed by the Soviet Union and
China's recognition of that shift. At the levels of both perceptions
and policy, Chinese policy makers spent much of 1983 coming to
terms with the changes in the superpower balance and the implications for U.S.-PRC relations. Only when that process was complete
could China's U.S. policy become more accommodating.

RESTORED AMERICAN CONFIDENCE AND
THE REEVALUATION OF U.S. CHINA POLICY

Reagan had entered office fearful that the United States lacked
both the spirit and the strength to resist Soviet expansionism. But
by his third year in office, his attitude had begun to change.[1] Espe-

cially important in this regard were developments in U.S. defense policy. In March, Reagan declared his intent to develop a space-based missile defense system—the Strategic Defense Initiative (SDI). Critics of SDI argued that the proposal was fanciful and totally unrealistic, but the president placed great hope in its ability to contribute to U.S. security. More important, the United States was responding to perceived U.S. deficiencies in the strategic balance by concentrating on its strength—technological superiority. Thus, the emphasis on technology in the arms race fostered White House confidence in U.S. security vis-à-vis the Soviet Union.

Other aspects of the U.S. defense program also suggested U.S. resurgence. In 1983, Congress supported the administration's basic defense program. Resisting the growing nuclear-freeze movement, the administration defeated congressional attempts to curtail funding of the controversial B-1 strategic bomber, and it secured congressional funding for development of the MX missile, the next generation of U.S. ICBMs. Shortly thereafter, the president observed that now that there was bipartisan congressional support for strategic modernization, America had "finally begun to forge a national consensus for peace and security."[2]

Equally significant in restoring the administration's confidence was the October invasion of Grenada. For the first time since the Vietnam War, U.S. use of force created minimal domestic contention. "I have been more sure than I've ever been that we Americans . . . will keep freedom and maintain peace," the president declared in the aftermath of the invasion. Democrats and Republicans sent "a message to the world that . . . when our country is threatened we stand shoulder to shoulder in support of our men and women in the Armed Forces."[3]

Finally, relations with Europe were developing well. The most significant issue affecting both alliance relations and East-West security trends was the NATO decision to deploy Pershing II missiles in Western Europe. This policy was highly controversial in West Germany, where the peace movement threatened to topple the Kohl government, which would have undermined NATO unity and the prospects for Pershing II deployment. But in May at Williamsburg, Virginia, the NATO countries reaffirmed their intent to deploy the Pershing II by the end of the year should the INF negotiations fail to secure an agreement. Then the conservative Kohl government won reelection, and by winter the United States had deployed the Pershing II in West Germany. When Moscow retaliated by withdrawing from the INF negotiations, the NATO consensus held fast, underscoring the new trend in East-West military relations. The final communiqué of the December meeting of the North Atlantic Council held the Soviet Union fully responsible for the East-West stalemate and reaffirmed NATO's intent to continue Pershing II deployment should Moscow fail to compromise. Reagan reported in his 1984 State of the Union Address that for the NATO countries, 1983 had been "a banner year for political courage."[4]

Equally important, economic developments bolstered the administration's strategic confidence. By 1982, inflation had fallen from the double-digit numbers of the late 1970s and early 1980s to 3.9 percent. The last quarter of 1982 saw an annual rate of inflation of 1.1 percent. With inflation under control, the administration appeared to be laying the foundations for greater national economic power. In contrast to the decline in GNP in 1982, in 1983, the economy grew by 3.5 percent and unemployment had begun to fall.

Soviet domestic and foreign policy developments also contributed to U.S. strategic optimism. Although the true extent of the Soviet Union's economic difficulties would not be known for a number of years, it was clear by 1983 that while the U.S. economy was on the rebound, the Soviet economy was deteriorating. And in Afghanistan the Soviet Army had become bogged down in an intractable and protracted war. In 1983, when the Afghan resistance forces escalated the scale of their attacks on Soviet forces and expanded the range of their operations, Soviet casualties increased. The State Department estimated that by the end of the four-year occupation in late 1983, 17–20,000 Soviet soldiers had been killed or wounded. A large-scale Soviet offensive to counter this trend failed completely.

The occupation of Afghanistan appeared to be the last hurrah of Soviet expansionism. Growing economic pressures, the struggle in Afghanistan, and perhaps even the trend in U.S. foreign policy dissuaded Moscow from launching similar military initiatives. "There have been no new Afghanistans, Angolas, or Nicaraguas on this administration's watch," Secretary of State Shultz could boast in late 1984, looking back on President Reagan's first four years in office.[5]

Moscow was also in the midst of a succession crisis. In November 1982, Leonid Brezhnev died and was succeeded by Yuri Andropov. But Andropov, who was both aged and increasingly sick, died in February 1984, only to be succeeded by the aging K. U. Chernenko. The inevitable passing of the Soviet gerontocracy was finally occurring, creating domestic paralysis and further undermining Moscow's global capabilities. After Andropov died in February, Under Secretary of State Lawrence Eagleburger observed that since early 1983, the Soviet leadership had been "confused and disorderly," and that "by and large the Soviet decision-making process ha[d] been in neutral, at best."[6] The Soviet Union's global capabilities and stature were clearly declining.

These domestic and international developments were reflected in the Reagan administration's increasingly sanguine view of U.S.-Soviet relations. In February 1983, Shultz argued that the president had been "brilliantly successful in turning around the defense strength of the United States." Although the battle continued, it was "certainly joined right now."[7] By August, President Reagan was exulting that the country was "on the right track again. As a nation, we've closed the books on a long, dark period of failure and self-doubt and set a new course." He had kept his pledge to restore America's military posture, Reagan declared. U.S. military forces were "back on their feet again." Indeed, "I think we've closed, largely, that window of vulnerability," he said in December.[8] Only a short time earlier, he had believed that Soviet ICBM superiority significantly undermined U.S. security by making U.S. land-based strategic forces vulnerable to a Soviet first strike.

The turnaround in administration thinking was complete by early 1984. "Three years ago we embraced a mandate from the American people to change course, and we have. . . . we halted America's decline," Reagan said in January. "America's defense policy is more credible and it is making the world a safer place—safer because there is less danger that the Soviet leadership will underestimate our strength or question our resolve."[9] In April, the president argued: "The simple fact is that in the last half of the 1970s, we were not deterring, as events from Angola to Afghanistan made clear. Gone are the days when the United States was perceived as a rudderless superpower, a helpless hostage to world events. American leadership is back."[10]

Complementing and reinforcing this fundamental change in the president's strategic outlook was the appointment of George Shultz as secretary of state. Shultz differed from Haig in two important respects. First, he was less prone than Haig to dramatize the Soviet threat and publicly dwell on U.S. strategic weakness. Whereas Haig emphasized the challenge of Soviet power and the necessity for urgent measures to provide for U.S. security, Shultz stressed American accomplishments in reversing the trend in the strategic balance and expressed greater confidence in U.S. capability. Shultz's relative composure enabled Washington to negotiate with both the Soviet Union and U.S. allies with greater leverage. Whereas Haig's posture magnified the importance of stable alliances in U.S. security, thereby encouraging U.S. allies to seek quids pro quo for cooperation, Shultz's equanimity fostered a more effective U.S. negotiating posture vis-à-vis the allies of the United States, including China.

Secondly, Shultz's more sanguine view of the Soviet threat encouraged him to assign reduced importance to China's strategic value and to the Kissingerian logic of the strategic triangle. Although Shultz clearly recognized that China was an important regional power and valued the U.S.-PRC relationship, he tended to discount China's influence on the global balance, observing that the United States appreciated its "constructive *regional* role." Moreover, to the extent that Shultz focused on U.S. security policy in Asia, he placed greater emphasis on U.S.-Japan relations than on U.S.-PRC relations. Thus, in contrast to Haig, who believed that for U.S. security interests, China might be "the most important country in the world," Shultz was less inclined to seek strategic cooperation at the expense of other U.S. interests. In this respect, unlike Haig, he was in agreement with other leading administration officials in both the Defense Department and the White House. Although some State Department and embassy officials remained reluctant to antagonize Chinese leaders, there was now a consensus among the administration's senior policy makers regarding the limited role of China in U.S. security policy, and a corresponding willingness to incur Chinese criticism.[11]

In important respects, then, Shultz's perspective on China was similar to Carter's and Vance's in the 1977–78 period. But unlike that of Carter and Vance, Shultz's tenure corresponded with significant improvement in the U.S.-Soviet balance of power, which enabled the administration to sustain a policy resistant to Chinese pressure for compromise. The combination of the developing trend in the superpower balance and Shultz's personal view of China produced a less accommodating policy toward U.S.-PRC conflicts of interest.

CHINA'S CHANGING VIEW OF THE SUPERPOWER BALANCE

China's reevaluation of the U.S.-Soviet strategic balance in 1983 was crucial to the development of U.S.-PRC relations. By the end of the year, Chinese leaders concluded that the United States had gained the upper hand in U.S.-Soviet relations. During this same period, the increasing inertia in Soviet leadership and continued Sino-Soviet rapprochement had improved China's strategic position. But this positive trend in Sino-Soviet relations could not offset the impact of the transformation in U.S. security on U.S.-PRC relations and on China's reduced negotiating leverage regarding ongoing conflicts of interests.

When the post-communiqué period began, China held to the view of U.S.-Soviet relations that had contributed to its successful effort to compel Washington to compromise on arms sales to Taiwan. In September, an analyst writing in the journal *Shijie jingji yu zhengzhi neican* argued that Reagan's anti-Soviet position and continuing U.S. economic and military problems had weakened the U.S. pro-Taiwan lobby, and that the United States could not but "emphasize maintaining and developing U.S.-China relations." The Reagan administration did not "dare brave a crisis in which U.S.-China relations could go backward and rupture," Jin Zujie claimed. Washington "had no choice" but to compromise in order to achieve the goals of the August 17 communiqué, and it would continue to base its China policy on strategic considerations.[12] In the fall, Wang Baoqin and Xu Lei, two leading Chinese analysts, argued that because of U.S. economic problems and tensions in relations with Western European and Third World countries, the capacities of the United States continued to "fall short of its ambition and strategically it is even more in need of China." Reagan had agreed to the joint communiqué because he feared that a bilateral crisis would lead China to improve relations with the Soviet Union and harm U.S. global strategy. In the future, although they foresaw a slim possibility that the Reagan administration might adopt policy harmful to Chinese interests, the analysts argued that the priority the United States attached to its "strategy of uniting with China to resist the Soviet Union" might increase but would not diminish.[13]

This same trend continued through the winter. In February 1983, Ding Xinghao of the Shanghai Institute of International Studies wrote that in 1982, the Reagan administration had "weighed the pluses and minuses" of an ongoing crisis in U.S.-PRC relations and, considering its strategic interests, "could not but make concessions on the Taiwan issue" and agree to the August 17 communiqué. In 1983, U.S. "recognition of its strategic interests" obliged Washington to continue to "develop relations" with China. A "power decline" had left the United States unable to "rely on itself to obtain national security," and the "dominant policy faction" in the administration recognized that the Taiwan issue "definitely" could not be allowed to become entwined in other issues and "to harm relations . . . to the extent that it would damage common interests."[14] Wang Shuzhong agreed that U.S. weakness had compelled the White

House to make a series of concessions on Taiwan since January 1981, and that the joint communiqué reflected U.S. strategic necessity. But he was less optimistic about President Reagan relinquishing his pro-Taiwan policies. Thus, China might have to maintain its belligerent posture: "If the United States does not change its hegemonistic policy of interfering in China's domestic affairs" it would not be possible "to eliminate crises in U.S.-China relations."[15]

During this same period, however, China's view of U.S.-Soviet relations was beginning to evolve. Chinese analysts were beginning to observe that although the United States remained troubled by serious problems and had not established an advantageous trend in U.S.-Soviet relations, it was no longer in such a passive position vis-à-vis the Soviet Union. In this analysis, both superpowers were beset with intractable economic and diplomatic problems and mutually intent on achieving "hegemonism."

This analysis first appeared in early 1983 in *Guoji wenti yanjiu*. Li Ning of the Institute of International Studies argued that Moscow faced a decaying economy and serious difficulties in Poland and Afghanistan, as well as in its Cambodia policy. Its foreign adventures had placed it in "an isolated position that it was incapable of casting off." Thus, Soviet expansion "could not but be somewhat restrained, and even when the United States closed in on certain regions or problems," such as in the Middle East, Moscow was often able to "attempt nothing and accomplish nothing." Nevertheless, Moscow responded with a "counterattack" and refused to make concessions; there would be no respite from its hegemonic policies. As for Washington, the "deepening" U.S. "economic crisis influenced Reagan's ability to expand military power, such that the defense budget did not increase as planned." Moreover, the Democratic Party had gained in the midterm elections, and the antiwar forces were gaining ground. In Europe, Washington faced opposition to waging "economic war" against the Soviet Union.[16] Huan Xiang, head of the State Council's Center for International Studies, similarly argued that both superpowers were "beset with difficulties" and poor economic conditions. Washington faced massive budget and trade deficits, as well as high unemployment, while the Soviet Union had failed to fulfill its five-year plan. Given their mutual weakness, neither was "capable of freely and without restraint utilizing its massive military power."[17]

This perception of disarray in both superpowers continued through midyear. The U.S. economy, although recovering, remained troubled, and U.S. relations with Western Europe were riddled with

economic conflict and difficulties surrounding the appropriate response to Soviet deployment of SS20s in Europe. An analyst at the
Defense Ministry's Beijing Institute for International Strategic Studies considered the United States still somewhat disadvantaged in
superpower relations: "The situation of the United States taking the
offensive while being defensive and the Soviet Union taking the defense while being on the offensive can frequently reappear again."[18]

Coinciding with this perception of superpower floundering was
increased momentum in Sino-Soviet rapprochement. After Brezhnev died in November 1982, his successor, Andropov, expressed
more interest in improved relations with China. In March 1983, following the second round of Sino-Soviet normalization talks and a
meeting between Soviet Foreign Minister Andrei Gromyko and PRC
Vice Minister of Foreign Affairs Qian Qichen, Moscow stressed the
possibility of improved relations. Although China approached Sino-
Soviet détente with considerable caution, there was no mistaking
Soviet interest in ameliorating tension with China in response to
increased U.S.-Soviet tension.[19]

Moscow's interest in Sino-Soviet rapprochement and Chinese perceptions of superpower weakness and rivalry led Beijing to continue
to assign China an important role in the superpower struggle. In the
most detailed analysis of this thinking, analysts from the Institute
of Contemporary International Relations argued in *Shijie jingji yu
zhengzhi neican* that both superpowers were experiencing "serious
difficulties," and that through the 1980s, there would not be any
"fundamental change" in the "balance of economic and military
power." Superpower dominance had declined, and there was "a tendency" among Second World countries to "be independent and keep
the initiative in their own hands," as well as a trend in "the world
power structure . . . toward multipolarity." In this context, although
the PRC was the "weakest side" in the "trilateral confrontation," it
"[held] the balance and a deviation to one side [would] produce a
basic change in the balance of power." In the "trilateral contention,"
the superpowers were on par with each other, so each "look[ed] to
bring China to its side." Ultimately, the "trilateral relationship" was
advantageous to the "realization of the three strategic tasks of anti-
hegemonism, speeding up the construction of the four moderniza-
tions, and making Taiwan return to the motherland."[20]

Before long, however, the cumulative effect of changes in U.S.-
Soviet relations compelled China to reevaluate its own strategic
value to the United States. When President Reagan announced his
Strategic Defense Initiative, a *Xinhua* commentary characterized

the proposal as an "attempt to outrace the Soviet Union to gain superiority."[21] At the May Williamsburg summit of the seven advanced market economies, Washington secured a public commitment from West Germany, Italy, and England to deploy Pershing II intermediate-range missiles and cruise missiles on their territory by the end of the year if Moscow and Washington did not first conclude a treaty covering the missiles. *Xinhua* observed that the agreement amounted to "a powerful support to the United States in its . . . negotiations with the Soviet Union." Washington was apparently overcoming its inability to impose policy on its allies.[22] Then, during the summer, the administration defeated efforts to curtail funding for the B-1 bomber and secured funding for the MX missile and, for the first time since 1969, production of chemical weapons. When Congress approved deployment of 100 MX missiles, one PRC analyst observed that "after many twists and turns, ... the heated disputes over the deployment of the MX missiles have, after all, been brought to an end."[23]

Huan Xiang summed up the new Chinese perspective. In contrast to his negative assessment in January, he argued in August that since Reagan had taken office, Washington had "adopted a number of steps to resolutely destroy the nuclear strategic balance." Huan also argued that the United States now sought regional superiority. In Central America, it had "greatly strengthened its powerful military and political pressure, determined to reestablish its hegemony." In the Middle East, the Reagan administration had used Israel to "launch an offensive." In contrast, over the same period, Moscow had "attempted nothing and accomplished nothing"; it was only able to "try to secure its Middle East position." Reagan could thus claim "definite achievements" toward "restoration of U.S. global hegemony." Huan was even optimistic on the U.S. economy, arguing that by early 1983, the post-1980 economic downturn had ended, that in the "new period," there was "some momentum" to the recovery, and that this momentum might even increase.[24]

Regarding Soviet prospects, Huan acknowledged that Andropov sought to implement extensive economic reform, "but in view of the current and future situations, the difficulties he encounters are relatively large." In international affairs, Moscow faced "increasingly heated resistance from the United States." Huan ended his brief discussion of the Soviet Union by saying, "as for Soviet economic weaknesses, . . . everyone is very well informed and thus there is no need to reiterate."[25]

During this same period, Ding Xinghao presented the first analysis in *Shijie jingji yu zhengzhi neican* questioning China's strategic importance. Whereas in February, Ding had been confident that Washington would continue to soft-pedal the Taiwan issue in order to maximize cooperation with China, by August, he had reconciled himself to George Shultz's March assessment of China's limited strategic role and his equanimity about ongoing U.S.-PRC tension. China's role in U.S. global strategy had "relatively declined" in part because the "world situation was relatively stable," so the U.S. "need for China to check the Soviet Union" lacked "urgency." So long as nothing analogous to the Soviet invasion of Afghanistan occurred, the "position of the 'China factor' in U.S. strategy to resist the Soviet Union [would] not seem very important."[26]

This analytical trend gained further support after U.S. troops invaded Grenada on October 25. This event eliminated any Chinese doubt regarding lingering U.S. passivity. *Xinhua* declared that the "invasion removed the veil over U.S. policy"; the United States had resorted to war to ensure its "hegemonic position" in the Caribbean. There was also momentum in U.S. policy, for the invasion "sent a shockwave" through Central America, creating worries over whether the "invasion [would] repeat itself" in the region. *Xinhua* reluctantly acknowledged that for the most part the invasion had been a domestic success for the administration.[27] The second important development occurred in November when Pershing II missiles arrived in Europe and Moscow withdrew from the INF negotiations. The Soviet Union's European policy was a failure, inasmuch as Washington had defeated Moscow's campaign to divide the NATO allies.

These developments created a consensus in China that Washington had the upper hand vis-à-vis Moscow. In the November issue of *Shijie jingji yu zhengzhi neican*, He Fang wrote that the combination of the recovering U.S. economy, the easing of the post-Vietnam / Watergate syndrome, and increasing U.S. nationalistic pride with the "daily deterioration" of the Soviet economic system and the entrenchment of conservatives in the Soviet bureaucracy created a widening gap between the superpowers. Moscow was facing an "unfavorable situation"; the "burden of strategic competition . . . and foreign expansion" was "too heavy." The USSR was "gasping for breath." It had sunk into a "passive situation" and needed a strategic "breathing spell" to carry out domestic consolidation. In these circumstances, the United States believed that "through arms competition and increased pressure" it could either "force the Soviet Union to make significant concessions" or "at least significantly weaken" it. Thus, over three years, the United States had increased defense expenditures by an average of 9 percent per year and funded the MX missile and the B-1 bomber. Moreover, in "key regions," U.S. policy had moved from "post-Vietnam retrenchment" to increasing military pressure on Soviet positions.[28]

In the December issue of *Shijie jingji yu zhengzhi neican*, Li Ning developed He Fang's analysis. In January, Li had noted continued U.S. economic problems and significant opposition from Congress and the peace movement to Reagan's defense policies. Now he argued that the U.S. economy had begun to recover, and that Reagan's prestige and reelection prospects had improved. In Europe, conservative forces had improved their position too, making the Soviet peace offensive ineffective, and Washington had secured Western European cooperation in the deployment of the Pershing II missile. Overall, the "basis of the U.S.-Soviet stalemate" had changed, and "over the past half-year" the trend in superpower relations had favored the United States. Washington believed the situation to be advantageous to itself and saw unusual opportunities compelling the Soviet Union to make concessions. In his institute's *gongkai* (open) journal, Li wrote that U.S. confidence had increased. Washington had finally overcome the "Vietnam War syndrome" and the "aftereffect of Watergate."[29]

Renmin ribao reached similar conclusions. In a "year-end review," it reported that in Europe, the NATO countries had "temporarily got the upper hand." The invasion of Grenada was "the most striking event this year," and the most serious military operation the United States had carried out since the Vietnam War. The operation revealed that Washington "would never hesitate to take the risk of military involvement in regional conflicts." Overall, since Reagan had assumed office, Washington had "taken the initiative to counteract Soviet influence . . . and proceeded to put an end to the previous passive situation." In contrast, Moscow was "beset with various difficulties at home and abroad, and its expansionist momentum can no longer be as swift and violent as in the 1970s."[30]

Within one year, Chinese policy analysts had perceived a fundamental transformation in U.S.-Soviet relations. Whereas at the end of 1982, the United States had faced the Soviet challenge from a "passive position," by the end of 1983, Washington had taken the offensive, and the Soviet Union was defensive and passive. Most striking was the fact that Washington had taken the initiative without out Chinese assistance; it had improved its position *at the same time* that U.S.-PRC relations remained tense because of Beijing's dissatisfaction with U.S. China policy. Among the many indications of U.S. resolve—including economic developments, defense spending, the use of force in Grenada, and improved NATO relations—this convergence of developing U.S. global authority with instability in U.S.-PRC relations clearly indicated that Washington was no longer in great need of stable U.S.-PRC relations. Beijing could not count on U.S. strategic vulnerability to ensure U.S. conciliation.

China's foreign policy specialists made this analytical connection in *Shijie jingji yu zhengzhi neican*. He Fang and Li Ning agreed that in the context of developing U.S. authority, Washington no longer saw the world as multipolar; it had adopted a bipolar perspective, in which China assumed reduced strategic importance. Li argued that in the bipolar perspective, U.S. focus on China had "relatively de-clined." Corresponding with its improved strategic position during the past six months, "in the past half-year or more" the United States had ceased viewing China as a global power and now saw it as an Asian power, and that even as an Asian power, its "position ha[d] somewhat declined." The Reagan administration saw China as militarily "relatively weak" and believed that "past estimates of Chinese power were inadequate." Moreover, in the context of U.S. strategic momentum and China's reduced importance, administra-tion concern over Sino-Soviet rapprochement had eased, further di-minishing China's importance.[31] He Fang argued that the changes in U.S.-Soviet relations could not but influence "so-called triangular relations" between China, the United States and the Soviet Union. Washington would "no longer pay such attention to the strategic role of other powers," including China. Looking back over 1983, he observed that this shift "not only obstructed the development of U.S.-PRC relations, but also led relations to go downhill." Specifi-cally, U.S. policy toward new conflicts and Taiwan reflected greater U.S. "rigidity."[32]

By the end of 1983, China knew more about the U.S. strategic posture and reappraised its own importance to U.S. security. This change enhanced the credibility of signals from Washington that it was resolved to endure U.S.-PRC tension. Beijing understood that it was in no position to threaten Washington with deteriorated rela-tions, and that the United States was well positioned to call China's bluff.

China's gradual reevaluation of the U.S. strategic posture was re-flected in its U.S. policy. By the end of 1983 and early 1984, Beijing had grasped the Reagan administration's reevaluation of China's strategic importance and reconciled itself to a subsidiary role in U.S.

security policy, and thus to the necessity for compromise. Stable U.S.-PRC political relations and a context for the institutionalization of U.S.-PRC relations first begun during the Carter administration were the result.

China's changing strategic circumstances during this period were also reflected in the fate of its "independent foreign policy." In September 1982, Party Secretary Hu Yaobang declared China would adopt a evenhanded policy toward the superpowers. China's policy would reflect case-by-case analysis, and it would be politically and strategically independent of both the Soviet Union and the United States.[33] Following China's successful effort during 1981–82 at eliciting U.S. compromise on Taiwan, and Washington's heightened concern about Soviet power, it is not surprising that Chinese leaders exhibited greater confidence in their foreign policy and declared their "independence" from alignment with the United States. Yet no sooner had Hu Yaobang announced China's new policy than the strategic conditions that had elicited it began progressively to disappear. Except in propaganda, China never implemented its "independent foreign policy." Rather, during the remaining years of the 1980s, across a wide range of issues, China moved significantly closer to the United States, seeking and developing unprecedented U.S.-PRC strategic, economic, and cultural cooperation.

Renewed Stability in U.S.-PRC Relations

After the August 17 communiqué, China continued to press for U.S. concessions on a range of issues. As one U.S. statesmen recalled, the Chinese "were at us for everything," no matter how minor the affront to Chinese sensibilities.[34] The United States, on the other hand, shifted to a far less compliant posture. While it accommodated PRC sensitivity on Taiwan by scrupulously abiding by existing agreements and was quite forthcoming on trade and military issues when it served U.S. interests, on conflictual issues, the Reagan administration consistently adopted measures that bluntly signaled its firm resolve not to succumb to Chinese pressure. There was no intent to be provocative. But Washington would not compromise to secure conflict-free relations. This was clear both of the Taiwan issue and of new issues in U.S.-PRC relations. But by the end of the year, Washington's policy shift and Beijing's own recognition of the transformation of the superpower balance had led China to adjust its U.S. policy by adopting a more accommodating posture on conflicts of interest. China even adopted a conciliatory policy on the

Taiwan issue, reconciling itself to a level of U.S. arms sales far above what it had expected.

"TRIP DIPLOMACY" AND THE SHELVING
OF THE TAIWAN ISSUE

After the signing of the August 17 communiqué, China immediately put Washington on notice that it would not tolerate any U.S. insensitivity to PRC interests. When Ambassador Arthur Hummel met with Deng Xiaoping on August 17, Deng told him that China expected a quantitative reduction of 20 percent annually in U.S. arms sales to Taiwan, leading to an end to sales after five years.[35] China had not dropped its demand for an early end to all U.S. arms sales to Taiwan. Rather than celebrating the resolution of the conflict and looking forward to improved U.S.-PRC relations, a *Renmin ribao* editorial, provocatively titled "Strictly Adhere to the Agreement, Remove Obstacles," warned that although the communiqué broke the deadlock over U.S. arms sales to Taiwan, this "did not mean that the problem has been completely resolved." Instead, the "dark clouds hanging over U.S.-China relations have still not been completely cleared away." If Washington based its China policy on the Taiwan Relations Act, U.S.-PRC relations "would not only not develop, but would certainly once again face a serious crisis."[36] Similarly, Chinese Ambassador Chai Zemin praised the communiqué but insisted that "this does not mean the entire issue has been totally solved." He warned that China would vigilantly monitor U.S. compliance with the communiqué, declaring that the new issue was "how to carry out all the principles and commitments . . . honestly and thoroughly." Only "through the implementation of these principles and commitments would Sino-American relations develop smoothly."[37]

In the fall, China became increasingly strident in response to U.S. policy. Foreign Minister Huang Hua criticized Americans who "cherish the fond dream of creating 'two Chinas' or 'one China, one Taiwan,' and stubbornly regard Taiwan as the U.S. 'unsinkable aircraft carrier' in Asia." He warned that if U.S. policy were "swayed by such people, the political basis" of U.S.-PRC relations "would be completely undermined."[38] A *Renmin ribao* commentary attacked Reagan's commitment to the Taiwan Relations Act and his insistence that U.S. arms sales to Taiwan would decline only if the PRC maintained its commitment to peaceful reunification. It charged that Reagan had "completely violated the spirit" of the August 17 communiqué, and that his approach conflicted with his "words about . . . improving relations with the PRC. The Chinese people will absolutely not agree with views like these." The editorial closed by expressing the hope that the U.S. government would "clear away interference, abide by the agreement, and tangibly implement . . . the communiqué, so that Sino-U.S. relations will be able to continue to develop."[39]

This was the atmosphere in which two U.S. delegations visited Beijing. The first, led by Treasury Secretary Donald Regan in mid December, sought expanded trade relations with China, which would presumably benefit Chinese modernization. Nevertheless, Finance Minister Wang Bingqian not only complained about restrictions on trade and technology transfer but, in a reference to the Taiwan issue, argued that "dark clouds hanging over the political aspect of . . . relations" were "detrimental to the development of economic cooperation and trade." Although China sought expanded trade, it would not drop its outspoken opposition to U.S. policy on Taiwan.[40]

Secretary of State Shultz's February 1983 visit to Beijing fared no better. Shultz reiterated U.S. intentions to promote U.S.-PRC relations and abide by the provisions of the August 17 communiqué. Yet he repeatedly stated that his purpose in coming to China was to "exchange views" and have a "dialogue" with Chinese leaders—he had not come with new initiatives aimed at easing PRC dissatisfaction. Indeed, he had earlier decided that he would not make any concessions simply to ensure a successful visit. Chinese leaders were clearly disappointed, and the result, as Assistant Secretary of State Paul Wolfowitz recalled, was that Shultz had a "very tough visit." Another participant in the delegation recalled that it was a "rough trip . . . it was not a picnic."[41]

Shultz held "friendly and frank" conversations with Premier Zhao, "frankly exchanged views" with Deng Xiaoping, and conducted eight hours of talks with Foreign Minister Wu Xueqian in a "serious and frank manner." He listened while Chinese leaders repeatedly complained of U.S. policy on Taiwan, particularly regarding Washington's interpretation of the joint communiqué, its treatment of Taiwan's diplomatic presence in the United States, and the level of U.S. arms sales to Taiwan. Shultz also heard Deng's protests on the Hu Na incident and on the Huguang Railway Bonds issue (discussed below), as well as a protest from Vice Foreign Minister Han Xu on U.S.–South Korean joint military exercises under way at the time. At the end of the trip, Chinese officials praised Shultz's "patience in listening to the views of others."[42] *Renmin ribao* warned, however, that "to further improve relations, it is imperative to remove the chief obstacle of the Taiwan question; the United States has not strictly observed the provisions of the 'August 17' communiqué and the Taiwan Relations Act is a serious stumbling block in the way of U.S.-PRC relations."[43] In addition, Beijing again turned aside Reagan's invitation to Premier Zhao Ziyang to visit Washington in the summer or autumn, again insisting that the date be worked out through diplomatic channels.[44]

Shultz had believed that Chinese badgering would have to stop if relations were to develop and the two sides were to get any work done. Thus, in his conversations in Beijing, he insisted that although there were some things the United States could do, there were also things it could not do; China would have to reconcile itself to the limits of U.S. flexibility. On the issue of arms sales to Taiwan, he insisted that the United States would abide by both the Taiwan Relations Act and the August 17 communiqué. He further maintained that although the overall trend would conform to U.S. commitments in the communiqué, Washington might actually increase arms sales in a particular year, as it had indicated during the negotiations. After an extended period of U.S. efforts to reach agreement through mutual compromise, Shultz communicated a new policy establishing U.S. resistance to accommodating incessant Chinese demands.[45]

After Shultz left China, he publicly signaled U.S. equanimity about tension in U.S.-PRC relations. He insisted that "progress in U.S.-China relations need not come at the expense of . . . our close unofficial relationship with the people of Taiwan" and that Washington's commitment to a decline in U.S. arms sales to Taiwan was tied to the level of tension across the Taiwan Strait. Shultz also indicated that Washington could endure Chinese belligerence. Although U.S. policy might cause friction with the PRC, "frustrations and problems" in U.S. relations with China were "inevitable." They would arise "not only out of differences concerning Taiwan but out of the differences between our two systems."[46]

Shultz also publicly expressed the administration's new assessment of China's strategic importance. In a widely covered speech in San Francisco, Shultz stressed that the United States saw Japan as its most important Asian security partner. In contrast to the assessments of previous U.S. administrations, he downgraded China's importance as a regional power. Beijing was perturbed by Washington's reappraisal of Chinese power, and Chinese diplomats and policy analysts expressed concern that the United States failed to appreciate China's importance.[47]

Shortly thereafter, Washington announced that the projected level of U.S. arms sales to Taiwan for 1983 and 1984 would decrease by only U.S. $20 million each year, and that the benchmark year used to determine the reduction in future sales was 1979, the year in which the largest quantity of arms had been transferred to Taiwan since normalization. Furthermore, the administration had calculated the amount of the 1979 sales in 1983 dollars, which made the base amount $800 million.[48]

The United States was abiding by both the letter of the August 17 communiqué and the negotiating history. During the negotiations, Ambassador Hummel had refused to discuss dollar amounts, allowing the United States the flexibility to consider inflation when calculating the annual trend in arms sales.[49] Nonetheless, Beijing quickly responded to Washington's complacency about Chinese discontent. Soon after Shultz left China, Beijing issued a formal protest charging that President Reagan had "gravely distorted" the terms of the joint communiqué. This was the first formal protest against the president's remarks since he took office. A *Xinhua* commentary charged that Reagan's position amounted to a "denial" of "commitments" made in the communiqué and a "serious retrogression" in U.S. policy. Beijing then complained about the level of arms sales, the prospective long-term trend of annual $20 million reductions, and the U.S. consideration of inflation. Ambassador Hummel was summoned to the Foreign Ministry to receive "representations" charging that the projected arms sales "greatly exceed[ed]" those of previous years and were "at variance with the stipulations" of the joint communiqué.[50]

China's counterattack continued when a U.S. House of Representatives delegation led by Speaker Thomas P. O'Neill, Jr., visited Beijing. Deng told the delegation that action was required to remove the obstacles to developing U.S.-PRC relations, and Premier Zhao insisted that he was dissatisfied with U.S.-PRC relations, and that conditions had "not been improved after the joint communiqué . . . and Secretary of State George Shultz's . . . visit last February."[51] Peng Di, Xinhua's senior Washington correspondent, complained about all these issues and warned that "the situation demands action. Does the United States wish to see its relations with China improve or turn sour . . . ?" He charged that U.S. arms sales to Taiwan "cloud[ed] the prospects" of relations and asked "whether these and other actions meant that the United States had "crossed the Rubicon" and was "working obstinately for a retrogression" in U.S.-PRC relations? As far as the U.S.-PRC summit was concerned, China was still holding it hostage to U.S. concessions. Premier Zhao told Australian journalists that he had "no specific plans to visit the United States," and that Chinese leaders were "not satisfied with the present state of U.S.-China relations."[52]

This was the context in which Secretary of Commerce Malcolm Baldridge arrived in Beijing on May 21. The day before he arrived, Ambassador Hummel was summoned to the Foreign Ministry over the Hu Na affair.[53] Unlike Secretary Shultz, however, Baldridge arrived in China with an economic initiative that pleased his hosts. On his way to China, Baldridge received President Reagan's permission to announce that Washington had changed China's export category, moving it from category "P" to category "V." China would now be formally treated like India and other friendly nonaligned countries, and its access to sophisticated Western technology would expand.

President Reagan had agreed to change China's trade status in early 1981 in advance of Secretary Haig's visit to Beijing. Nonetheless, formal implementation of this decision occurred only after extensive debate within the administration. Secretary Shultz was one of the main proponents of the change. In February, he had heard Chinese complaints about U.S. restraints on technology transfer, and he believed that, unlike arms sales to Taiwan and other conflictual issues, this area was one in which the United States could do something to help China. After he returned to Washington, he worked with officials from the White House and the Commerce Department to change China's trade status. There was energetic opposition to the proposal in the Department of Defense from Richard Perle and other officials concerned with technology leakage. Yet DOD officials responsible for policy issues, including Richard Armitage, supported the move. As one participant recalled, DOD was "schizophrenic" on this issue. Nevertheless, Secretary of Defense Weinberger believed that technology leakage was a paramount issue, and he did not support liberalizing exports to China. Ultimately, he failed to generate a DOD position on the issue, and the decision fell to the president. Baldridge continued to press for the change from a secure room in the U.S. embassy in Tokyo just prior to his departure for Beijing, and at the last minute, the president concurred with his State Department and National Security Council advisers; he put aside the issue of technology leakage and agreed to the reclassification.[54]

Chinese leaders "welcomed" Baldridge's visit, characterizing it as "quite successful." Beijing was pleased that the two sides had reached numerous agreements that would ease Chinese access to U.S. technology. Moreover, U.S. embassy officials observed that in the aftermath of the visit, their dealings with Chinese officials became friendlier, and they developed greater access to Chinese offices.[55]

Nevertheless, during and after Baldridge's visit to Beijing, Chinese officials remained skeptical that the administration would truly implement a more liberalized trade policy. They expressed suspicions that U.S. promises to provide China with access to U.S. technology would remain unfulfilled—that there would be "loud thunder, but little rain."[56] Moreover, while seeking better trade relations, Beijing did not drop its strong opposition to other aspects of U.S. policy—it sought the benefits of expanded trade without modification of its assertive policy on other issues, including Taiwan. Accordingly, Premier Zhao again did not accept President Reagan's invitation to visit Washington, and Deng signaled his dissatisfaction by failing to meet with Baldridge.[57]

This trend continued throughout the summer. Premier Zhao set the tone in his June 6 report to the opening session of the sixth National People's Congress. The United States, he charged, continued to sell arms to Taiwan "in serious violation of all" of the U.S.-PRC communiqués. He warned that Beijing would "never tolerate any infringement on China's sovereignty or any interference in its internal affairs." The United States "should strictly observe" the communiqués and "stop doing anything that harm[ed]" U.S.-PRC relations. This was the only way to ensure "sound development" of relations.[58] In July, Ambassador Zhang Wenjin made a "strong protest" and expressed China's "grave concern" at the U.S. announcement that it would sell Sparrow and Standard missiles to Taiwan. He charged that in quality and quantity the sale exceeded previous sales and was an "open violation" of the August 17 communiqué. The protest also contained China's first public complaint over Washington's refusal to consult with Beijing over arms transfers to Taiwan. "If there is no examination of the . . . specific items," it insisted, the U.S. commitment not to improve the quality of arms sold to Taiwan would become "unverifiable empty talk."[59] In early August, Foreign Minister Wu Xueqian belittled U.S. claims that the amount of arms sold to Taiwan had been reduced, and charged that the reduction called for in the August 17 communiqué "should not be a matter of one dollar, or even ten dollars. It should be a substantial reduction."[60]

But during this same period, the United States reinforced Secretary Shultz's effort to persuade Beijing that continued conflict would be useless. In June, just after the Williamsburg conference, which played such a significant role in Beijing's reassessment of U.S.-Soviet relations, Washington indicated that it was prepared to wait indefinitely for China to accommodate itself to U.S. policy. As the president prepared to visit a number of Asian countries, the question of whether he should also visit China arose within the administration. Although the president's political advisers, including Michael Deaver, promoted such a visit and feared the political backlash should he not visit Beijing, State Department and National Security Council officials argued that protocol required that Premier Zhao first visit Washington and that it would be unseemly and counterproductive for the United States to appear too eager for a Beijing summit. The president sided with his foreign policy advisers, amending a State Department memo to express his personal objection to visiting China unless Zhao first came to Washington. Shortly thereafter, Shultz arranged a meeting with the Chinese ambassador and explained that although the president would be in Asia, he would not visit China. Shultz explained that Reagan would like to go to China, but that he would wait until Zhao had visited Washington. In so doing, Shultz signaled U.S. indifference toward China's policy of holding the summit and stable relations hostage to U.S. concessions. Later, during the summer, the administration received indications that Beijing was reconsidering its posture toward a Washington summit.[61]

Moreover, during this same period China perceived that the Reagan administration had consolidated its position in domestic politics, and that there was a real possibility that China would have to deal with it through 1988. Not only was the administration turning around the U.S.-Soviet balance of power and reevaluating China's strategic importance, it was also relatively popular at home. Chinese leaders could not count on another in the sequence of frequent presidential successions since Watergate.[62] In this strategic and bilateral context, Beijing was developing an interest in compromise.

The summer of 1983 was a crucial period in the transformation of U.S.-PRC relations. By the time Secretary of Defense Caspar Weinberger visited Beijing in late September, Deng Xiaoping had decided to take a significant step to improve relations; he personally approved of President Reagan's offer of a Washington summit, and Premier Zhao informed Weinberger that he wanted to visit the United States in January 1984. Moreover, senior-level military exchanges, which China had suspended since mid 1981, seemed back on track.

Chinese Defense Minister Zhang Aiping agreed to visit the United States. And in contrast to China's previously aloof attitude toward military relations, there were productive working sessions between the two militaries.[63]

Nonetheless, Weinberger received, at best, a "correct" welcome by the Chinese military leadership, and he was unable to elicit their views of the strategic environment or of the Soviet Union, despite having made a lengthy and fairly comprehensive presentation of the U.S. perspective. As for cooperation on technology, Chinese leaders maintained a disinterested posture. Prior to his arrival in Beijing, Weinberger had indicated his interest in an arms-sales agreement, and Chinese leaders saw no reason to appear too eager to agree. When Zhang Aiping finally advanced a proposal for purchasing U.S. weaponry, he put forth an open-ended set of principles suggesting Chinese access to a wide range of equipment, without any specificity or consideration of mission, and permitting China to negotiate directly with U.S. companies without case-by-case review. Although Weinberger reported that Washington was willing to cooperate with Beijing to improve China's anti-tank and air defense capabilities and U.S. negotiators tried to focus the discussion on specific items on China's 1981 "wish list," Chinese leaders remained solely interested in a broad framework implying U.S. acquiescence to Chinese purchases of extensive U.S. hardware and technology.[64]

Chinese civilian leaders were just as rigid as the military leaders on both political issues and military relations. Although they had agreed to the Washington summit, they continued to object strongly to U.S. policy. Deng Xiaoping told Weinberger that while mutual understanding was important, it was even more important to eliminate basic obstacles and resolve substantive matters. He held that the "crux of the matter is the Taiwan issue," and that once this was resolved, the major obstacle in U.S.-PRC relations would have been removed. Premier Zhao, while pleased at U.S. liberalization of technology exports to China, repeatedly and forcefully stressed that the Taiwan issue was the obstacle to improved relations and expressed caution regarding military cooperation.[65]

Weinberger was faced with an unpleasant choice. On the one hand, he could accept the Chinese proposal for open-ended cooperation with respect to military technology, which would give him his "successful" visit and ostensibly advance U.S.-PRC security cooperation. But this option would likely lead to later problems, since China might well badger the United States to fulfill its apparent commitment to sell it sensitive technology. In addition, it would mislead China's neighbors about the true extent of U.S. willingness to cooperate with the PRC. At the urging of his Pentagon adviser Richard Armitage, Weinberger agreed with officials from the National Security Council and the State Department and resisted Chinese pressure. He left China without an agreement to cooperate in military technology.[66] Although Weinberger's decision was personally less fulfilling and elicited the expected negative media coverage, it reflected what U.S. advisers believed to be good policy, and, equally important for the development U.S.-PRC relations, it sent the same message to Chinese leaders that they had been hearing since the Shultz visit in February; Washington did not require agreements with Beijing, and it would not compromise simply to mollify Chinese irritation.

Chinese leaders might thus have agreed to a January summit in Washington, but they had yet to abandon their belief that Chinese-contrived tension would elicit U.S. compromises on political and military relations. Zhang Aiping's most forthcoming remarks during the Weinberger visit merely expressed interest in Weinberger's suggestion that China might consider purchasing U.S. air-defense equipment and anti-tank weaponry and allowed that the talks were a "good beginning" and "set the stage" for expanded relations. He did not, however, give up his demand for an open-ended agreement on principles.[67]

Beijing's confrontational posture over Taiwan continued into October when Foreign Minister Wu visited the United States. Just before his departure for Washington, Wu insisted that if the United States "truly desire[d] to see a peaceful settlement of the Taiwan question," it should "refrain from having any official or *semi-official* relations with Taiwan." In his meeting with U.S. officials, he reiterated China's stance that Washington was not adhering to the communiqué.[68] In response, Secretary of State Shultz reiterated that the two sides would continue to have differences, and that such differences were "normal in any relationship," particularly in U.S.-PRC relations. U.S. officials also reaffirmed Washington's intention to consider inflation when calculating the base amount against which future quantitative reductions in U.S. arms sales would be pegged. Wu thus warned that "the obstacles yet to be overcome" to smooth development of relations "must be removed" and asserted that once the obstacles were removed, there would be "far greater results" in U.S.-PRC relations. In Chicago, he insisted that there had not been "plain sailing," and that there were still "difficulties and obstacles" in U.S.-PRC relations. In particular, U.S. sales of "large quantities" of arms to Taiwan amounted "to actually encouraging the Taiwan authorities not to join us in . . . peaceful reunification. . . . This naturally meets our firm opposition."[69]

China was trying one last time before Premier Zhao's forthcoming visit to Washington to test the willingness of the United States to alter its Taiwan policy. When the United States declined to accommodate PRC demands, Beijing had to decide whether Zhao's visit would be fraught with tension or would reestablish stable cooperation.

At this late date, a Chinese leadership debate over U.S.-PRC relations intensified. The immediate issue was a proposed U.S. Senate resolution on the future of Taiwan. In March 1983, when the issue was first raised in the Senate Foreign Relations Committee, Beijing made "serious representations" to the administration, demanding that it influence the proceedings. When, on November 15, the committee passed the resolution, which called for peaceful resolution of the conflict between Taiwan and the mainland in conformity with the Taiwan Relations Act and the wishes of the people on Taiwan, Beijing threatened retaliation, suggesting that the summit was in jeopardy. Its official protest warned that the resolution could "only raise new obstacles in the relations between the two countries and bring greater damage to them. The Chinese Government strongly urges the U.S. Government to immediately take effective measures to prevent further aggravation of the situation. The Chinese Government expects an explicit reply from the U.S. Government."[70]

In this context, Party Secretary Hu Yaobang challenged the new trend in China's U.S. policy. He insisted that if Reagan's reply to China's protest over the congressional resolution on the future of Taiwan was "not satisfactory," then Beijing would "have to reconsider if the exchange of visits between Premier Zhao and President Reagan can materialize." And as late as December, President Li Xiannian and a majority of his colleagues in the Leading Group on Foreign Affairs of the Central Committee opposed the Zhao visit to Washington and the adoption of a more conciliatory U.S. policy.[71]

But the futility of conflict persuaded Deng Xiaoping to overrule the opposition to China's new policy, and Zhao would travel to Washington as promised. Although the president did not distance himself from the Senate resolution, Foreign Minister Wu accepted the White House's posture. "Now that the U.S. . . . has made clarifications and promises, we expect the U.S. to fulfill its promise by concrete actions," he declared.[72] The final shift in China's U.S.

policy was readily apparent when Zhao stated that the purpose of his visit to the United States was to "*stabilize* relations."[73]

Consequently, when Zhao visited Washington in January 1984, he never publicly raised the issue of U.S. arms sales to Taiwan or other contentious aspects of the Reagan administration's policy. Rather, he acquiesced to the U.S. face-saving device of having only unofficial relations with Taiwan, declaring:

> President Reagan said that Taiwan is an old friend. I have expressed the hope that he was referring to the people of Taiwan but not the authorities of Taiwan. I also said that I believe that he was referring to people-to-people relations but not official relations. . . . President Reagan said again and again that he will not throw over old friends in order to make new ones. This means he regards China as a friend. . . . China has never interfered in the internal affairs of other countries merely for the sake of old friends. This is our principle. And I believe this also conforms to the values of the United States.[74]

Overall, he concluded that he was "satisfied with the results of the visit" and that it would "produce a positive influence" on U.S.-PRC relations. He was now "full of confidence" that there would be "steady and sustained development of U.S.-China relations."[75]

China's U.S. policy had evolved from accentuating conflicts of interest to stressing cooperative relations. Reagan's reception in China in April was the culmination of this development, and Chinese leaders "took every effort" to make it a success. Thus, despite the president's expectation that Chinese leaders would repeatedly criticize U.S. policy on Taiwan, the April 1984 Beijing summit took place in an atmosphere of nearly conflict-free U.S.-PRC relations. Although Foreign Minister Wu Xueqian complained to Secretary of State Shultz about the rate of decline in U.S. arms sales to Taiwan, Shultz simply noted that the United States had been abiding by the August 17 communiqué and intended to continue doing so. The administration stressed that the communiqué called for "gradual reduction," and that that was what would take place. Similarly, the president repeatedly maintained that there were "differences between us that should be neither glossed over or denied," reinforcing Washington's relaxed attitude toward conflict with China.[76]

Beijing did not allow these differences to interfere with the president's visit. Premier Zhao observed that China was pleased with U.S. contributions to the recent improvement in relations. Expressing a new formulation of Beijing's policy, his central point was that the Taiwan problem, rather than disrupting present-day relations, "*might* cause a serious setback" in relations if it were mishandled. In his speech at the farewell banquet, he said that he and Reagan had held "friendly" and "constructive talks in a candid and amicable atmosphere." He did not even mention Taiwan, but stressed the prospects for expanding economic and technical cooperation. In an unusual gesture, Deng Xiaoping held a working meeting with Reagan that lasted an hour and forty minutes, which he characterized as a "big success" that had made "great progress." Li Xiannian went so far as to host a private dinner for the president. Both leaders refrained from raising the Taiwan issue or any difference in relations.[77]

NEW CONFLICTS IN U.S.-PRC RELATIONS

The evolving trend in U.S.-PRC conflict over Taiwan also characterized Chinese policy toward a number of new issues involving human rights, legal conflicts, and Chinese and Taiwanese participation in international organizations. In each case, China adopted a relatively bellicose tone, suggesting the possibility of significant retaliation. But as the year progressed and as the change in U.S.-Soviet relations became increasingly apparent, Beijing accommodated itself to U.S. policy. As with developments in U.S.-PRC tension over Taiwan, the final catalyst persuading Beijing to drop the other outstanding conflictual issues was its interest in a successful U.S.-PRC summit.

The first of the new issues to disrupt relations was the Huguang Railway Bonds case. In November 1979, a class-action suit was filed against the People's Republic of China on behalf of the holders of the bonds, which were issued in 1911, the last year of the Qing dynasty. The suit demanded that China pay to the plaintiffs the principal and the interest on the bonds. Claiming sovereign immunity, China did not appear in court. In early February 1983, the court issued a default judgment against Beijing, stipulating that it pay the plaintiffs more than U.S. $40 million. The court further ruled that if Beijing did not comply with the judgment, it would seize PRC property in the United States.

Beijing responded by presenting Secretary of State Shultz with an aide-memoire, during his February visit to Beijing, charging that the State Department had "shirked its responsibility." The PRC said it expected the U.S. administration to "handle the case properly so that Sino-U.S. relations and normal trade and economic exchanges may not be impaired." Deng personally raised the issue with Shultz, linking his personal prestige with the outcome of the dispute. Chinese behavior suggested that the bonds issue might be a "total disaster" for the relationship.[78]

The U.S. posture was based on the legal issues, and there was little anxiety expressed over PRC concerns. The State Department explained to Chinese diplomats that only the courts could rule on the validity of a sovereign immunity defense, and that China would have to argue its case based on U.S. law. When Beijing refused to appear in court, Washington noted that sovereign immunity was "not absolute," and that states "may be sued for actions taken in commercial capacity." Rather than offer the court its opinion, the State Department merely stated that it had no position on the legal merits of the case, and that it hoped China would act in accordance with U.S. legal procedures.[79]

For two months after the judgment was issued, China attacked the entire proceedings. But by September 1983, after Zhao had accepted President Reagan's invitation to visit Washington, it had decided to work within the U.S. legal system, hiring U.S. lawyers to represent it in court. Similarly, Chinese media were now discussing the case on its legal merits. The United States, now that China had compromised, supported the PRC against the plaintiffs through a friend of the court brief asking the court to set aside the default judgment.[80]

China followed a similar policy regarding the conflict over the Reagan administration's May 1983 decision not to object to Pan American World Airways' decision to recommence service to Taiwan. The airline had suspended its service to Taipei in 1978 when it sought permission from Beijing to serve the mainland. When Pan Am first suggested its interest in resuming service to Taiwan, some U.S. officials suggested that it incorporate a new airline to service Taiwan with aircraft displaying a distinct name and logo. Eventually, however, the administration supported Pan Am's request, justifying its decision on the basis of China's consent at the time of normalization that Washington would conduct civil aviation matters with Taipei through the American Institute in Taiwan, its de facto embassy.[81]

Ambassador Hummel was once again summoned to the Foreign Ministry to receive China's "solemn position" opposing the decision. When Washington ignored Beijing's plea and Pan Am began service to Taiwan in June, China lodged a "strong protest." Beijing charged that because international airline routes are government-regulated, Pan Am's Taiwan route was not merely a commercial activity but must be approved by the PRC, the sole legal government of China, which included Taiwan. Insisting that it was "futile for the U.S. Government to belittle the political implications of such authorization and shed . . . responsibility," it warned that failure to respect PRC sovereignty would "inevitably cause damage" to U.S.-PRC relations. The U.S. side would "be held fully responsible."[82]

China's Civil Aviation Administration held that insofar as China had granted approval to Pan Am to service the mainland on the condition that it terminated its service to Taiwan, Washington should assign another airline the U.S.-PRC route. Indeed, Beijing suggested that it would cancel Pan Am's right to serve the PRC should the administration not comply with the PRC demand. But in response to U.S. warnings that Washington would retaliate by cancelling China's service to the United States, Chinese leaders reconciled themselves in the fall to Pan Am service to both China and Taiwan. Beijing retaliated by merely denying Pan Am overflight of Chinese territory on flights to Hong Kong and emergency landing rights in Guangzhou.[83]

Thus, toward the end of the year, China shelved divisive issues that it had allowed to disrupt relations. Similarly, in December, when China completed its reassessment of the superpower balance, and as the Washington summit approached, Beijing decided to resolve the remaining issues that threatened to undermine a fully successful summit.

The first of these remaining issues was the case of Hu Na, a Chinese tennis player who had sought political asylum in the United States. The initial reaction of officials at the State Department's China Desk was to deny her asylum status and have her return to China. They accepted the assurances of Chinese leaders that Hu would not suffer any reprisals. A battle then developed between the Bureau of Human Rights, which had the responsibility for issuing an advisory to the Bureau of Immigration and Naturalization, and the East Asia Bureau. Not only were officials at Human Rights shocked that the China specialists would send Hu back to China, they also argued that on legal grounds, she had an obvious case for asylum. Simply because she had asked for asylum, she had a "reasonable fear" that she would face persecution should she return. Moreover, should the administration deny her asylum, the case would likely remain in the courts, and thus in the newspapers, for an extended period, creating political trouble for the president in conservative circles. Faced with this situation, East Asia Bureau officials suggested alternative, less offensive methods to permit her to stay in the United States, such as granting her regular immigrant status. Alternatively, they hoped she would agree to go to Taiwan. These options required Hu Na's cooperation, for they would have required her to drop her request for political asylum, but there was no suggestion from her lawyers that she was prepared to compromise. Despite the efforts of the East Asia specialists to finesse this issue in the interests of stable U.S.-PRC relations and Shultz's desire to avoid confrontation, Shultz ultimately supported the position of the Bureau of Human Rights that the United States grant Hu political asylum.[84]

During the eight months it took the administration to reach a decision, China gradually increased the severity of its demands that Hu Na be returned to China. When Hu requested asylum in the summer of 1982, the Chinese ambassador called for her return to China, and Beijing warned that the incident was "sure to adversely affect the cultural exchanges" between the United States and China. Shortly thereafter, on the very day that the August 17 communiqué was issued, Chinese leaders warned Ambassador Hummel of the "gravity" of the issue.[85] As with the Huguang Bonds issue, when Deng met with Shultz in Beijing in February 1983, he demanded that Hu be returned to China, tying his personal prestige to the outcome of the dispute. Moreover, Hu frequently played tennis with Priemier Wan Li, and Chinese leaders had guaranteed her safety should she return to Beijing.[86]

When Washington granted Hu Na asylum, China cancelled the remaining exchanges called for in the U.S.-PRC cultural agreement. It also warned the United States against taking further hostile acts against China, summoning Hummel to the Foreign Ministry at 8:30 P.M. and presenting him with a "strong protest" at this "grave political incident long premeditated and deliberately created by the United States." It threatened that China would retaliate against future incidents, insisting that it would "never, for the sake of relations with the United States, abandon its principled stand of safeguarding its state sovereignty and national dignity," and that how relations developed was "dependent" on U.S. behavior.[87] A *Renmin ribao* commentary asserted that U.S. officials had "made a whole series of moves that hurt the Chinese people's dignity, feelings and interests" and that the United States was "bound to cause damage" to U.S.-PRC relations if it handled other issues with a similar disregard for Chinese attitudes. "The United States . . . must think over its choice carefully!" it warned.[88] Nevertheless, in October, Foreign Minister Wu Xueqian expressed an interest in reopening negotiations over cultural exchanges, and discussions began in December, just prior to Premier Zhao's arrival in the United States. China had acquiesced to U.S. policy on political asylum.[89]

In December, too, China also reconciled itself to U.S. policy on Taiwan's membership in the Asian Development Bank (ADB) and congressional statements on Taiwan and U.S.-Taiwan relations. In February 1983, Beijing had declared its intention to request admission to the ADB and demanded that Taiwan be ousted. It maintained that because Washington had recognized the People's Republic of China as the sole legitimate government of China, it must also support Beijing's "demand for the expulsion of the Taiwan authorities" from the bank. Beijing argued that the bank's constitution required that membership be open only to members of the United Nations.[90]

In Washington, the reaction among many officials was "here we go again." China was challenging U.S. policy in an area in which the administration would not bend, and that would thus require firm diplomacy. Some China specialists hoped Taiwan would adopt a conciliatory attitude, such as accepting membership within the PRC delegation, or withdraw in protest against PRC membership, thus resolving the issue. But Treasury Secretary Donald Regan and Assistant Secretary of State Paul Wolfowitz adopted an uncompromising position, which determined U.S. policy.[91] Although the United States reiterated its recognition of the PRC as the sole legal government of China and its opposition to a "two-Chinas" policy and conceded Chinese membership credentials, it insisted that if Taiwan were ousted from the ADB, Washington would end its financial contribution to the bank. The State Department maintained that ousting Taiwan "would have serious implications for continued U.S. participation and funding for the Asian Development Bank."[92]

The United States and China were now at odds over a fundamental issue—the role of Taiwan in international organizations. When the United States refused to budge, China went on the offensive. In May, when the ADB's annual meeting was in session, an article in *Renmin ribao* insisted that "the Taiwan authorities cannot find any excuse to pretend to be the Chinese government. Therefore, they are no longer qualified to be a member of the bank." It further warned that the United States "would be well advised to treasure the friendship between the Chinese and American peoples [and] abandon its erroneous policy."[93] After U.S. Treasury Secretary Regan reminded the ADB delegates of strong U.S. opposition to ousting Taiwan, the meeting adjourned without considering the PRC membership request. Beijing declared that "after ten years of ups and downs, Sino-American relations leave much to be desired, snagged as they are on the Taiwan issue." Washington had not given up "its policy of two Chinas or one China and one Taiwan," and it continued to regard "the island as an 'unsinkable aircraft carrier.' Its insistence on keeping Taiwan in the bank is another manifestation of this erroneous U.S. policy."[94]

The polemics quieted down during the summer, but in November, the U.S. Congress passed a foreign aid appropriations bill that stipulated that the "Republic of China" should remain a full member of the bank, regardless of PRC membership. Ambassador Hummel was summoned to the Foreign Ministry to be read a "serious protest" "emphatically" calling upon the United States "to stop all attempts at creating 'two Chinas.' Otherwise, [Washington would] not be able to shirk the responsibility for the serious consequences arising therefrom."[95] A highly charged *Renmin ribao* commentary alleged that the bill was a "wanton act violating Chinese sovereignty" and "odious and brazen on the point of creating "two Chinas." Should the president sign the bill, "it would constitute an open renunciation of the fundamental principles underlying the establishment of Sino-U.S. diplomatic relations and of the solemn commitment made by the U.S. Government in various . . . joint communiqués," *Renmin ribao* declared. "Whither does the U.S. Government intend to lead relations between the two countries?" it asked pointedly. The commentary closed with a clear challenge to the administration:

> The dark clouds over Sino-U.S. relations have never been completely cleared away, and now, no sooner have signs of improvement come into sight than a new threat looms ahead. There are always some people in the United States who . . . judge that no matter how arbitrarily they act, the Chinese Government . . . will always swallow the bitter pills they concoct. This is a dangerous game. If this is allowed to continue, immeasurable damage will be done to Sino-U.S. relations. The U.S. Government will bear sole responsibility for such serious consequences.[96]

Although President Reagan disassociated himself from the "Republic of China" language in the aid bill and reiterated recognition of the PRC as the "sole legal government of China," he defied Beijing's warning and signed the bill, saying that he "firmly believed that we must continue the valuable and productive unofficial relations with the people of Taiwan and I strongly support efforts to ensure their continued participation in the Asian Development Bank."[97]

In early December, as Premier Zhao prepared to visit Washington, China finally compromised. Beijing allowed that Taiwan could remain a member of the ADB if the Republic of China flag was not displayed at bank headquarters and if Taipei agreed not to use "Republic of China" as its membership title. The first indication of this change was evident less than one week after Reagan's statement. Although *Renmin ribao* complained that Reagan's clarification was unsatisfactory and suggested that his support for Taiwan's membership in the ADB was inconsistent with U.S. recognition of the PRC, it retreated to the position that if the United States actually respected the "one-China" policy, it did not have any reason "to maintain support for the continued presence of Taiwan in the Asian Development Bank *under the name 'Republic of China.'*" In Washington, Zhao said that China would participate in international organizations with representatives from Taiwan using the name "Taiwan, China," thus personally acquiescing to U.S. policy on the ADB.[98] Furthermore, Foreign Minister Wu accepted the White House's position on the objectionable congressional resolution. "Now that the president . . . has made clarifications and promises, we expect the U.S. to fulfill its promise by concrete actions," Wu declared.[99]

Zhao Ziyang's visit to Washington was a great success, and both sides now looked forward to President Reagan's April visit to Beijing. Nevertheless, one minor issue threatened to create conflict at the summit. Although Beijing had earlier accepted the U.S. position regarding Pan American World Airways, it had yet to grant Northwest Airlines permission to service China. As part of the 1980 U.S.-PRC civil aviation agreement, Beijing agreed to allow two U.S. carriers access to China. But Northwest was still serving Taiwan, and since early 1983, Beijing had refused to grant Northwest an operating license. But U.S. officials convinced Chinese authorities that if the Northwest Airlines negotiators left Beijing without an operating license, Chinese service to the United States would be curtailed, affecting the forthcoming Beijing summit. Just when the Northwest representatives were scheduled to depart China, Beijing compromised. Although China only granted Northwest a six-month permit, the airline began service to China and maintained its Taiwan service.[100]

U.S.-PRC relations were thus bedeviled by a host of new conflicts in 1983. As with the conflict over U.S. arms sales to Taiwan, in each case Washington adopted an uncompromising position, suggesting its reassessment of the value of conflict-free U.S.-PRC relations to

U.S. security and establishing its resolve to endure PRC threats and risk PRC retaliation. This policy shift combined with China's gradual reappraisal of the U.S.-Soviet balance of power to persuade Chinese leaders that efforts to impose compromises on the United States concerning both Taiwan and the new conflicts in relations would fail and only lead to counterproductive tension. Such tension could have continued indefinitely, but by the end of 1983, coinciding with Beijing's full understanding of the changes in the superpower balance and with the upcoming U.S.-PRC summits, Beijing backed down from its threats to disrupt relations.

This change in China policy coincided with improving Sino-Soviet relations. Nevertheless, as has been the case since the first stages of U.S.-PRC rapprochement, the asymmetry between U.S. and Chinese capabilities imposed on Beijing relatively greater vulnerability to Soviet power. Moreover, the developments in 1983 in the U.S.-Soviet strategic balance had exacerbated the asymmetries between China and the United States, thereby undermining the value of improving Sino-Soviet relations in China's U.S. policy. Thus, by the end of the year, it was clear that continued U.S.-PRC conflict not only did not serve China's interests in U.S.-PRC relations, but undermined China's position in the Sino-Soviet conflict. In the circumstances, Beijing moved to defuse the remaining conflicts and, as Zhao Ziyang put it before he left for Washington, "stabilize" U.S.-PRC relations.

Consolidating U.S.-PRC Relations: Military, Economic, and Educational Exchanges

Once Beijing reconciled itself to U.S. China policy, the two sides were able to develop substantial cooperation on a wide range of issues. This occurred despite Beijing's continued dissatisfaction with Washington's interpretation and implementation of the August 17 communiqué.

One of Secretary of State Shultz's first steps in China policy was to order a review of the negotiations leading to the August 17 communiqué and to direct his staff to look for policy that would enable the United States simultaneously to fulfill its obligations under the Taiwan Relations Act and the August 17 communiqué. Much to the consternation of the State Department's China specialists, officials at the Bureau of Politico-Military Affairs discerned that Washington had not made any commitments to Beijing concerning the quality of *technology* transferred to Taiwan. Washington could thus license the sale of advanced technology to Taiwan without violating the terms of the communiqué. Moreover, "creative application" of the August communiqué justified the administration's decisions to sell Taiwan weaponry that had been licensed for export prior to 1979, but not delivered, and, in accordance with the negotiating record, to sell Taiwan advanced versions of weapons that had been transferred prior to 1979 but were no longer manufactured.[101]

Thus, in the mid 1980s, U.S. corporations received licenses to sell advanced weaponry and military technology to Taiwan. General Dynamics sold the technology for Taiwan to upgrade its forty-year-old frigates, which permitted Taiwan to build a Perry-class fast frigate that would improve Taiwan's anti-submarine warfare capability. Washington also sold Taiwan C-130 transport planes to replace the C-119 transport and an improved version of the M-48 tank. The export license for the C-130 transport had been granted prior to 1979 and the original M-48 tank had gone out of production. Washington used similar justifications for the sale of laser-guided bombs, Maverick missiles, Harpoon anti-ship missiles, the Standard air-defense system, and other weaponry. The most sensitive decision concerned the license to export technology to Taiwan enabling it to build an advanced military aircraft. Not only was the issue "bitterly fought out" in the administration, but all sides to the debate recognized the possibility that, unlike past transfers, U.S. transfer to Taiwan of advanced aircraft technology might well elicit significant Chinese retaliation. But not only did Taiwan need a modern aircraft, but should it not develop its own aircraft, the Taiwan Relations Act might ultimately require the sale of the F-16, which would certainly do even greater damage to U.S.-PRC relations. Technology transfer was thus the lesser of two evils, and Secretary of State Shultz agreed to the sale. Nonetheless, the transfer was designed to minimize PRC opposition. The technology permitted Taiwan to develop a "defensive" F-16, designed for less range but faster climbing power.[102]

There were also U.S.-PRC differences over the pace of reduction in quantity of U.S. arms sales to Taiwan. On the one hand, Washington continued to insist that the trend reflected an appropriately gradual rate of decline of approximately $20 million per year. This figure, however, measured the value of new government agreements plus commercial deliveries. Based on the value of total transfers (governmental plus commercial deliveries), during the last four years of the Reagan administration, the value of military deliveries to Taiwan increased every year. Total transfers in 1988 were worth nearly 70 percent more than those in 1984.[103] It is thus not surprising that

Beijing was unhappy with the pace of reduction of U.S. arms sales to Taiwan.

Beijing protested Washington's policy on all of these issues, and Washington's consistent reply was that it was abiding by the terms of the communiqué. In 1986, China finally responded publicly. But it avoided a threatening posture. An article in a relatively low-profile journal complained about the quantity and quality of U.S. arms and technology sales to Taiwan, but it refrained from making even the mildest threat of retaliation. Party Secretary Hu Yaobang also complained about U.S.-Taiwan military relations, but adopted the familiar posture that there would only be repercussions on relations if U.S. policy continued for "a long period of time."[104]

Ultimately, however, there was little China could do to persuade the United States to change its Taiwan policy, because its negotiating leverage over U.S. policy had further declined in the 1980s. The momentous Soviet concessions in the INF negotiations and the serious deterioration of the Soviet economy in the late 1980s underscored the extent to which Moscow no longer posed a significant immediate challenge to U.S. security. By the end of the Reagan administration, this trend had become so salient that the very basis for U.S.-PRC strategic cooperation—the Soviet global threat—had significantly diminished. Moreover, the consolidation of U.S.-Soviet détente further reduced the importance of China in U.S. security policy. The resulting erosion of Chinese leverage was so great that Beijing was compelled to accept the status quo in U.S.-Taiwan relations to obtain the benefits of U.S.-PRC cooperation.

But while the Reagan administration took advantage of its enhanced position in U.S.-PRC relations, it never wavered from its commitment to recognition of the PRC as the government of China. Formal and declaratory U.S. policy adhered to the pattern established by Secretary of State Haig early in the administration. Moreover, during his March 1987 visit to China, Secretary of State Shultz supported Beijing's efforts to develop ties between Taiwan and the mainland and prodded Taipei to accelerate the lifting of controls on people on Taiwan seeking contact with mainland Chinese. In Shanghai, he declared that the United States welcomed "indirect trade and increasing people-to-people interchange" between Taiwan and the mainland.[105] Washington thus offered Beijing some consolation for its acquiescence to ongoing U.S.-Taiwan military relations.

In this context of minimal U.S. sensitivity to PRC interests, economic relations and military, educational, and scientific exchanges nonetheless flourished. Now that the two sides had established a modus vivendi on the Taiwan issue, the relationship could move beyond mere strategic alignment against the Soviet Union, and each side could pursue a host of other interests. Turning from their approach in the 1970s, when Beijing and Washington had pursued economic and military cooperation for their symbolic value in developing political and strategic relations, they now sought nonstrategic cooperation for its direct contribution to each side's interests. Thus, the process of institutionalizing U.S.-PRC relations, which had begun during the Carter administration after normalization, was now adopted by the Reagan administration under more favorable political circumstances.

THE CONSOLIDATION OF U.S.-PRC MILITARY
AND SECURITY COOPERATION

One of the most significant efforts at institutionalizing support for U.S.-PRC cooperation involved development of military relations. This relationship was one of the more complex and least understood aspects of U.S.-PRC Cold War cooperation. Clearly, the immediate basis for cooperation was the shared perspective on the Soviet military threat. In the short term, by heightening Soviet security concerns, consolidated military relations contributed to Chinese and U.S. ability to resist Soviet pressure. Moreover, both sides foresaw that greater Chinese military capability would undermine Soviet ability to consolidate Moscow's considerable advantage in the Sino-Soviet military balance and would exacerbate the Soviet Union's defense burden.

Nonetheless, the long-term political payoffs held even greater potential for stable U.S.-PRC cooperation. First, the development of military relations would enable the two militaries to become better acquainted with each other's operating procedures and strategic planning and enable both sides to plan for the future with less uncertainty. This would help reduce the potential for unnecessary conflict arising from miscalculation of each other's intentions. Second, the overall technological sophistication of Chinese soldiers would benefit from exposure to Western equipment. Third, the Chinese military elite would gain valuable information toward the reform of PLA management and military doctrine. Finally, developed U.S.-PRC military ties would promote in both military bureaucracies an interest in overall stable relations, insofar as it would permit U.S. and Chinese officials to maintain and even expand their ties with their counterparts.[106]

The first steps in military relations occurred when Harold Brown visited China in January 1980. Chinese Defense Minister Geng Biao paid a reciprocal visit later in the year, and the Carter administration eased restrictions on dual-use exports to China. During the early Reagan administration, Beijing held further military cooperation hostage to the Taiwan issue, but now that China was content to abide by the status quo in U.S.-Taiwan relations, U.S.-PRC military relations moved forward. Secretary Weinberger's September 1983 visit to Beijing was the first step toward reestablishing momentum in military relations. Although the Taiwan issue continued to obstruct full development of relations, his visit laid the groundwork for a resumption of high-level exchanges, reciprocal visits by lower-level functionaries, and U.S. arms sales to China.

In the aftermath of Reagan's April 1984 visit to Beijing, U.S.-PRC military relations quickly developed. Unlike the Carter administration, the Reagan administration engaged in little or no debate over the value of military exchanges with China. Once Chinese leaders decided to move forward, military relations rapidly developed. Regarding high-level exchanges, Chinese Defense Minister Zhang Aiping reciprocated the 1983 Weinberger visit with a June 1984 visit to Washington. By the end of the Reagan administration, the chairman of the Joint Chiefs of Staff and various U.S. service secretaries and chiefs had visited Beijing, and their Chinese counterparts had all visited Washington. As a result, when Weinberger returned to Beijing in 1987, he held much more fruitful discussions with Chinese leaders than he had in 1983.[107]

Parallelling these senior-level exchanges were significant developments among functional units. The highest-profile developments were the operational contacts between Chinese and U.S. naval vessels in the South China Sea in 1986 and the port call to Qingdao by three U.S. naval vessels in November 1986. Equally important were the exchanges between U.S. and Chinese military delegations specializing in such areas as logistics, management, maintenance, and military medicine.[108] This combination of high-level and functional exchanges was the culmination of the Carter administration's efforts to develop institutional ties between the two militaries.

The two sides also entered into an arms-sales relationship. For the United States, arms sales to China contributed to its ability to defend itself against the Soviet Union and consolidated the security relationship, thereby creating additional burdens on Soviet diplomacy and defense planning. For China, access to Western military technology enabled it to improve its defense capability at a more rapid rate than would otherwise have been possible and to enhance

China's overall technology capabilities as its engineers learned from the production process. But there were limits to the arms-sales relationship. There were four categories of military technology that the United States would not sell to China: technology that would improve Chinese capability regarding strategic missiles, nuclear weapons, intelligence, and anti-submarine warfare. And within these constraints, Washington would only sell China defensive equipment that would not threaten U.S. allies in the region or alter the mainland-Taiwan military balance, thereby invoking the Taiwan Relations Act.[109] In addition, China possessed limited amounts of foreign exchange and thus preferred to buy the technology and production capabilities rather than purchase large quantities of finished products.

Within these constraints, China and the United States were able to develop an arms-transfer relationship. In June 1984, the United States granted China eligibility for the U.S. Foreign Military Sales program. By the end of the Reagan administration, the two sides had reached agreements calling for the United States to sell China four military technology programs: a modernization package for a large-caliber artillery plant, MK 46 Mod 2 anti-submarine torpedoes, artillery-locating radar, and an advanced avionics package for China's F-8 interceptor jet. Negotiations also were taking place concerning other military equipment.[110]

In addition to developing bilateral military cooperation, the resolution of the Taiwan issues made possible further development of intelligence cooperation. In February 1984, less than two months after Premier Zhao Ziyang's visit to Washington, Director of Central Intelligence William Casey secretly visited Beijing, becoming the second director of the CIA to visit China. He held a successful round of meetings with the head of Chinese intelligence and the Chinese foreign minister concerning such issues as Afghanistan and the Soviet Union. By this time, the United States was purchasing much of the military matériel it was providing to the resistance forces in Afghanistan directly from China. The Reagan administration also expanded intelligence sharing with China regarding the Soviet nuclear weapons program. During the mid 1980s, the United States established in China additional monitoring equipment, which Chinese technicians used to monitor Soviet nuclear tests, providing copies of the data to the United States. There was even cooperation regarding developments in Central America. When the Reagan administration sought covert Chinese cooperation in arming the U.S.-supported Contras in their war with the Nicaraguan Sandinista government, Beijing was pleased to comply. The chief of the military mission at the Chinese embassy in Washington negotiated the cooperation with White House officials.[111]

THE DEVELOPMENT OF ECONOMIC AND EDUCATIONAL TIES

U.S.-PRC economic relations also flourished during this period. Building on the objectives and the accomplishments of the Carter administration, the Reagan administration encouraged the development of trade relations. Most important was its decision to reclassify China to export category "V" immediately prior to Secretary of Commerce Baldridge's May 1983 visit to China. Although the Carter administration had liberalized exports controls by moving China from export category "Y," comprised of Soviet-bloc countries, to category "P," which permitted enhanced Chinese access to nonlethal military equipment, further liberalization by the Reagan administration provided the additional stimulus required for expanded trade.

As noted earlier, China clearly had the most to gain from expanded economic relations, insofar as it would gain access to advanced technology and the foreign currency required to purchase the technology. The United States would also gain, however, insofar as economic relations would promote stable political relations and continued economic and political reform in China. Similarly, U.S.-PRC trade would benefit various economic sectors in the United States, creating domestic support for stable relations. The harm done by Chinese imports to specific U.S. industries and concern in the Defense Department over technology leakage nonetheless made expanded trade with the PRC contentious in the United States.

The new U.S. technology-export regulations for China established three categories of items—a green zone, a yellow zone, and a red zone. The debate within the administration concerned which technology could be included in the green zone and thus receive export licenses without prior interagency review. The debate intensified as the president's April 1984 summit neared. DOD officials concerned with policy issues and the Commerce and State Departments wanted to offer China an attractive list of available high-technology items. But other DOD officials, including Richard Perle, continued to argue for a relatively restrictive green-zone list. As in the past, Weinberger was unable to bring the issue to closure, and the final decisions on many items were only made when the president was traveling to China on Air Force One.[112]

These debates continued throughout Reagan's two terms. Beijing frequently complained that Washington unnecessarily withheld from China technology desirable for Chinese industrial modernization.[113] Nonetheless, these disputes affected only the margins of trade relations; trade flourished during the Reagan administration, and both sides realized important benefits.

By the end of the Reagan administration, the United States had become a major market for Chinese exports. Indeed, Chinese textile exports to the United States developed into a major source of Beijing's foreign exchange, despite recurring friction in the textile negotiations. As in earlier years, in both 1983 and 1986, negotiations broke down over U.S. quotas on China's textile exports, and Washington unilaterally imposed quotas on additional categories, so that by 1986, over 90 percent of Chinese textile imports were subject to controls. Nevertheless, China adjusted to the new restrictions and the importance of its textile exports to the United States continued to grow.

U.S.-PRC economic relations also promoted Chinese modernization and technology transfer to China through trade and direct U.S. investment in China. Not only did the Chinese economy profit from the development of a more modern industrial plant, foreign investment also promoted technology transfer through the training of Chinese employees and accumulation of foreign reserves through sales of the final products to foreign markets. By the end of the Reagan administration, the United States was the largest investor in the Chinese economy, easily surpassing total Japanese investment. Most of the U.S. investment was in oil exploration and in hotel and manufacturing projects.[114]

Various sectors of the U.S. economy also benefited from U.S.-PRC trade. By 1989, the United States annually exported nearly $6 billion of goods to China. U.S. wheat exporters, fertilizer producers, aircraft manufacturers, and timber companies were the major beneficiaries. In 1988–89, for example, China purchased one-sixth of all U.S. fertilizer production and was the largest purchaser of U.S. wheat. U.S. importers also benefited from trade relations. U.S. retailers and ultimately the American consumer benefited from access to inexpensive Chinese apparel and toys.[115] U.S.-PRC economic relations had created a number of groups possessing an interest in stable relations.

There was one issue, however, where economic cooperation conflicted with strategic interests, thus requiring protracted negotiations and compromise—U.S.-PRC cooperation on the development of the Chinese nuclear energy industry. The negotiations over this agreement underscore the difference between purely economic negotiations and negotiations involving strategic interests, showing the importance of asymmetrical strategic interests in determining the outcome of negotiations.[116]

There certainly were complementary interests encouraging cooperation in the nuclear-energy field. In the early 1980s, there was growing interest in the United States in exporting nuclear energy technology to China. The U.S. nuclear energy industry had been in steady decline, and it was hoped that the Chinese market would enable it to survive. U.S.-PRC cooperation in nuclear energy also seemed an ideal way for the United States to consolidate relations after a period of considerable bilateral turmoil and at a time when the administration remained concerned about Soviet power. And the advantage for China was obvious—its infant nuclear energy industry would benefit from access to U.S. technology.

Nevertheless, U.S.-PRC cooperation in nuclear energy production turned out to be a very controversial issue. Because China was not a signatory to the Nuclear Non-Proliferation Treaty (NPT), a bilateral agreement delineating the restrictions on the use and export of U.S. nuclear technology by China was required for American companies to export such technology to China. The United States first discussed with China cooperation in nuclear energy during Secretary of State Haig's June 1981 visit to Beijing and proposed a formal agreement in September 1981, but owing to the tension in relations during the early part of the Reagan administration, neither side actively pursued the matter until 1983.[117] In late 1983, after China joined the International Atomic Energy Agency, the United States raised the subject again, but China still refused to sign the NPT. Most important, its assistance to Pakistan's nuclear-weapons program indicated that it could not be trusted with U.S. nuclear technology. Under these circumstances, the Reagan administration needed firmer Chinese commitments regarding nonproliferation and Sino-Pakistani relations in order to secure congressional approval of a U.S.-PRC nuclear cooperation agreement.

Chinese cooperation required high-level leadership statements committing China to nonproliferation. During Reagan's April 1984 visit to Beijing, Zhao Ziyang stated that Chinese leaders did "not advocate or encourage nuclear proliferation. We do not engage in it ourselves nor do we help other countries to develop nuclear weapons." This and similar statements, including private assurances regarding future Chinese adherence to this policy, were sufficient to secure the president's initials on the agreement. Nonetheless, U.S. intelligence continued to report covert Chinese assistance to Pakistan's nuclear program. Chinese leaders were evidently distorting the facts in order to reach agreement.

It was clear that China was not going to end its assistance program to Pakistan in order to gain access to U.S. nuclear energy technology. Not only did Beijing already have access to French, German, British, and Japanese technology, but compromise on this issue would require China to sacrifice its security position in South Asia for the sake of economic and technology interests. By the mid 1970s, Pakistan was the PRC's remaining security partner in a region where China had fought a war against India in 1962, and Beijing was apparently intent on guaranteeing Pakistan's military security against far more powerful India by aiding its nuclear program. Gaining access to U.S. nuclear technology was an insufficient inducement for China to end its assistance to Pakistan. Hence, it was up to the Reagan administration either to forgo an agreement with China on exports of nuclear technology or compromise by sacrificing its nonproliferation objectives, thus incurring criticism from domestic groups that regarded ending the proliferation of nuclear weapons as more important than U.S.-PRC cooperation.[118] Ultimately, motivated by both foreign policy and domestic economic interests, the Reagan administration accepted the political and foreign policy costs of the agreement, accepting Chinese assurances at face value and disregarding Chinese transfers of nuclear technology to Pakistan. The administration signed the agreement and submitted it to Congress in July 1985, where it was ultimately approved.

Complementing expanded U.S.-PRC cooperation in military and economic relations was the continued expansion of U.S.-PRC educational exchanges. Indeed, the one area that had not been affected by the heightened political tension over Taiwan was China's interest in using U.S. universities to train its next generation of scientists. Beijing had already developed a stake in education exchanges in 1979–80, and it was not about to disrupt them over U.S.-Taiwan relations, notwithstanding its refusal to develop trade relations while the Taiwan issue remained unresolved. By 1983, nearly twenty thousand students and senior scholars from the PRC had studied in the United States. The vast majority specialized in the physical, health, and computer sciences and in engineering. This trend continued throughout the Reagan administration's second term. The Chinese government reported that by early 1988, over 36,000 scholars had visited the United States. At this time, two-thirds of all PRC students studying abroad were in the United States. China clearly benefited from this relationship—of the 36,000 visitors to U.S. academic institutions through early 1988, nearly 9,000 had returned to China.[119]

Thus, after China reconciled itself to U.S. policy on Taiwan, U.S.-PRC relations developed along a number of paths fruitful of long-term stability and consolidated political relations. Moving beyond strategic cooperation, expanded relations allowed various sectors of each government bureaucracy and society to develop interests in stable U.S.-PRC cooperation. Prior to normalization, and largely until 1983, the interest in relations was limited to the individual leaders and a limited number of specialists on the other country. By 1988, significant elements in both countries had developed a stake in bilateral relations.

This is not to say that during this period the relationship did not experience difficulties. Insofar as there were new points of contact, there were also new issues to differ about. China continued to complain about U.S. quotas on Chinese textile exports to the United States, and trade relations led to trade imbalances, first to the detriment of China and then to the detriment of the United States. The interplay of different cultural and leadership attitudes toward research also gave rise to problems in early educational exchanges. And as China expanded its sale of weapons to Third World countries, including the sale of Silkworm Missiles to Iran and CSS2 intermediate-range ballistic missiles to Saudi Arabia, doubts emerged in the United States over the wisdom of military-related technology transfer to China. In 1987, Washington temporarily suspended its review and liberalization of its controls on technology exports to China. Similarly, in the context of the demise of the Soviet threat, burgeoning U.S-Soviet détente, and the first signs of the end of the Cold War, the American public focused its attention on China's human rights policy, and it did not like what it saw. Thus, beginning in 1987, human rights emerged as an issue in U.S.-PRC relations.[120]

On balance, however, the development of new cooperative ties made a significant contribution to stable U.S.-PRC relations. To the extent that new issues arose in the relationship, there were significant interests on both sides seeking to contain the conflict and prevent it from undermining cooperative relations. By the end of the Reagan administration, Beijing and Washington had developed such a stake in the relationship that even the demise of the strategic imperative for cooperation did not lead either to lack of interest in either country or to stagnant bilateral relations. In retrospect, this was perhaps the greatest achievement in U.S.-PRC relations since rapprochement. For over twenty years, the two countries had managed to navigate the hazards of an exceedingly complex relationship to lay the foundation for a relationship that could withstand the vicissitudes of international circumstances and security interests, so that relations developed independent of strategic considerations. For two countries that had the potential to wreak havoc on each other and on the world, this was a worthy accomplishment.

Conclusion

The irony of the Reagan administration's China policy is that the American president most personally attached to Taiwan, and a president more suspicious of Beijing than any president since Richard Nixon, developed the most successful U.S. policy toward the PRC since the original rapprochement between the two countries. Not only did Ronald Reagan's China policy serve U.S. interests in developing stable and cooperative relations at minimal costs to other U.S. interests, he also developed bipartisan support for it. Moreover, there is further irony in the fact that policies that were divisive and destructive of bipartisan support for Reagan's defense policies were a basic source of this success. His advocacy of the MX missile and simultaneous development of both the B-1 and B-2 bomber, his deployment of Pershing II missiles in Europe, and his Strategic Defense Initiative all aroused significant domestic opposition. But his decision to implement these policies was a major factor in promoting U.S. objectives vis-à-vis China.

There is also irony in the development of China's U.S. policy. China's ultimate inability to overcome U.S. steadfastness on Taiwan and extract additional U.S. concessions reflected the emergence of a U.S. policy toward the Soviet Union that Chinese leaders had been advocating since the early 1970s. China had long sought the resurgence of U.S. will to contain Soviet "hegemonism." Now that the United States had adopted China's preferred policy, Chinese leaders were compelled to adjust to China's reduced international influence and adopt a more compliant posture on significant Chinese foreign policy interests. Moreover, once China was compelled to shelve the Taiwan issue, it developed a foreign policy far more conducive to its national interest. After years of battling the United States over Taiwan, the PRC developed significant access to the economies of the advanced industrial countries, which did far more for China's national interest than any U.S. concession on Taiwan could ever do.

These developments in U.S.-PRC relations reflected the inherent asymmetries in U.S.-PRC relations. Yet they also revealed the extent to which mutually beneficial relations were obtainable despite significant conflicts of interests. Through the 1980s, Washington and Beijing never fully resolved many of the issues that had plagued relations since the first days of rapprochement. But their statesmen succeeded in developing policies that enabled the United States and China to cooperate notwithstanding those differences.

CHAPTER 8

Conclusion

NEGOTIATING COOPERATION

By the end of the 1980s, Americans and Chinese had established extensive political, military, economic, and cultural cooperation. This development was particularly remarkable insofar as for the twenty years of the 1950s and 1960s U.S.-PRC relations had been frozen in deep mistrust and hostility. This remarkable transformation in U.S.-PRC relations not only benefited both sides strategically but also established the basis for long-term cooperation in a wide range of nongovernmental activities.

But during the twenty years of U.S.-PRC cooperation, there were also extensive negotiations over serious conflicts of interest. For cooperation to occur, Washington and Beijing had to manage these conflicts to avoid escalated tension. These were very successful negotiations. Although there were periods of heightened tension, at no time did either side allow the tension to dominate the relationship and lead to setbacks.

Many factors contributed to the stable development of U.S.-PRC cooperation. Foremost among these was the common U.S. and Chinese interest in resisting Soviet power. This interest brought the two countries together in the early 1970s and promoted cooperation until the end of the 1980s. Nonetheless, security concerns affected each state differently, and their effect on each changed over time. The result was that the relative security of the two countries was constantly shifting, thus creating a shifting interest in cooperation and distinct negotiating outcomes as the cost each side was willing to incur to maintain cooperation evolved.

In the United States, increased concern for Soviet power invariably led U.S. policy makers to search for ways to expand U.S.-PRC cooperation and increased their willingness to consider compromise of long-held U.S. positions. This was the case during the early Nixon years, the Ford administration, and the later years of the Carter administration and the early years of the Reagan administration. The reverse also occurred. When the United States appraised the trend in U.S.-Soviet relations relatively optimistically, it preferred stalemated negotiations to compromise. At the height of détente under the Nixon administration, in the early part of the Carter administration, and after 1982 in the Reagan administration, American resistance to compromise vis-à-vis China reflected policy makers' positive assessment of the trend in U.S.-Soviet relations. The Ford administration consistently viewed Soviet policy with alarm, and was thus consistently dissatisfied with stagnant U.S.-PRC relations.

Chinese decision makers were similarly affected by changes in the international environment; China's policy toward the United States reflected its appraisal of the trend toward either strategic parity or asymmetry in U.S.-Soviet relations, particularly as perceived by U.S. policy makers, as well as of the immediacy of the Soviet threat to China. But unlike the United States, China lacked the ability to improve its security by mobilizing internal resources. Changes in Chinese defense spending could not even begin to offset Soviet military power aimed at China. Moreover, given the state of Sino-Soviet relations, China could not reduce the Soviet threat without making unacceptable compromises. Neither the PRC's defense policy nor its Soviet policy could affect China's basic international condition. China's security was thus far more dependent on external circumstances than that of the United States.

The contrast between U.S. and Chinese power affected China's relative security situation in two ways. First, developments in U.S.-Soviet relations had a much greater impact on Chinese security than developments in Sino-Soviet relations had on U.S. security. China attentively watched superpower relations, because daily events could affect Chinese security; the United States watched Sino-Soviet relations because the *potential* for change cautioned against complacency. Second, China's relative weakness vis-à-vis both superpowers, including its limited ability to improve its military capability, and the correspondingly greater threat of Soviet power to China made the PRC more dependent on U.S.-PRC security cooperation than the United States; isolation would weigh significantly more on Beijing than on Washington.

These differences in U.S. and Chinese security circumstances had a profound effect on China's U.S. policy. When Chinese leaders believed that Washington assessed the U.S.-Soviet balance confidently, as it did during the superpower détente of the early 1970s, the early years of the Carter administration, and the later years of the Reagan administration, Beijing was forced to adopt a compliant posture toward U.S. policy that undermined Chinese interests. This explains China's strategic decision, motivated by Soviet and Vietnamese policy in Indochina in the context of relative U.S. complacency about the Soviet Union, to compromise in 1978 on U.S. arms sales to Taiwan for the sake of normalizing U.S.-PRC relations. It also explains the response of the PRC to U.S. policy on arms sales to Taiwan in the mid 1980s. When Beijing ultimately understood that the U.S. strategic advantage enabled Washington to resist compromise with China, it reconciled itself to U.S. policy.

This dynamic also meant that Beijing acquired leverage only when strategic circumstances created heightened U.S. interest in cooperation with China. This was the case during the Ford administration, when Chinese leaders tried to use domestic instability in the United States and the inertia in U.S. foreign policy to pressure Henry Kissinger into early normalization of U.S.-PRC relations. Similarly, during the early years of the Reagan administration, Washington's alarm over the momentum of Soviet expansionism and the deterioration of U.S. military capability made U.S. decision makers, particularly Secretary of State Alexander Haig, vulnerable to Chinese pressure and encouraged them to adjust U.S. policy toward Taiwan in order to stabilize U.S.-PRC relations.

China's U.S. policy during the 1970s and 1980s was thus a function of evolving U.S. attitudes toward U.S.-Soviet relations. In U.S.-PRC negotiations, China was fundamentally a reactive state with extremely limited ability to take the initiative in bilateral relations. Chinese negotiators could only wait until international circumstances provided opportunities to achieve Beijing's foreign policy objectives, including increased U.S. disengagement from Taiwan.

Chinese weakness was also apparent in the different U.S. and Chinese objectives in cooperation. Whereas the United States sought cooperation in order to promote both U.S. security and détente with the Soviet Union, China's objective in strategic cooperation was solely to develop security through participation in an anti-Soviet coalition. In the 1970s and 1980s, the PRC was generally too weak to try to negotiate reduced conflict with Moscow, despite U.S.-PRC cooperation. Beijing's frequent complaints that the United States stood on China's shoulders to negotiate improved relations with Moscow thus reflected Chinese weakness as much as they did U.S. policy. Because Beijing simply lacked a corresponding ability to develop Sino-Soviet relations, it could not retaliate with similar tactics and was reduced to complaining and lobbying for changes in U.S. policy.[1]

But despite Chinese weakness, Beijing was able to make significant progress toward its objective of detaching the United States from Taiwan. To a significant extent, this success resulted in the emergence of a more equitable balance of leverage between the United States and China, which occurred when American leaders were willing to compromise because they believed that the United States faced a serious challenge from the Soviet Union. When such a balance occurred, the outcome was not stalemate but U.S. compromise. This was because the interests at stake with respect to Taiwan were not symmetrical. Whereas American interest in Taiwan reflected the legacy of a historical commitment, ideological affinity, domestic politics, and a general concern for U.S. security interests in Asia, Chinese interest involved enduring and vital security considerations and intense nationalist emotions. Thus, when strategic factors created a semblance of balance in U.S.-PRC bargaining relations, as during the early Reagan administration, this asymmetry apropos of Taiwan encouraged Washington to adopt a relatively conciliatory posture. In the circumstances, because concessions were relatively less damaging to U.S. interests, it was possible for China to compel U.S. policy makers to compromise on U.S. policy toward Taiwan.

By the end of the 1980s, however, China had failed to secure its final objective—the strategic isolation of Taiwan. Despite all Beijing's considerable efforts, Washington continued to sell advanced weapons and military technology to Taiwan. Similarly, Beijing had to give up its objective of securing an explicit U.S. agreement that Taiwan was Chinese territory. China simply never developed the leverage to compel the United States to "abandon" Taiwan; even the intense conditions of superpower Cold War rivalry could not generate sufficient Chinese leverage. However, China never relinquished its objective. Rather, it was compelled to wait for more favorable circumstances. Given the limits of its leverage during the height of superpower tension in the 1970s and 1980s, such circumstances will likely only occur when China becomes strong enough to end its dependence on other countries for its security—when its develops a truly "independent foreign policy."

Nonetheless, international factors and considerations of national interest do not provide a full explanation of U.S.-PRC negotiations during the 1970s and 1980s. Other factors intervened to influence

U.S. and Chinese policy on conflicts of interest. Domestic politics was certainly an influential factor in policy making. By all accounts, both Richard Nixon and Gerald Ford wanted to enhance U.S. security during their respective presidencies by normalizing relations with China, but domestic politics nonetheless led both presidents to defer normalization. President Nixon wanted to complete his second term in office; President Ford wanted to win election to a second term as president. Presidential transitions also affected U.S. policy. During the early period of his presidency, President Carter held a more sanguine view of the Soviet Union than President Ford had done, and this difference created a change in U.S. policy toward China. Similarly, despite the hardening of the Carter administration's Soviet policy, President Reagan was far more concerned with Soviet power than President Carter had been. This difference was reflected in the Reagan administration's initial willingness to compromise on U.S. arms sales to Taiwan, and then in its greater interest in developing military cooperation with China.

But even the role of domestic politics in U.S.-PRC relations reflected the disparity in each country's capabilities and strategic circumstances. Ultimately, China's strategic vulnerability and dependence on U.S.-PRC cooperation minimized the importance of domestic politics in Chinese foreign policy. Even when Chinese radicals pressed their ideological attack on Chinese foreign policy makers during the mid 1970s, they were prevented from participating in diplomacy and obliged to limit their attention to U.S.-PRC cultural and economic relations. Similarly, despite the high stakes involved, the wide range of policy issues in debate, and the greater participation of radical politicians in China's U.S. diplomacy, the succession from Mao to Deng in 1976–77 had only an almost imperceptible impact on China's U.S. policy. Chinese vulnerability to the Soviet threat and the uncertainty over U.S. resistance to Soviet expansion created the imperative of U.S.-PRC cooperation, and thus the need to resist domestic incentives to change foreign policy.

Moreover, China's relative strategic weakness affected the role of U.S. domestic politics in U.S.-PRC relations. Because the cost of heightened U.S.-PRC tension would disproportionately affect China, the Ford administration was able to resist Chinese pressures to normalize relations during a period of U.S. strategic vulnerability. The Ford administration imposed the international costs of President Ford's domestic political vulnerability on China, expressed as deferred normalization of relations and Chinese leaders' acquiescence to this, despite their expectation that the United States would accept Chinese conditions and normalize relations during Nixon's second term.

Miscalculations and individual perspectives further complicated the role of security circumstances in Chinese and U.S. policy making. Beijing miscalculated the value the Reagan administration assigned to U.S.-PRC cooperation in the aftermath of the negotiations leading to the August 17 communiqué. China's negotiating position on U.S. arms sales to Taiwan and a host of new issues in U.S. relations, such as Taiwan's participation in the Asian Development Bank, was predicated on China's outdated view that the United States would continue to compromise to maintain stable U.S.-PRC relations, as it had during the first eighteen months of the Reagan administration. U.S.-PRC conflict through the end of 1983 reflected the two countries contrasting assessments of American security, and thus of the U.S. inclination to compromise. Indeed, China's declaration of its "independent foreign policy" reflected the same miscalculation that given heightened superpower conflict, and with neither side assured of obtaining the advantage, China's value to both countries would increase, thus enabling it to adopt a more independent posture. Both the PRC's U.S. policy and its "independent foreign policy" were, however, based on outdated assumptions, and after a year of counterproductive conflict, except insofar as it enabled China to reassess its leverage, Beijing abandoned its bargaining offensive and adopted a relatively acquiescent U.S. policy. Furthermore, except in rhetoric, Beijing never implemented its independent foreign policy. Throughout the 1980s, China sought and developed consolidated military and security relations with the United States and developed closer economic relations with the United States than with any other country.

In the United States, the personal and shifting perspectives of policy makers on both U.S. security and China's strategic importance affected policy making. Jimmy Carter's initial disinclination to distrust Soviet intentions led him to alter the course of U.S.-PRC policy set by Nixon and Ford. Subsequently, his reevaluation of the Soviet threat led him to restore the policy of his predecessors. The Soviet Union had not changed between 1975 and 1978; rather, the American president's view of the Soviet Union changed. Each change led to a corresponding reappraisal of U.S.-PRC cooperation, and thus a corresponding change in China policy.

President Reagan's personal intervention in policy making and the transition to Alexander Haig and then to George Shultz as secretary of state in the Reagan administration had equally significant repercussions on U.S. China policy. Haig believed that the Soviet threat was all-encompassing, and that China was a vital element in reducing that threat. Haig's preoccupation with China encouraged Beijing to try to extract maximum concessions from Washington and led Haig to be willing to pay a high cost for U.S.-PRC cooperation. Ronald Reagan's decision in July 1982 to resist Haig's advice and follow his own policy inclination reveals the importance of personal perspectives on the outcome of negotiations. Similarly, George Shultz restored greater prudence to U.S.-China policy. He assessed the advantages of the United States in dealing with China differently, so that U.S. policy exhibited more restraint in response to Chinese demands under his guidance.

The importance of these developments in U.S. policy making underscores the inconsistency in U.S. policy toward China during the Cold War. The combination of American power and democracy created a foreign policy that was far less predictable than that of China. Over the twenty years of U.S.-PRC cooperation, the United States had three successions and four presidents. In contrast, China had only one succession and two preeminent leaders. Moreover, in contrast to the United States, where presidents and their foreign policy advisers often come from outside the existing policy making structure, may not share the views of their predecessors, and will often prefer to chart their own courses, in China, preeminent leaders arise through a patronage system and thus tend to share the predilections of their predecessors. Moreover, China's foreign policy elite remained stable across successions. The transition from Mao to Deng did not, therefore, produce changes in China's assessment of its security situation and of U.S.-Soviet relations. In consequence, Beijing's conditions for normalization of relations did not change either. Elite transitions and idiosyncratic policy perspectives in China affected U.S.-PRC relations far less than such factors in the United States did.

The importance of domestic politics in U.S. foreign policy making was reflected in the close attention that Chinese leaders paid to changes both in American politics and in the U.S. policy-making elite and in their efforts to influence the relationship among U.S. policy makers. Chinese understanding of President Ford's domestic difficulties and of the potential implications of the change in policy makers in November 1975 affected Chinese policy toward the United States, including Chinese policy expressed in the December 1975 U.S.-China summit. Similarly, the evolution of China's negotiating policy toward the Reagan administration in 1981–82 was influenced by Beijing's understanding of the changing role of Alexander Haig in the policy-making process and his replacement by George Shultz. Thus, China took into account the American policy-making process when making U.S. policy. Moreover, at times, Chinese leaders tried to influence that process. Beijing's publicity for the views of James Schlesinger and its efforts during the Ford administration to arrange for him to visit Beijing appeared designed to bolster his authority in U.S. policy making. Its 1977 invitation to Zbigniew Brzezinski to visit China had a similar objective. In each case, Chinese leaders sought to bolster the authority of the U.S. policy maker most inclined to develop relations with China. In contrast, the combination of the greater policy-making centralization in China and the secrecy surrounding Chinese elite conflict meant that U.S. policy makers rarely, if ever, tailored U.S. policy in response to developments in Chinese domestic politics.[2]

Finally, it is important to note just how little ideology affected U.S.-PRC negotiations. Concerning U.S. policy, in 1975, Ronald Reagan opposed Gerald Ford's China policy partly because he was ideologically inclined to resist sacrificing Taiwan's interests for the sake of better U.S.-PRC relations. But it was political considerations that persuaded the president to defer normalization of relations. When Reagan became president, his opposition to communism did not deter him from seeking closer U.S.-PRC relations. He simply did not want to sacrifice U.S.-Taiwan relations. Moreover, the strategic importance of U.S.-PRC relations compelled even him to adjust U.S. policy on arms sales to Taiwan. Other than the partial exception of U.S. policy during the 1975–76 presidential campaign, ideology never inhibited U.S. leaders from seeking strategic, economic, and cultural cooperation with China.

In a predicament similar to Ronald Reagan's, Chinese leaders found it hard to accept even the need to rely on the United States to protect Chinese security. The United States had not only been a strategic adversary throughout the 1950s and 1960s, it was and remained an ideological adversary. China's leaders in the 1970s and 1980s were Marxist-Leninist revolutionaries who believed in the necessity for struggle against capitalist-inspired imperialism and in the innate threat posed to socialism by capitalist countries. To have to cooperate with the world's most powerful capitalist country was both discomfiting and politically threatening. Chinese cooperation with the United States undermined one of the foundations of the legitimacy of the Communist Party of China both during the Maoist period, when radical ideology was very influential in domestic politics, and in the post-Mao period, when China's pragmatic dependence on the United States extended from security to economics. It is thus not surprising that the more ideologically doctrinaire Chinese leaders, who were not responsible for foreign policy, tried to use China's U.S. policy to weaken the power of their political adversaries in the elite politics of the 1970s and 1980s.

Ultimately, however, China's strategic vulnerability minimized the role of ideology in China's U.S. policy. Even when Chinese radicals pressed their ideological attack on Chinese moderates in the Foreign Ministry during the mid 1970s, China's U.S. policy did not evince any interest in reversing the trend of cooperation with the United States. During the 1980s, China's policy toward strategic cooperation, textile negotiations, and educational exchanges reflected minimal ideological influence.[3]

The exception to this was Mao's personal ideological impact on Chinese international trade and culture policies. Mao made strategic policy as a strategic realist, but he made economic and cultural policy as a socialist revolutionary. After Mao died, China's policy on the full range of nonstrategic interactions with Western countries was transformed. Nonetheless, the distinction between economic and strategic policy is instructive. In matters of war and peace, alignment policy, and strategic cooperation, Mao was a realist. He was able to isolate the effect of his ideologically motivated policies to areas that did not affect China's immediate strategic situation. Moreover, Mao's economic and cultural policies were not part of his U.S. policy. They reflected a posture toward the entire global community rather than a special ideological challenge posed by the United States. Mao looked on the United States as a distinct strategic actor in international politics and developed a U.S. policy that reflected America's unique role in Chinese security. Indeed, Beijing's policy on U.S.-Taiwan relations, an issue that elicited instinctual ideological, political, and nationalist passions in China, was one of the most realistic of Mao's foreign policies.

The preceding chapters provide six case studies of U.S.-PRC negotiations. Each case is characterized by a distinct combination of international and domestic factors affecting policy making in Washington and Beijing and the resulting negotiating outcome. No single factor can explain the changing dynamics of U.S.-PRC relations during the 1970s and 1980s. During these twenty years, a changing combination of variables came together to produce a number of distinct bilateral outcomes. The most that can be said is that leaders in both countries first considered their respective country's strategic circumstances when making policy, and that they preferred to make policy based on these factors. When policy makers disagreed over policy, there was no dispute over the importance of strategic considerations. Rather, they simply held competing strategic perspectives. When domestic politics did influence policy, policy makers considered it an obstacle to implementing their preferred, internationally derived foreign policies.

American and Chinese Approaches to Negotiations

The twenty years of U.S.-PRC negotiations reveal each side's distinct approach to negotiating conflicts of interest. With the exception of the later Reagan years, whenever China placed the Taiwan issue on the agenda, Washington approached the issue as a problem requiring solution. The most pressing concern of the United States was developing U.S.-PRC strategic cooperation, and U.S.-Taiwan relations were, for the most part, considered an obstacle to that objective. American policy makers also believed that Chinese leaders shared their interest in maximizing cooperation, and that they were prepared to work with the United States to solve the "Taiwan problem." If correctly managed, they believed, the Taiwan issue would not interfere in U.S.-PRC strategic cooperation.

American policy makers thus frequently entered into U.S.-PRC negotiations without a clear concept of what U.S. negotiating objectives were and what the negotiating strategy best able to secure those objectives might be. Rather, they perceived the negotiations as an opportunity for American and Chinese leaders to resolve a dispute that prevented their two countries from pursuing their common interest in cooperation against the Soviet Union. U.S. diplomats tended to ask what U.S. concessions were necessary to develop and maintain cooperation.

Chinese leaders, on the other hand, consistently viewed the negotiations as an adversarial process, in which they were determined to extract from the United States as many concessions as possible on U.S.-Taiwan relations without significantly affecting China's immediate security interests. In contrast to U.S. negotiators, Chinese negotiators pursued two sets of interests simultaneously—strategic cooperation and recovery of Taiwan. Although they clearly placed a higher priority on promoting Chinese security against the Soviet Union, they never lost sight of their interest in detaching the United

States from Taiwan. In contrast to U.S. negotiators, Chinese negotiators asked what the maximum they could achieve in the negotiations was.

These contrasting positions also help to explain each country's distinct approach to the bilateral relationship. Throughout the 1970s and 1980s, the United States considered strategic cooperation with the PRC the sole vital interest between the two countries. China, on the other hand, considered strategic cooperation as merely the most pressing objective among a host of other very important Chinese objectives in U.S.-PRC relations. Thus, where the United States sought to project an image of solidarity and promote positive developments, China often felt that tension was a positive factor if it helped to achieve other Chinese objectives, such as detaching the United States from Taiwan.

For the United States, cooperation with the PRC was an element in U.S. leadership of a worldwide anti-Soviet coalition. Beijing, however, rejected the concept of Chinese participation in a U.S.-led coalition. Participation in a U.S.-led coalition implied loss of Chinese initiative, and thus acquiescence to the status quo in U.S.-Taiwan relations. It would also imply Chinese acknowledgement of China's subordinate status in the global balance, which would undermined China's self-image and the stature of its leaders in domestic politics. If nothing else, the rhetoric of the independent foreign policy served to mask the reality of China's dependence on cooperating with the United States in resistance to Soviet power.

The one exception to this pattern occurred just days before Deng Xiaoping's visit to the United States in January 1979, when the Chinese leader acknowledged Chinese poverty and said that China wanted to "unite" with United States and Japan. Only then would China "carry weight" in the anti-Soviet struggle.[4] The possibility of the Soviet Union attacking China in response to China's imminent invasion of Vietnam had compelled Deng to swallow Chinese pride and even risk domestic criticism in order to bolster Chinese security.

One negotiating strategy that China frequently employed in its unrelenting effort to recover Taiwan was its willingness to forgo agreement rather than accept an unsatisfactory agreement. When Chinese leaders found themselves in a poor bargaining position regarding Taiwan, rather than discussing the issue, they sidestepped it, dropping it from the agenda. They thus retained the option of raising the issue and reaching agreement on it at another time without the encumbrance of prior commitments. This was the case dur-

ing the Nixon and Kissinger visits to China and during the normalization negotiations in 1978. Chinese leaders' readiness to avoid the
Taiwan issue and other troublesome aspects of negotiations, such as
the arms-sales issue, did not reflect Beijing's lack of interest in Taiwan or its willingness to shelve contentious issues in order to promote security cooperation, but rather recognition of China's lack of
leverage at that particular time. Whereas U.S. statesmen often interpreted such Chinese flexibility as reflecting the strategic acumen or
realistic perspective of the leaders of the PRC, it actually reflected
their immediate negotiating strategy apropos of a vital Chinese
interest.

The contrasting approach to the bilateral relationship also affected the course of negotiations. China was often content to defer
compromise and agreement until it extracted maximum U.S. concessions; it never compromised until it had to, often at the last
minute. It adopted an "optimizing" bargaining strategy, often characteristic of revolutionary societies. But whereas China rejected
compromise until necessary, the United States adopted its problem-
solving approach and presented China with a succession of conciliatory proposals, hoping to elicit Chinese compromise and renewed
cooperation. The United States adopted an "accommodative" approach to resolving conflict.[5] In such circumstances, Chinese leaders acquiesced only when the United States refused to make additional concessions, leaving them with the choice of either compromise or escalated conflict. Beijing always chose compromise.
This process characterized the negotiations over each of the three
communiqués and the negotiations over Taiwan and other contentious issues in 1983. It has also characterized U.S.-China economic
negotiations.[6]

Whereas China was content to let negotiations continue, the
United States frequently relied on deadlines to elicit Chinese concessions and to bring the negotiations to an end. Deadlines worked
to U.S. advantage during Kissinger's first visit to China in July 1971,
Nixon's July 1972 visit to Beijing, the 1978 normalization negotiations, and the 1981–82 negotiations over U.S. arms sales to Taiwan.
The United States also employed deadlines in the negotiations over
the various textile agreements. After observing U.S.-PRC negotiations over an extended period of time, one Chinese diplomat observed that use of a deadline was a typical U.S. negotiating tactic.[7]

But even when deadlines compelled China to compromise and
reach agreement, it would reopen negotiations at a later date. China
does not "agree to disagree." If an agreement is preferable to no

agreement, rather than reach a comprehensive agreement that commits China to unsatisfactory conditions, Chinese leaders prefer a partial agreement. This allows them to defer negotiations over other issues to a later time when China may be better positioned to achieve their objective. As with China's negotiating style in business transactions, "nothing is ever final" in U.S. diplomatic negotiations with China.[8] Shortly after the normalization of relations, for example, Beijing reopened the arms-sales issue, and after the communiqué of August 17, 1982, it continued to press for more U.S. concessions on arms sales to China. Thinking the existing agreement had resolved an issue, however, U.S. policy makers believed that if they could only calm Chinese suspicions of U.S. intentions, the prior agreement would suffice, and new negotiations would not be necessary. Alexander Haig fell victim to this illusion.

Over the twenty years of negotiations, these dynamics produced the long-term trend of a succession of U.S. concessions to Beijing. China adopted "salami tactics" on the Taiwan issue. In each round of the negotiations, it tried to slice a little more off of the U.S. position. By the middle of the Reagan administration, the United States had moved a significant distance from its original policy on Taiwan.[9]

To a great extent, these differing negotiating styles, the bilateral dynamics, and the long-term characteristics of the negotiations can be explained by each country's distinct position on the Taiwan issue. As both the weaker and dissatisfied power, China required U.S. concessions to achieve its objective, but could only take the diplomatic offensive when its strategic circumstances permitted. The United States, on the other hand, was the status-quo state. Because Washington began negotiating in 1969 on the basis of its preferred position, it was content to focus on U.S.-PRC strategic cooperation against the Soviet Union and to push the Taiwan issue off the agenda. Washington was thus usually on the defensive in U.S.-PRC negotiations, unprepared for periodic Chinese efforts to pressure it to change its Taiwan policy.

From Cold War Cooperation to Conflict and Cooperation in the Post–Cold War Era

Despite each side's interest in optimizing its position on Taiwan, and despite all of the international and domestic factors influencing policy making in Washington and Beijing, from 1969 to 1989 the United States and China successfully managed their bilateral conflicts. Diplomats in Washington and Beijing deserve credit for this significant accomplishment. American and Chinese leaders had the requisite political courage and imagination to create mutually satisfactory solutions to difficult issues.

But these leaders had to manage the Taiwan issue because their countries faced the common imperative of cooperation. The United States and China viewed the Soviet Union as very dangerous, and each sought strategic cooperation to improve their respective security. Taiwan was never unimportant, but it was always less important. These conditions compelled both sides to focus on cooperation, rather than conflict, and to minimize contention. The challenge for Beijing was thus to achieve its objective regarding Taiwan without disturbing U.S.-PRC cooperation. The United States sought to maintain ties with Taiwan while simultaneously developing U.S.-PRC cooperation.

Throughout this period, even the domestic politics of both countries favored conflict management. Leaders in both Beijing and Washington could not afford the charge of having "lost" a key strategic ally. Although President Ford feared legitimating Ronald Reagan's charge that he was "abandoning Taiwan," the dominant sentiment throughout the 1970s and 1980s in the United States was that the White House could not allow the Taiwan issue to jeopardize U.S.-PRC cooperation. Alexander Haig recalls warning Reagan about just this issue and the risk of eliciting charges from Democrats of having "lost China."[10]

Chinese leaders faced a similar imperative. Despite their anti-imperialist ideology and their opposition to collaboration with capitalist countries, Chinese radicals did not dare upset U.S.-PRC relations during the summer of 1976 when Chairman Mao was incapacitated. Jiang Qing and her radical colleagues could not develop a reputation for strategic irresponsibility if they hoped to survive the succession. Indeed, Hua Guofeng adopted a conciliatory stance toward Taiwan and U.S.-PRC relations during the summer of 1976 and after Mao died that September. Because of his background as a beneficiary of the Cultural Revolution, he needed to establish his ability to manage U.S.-PRC relations.

The development of strategic cooperation thus did not reflect a "special relationship" between China and the United States. Rather, U.S.-PRC strategic cooperation and the negotiations over Taiwan and other contentious issues reflected heightened superpower tension, significantly shifting superpower capabilities, and perception by the United States and China of a common threat.

The characteristics of U.S.-PRC negotiations during the 1970s and

1980s do not apply to the 1990s. Political cleavages and economic disaster crippled what was once the Soviet Union and is now a much weaker Russia. Without the Soviet Union, there is no longer a common threat creating the necessity for U.S.-PRC cooperation. The demise of the Soviet Union has created the post–Cold War era. International relations have been transformed, including U.S.-PRC relations.[11]

The most obvious and significant repercussion of this transformation has been the inability of Washington and Beijing to manage conflicts of interest with minimal impact on cooperative relations. The Chinese Communist Party's violent repression of the Chinese democratic movement in 1989 led to the disruption of cooperation in diplomatic, military, economic, and cultural relations. Although the June 1989 Beijing massacre was the most public display of Chinese government repression since 1949, U.S. leaders and the American public have always strongly objected to Beijing's human rights policies. But whereas during the 1970s and 1980s the development of cooperative relations was unaffected by differences over human rights, they have become the most salient issue in U.S.-PRC relations in the post–Cold War era, absent the imperative for cooperation against the Soviet Union.

This same post–Cold War process has shaped the entire agenda of U.S.-PRC relations. Serious conflict has developed over various trade issues and over weapons proliferation. Whereas in the 1970s and 1980s, the agenda was cooperation, and conflict required careful management, in the 1990s, the agenda is dominated by conflicts of interest. The challenge for Washington and Beijing is to deal with these conflicts of interests while simultaneously maintaining at least minimal cooperation. In the post–Cold War era, there will be persistent conflict and only limited and tentative cooperation in U.S.-PRC relations.

The contrast between the Cold War and post–Cold War eras of U.S.-PRC relations is clear in the changed impact of domestic politics on policy making. Whereas in the 1970s and 1980s, domestic politics in Washington and Beijing encouraged compromise solutions to conflicts of interest, in the 1990s, domestic politics in both countries imposes political cost on leaders suggesting compromise. In the absence of an immediate threat, the value of strategic cooperation is reduced, so that opposition politicians no longer have to refrain from using U.S.-PRC relations to weaken political adversaries. After the Cold War, opposition politicians in Beijing and Washington can adopt irresponsible policy positions designed to weaken incumbents, confident that policy makers will either resist the pressure to change policy or that policy change will have a minimal impact on immediate security concerns.

Post–Cold War U.S.-PRC cooperation has been undermined by the wider range of policy choice in both countries and the heightened salience of domestic politics with respect to the policy-making process. Nevertheless, both sides continue to have an interest in cooperation. Washington must cooperate with China to control the spread of ballistic missiles and nuclear weapons and to resolve conflicts in Indochina and on the Korean Peninsula. Beijing must cooperate with Washington to maintain its access to the U.S. market, a primary source of China's foreign exchange. Most important, the United States and China must cooperate to avoid the development of an adversarial relationship, which was so costly to both sides during the 1950s and 1960s.

But in contrast to the situation in the 1970s and 1980s, U.S. and Chinese interests in cooperation are not common interests. Rather, U.S.-PRC cooperation is primarily required to resolve conflicts of interest. Moreover, the issues at stake in the 1990s are less pressing than the immediate security interests of the Cold War were. Both of these factors make U.S.-PRC cooperation more difficult to achieve during the post–Cold War era than it was during the Cold War.

Thus far, however, despite polemics, Chinese and American leaders have managed to maintain important elements of cooperation. President Bush resisted often-partisan opposition to maintaining most-favored-nation trade status for Chinese exports to the United States. President Clinton abandoned his campaign-driven China policy and ultimately adopted the China policy of the Bush administration. Despite the pressure of succession politics, Chinese leaders have resisted demands from Chinese conservatives to reject compromise and have limited exports of missile and nuclear technologies and contributed to stability in Indochina and the Korean Peninsula. Most revealing, both sides have managed to avoid excessive conflict over Taiwan, despite expanded U.S.-Taiwan military relations and growing support on Taiwan for declaring itself an independent country. U.S.-PRC cooperation in the post–Cold War era is very difficult, but it remains an important and obtainable objective.

But to the extent that Chinese and U.S. leaders have been able to maintain the bare essentials of cooperation, they have benefited from the successes of their predecessors. In the 1990s, American and Chinese leaders have reached out to a variety of domestic interests to overcome the obstacles to cooperation. Most important, ten years of economic relations during the Carter and Reagan administrations and the leadership of Deng Xiaoping created significant U.S. and Chinese domestic interests with a stake in cooperation. Intellectuals in both countries also gained from exchanges and continue to promote cooperation. And despite the post-1989 suspension of military exchanges, U.S. and Chinese military leaders had benefited from cooperation and helped check the trend toward escalated conflict.

It is hard to imagine that even minimal U.S.-PRC cooperation could have survived the 1989 Beijing massacre had American and Chinese leaders not laid the foundations of cooperation during the previous twenty years. The basis for the development of U.S.-PRC relations in the 1970s and 1980s does not exist in the 1990s, but the legacy of American and Chinese diplomats negotiating for cooperation continues to shape relations in the post–Cold War era.

Appendixes

U.S.-PRC Joint Communiqués

The Shanghai Communiqué
(February 27, 1972)

JOINT COMMUNIQUÉ BETWEEN
THE PEOPLE'S REPUBLIC OF CHINA
AND THE UNITED STATES OF AMERICA

President Richard Nixon of the United States of America visited the People's Republic of China at the invitation of Premier Chou En-lai [Zhou Enlai] of the People's Republic of China from February 21 to February 28, 1972. Accompanying the President were Mrs. Nixon, U.S. Secretary of State William Rogers, Assistant to the President Dr. Henry Kissinger, and other American officials.

President Nixon met with Chairman Mao Tse-tung [Mao Zedong] of the Communist Party of China on February 21. The two leaders had a serious and frank exchange of views on Sino–U.S. relations and world affairs.

During the visit, extensive, earnest, and frank discussions were held between President Nixon and Primier Chou En-lai on the normalization of relations between the United States of America and the People's Republic of China, as well as on other matters of interest to both sides. In addition, Secretary of State William Rogers and Foreign Minister Chi P'eng-fei [Ji Pengfei] held talks in the same spirit.

President Nixon and his party visited Peking [Beijing] and viewed cultural, industrial and agricultural sites, and they also toured

Hangchow [Hangzhou] and Shanghai where, continuing discussions with Chinese leaders, they viewed similar places of interest.

The leaders of the People's Republic of China and the United States of America found it beneficial to have this opportunity, after so many years without contact, to present candidly to one another their views on a variety of issues. They reviewed the international situation in which important changes and great upheavals are taking place and expounded their respective positions and attitudes.

The U.S. side stated: Peace in Asia and peace in the world requires efforts both to reduce immediate tensions and to eliminate the basic causes of conflict. The United States will work for a just and secure peace: just, because it fulfills the aspirations of peoples and nations for freedom and progress; secure, because it removes the danger of foreign aggression. The United States supports individual freedom and social progress for all the peoples of the world, free of outside pressure or intervention. The United States believes that the effort to reduce tensions is served by improving communication between countries that have different ideologies so as to lessen the risks of confrontation through accident, miscalculation or misunderstanding. Countries should treat each other with mutual respect and be willing to compete peacefully, letting performance be the ultimate judge. No country should claim infallibility and each country should be prepared to re-examine its own attitudes for the common good. The United States stressed that the peoples of Indochina should be allowed to determine their destiny without outside intervention; its constant primary objective has been a negotiated solution; the eight-point proposal put forward by the Republic of Vietnam and the United States on January 27, 1972, represents a basis for the attainment of that objective; in the absence of a negotiated settlement the United States envisages the ultimate withdrawal of all U.S. forces from the region consistent with the aim of self-determination for each country of Indochina. The United States will maintain its close ties with and support for the Republic of Korea; the United States will support efforts of the Republic of Korea to seek a relaxation of tension and increased communication in the Korean peninsula. The United States places the highest value on its friendly relations with Japan; it will continue to develop the existing close bonds. Consistent with the United Nations Security Council Resolution of December 21, 1971, the United States favors the continuation of the cease-fire between India and Pakistan and the withdrawal of all military forces to within their own territories and to their own sides of the ceasefire line in Jammu and Kashmir; the

United States supports the right of the peoples of South Asia to shape their own future in peace, free of military threat, and without having the area become the subject of great power rivalry.

The Chinese side stated: Wherever there is oppression, there is resistance. Countries want independence, nations want liberation and the people want revolution—this has become the irresistible trend of history. All nations, big or small, should be equal; big nations should not bully the small and strong nations should not bully the weak. China will never be a superpower and it opposes hegemony and power politics of any kind. The Chinese side stated ' that it firmly supports the struggles of all the oppressed people and nations for freedom and liberation and that the people of all countries have the right to choose their social systems according to their own wishes and the right to safeguard the independence, sovereignty and territorial integrity of their own countries and oppose foreign aggression, interference, control and subversion. All foreign troops should be withdrawn to their own countries.

The Chinese side expressed its firm support to the peoples of Vietnam, Laos, and Cambodia in their efforts for the attainment of their goal and its firm support to the seven-point proposal of the Provisional Revolutionary Government of the Republic of South Vietnam and the elaboration of February this year on the two key problems in the proposal, and to the Joint Declaration of the Summit Conference of the Indochinese Peoples. It firmly supports the eight-point program for the peaceful unification of Korea put forward by the Government of the Democratic People's Republic of Korea on April 12, 1971, and the stand for the abolition of the "U.N. Commission for the Unification and Rehabilitation of Korea." It firmly opposes the revival and outward expansion of Japanese militarism and firmly supports the Japanese people's desire to build an independent, democratic, peaceful and neutral Japan. It firmly maintains that India and Pakistan should, in accordance with the United Nations resolutions on the India-Pakistan question, immediately withdraw all their forces to their respective territories and to their own sides of the ceasefire line in Jammu and Kashmir and firmly supports the Pakistan Government and people in their struggle to preserve their independence and sovereignty and the people of Jammu and Kashmir in their struggle for the right of self-determination.

There are essential differences between China and the United States in their social systems and foreign policies. However, the two sides agreed that countries, regardless of their social systems, should conduct their relations on the principles of respect for the sovereignty and territorial integrity of all states, non-aggression against other states, non-interference in the internal affairs of other states, equality and mutual benefit, and peaceful coexistence. International disputes should be settled on this basis, without resorting to the use or threat of force. The United States and the People's Republic of China are prepared to apply these principles to their mutual relations.

With these principles of international relations in mind the two sides stated that:

—progress toward the normalization of relations between China and the United States is in the interests of all countries;

—both wish to reduce the danger of international military conflict;

—neither should seek hegemony in the Asia-Pacific region and each is opposed to efforts by any other country or group of countries to establish such hegemony; and

—neither is prepared to negotiate on behalf of any third party or to enter into agreements or understandings with the other directed at other states.

Both sides are of the view that it would be against the interests of the peoples of the world for any major country to collude with another against other countries, or for major countries to divide up the world into spheres of interest.

The two sides reviewed the long-standing serious disputes between China and the United States. The Chinese side reaffirmed its position: The Taiwan question is the crucial question obstructing the normalization of relations between China and the United States; the Government of the People's Republic of China is the sole legal government of China; Taiwan is a province of China which has long been returned to the motherland; the liberation of Taiwan is China's internal affair in which no other country has the right to interfere; and all U.S. forces and military installations must be withdrawn from Taiwan. The Chinese Government firmly opposes any activities which aim at the creation of "one China, one Taiwan," "one China, two governments," "two Chinas," and "independent Taiwan" or advocate that "the status of Taiwan remains to be determined."

The U.S. side declared: The United States acknowledges that all Chinese on either side of the Taiwan Strait maintain there is but one China and that Taiwan is a part of China. The United States Government does not challenge that position. It reaffirms its interest in a peaceful settlement of the Taiwan question by the Chinese themselves. With this prospect in mind, it affirms the ultimate objective of the withdrawal of all U.S. forces and military installations from Taiwan. In the meantime, it will progressively reduce its forces and military installations on Taiwan as the tension in the area diminishes.

The two sides agreed that it is desirable to broaden the understanding between the two peoples. To this end, they discussed specific areas in such fields as science, technology, culture, sports and journalism, in which people-to-people contacts and exchanges would be mutually beneficial. Each side undertakes to facilitate the further development of such contacts and exchanges.

Both sides view bilateral trade as another area from which mutual benefits can be derived, and agreed that economic relations based on equality and mutual benefit are in the interest of the people of the two countries. They agree to facilitate the progressive development of trade between their two countries.

The two sides agreed that they will stay in contact through various channels, including the sending of a senior U.S. representative to Peking from time to time for concrete consultations to further the normalization of relations between the two countries and continue to exchange views on issues of common interest.

The two sides expressed the hope that the gains achieved during this visit would open up new prospects for the relations between the two countries. They believe that the normalization of relations between the two countries is not only in the interest of the Chinese and American peoples but also contributes to the relaxation of tension in Asia and the world.

President Nixon, Mrs. Nixon and the American party expressed their appreciation for the gracious hospitality shown them by the Government and people of the People's Republic of China.

Joint Communiqué on the Establishment of Diplomatic Relations Between the United States of America and the People's Republic of China,
(January 1, 1979)

The United States of America and the People's Republic of China have agreed to recognize each other and to establish diplomatic relations as of January 1, 1979.

The United States of America recognizes the Government of the

People's Republic of China as the sole legal Government of China. Within this context, the people of the United States will maintain cultural, commercial, and other unofficial relations with the people of Taiwan.

The United States of America and the People's Republic of China reaffirm the principles agreed on by the two sides in the Shanghai Communiqué and emphasize once again that:

—Both wish to reduce the danger of international military conflict.

—Neither should seek hegemony in the Asia-Pacific region or in any other region of the world and each is opposed to efforts by any other country or group of countries to establish such hegemony.

—Neither is prepared to negotiate on behalf of any third party or to enter into agreements or understandings with the other directed at other states.

—The Government of the United States of America acknowledges the Chinese position that there is but one China and Taiwan is part of China.

—Both believe that normalization of Sino-American relations is not only in the interest of the Chinese and American peoples but also contributes to the cause of peace in Asia and the world.

The United States of America and the People's Republic of China will exchange Ambassadors and establish Embassies on March 1, 1979.

United States–China Joint Communiqué on United States Arms Sales to Taiwan
(August 17, 1982)

1. In the Joint Communiqué on the Establishment of Diplomatic Relations on January 1, 1979, issued by the Government of the United States of America and the Government of the People's Republic of China, the United States of America recognized the Government of the People's Republic of China as the sole legal government of China, and it acknowledged the Chinese position that there is but one China and Taiwan is part of China. Within that context, the two sides agreed that the people of the United States would continue to maintain cultural, commercial, and other unofficial relations with the people of Taiwan. On this basis, relations between the United States and China were normalized.

2. The question of United States arms sales to Taiwan was not settled in the course of negotiations between the two countries on

establishing diplomatic relations. The two sides held differing positions, and the Chinese side stated that it would raise the issue again following normalization. Recognizing that this issue would seriously hamper the development of United States–China relations, they have held further discussions on it, during and since the meetings between President Ronald Reagan and Premier Zhao Ziyang and between Secretary of State Alexander M. Haig, Jr., and Vice Premier and Foreign Minister Huang Hua in October, 1981.

3. Respect for each other's sovereignty and territorial integrity and non-interference in each other's internal affairs constitute the fundamental principles guiding United States–China relations. These principles were confirmed in the Shanghai Communiqué of February 28, 1972, and reaffirmed in the Joint Communiqué on the Establishment of Diplomatic Relations which came into effect on January 1, 1979. Both sides emphatically state that these principles continue to govern all aspects of their relations.

4. The Chinese government reiterates that the question of Taiwan is China's internal affair. The Message to Compatriots in Taiwan issued by China on January 1, 1979, promulgated a fundamental policy of striving for peaceful reunification of the Motherland. The Nine-Point Proposal put forward by China on September 30, 1981, represented a further effort under this fundamental policy to strive for a peaceful solution to the Taiwan question.

5. The United States Government attaches great importance to its relations with China, and reiterates that it has no intention of infringing on Chinese sovereignty and territorial integrity, or interfering in China's internal affairs, or pursuing a policy of "two Chinas" or "one China, one Taiwan." The United States Government understands and appreciates the Chinese policy of striving for a peaceful resolution of the Taiwan question as indicated in China's Message to Compatriots in Taiwan issued on January 1, 1979, and the Nine-Point Proposal put forward by China on September 30, 1981. The new situation which has emerged with regard to the Taiwan question also provides favorable conditions for the settlement of United States–China differences over the question of United States arms sales to Taiwan.

6. Having in mind the foregoing statements of both sides, the United States Government states that it does not seek to carry out a long-term policy of arms sales to Taiwan, that its arms sales to Taiwan will not exceed, either in qualitative or in quantitative terms the level of those supplied in recent years since the establishment of diplomatic relations between the United States and China, and that it intends to reduce gradually its sales of arms to Taiwan,

leading over a period of time to a final resolution. In so stating, the United States acknowledges China's consistent position regarding the thorough settlement of this issue.

7. In order to bring about, over a period of time, a final settlement of the question of United States arms sales to Taiwan, which is an issue rooted in history, the two governments will make every effort to adopt measures and create conditions conducive to the thorough settlement of this issue.

8. The development of United States–China relations is not only in the interests of the two peoples but also conducive to peace and stability in the world. The two sides are determined, on the principle of equality and mutual benefit, to strengthen their ties in the economic, cultural, educational, scientific, technological and other fields and make strong, joint efforts for the continued development of relations between the governments and peoples of the United States and China.

9. In order to bring about the healthy development of United States–China relations, maintain world peace and oppose aggression and expansion, the two governments reaffirm the principles agreed on by the two sides in the Shanghai Communiqué and the Joint Communiqué on the Establishment of Diplomatic Relations. The two sides will maintain contact and hold appropriate consultations on bilateral and international issues of common interest.

Taiwan Relations Act

Taiwan Relations Act
(Public Law 96-8, April 10, 1979)

An Act

To help maintain peace, security, and stability in the Western Pacific and to promote the foreign policy of the United States by authorizing the continuation of commercial, cultural, and other relations between the people of the United States and the people on Taiwan, and for other purposes.

Be it enacted by the Senate and House of Representatives of the United States of America in Congress assembled,

SHORT TITLE

Section 1. This Act may be cited as the "Taiwan Relations Act."

FINDINGS AND DECLARATION OF POLICY

Section 2.
(a) The President having terminated governmental relations between the United States and the governing authorities on Taiwan recognized by the United States as the Republic of China prior to January 1, 1979, the Congress finds that the enactment of this Act is necessary—

(1) to help maintain peace, security, and stability in the Western Pacific; and

(2) to promote the foreign policy of the United States by authorzing the continuation of commercial, cultural, and other relations between the people of the United States and the people on Taiwan.

(b) It is the policy of the United States—

(1) to preserve and promote extensive, close, and friendly commercial, cultural, and other relations between the people of the United States and the people on Taiwan, as well as the people on the China mainland and all other peoples of the Western Pacific area;

(2) to declare that peace and stability in the area are in the political, security, and economic interests of the United States, and are matters of international concern;

(3) to make clear that the United States decision to establish diplomatic relations with the People's Republic of China rests upon the expectation that the future of Taiwan will be determined by peaceful means;

(4) to consider any effort to determine the future of Taiwan by other than peaceful means, including by boycotts or embargoes, a threat to the peace and security of the Western Pacific area and of grave concern to the United States;

(5) to provide Taiwan with arms of a defensive character; and

(6) to maintain the capacity of the United States to resist any resort to force or other forms of coercion that would jeopardize the security, or the social or economic system, of the people on Taiwan.

(c) Nothing contained in this Act shall contravene the interest of the United States in human rights, especially with respect to the human rights of all the approximately eighteen million inhabitants of Taiwan. The preservation and enhancement of the human rights of all the people on Taiwan are hereby reaffirmed as objectives of the United States.

IMPLEMENTATION OF UNITED STATES POLICY
WITH REGARD TO TAIWAN

Section 3.

(a) In furtherance of the policy set forth in section 2 of this Act, the United States will make available to Taiwan such defense articles and defense services in such quantity as may be necessary to enable Taiwan to maintain a sufficient self-defense capability.

(b) The President and the Congress shall determine the nature and quantity of such defense articles and services based solely upon their judgment of the needs of Taiwan, in accordance with procedures established by law. Such determination of Taiwan's defense needs shall include review by United States military authorities in connection with recommendations to the President and the Congress.

(c) The President is directed to inform the Congress promptly of any threat to the security or the social or economic system of the people on Taiwan and any danger to the interests of the United States arising therefrom. The President and the Congress shall determine, in accordance with constitutional processes, appropriate action by the United States in response to any such danger.

APPLICATION OF LAWS; INTERNATIONAL AGREEMENTS

Section 4.

(a) The absence of diplomatic relations or recognition shall not affect the application of the laws of the United States with respect to Taiwan, and the laws of the United States shall apply with respect to Taiwan in the manner that the laws of the United States applied with respect to Taiwan prior to January 1, 1979.

(b) The application of subsection (a) of this section will include, but shall not be limited to, the following:

(1) Whenever the laws of the United States refer or relate to foreign countries, nations, states, governments, or similar entities, such terms shall include and such laws shall apply with respect to Taiwan.

(2) Whenever authorized by or pursuant to the laws of the United States to conduct or carry out programs, transactions, or other relations with respect to foreign countries, nations, states, governments, or similar entities, the President or any agency of the United States Government is authorized to conduct and carry out, in accordance with section 6 of this Act, such programs, transactions, and other relations with respect to Taiwan (including, but not limited to, the performance of services for the United States through contracts with commercial entities on Taiwan), in accordance with the applicable laws of the United States.

(3) (A) The absence of diplomatic relations and recognition with respect to Taiwan shall not abrogate, infringe, modify, deny, or otherwise affect in any way any rights or obligations (including but not limited to those involving contracts, debts, or property interests of any kind) under the laws of the United States heretofore or hereafter acquired by or with respect to Taiwan.

(B) For all purposes under the laws of the United States, including actions in any court in the United States, recognition of the People's Republic of China shall not affect in any way the ownership of or other rights or interests in properties, tangible and intangible, and other things of value, owned or held on or prior to December 31, 1978, or thereafter acquired or earned by the governing authorities on Taiwan.

(4) Whenever the application of the laws of the United States depends upon the law that is or was applicable on Taiwan or compliance therewith, the law applied by the people on Taiwan shall be considered the applicable law for that purpose.

(5) Nothing in this Act, nor the facts of the President's action in extending diplomatic recognition to the People's Republic of China, the absence of diplomatic relations between the people on Taiwan and the United States, or the lack of recognition by the United States, and attendant circumstances thereto, shall be construed in any administrative or judicial proceeding as a basis for any United States Government agency, commission, or department to make a finding of fact or determination of law, under the Atomic Energy Act of 1954 and the Nuclear Non-Proliferation Act of 1978, to deny an export license application or to revoke an existing export license for nuclear exports to Taiwan.

(6) For purposes of the Immigration and Nationality Act, Taiwan may be treated in the manner specified in the first sentence of section 202(b) of that Act.

(7) The capacity of Taiwan to sue and be sued in courts in the United States, in accordance with the laws of the United States, shall not be abrogated, infringed, modified, denied, or otherwise affected in any way by the absence of diplomatic relations or recognition.

(8) No requirement, whether expressed or implied, under the laws of the United States with respect to maintenance of diplomatic relations or recognition shall be applicable with respect to Taiwan.

(c) For all purposes, including actions in any court in the United States, the Congress approves the continuation in force of all treaties and other international agreements, including multilateral conventions, entered into by the United States and the governing authorities on Taiwan recognized by the United States as the Republic of China prior to January 1, 1979, and in force between them on December 31, 1978, unless and until terminated in accordance with law.

(d) Nothing in this Act may be construed as a basis for supporting the exclusion or expulsion of Taiwan from continued membership in any international financial institution or any other international organization.

OVERSEAS PRIVATE INVESTMENT CORPORATION

Section 5.

(a) During the three-year period beginning on the date of enactment of this Act, the $1,000 per capita income restriction in clause (2) of the second undesignated paragraph of section 231 of the Foreign Assistance Act of 1961 shall not restrict the activities of the Overseas Private Investment Corporation in determining whether to provide any insurance, reinsurance, loans, or guaranties with respect to investment projects on Taiwan.

(b) Except as provided in subsection (a) of this section, in issuing insurance, reinsurance, loans, or guaranties with respect to investment projects on Taiwan, the Overseas Private Insurance Corporation shall apply the same criteria as those applicable in other parts of the world.

THE AMERICAN INSTITUTE OF TAIWAN

Section 6.

(a) Programs, transactions, and other relations conducted or carried out by the President or any agency of the United States Government with respect to Taiwan shall, in the manner and to the extent directed by the President, be conducted and carried out by or through—

(1) The American Institute in Taiwan, a nonprofit corporation incorporated under the laws of the District of Columbia, or

(2) such comparable successor nongovernmental entity as the President may designate, (hereafter in this Act referred to as the "Institute").

(b) Whenever the President or any agency of the United States Governnment is authorized or required by or pursuant to the laws of the United States to enter into, perform, enforce, or have in force an agreement or transaction relative to Taiwan, such agreement or transaction shall be entered into, performed, and enforced, in the manner and to the extent directed by the President, by or through the Institute.

(c) To the extent that any law, rule, regulation, or ordinance of the District of Columbia, or of any State or political subdivision thereof in which the Institute is incorporated or doing business, impedes or otherwise interferes with the performance of the functions of the Institute pursuant to this Act, such law, rule, regulation, or ordinance shall be deemed to be preempted by this Act.

SERVICES BY THE INSTITUTE TO UNITED STATES CITIZENS ON TAIWAN

Section 7.

(a) The Institute may authorize any of its employees on Taiwan—

(1) to administer to or take from any person an oath, affirmation, affidavit, or deposition, and to perform any notarial act which any notary public is required or authorized by law to perform within the United States;

(2) to act as provisional conservator of the personal estates of deceased United States citizens; and

(3) to assist and protect the interests of United States persons by performing other acts such as are authorized to be performed outside the United States for consular purposes by such laws of the United States as the President may specify.

(b) Acts performed by authorized employees of the Institute under this section shall be valid, and of like force and effect within the United States, as if performed by any other person authorized under the laws of the United States to perform such acts.

TAX EXEMPT STATUS OF THE INSTITUTE

Section 8.

(a) The Institute, its property, and its income are exempt from all taxation now or hereafter imposed by the United States (except to the extent that section 11(a)(3) of this Act requires the imposition of taxes imposed under chapter 21 of the Internal Revenue Code of 1954, relating to the Federal Insurance Contributions Act) or by any State or local taxing authority of the United States.

(b) For purposes of the Internal Revenue Code of 1954, the Institute shall be treated as an organization described in sections 170(b)(1)(A), 170(c), 2055(a), 2106(a)(2)(A), 2522(a), and 2522(b).

FURNISHING PROPERTY AND SERVICES TO AND OBTAINING SERVICES FROM THE INSTITUTE

Section 9.

(a) Any agency of the United States Government is authorized to sell, loan, or lease property (including interests therein) to, and to perform administrative and technical support functions and services for the operations of the Institute upon such terms and conditions as the President may direct. Reimbursements to agencies under this subsection shall be credited to the current applicable appropriation of the agency concerned.

(b) Any agency of the United States Government is authorized to acquire and accept services from the Institute upon such terms and conditions as the President may direct. Whenever the President determines it to be in furtherance of the purposes of this Act, the procurement of services by such agencies from the Institute may be effected without regard to such laws of the United States normally applicable to the acquisition of services by such agencies as the President may specify by Executive order.

(c) Any agency of the United States Government making funds available to the Institute in accordance with this Act shall make arrangements with the Institute for the Comptroller General of the United States to have access to the books and records of the Institute and the opportunity to audit the operations of the Institute.

TAIWAN INSTRUMENTALITY

Section 10.

(a) Whenever the President or any agency of the United States Government is authorized or required by or pursuant to the laws of the United States to render or provide to or to receive or accept from Taiwan, any performance, communication, assurance, undertaking, or other action, such action shall, in the manner and to the extent directed by the President, be rendered or provided to, or received or accepted from, an instrumentality established by Taiwan which the President determines has the necessary authority under the laws applied by the people on Taiwan to provide assurances and take other actions on behalf of Taiwan in accordance with this Act.

(b) The President is requested to extend to the instrumentality established by Taiwan the same number of offices and complement of personnel as were previously operated in the United States by the governing authorities on Taiwan recognized as the Republic of China prior to January 1, 1979.

(c) Upon the granting by Taiwan of comparable privileges and immunities with respect to the Institute and its appropriate personnel, the President is authorized to extend with respect to the Taiwan instrumentality and its appropriate personnel, such privileges and immunities (subject to appropriate conditions and obligations) as may be necessary for the effective performance of their functions.

SEPARATION OF GOVERNMENT PERSONNEL
FOR EMPLOYMENT WITH THE INSTITUTE

Section 11.

(a) (1) Under such terms and conditions as the President may direct, any agency of the United States Government may separate from Government service for a specified period any officer or employee of that agency who accepts employment with the Institute.

(2) An officer or employee separated by an agency under paragraph (1) of this subsection for employment with the Institute shall be entitled upon termination of such employment to reemployment or reinstatement with such agency (or a successor agency) in an appropriate position with the attendant rights, privileges, and benefits which the officer or employee would have had or acquired had he or she not been so separated, subject to such time period and other conditions as the President may prescribe.

(3) An officer or employee entitled to reemployment or reinstatement rights under paragraph (2) of this subsection shall, while continuously employed by the Institute with no break in continuity of service, continue to participate in any benefit program in which such officer or employee was participating prior to employment by the Institute, including programs for compensation for job-related death, injury, or illness; programs for health and life insurance; programs for annual, sick, and other statutory leave; and programs for retirement under any system established by the laws of the United States; except that employment with the Institute shall be the basis for participation in such programs only to the extent that employee deductions and employer contributions, as required, in payment for such participation for the period of employment with the Institute, are currently deposited in the program's or system's fund or depository. Death or retirement of any such officer or employee during approved service with the Institute and prior to reemployment or reinstatement shall be considered a death in or retirement from Government service for purposes of any employee or survivor benefits acquired by reason of service with an agency of the United States Government.

(4) Any officer or employee of an agency of the United States Government who entered into service with the Institute on approved leave of absence without pay prior to the enactment of this Act shall receive the benefits of this section for the period of such service.

(b) Any agency of the United States Government employing alien personnel on Taiwan may transfer such personnel, with accrued allowances, benefits, and rights, to the Institute without a break in service for purposes of retirement and other benefits, including continued participation in any system established by the laws of the United States for the retirement of employees in which the alien was participating prior to the transfer to the Institute, except that employment with the Institute shall be creditable for retirement purposes only to the extent that employee deductions and employer contributions, as required, in payment for such participation for the period of employment with the Institute, are currently deposited in the system's fund or depository.

(c) Employees of the Institute shall not be employees of the United States and, in representing the Institute, shall be exempt from section 207 of title 18, United States Code.

(d) (1) For purposes of sections 911 and 913 of the Internal Revenue Code of 1954, amounts paid by the Institute to its employees shall not be treated as earned income. Amounts received by employees of the Institute shall not be included in gross income, and shall be exempt from taxation, to the extent that they are equivalent to amounts received by civilian officers and employees of the Government of the United States as allowances and benefits which are exempt from taxation under section 912 of such Code.

(2) Except to the extent required by subsection (a)(3) of this section, service performed in the employ of the Institute shall not constitute employment for purposes of chapter 21 of such Code and title II of the Social Security Act.

REPORTING REQUIREMENT

Section 12.

(a) The Secretary of State shall transmit to the Congress the text of any agreement to which the Institute is a party. However, any such agreement the immediate public disclosure of which would, in the opinion of the President, be prejudicial to the national security of the United States shall not be so transmitted to the Congress but shall be transmitted to the Committee on Foreign Relations of the Senate and the Committee on Foreign Affairs of the House of Representatives under an appropriate injunction of secrecy to be removed only upon due notice from the President.

(b) For purposes of subsection (a), the term "agreement" includes—

(1) any agreement entered into between the Institute and the governing authorities on Taiwan or the instrumentality established by Taiwan; and

(2) any agreement entered into between the Institute and an agency of the United States Government.

(c) Agreements and transactions made or to be made by or through the Institute shall be subject to the same congressional notification, review, and approval requirements and procedures as if such agreements and transactions were made by or through the agency of the United States Government on behalf of which the Institute is acting.

(d) During the two-year period beginning on the effective date of this Act, the Secretary of State shall transmit to the Speaker of the House of Representatives and the Committee on Foreign Relations of the Senate, every six months, a report describing and reviewing economic relations between the United States and Taiwan, noting any interference with normal commerical relations.

RULES AND REGULATIONS

Section 13. The President is authorized to prescribe such rules and regulations as he may deem appropriate to carry out the purposes of this Act. During the three-year period beginning on the effective date of this Act, such rules and regulations shall be transmitted promptly to the Speaker of the House of Representatives and to the Committee on Foreign Relations of the Senate. Such action shall not, however, relieve the Institute of the responsibilities placed upon it by this Act.

CONGRESSIONAL OVERSIGHT

Section 14.

(a) The Committee on Foreign Affairs of the House of Representatives, the Committee on Foreign Relations of the Senate, and other appropriate committees of the Congress shall monitor—

(1) the implementation of the provisions of this Act;

(2) the operation and procedures of the Institute;

(3) the legal and technical aspects of the continuing relationship between the United States and Taiwan; and

(4) the implementation of the policies of the United States concerning security and cooperation in East Asia.

(b) Such committees shall report, as appropriate, to their respective Houses on the results of their monitoring.

DEFINITIONS

Section 15. For purposes of this Act—
(1) the term "laws of the United States" includes any statute, rule, regulation, ordinance, order, or judicial rule of decision of the United States or any political subdivision thereof; and
(2) the term "Taiwan" includes, as the context may require, the islands of Taiwan and the Pescadores, the people on those islands, corporations and other entities and associations created or organized under the laws applied on those islands, and the governing authorities on Taiwan recognized by the United States as the Republic of China prior to January 1, 1979 and any successor governing authorities (including political subdivisions, agencies, and instrumentalities thereof).

AUTHORIZATION OF APPROPRIATIONS

Section 16. In addition to funds otherwise available to carry out the provisions of this Act, there are authorized to be appropriated to the Secretary of State for the fiscal year 1980 such funds as may be necessary to carry out such provisions. Such funds are authorized to remain available until expended.

SEVERABILITY OF PROVISIONS

Section 17. If any provision of this Act or the application thereof to any person or circumstance is held invalid, the remainder of the Act and the application of such provision to any other person or circumstance shall not be affected thereby.

EFFECTIVE DATE

Section 18. This act shall be effective as of January 1, 1979.

Approved April 10, 1979.

SOURCE: U.S., *Statutes at Large*, Vol. 93 (1979), pp. 14–21.

Reference Matter

Notes

Abreviations used in the following notes include:

AFP	Agence France-Presse
Basic Docs.	U.S. Department of State, *American Foreign Policy: Basic Documents, 1977–1980*
Current Docs.	U.S. Department of State, *American Foreign Policy: Current Documents* (various years)
DOD	U.S. Department of Defense
FBIS/PRC	U.S. National Technical Information Service, Foreign Broadcast Information Service, *FBIS Daily Report: China*
FBIS/SU	U.S. National Technical Information Service, Foreign Broadcast Information Service, *FBIS Daily Report: Soviet Union*
FBIS, *Trends*	U.S. National Technical Information Service, Foreign Broadcast Information Service, *Trends in Communist Media.*
FEER	*Far Eastern Economic Review*
JPRS	Joint Publications Research Service
Public Papers	U.S. National Archives, *Public Papers of the Presidents of the United States*
NYT	*New York Times*
SD Bull.	*State Department Bulletin*
WP	*Washington Post*
WSJ	*Wall Street Journal*

Chapter 1

1. Kissinger, *White House Years*, pp. 684–89, 705.

2. This is the understanding of cooperation, as distinct from harmony, adopted by Keohane in *After Hegemony*, pp. 51–54.

3. See Ikle, *How Nations Negotiate*, pp. 27, 30–35, for a discussion of redistributive bargaining.

4. See Snyder and Diesing, *Conflict Among Nations*, pp. 429–40, for a discussion of the interplay between security and negotiations in a triangular setting.

5. Ibid. See Snyder, "Security Dilemma," for a discussion of the sources of bargaining strength in negotiations between allies.

6. Ibid. For an early attempt by this author to address these issues in U.S.–China relations, see Robert S. Ross, "International Bargaining and Domestic Politics."

7. For an insightful discussion of the role of "signals" and "indices" in assessing resolve, see Jervis, *Logic of Images*, pp. 218–40.

8. Stein, *Why Nations Cooperate*, ch. 3, offers comprehensive discussion of the implications of bargaining with incomplete information or under misapprehension; see esp. pp. 70–73 for a discussion of "chicken" and "called bluff." In *Conflict Among Nations*, pp. 46–47, Snyder and Diesing discuss misperceptions in "called bluff," but from the perspective of the state with the dominate strategy. They correctly categorize it as an asymmetrical game, insofar as the outcome, in the absence of misperception, reflects the disparate capabilities of the players. See also, e.g., Jervis, *Logic of Images*; Harsanyi, "Advances in Understanding"; Nalebuff, "Rational Deterrence."

9. See Art, "Bureaucratic Politics," for a critique of the literature on bureaucratic politics, stressing its tendency to underestimate the power of the president. See Garrett, "U.S. Bureaucratic Politics and the Strategic Triangle," for a discussion of the importance of strategic perspectives for the personal policy preferences of decision makers regarding U.S. China policy.

10. For a discussion of realism as a first cut, see Keohane, "Theory of World Politics." The domestic-international negotiating dynamic is discussed in Putnam, "Diplomacy and Domestic Politics."

11. For a discussion of the role of domestic politics in Chinese foreign policy, see Robert S. Ross, "From Lin Biao to Deng Xiaoping."

12. The best works covering U.S.–China relations from 1949 to rapprochement are Barnett, *China and the Major Powers*, and Sutter, *China-Watch*. For a discussion of China's security perspective on the eve of the war, see Zhang Shuguang, "'Preparedness Eliminates Mishaps.'"

13. For a discussion of China's decision to enter the Korean War, see Goncharov, Lewis, and Xue, *Uncertain Partners*; Christensen, "Threats, Assurances, and the Last Chance for Peace." The classic statement of China's intentions in Korea remains Whiting, *China Crosses the Yalu*.

14. *Ta kung pao* (Hong Kong), May 18, 1987, in Foreign Broadcast Information Service, *Daily Report: China* (hereafter cited as *FBIS/PRC*), May 20, 1987, p. B3.

15. The best studies of the 1954 and 1958 crises are Stolper, *China, Taiwan and the Offshore Islands*; Tsou, "Mao's Limited War"; Gurtov, "Taiwan Strait Crisis Revisited"; Chang, "To the Nuclear Brink." For an analysis stressing Mao's domestic motives for initiating the 1958 conflict, see Christensen, "Domestic Mobilization and International Conflict." For an analysis of the role of Taiwan in the Sino-Soviet conflict, see Nelson, *Power and Insecurity*, pp. 40–45. See also the discussion of the Sino-Soviet polemics over peaceful transition to socialism and war in the nuclear age in Zagoria, *Sino-Soviet Conflict*, pp. 236–76, passim.

16. For a discussion of the U.S. strategy of coercion, see Chang, *Friends and Enemies*.

17. See ibid. for a discussion of U.S. attitudes toward the Sino-Soviet conflict and toward Chinese foreign policy in the mid 1960s.

18. Chang, "To the Nuclear Brink"; Stolper, *China, Taiwan and the Offshore Islands*.

19. See Christensen, "Domestic Mobilization and International Conflict."

20. For a discussion of China's foreign policy analysts and research institutions, including those that focus on the United States, see Shambaugh, "China's National Security Research Bureaucracy"; Shambaugh, *Beautiful Imperialist*.

Chapter 2

1. Freedman, *U.S. Intelligence and the Soviet Strategic Threat*, pp. 129–44, 151–59; 164–68; See also Prados, *Soviet Estimate*, pp. 195, 210, 221; Newhouse, *Cold Dawn*, pp. 168, 198, 201–2; 222–24; Smith, *Doubletalk*, pp. 212–13.

2. Freedman, *U.S. Intelligence and the Soviet Strategic Threat*, p. 145; Prados, *Soviet Estimate*, p. 194; Newhouse, *Cold Dawn*, p. 201, 204–5; 222–24; Smith, *Doubletalk*, pp. 118; Kissinger, *White House Years*, pp. 195–98, 203–4; U.S. Department of Defense (hereafter cited as DOD), *Defense Program and Budget: FY 1971*, pp. 40–42; DOD, *Annual Report: FY 1973*, pp. 30, 41, 45–46.

3. Kissinger, *White House Years*, pp. 195–98, 536–37, 541; Nixon, "Second Annual Foreign Policy Report to the Congress on United States Foreign Policy," in U.S. National Archives, *Public Papers of the Presidents of the United States: Richard Nixon, 1971* (hereafter cited as, e.g., *Public Papers . . . 1971*), pp. 308; Litwak, *Détente and the Nixon Doctrine*, p. 123; Gaddis, *Strategies of Containment*, p. 322; Newhouse, *Cold Dawn*, pp. 238–39.

4. Freedman, *U.S. Intelligence and the Soviet Strategic Threat*, p. 166; Smith, *Doubletalk*, pp. 104–5, 208–9, 212–13; Kissinger, *White House*

Years, pp. 145, 546–47. Moscow used similar tactics in negotiations for a U.S.–Soviet summit. It delayed setting a summit date, waiting until it received concrete U.S. arms-control concessions. Only after the July 1971 announcement of Nixon's plan to visit Beijing did Moscow begin to expedite the summit negotiations. See Kissinger, *White House Years,* pp. 766, 796, 835.

5. Nixon, *RN,* p. 390.

6. Herring, *America's Longest War,* pp. 222–23; Nixon, *RN,* 393–94.

7. Kissinger, *White House Years,* pp. 968–69.

8. Ibid., pp. 1017–19; 1026; 1099, 1105–6, 1195, 1302, 1311–13.

9. Ibid., p. 641.

10. See, e.g., Nixon's June 4, 1969, speech to the Air Force Academy in *Public Papers . . . 1969,* pp. 432–37; Nixon's July 1, 1970, conversation with American correspondents in *Public Papers . . . 1970,* pp. 557; Nixon, "Second Annual Report to the Congress on United States Foreign Policy," in *Public Papers . . . 1971,* pp. 224–26.

11. Nixon, "First Annual Foreign Policy Report to the Congress on United States Foreign Policy for the 1970's," in *Public Papers . . . 1970,* pp. 173, 180.

12. Nixon, "Second Annual Foreign Policy Report to the Congress on United States Foreign Policy," in *Public Papers . . . 1971,* pp. 305–7, 309.

13. *State Department Bulletin* (hereafter cited as *SD Bull.*), Sept. 20, 1971, pp. 300–301.

14. *Public Papers . . . 1971,* pp. 1063–64; *SD Bull.,* Nov. 29, 1971, pp. 613–14.

15. *SD Bull.,* Feb. 7, 1972, p. 146.

16. "Third Annual Report to the Congress on United States Foreign Policy," in *Public Papers . . . 1972,* pp. 195–97, 210, 212.

17. *SD Bull.,* June 26, 1972, p. 855.

18. *SD Bull.,* Feb. 5, 1973, p. 125.

19. Richard M. Nixon, "Fourth Annual Report to the Congress on United States Foreign Policy" (May 3, 1973), in *Public Papers . . . 1973,* pp. 357, 376. See also the late 1972 speeches of Secretary Rogers in, e.g., *SD Bull.,* Aug. 14, 1972, pp. 185–90; *SD Bull.,* Nov. 13, 1972, pp. 561–65.

20. Interview with U.S. government official; Litwak, *Détente and the Nixon Doctrine,* p. 123; DOD, *Annual Report: FY 1976,* pp. III 9–10.

21. Kissinger, *White House Years,* p. 179. On the administration's understanding of the implications of Soviet military preparations, see Kissinger's recollection of his discussion with Whiting in Kalb and Kalb, *Kissinger,* pp. 226–27. Whiting's account of this meeting is in Whiting, "Sino-American Détente." See also Hersh, *Price of Power,* pp. 357–59. On the cabinet meeting, see Safire, *Before the Fall,* p. 371.

22. China's growing fear of a Soviet attack in summer 1969 is revealed in Xiong, "Dakai Zhong Mei guanxi de qianzou," in *Zhonggong dangshi ziliao,* no. 42 (Xiong was a participant in the meetings of the marshals; his

recollection of the meetings is also excerpted under the title "Dakai Zhong Mei guanxi damen de qianzou," in *Liaowang*, no. 35, 1992). For an analysis of the escalating tension, see Wich, *Sino-Soviet Crisis Politics*. For a comprehensive discussion of Chinese motives for launching the border war, see Robinson, "Sino-Soviet Border Dispute."

23. For a discussion of the border talks, see *Dagong bao*, Jan. 9, 1970, in *FBIS/PRC*, Jan. 9, 1970, p. A1; *Washington Post* (hereafter cited as *WP*), Mar. 22, 1972; *WP*, May 3, 1972. On Soviet deployments, see Kissinger, *Years of Upheaval*, p. 46; *New York Times* (hereafter cited as *NYT*), Jan. 10, 1972. On the border skirmishes, see *WP*, Dec. 12, 1972; Garthoff, *Détente and Confrontation*, pp. 317–18.

24. The classic Chinese statement of its preference for Vietnamese tactics is Lin Biao, "Long Live the Victory of People's War," *Peking Review*, Sept. 3, 1965. For an analysis of this peace and of Sino-Vietnamese relations during this period, see Mozingo and Robinson, *Lin Piao on People's War*. For an extended analysis of this issue in Sino-Vietnamese relations, see Eugene K. Lawson, *Sino-Vietnamese Conflict*.

25. The best discussion of the 1971 South Asia crisis is Jackson, *South Asian Crisis*.

26. Kissinger, *Years of Upheaval*, pp. 52, 55; "Chou En-lai's Reports on the International Situation," pp. 123–24.

27. For a discussion of the Lin Biao affair and the politics of the early 1970s, see Jiang and Li, eds., *Lin Biao*; MacFarquhar, "Succession to Mao and the End of Maoism." For the Chinese government documents explaining the Lin Biao affair, see Kao, ed., *Lin Piao Affair*.

28. See Whiting, *Chinese Calculus*, pp. 200–205.

29. Xiong, "Dakai Zhong Mei guanxi de Qianzou," p. 80. For a discussion, see Naughton, "Third Front," esp. pp. 372–73. Note that this was also the period when Chinese were mobilized to "dig tunnels deep" in preparation for war.

30. This section and the discussion of the decisive role of Chairman Mao Zedong draws on Robert S. Ross, "From Lin Biao to Deng Xiaoping." Cf. Garver, *China's Decision*, ch. 4.

31. *Xinhua*, July 31, 1971, in *FBIS/PRC*, Aug. 2, 1971, pp. A5–7. See also the discussion of superpower collusion and U.S. aggressiveness in the article by a "certain naval unit," "Down with Hegemonism," *Renmin ribao*, Jan. 16, 1971, in *FBIS/PRC*, Jan. 18, 1971, pp. A1–2; and in the joint May 20, 1971, *Renmin ribao, Red Flag*, and *Liberation Army Daily* editorial "A Program for Anti-Imperialist Struggle," in *FBIS/PRC*, May 20, 1971, pp. A1–4. For additional discussions, see, e.g., *Xinhua*, Mar. 7, 1970, in *FBIS/PRC*, Mar. 9, 1970, pp. A11–13; *Xinhua*, Apr. 10, 1971, in *FBIS/PRC*, Apr. 12, 1971, pp. A1–3. For a full analysis of Lin's policy package, see Harding, "Political Trends in China Since the Cultural Revolution."

32. Zhou's thinking is discussed in Wang Li and Qiu Chengyun, "Lishi de gongxun," pp. 202–11. See also Xue, ed., *Dangdai Zhongguo waijiao*,

pp. 217–18. On the role of military leaders, see Editorial and Writing Organization of the Academy of Military Science, *Ye Jianying zhuanlue*, pp. 271–72; Xiong, "Dakai Zhong Mei guanxi de qianzou," pp. 70–71. For contemporary media articles defending the moderate line, see, e.g., "The Weak Can Defeat the Strong, the Small Can Defeat the Big," *Renmin ribao*, Jan. 17, 1971, in *FBIS/PRC*, Jan. 18, 1971, pp. A2–3; *Xinhua*, Apr. 25, 1971, in *FBIS/PRC*, Apr. 26, 1971, pp. A8–9; *Xinhua*, May 23, 1971, in *FBIS/PRC*, May 24, 1971, pp. A1–3. See also the secret speech by Zhou published in Taiwan. "Chou En-lai's Reports on the International Situation," pp. 116–20. See also Harding, "Political Trends in China Since the Cultural Revolution."

33. Mao Zedong, "Report to the Second Plenary Session of the Seventh Central Committee of the Communist Party of China," *Peking Review*, Nov. 29, 1968, pp. 8–9. On Zhou's participation, see Chen Dunde, *Mao*, pp. 82, 86–87. For the official report of the 1970 National Day celebration, see *Xinhua*, Sept. 30, 1978, in *FBIS/PRC*, Oct. 1, 1970, pp. B1–2. Snow's account is in his *Long Revolution*, pp. 3–5, 183. See also Garver, *China's Decision*, p. 137.

34. "Strive for New Victories," *FBIS/PRC*, Oct. 2, 1972, p. B2; *Xinhua*, Oct. 5, 1972, in *FBIS/PRC*, Oct. 6, 1972, p. A5.

35. The Chinese leadership apparently recognized this asymmetry. See the March 1973 secret speech by Zhou Enlai published in Taiwan as "Chou En-lai's Reports on the International Situation," p. 125.

36. Nixon, "Asia After Vietnam"; id., *RN*, pp. 341, 544; Morris, *Uncertain Greatness*, pp. 202–3; Newhouse, *Cold Dawn*, p. 220; Safire, *Before the Fall*, p. 368. At the same time, State Department officials developed an array of policy options designed to reduce bilateral tension and signal U.S. willingness to initiate a new direction in U.S.–PRC relations. Interviews with Marshall Green, Paul Kreisberg, Roger Sullivan, and other State Department officials.

37. Kissinger, *White House Years*, pp. 177–79, 191–92.

38. Wang Li and Qiu Chengyun, "Lishi de gongxun," p. 203.

39. Xue, ed., *Dangdai Zhongguo waijiao*, pp. 217–18.

40. This paragraph and the following paragraph are based on the following: Hu Shiyan, et al., eds., *Chen Yi zhuan*, pp. 614–15, 697; Xiong, "Dakai Zhong Mei guanxi de qianzou," pp. 61, 69–87; Editorial and Writing Organization of the Academy of Military Science, *Ye Jianying zhuanlue*, pp. 271–72; He, *Yuanshuai waijiaojia*, pp. 236–37; Chen Dunde, *Mao*, p. 10; Gong, *Kuayue*, p. 41.

41. Xiong, "Dakai Zhong Mei guanxi de qianzou," pp. 84–87; Wang, *Chen Yi de waijiao yishu*, p. 58.

42. For a discussion of this and other aspects of U.S.–PRC rapprochement, see Whiting, *Sino-American Détente*.

43. For a discussion of the theoretical aspects of this tactic, sometimes called "graduated reciprocation in tension reduction" (GRIT) and its impor-

tance in Soviet diplomacy leading to the 1955 Austrian State Treaty, see Larson, "Crisis Prevention and the Austrian State Treaty."

44. Kissinger, *White House Years*, pp. 180–82; interview with Richard Allen; Garthoff, *Détente and Confrontation*, p. 218; Xue, ed., *Dangdai Zhongguo waijiao*, p. 219.

45. For a close look at the relationship between the Sino-Soviet border tension and U.S. China policy, see Kissinger, *White House Years*, pp. 179–86. On NSSM-63, see Garthoff, *Détente and Confrontation*, p. 216. Kissinger's account fails to include the important meeting in San Clemente between Kissinger, Holdridge, and Allen S. Whiting, when Whiting pointed out Soviet construction of an airfield on the Sino-Soviet border and Soviet preparations for a conventional air attack and advised Kissinger to signal PRC leaders of U.S. disapproval of a Soviet attack, which the administration subsequently did. See Hersh, *Price of Power*, pp. 357–59. Whiting's account is in "Sino-American Détente," pp. 336–37. On the trade restrictions, see Kissinger, *White House Years*, pp. 173, 180.

46. Kissinger, *White House Years*, pp. 182–83, 184, 191; Garthoff, *Détente and Confrontation*, p. 220 n. 65.

47. Chen Dunde, *Mao*, p. 55; interview with William Rogers; Garrett, "Strategic Basis for Learning in U.S. China Policy," p. 48 n. 91; Szulc, *Illusion of Peace*, pp. 116–18; Kissinger, *White House Years*, pp. 181, 186–90.

48. Interview with Paul Kreisberg; Hersh, *Price of Power*, pp. 360–61. Author's emphasis.

49. Interview with U.S. government official.

50. Interview with John Holdridge; Xue, ed., *Dangdai Zhongguo waijiao*, p. 219.

51. For a full discussion of the impact of the invasion of Cambodia, see Robert S. Ross, "From Lin Biao to Deng Xiaoping." See also Xue, ed., *Dangdai Zhongguo waijiao*, pp. 219–20.

52. Wang Li and Qiu Chengyun, "Lishi de gongxun," p. 204. See also Xue, ed., *Dangdai Zhongguo waijiao*, p. 219. Kissinger's account is in *White House Years*, pp. 694–97.

53. Interview with U.S. government official; Kissinger, *White House Years*, pp. 698–99.

54. Kissinger, *White House Years*, pp. 699–701, 703–4.

55. On the role of Mao and Zhou Enlai in ping-pong diplomacy, see Qian, "Pingpang waijiao", esp. chs. 8, 9, 14, 15. See also Guan, "Zhou Enlai," pp. 23–25.

56. On unilateral U.S. initiatives during this period, see *SD Bull.*, May 3, 1971; *SD Bull.*, June 28, 1971, pp. 815–16; *WP*, Feb. 18, 1972; Kissinger, *White House Years*, pp. 723, 731–32; Nixon, *RN*, 549–50. Kissinger's discussions of the U.S.–PRC messages is the most complete. See *White House Years*, pp. 714, 724, 727.

57. Xue, ed., *Dangdai Zhongguo waijiao*, p. 220; Kissinger, *White House Years*, pp. 726–27. Note that China's analysis of these exchanges confirms

Kissinger's record, particularly regarding China's compromise on the agenda of the Beijing meetings.

58. Newhouse, *Cold Dawn*, p. 203; Smith, *Doubletalk*, p. 252; Kissinger, *White House Years*, pp. 830, 836.

59. Kissinger, *White House Years*, p. 768.

60. Ibid., pp. 822–23.

61. Gong, *Kuayue*, p. 103.

62. Ibid., pp. 103–4.

63. Ibid., pp. 104, 116–17; Wang Li and Qiu Chengyun, "Lishi de gong-xun," pp. 205–6.

64. Garthoff, *Détente and Confrontation*, p. 223.

65. Interview with W. R. Smyser.

66. Xue, ed., *Dangdai Zhongguo waijiao*, p. 221; Wei, "Jixinge mimi fang Hua neimu," p. 40; Solomon, *U.S.–PRC Political Negotiations*, pp. 14, 15.

67. Xue, ed., *Dangdai Zhongguo waijiao*, p. 221; Solomon, *U.S.–PRC Political Negotiations*, p. 14.

68. Xue, ed., *Dangdai Zhongguo waijiao*, p. 221.

69. Kissinger, *White House Years*, pp. 751–53, 759–60.

70. Xue, ed., *Dangdai Zhongguo waijiao*, pp. 221–22; interview with R. W. Smyser; Nixon's interview with Dan Rather is in *SD Bull.*, Jan. 24, 1972, pp. 79–80.

71. *NYT*, Aug. 5, 1971.

72. The following paragraphs are based on Kissinger, *White House Years*, pp. 777–84; Wei, "Jixinge dier ci fang Hua."

73. Kissinger, *White House Years*, p. 783; interviews with Paul Kreisberg and John Holdridge.

74. Chinese leaders could draw some satisfaction from the Chinese-language text of the communiqué. Although the English-language version uses "acknowledge," the Chinese version uses the characters *renshi*, which can imply both recognition and acceptance, rather than simply acknowledgement. Hence, despite the English wording of the text, Beijing can argue that the Shanghai communiqué commits the United States to a policy that recognizes that Taiwan is part of China. Nonetheless, insofar as both versions of the Shanghai communiqué are equally correct, the ambiguous U.S. position is valid. For the Chinese-language version, see Dong, *Zhong Mei Guanxi ciliao xuanbian*, pp. 3–8.

75. Wei, "Jixinge dier ci fang Hua," p. 70; Xue, ed., *Dangdai Zhongguo waijiao*, p. 222.

76. Interviews with Marshall Green, Harvey Feldman, and other State Department officials; Kissinger, *White House Years*, p. 773. See also *NYT*, July 21, 1971; Rogers's Aug. 2 announcement is in *SD Bull.*, Aug. 23, 1971, p. 193.

77. Interviews with Secretary of State William Rogers and Harvey Feldman.

78. Interviews with Marshall Green, Harvey Feldman, and other former U.S. officials; Bush, *Looking Forward*, pp. 112–13. Kissinger maintains that

the U.N. vote occurred "a week earlier than expected." *White House Years,* pp. 773, 784. But a later U.N. vote would not have changed the impact of his visit to China.

79. Interviews with Marshall Green, Harvey Feldman, and other former U.S. officials; Kissinger, *White House Years,* pp. 773, 775.

80. Kissinger, *White House Years,* pp. 913–18.

81. *NYT,* Feb. 13, 1972, cited in Vertzberger, *China's Southwestern Strategy,* p. 58.

82. *SD Bull.,* Jan. 24, 1972, pp. 83–84.

83. *NYT,* Feb. 29, 1972; *WP,* Feb. 6, 1972, interview with State Department officials.

84. Newhouse, *Cold Dawn,* p. 238.

85. Kissinger, *White House Years,* p. 768; Garthoff, *Détente and Confrontation,* pp. 232–33.

86. Interviews with Secretary of State William Rogers and Roger Sullivan.

87. Lu, *Waijiao jubu,* p. 109; Kissinger, *White House Years,* pp. 1060–62. See also Nixon, *RN,* pp. 560–64.

88. Solomon, *U.S.–PRC Political Negotiations,* p. 21; Wei, "Nikesen Zongtong fang Hua," p. 95.

89. Xue, ed., *Dangdai Zhongguo waijiao,* pp. 223–24; Wei, "Nikesen Zongtong fang Hua," pp. 90–95.

90. The course of the negotiations is documented in Kissinger, *White House Years,* pp. 1075–80; Wei, "Jixinge dier ci fang Hua," pp. 89–96.

91. Ibid., pp. 1082–83.

92. Interviews with Marshall Green and John Holdridge.

93. Solomon, *U.S.–PRC Political Negotiations,* p. 21.

94. Yin, "Bali de Mimi," pp. 188–89; Walters, *Silent Missions,* pp. 545–46; Kissinger, *White House Years,* pp. 1103–4.

95. Interview with Alexander Haig.

96. Diplomatic History Research Office, ed., *Zhou Enlai waijiao,* p. 624. Regarding Vietnamese isolation, note that Nixon received China's "ping-pong diplomacy team" at the White House just as Vietnam was engaged in its 1972 spring offensive. See Turley, *Second Indochina War,* p. 147. For a discussion of the impact of the U.S.–PRC opening on Vietnamese interests, see Garver, "Sino-Vietnamese Conflict and the Sino-American Rapprochement."

97. Kissinger, *White House Years,* p. 1073; Wang Li and Qiu Chengyun, "Lishi de gongxun," pp. 206–7; Wei, "Nikesen Zongtong fang Hua," p. 89; Xue, ed., *Dangdai Zhongguo waijiao,* p. 225.

98. Gong, *Kuayue,* pp. 205–6.

99. Solomon, *U.S.–PRC Political Negotiations,* p. 17; interview with Roger Sullivan and other U.S. officials.

100. Gong, *Kuayue,* p. 103.

101. Ibid., pp. 205–6.

102. Ibid.; Solomon, *U.S.–PRC Political Negotiations,* p. 30.

103. Gong, *Kuayue*, pp. 205–6.

104. Xue, ed., *Dangdai Zhongguo waijiao*, p. 225; Dou, ed., *Zhongguo Renmin Gongheguo duiwai guanxi gaishu*, p. 107; Gong, *Kuayue*, pp. 205–6.

105. Yin, "Bali de mimi," pp. 192–93; Solomon, *U.S.–PRC Political Negotiations*, pp. 23, 35, 48, 50.

Chapter 3

1. Nixon, *RN*, pp. 783, 815, 823. Emphasis in original.

2. *SD Bull.*, Oct. 1, 1973, pp. 425–26.

3. William Rogers, "The Necessity for Strength in an Era of Negotiations," Apr. 23, 1973, in *SD Bull.*, May 14, 1973, p. 590.

4. Gerald Ford, "The National Interest and National Strength," Apr. 15, 1975, in *SD Bull.*, May 5, 1975, pp. 572–75.

5. Freedman, *U.S. Intelligence and the Soviet Strategic Threat*, pp. 169–71; DOD, *Annual Report: FY 1975*, pp. 5–6, 30, 43–44, 46–47; DOD, *Annual Report: FY 1977*, pp. 48–49, 52–53.

6. Garthoff, *Détente and Confrontation*, p. 856.

7. *SD Bull.*, Oct. 14, 1974, pp. 504–19.

8. *SD Bull.*, Feb. 18, 1974, pp. 157–58.

9. Gelman, *Brezhnev Politburo and the Decline of Détente*, pp. 163–64.

10. *SD Bull.*, p. 393.

11. Garthoff, *Détente and Confrontation*, pp. 488–89.

12. *SD Bull.*, Oct. 13, 1975, p. 575; Jackson, "Thai–U.S. Security Relations," p. 165.

13. "Address Before a Joint Session of Congress," Apr. 10, 1975, *SD Bull.*, Apr. 28, 1975, pp. 533–36.

14. Legum, "Angola," pp. 583–84, 587–88, 599; Garthoff, *Détente and Confrontation*, p. 513.

15. U.S. Senate, *Angola*, pp. 7–8.

16. See, e.g., Barnett, *China and the Major Powers*, p. 207; Oksenberg, "Dynamics of the Sino-American Relationship," pp. 72–73; Harding, *Fragile Relationship*, p. 51.

17. Jia, *Mao*, pp. 338–39.

18. Interview with a well-informed Chinese source. *Reference News* is the daily Chinese translation of foreign media reports, which is published in three versions, according to the sensitivity of the material, and distributed internally through work units. Mao was suggesting that Jiang read the most sensitive version.

19. Cf. works cited in n. 16 above.

20. Party History Research Office, *Zhongguo Gongchandang lishi dashiji*, pp. 308–9; Lin, *Zhou Enlai*, pp. 259–61.

21. Party History Research Office, *Zhongguo Gongchandang lishi dashiji*, p. 309; Jia, *Mao*, pp. 327; Lin, *Zhou Enlai*, p. 266.

22. Jia, *Mao*, pp. 320, 322; Party History Research Office, *Zhongguo Gongchandang lishi dashiji*, pp. 306–7.

23. Ye, "Jiefang hou de Jiang Qing," p. 58; Hao and Duan, eds., *Zhongguo Gongchandang liushinian*, p. 636.

24. Jia, *Mao*, pp. 335, 340–41; Hao and Duan, eds., *Zhongguo Gongchandang liushinian*, pp. 639–40. Party History Research Office, *Zhongguo Gongchandang lishi dashiji*, pp. 310; Lin, *Zhou Enlai*, p. 285.

25. Jia, *Mao*, pp. 338–40.

26. Ibid., pp. 345–51.

27. Ibid., pp. 329–32; Lin, *Zhou Enlai*, pp. 313–14.

28. Jia, *Mao*, p. 355; Party History Research Office, *Zhongguo Gongchandang lishi dashiji*, p. 317.

29. Jia, *Mao*, pp. 304–6.

30. Gong, *Kuayue*, pp. 212–13; Jia, *Mao*, pp. 306–7; interview with a well-informed Chinese source.

31. Jia, *Mao*, pp. 307–08.

32. Ibid., p. 310.

33. For a revealing discussion of Mao's deteriorating health as well as his persistent political authority, see Li, *Private Life of Chairman Mao*; Zhang Yufeng, "Anecdotes of Mao Zedong and Zhou Enlai in Their Later Years," *Guangming ribao*, Dec. 26, 1988, in *FBIS/PRC*, Jan. 27, 1989, pp. 16–19. For a discussion of the role of the preeminent leader in China's foreign policy during the 1970s and 1980s, see Robert S. Ross, "From Lin Biao to Deng Xiaoping."

34. Gong, *Kuayue*, pp. 116–17; Zhang Ping, "Zhou Enlai," p. 576. The snails episode is reported in Terrill, *White-Boned Demon*, p. 343.

35. "Chiang Ch'ing's Address to Diplomatic Cadres," pp. 542–45.

36. Han et al., "Wei Zhong Mei guanxi zhengchanghua," pp. 513–15; Zhu, *Dashi furen huiyilu*, pp. 237–43.

37. *WP*, Aug. 17, 1973; ibid., Aug. 1, 1973.

38. *NYT*, Jan. 19, Jan. 22, Mar. 23, Mar. 29, May 3, and May 28, 1974; *WP*, Oct. 15, 1974.

39. *WP*, Dec. 28, 1975, *NYT*, Dec. 28, 1975. For an in-depth analysis of the release of the helicopter pilots, see Lieberthal, *Sino-Soviet Conflict in the 1970s*, pp. 126–33.

40. Jia, *Mao*, p. 342.

41. Robert S. Ross, *Indochina Tangle*, p. 65. For a fuller discussion of Soviet-Vietnamese relations during this period, see ibid., pp. 30–32, 56–62, 86–93.

42. U.S. Senate, *Angola*, pp. 184–85; Valenti, "Soviet Decision-Making," p. 103; Garthoff, *Détente and Confrontation*, p. 514.

43. *Xinhua*, Oct. 3, 1973, in *FBIS/PRC*, Oct. 4, 1973, pp. A3–15; *Xinhua*, Sept. 26, 1975, in *FBIS/PRC*, Sept. 29, 1975, p. A3.

44. Ren Guping, "Year of Turbulence, Year of Victory," *Renmin ribao*, Jan. 8, 1975, in *FBIS/PRC*, Jan. 9, 1975, pp. A3–4; Foreign Broadcast Infor-

mation Service, *Trends in Communist Media* (cited hereafter as FBIS, *Trends*), Dec. 31, 1975, pp. 4–5.

45. *Xinhua*, Nov. 7, 1975, in *FBIS/PRC*, Nov. 10, 1975, pp. A1–2; Fan Xiuqu, "The Détente Fraud Does Not Work," *Renmin ribao*, July 19, 1975, in *FBIS/PRC*, July 21, 1975, p. A11; interviews with U.S. government officials.

46. Bush, *Looking Forward*, p. 143.

47. FBIS, *Trends*, Nov. 12, 1975, pp. 1–2; interviews with various U.S. officials; Solomon, *Chinese Political Negotiating Behavior*, pp. 52–53.

48. FBIS, *Trends*, May 12, 1976, p. 1–2.

49. FBIS, *Trends*, May 12, 1976, pp. 1–2, 6; June 4, 1976, pp. 6–7; July 30, 1975, pp. 5–6.

50. Jia, *Mao*, pp. 306–7, 342; Gong, *Kuayue*, pp. 212–13; interview with a well-informed Chinese source.

51. For a discussion of Chinese fears in the postwar era and the PRC's improving relations with the ASEAN states, see Robert S. Ross, *Indochina Tangle*. For an excellent discussion of unfulfilled Soviet efforts to penetrate the region, see Buszynski, *Soviet Foreign Policy and Southeast Asia*.

52. Interview with Gerald Ford.

53. Interview with U.S. government official; *WP*, Apr. 30, 1973, May 31, 1973; Solomon, *U.S.–PRC Political Negotiations*, p. 33.

54. Shi, ed., *Dangdai Zhongguo de duiwai jingji hezuo*, p. 320. See also Li Ping, "'Wenhua Da Geming' zhong de Zhou Enlai," p. 30.

55. *WP*, May 21, 1973; May 6, 1973; July 2, 1973; and July 16, 1973; *NYT*, Nov. 28, 1973.

56. Han et al. "Wei Zhong Mei guanxi zhengchanghua," p. 495; Gong, *Kuayue*, pp. 212–13. For a discussion of the agreement, see Garthoff, *Détente and Confrontation*, pp. 334–44.

57. *New York Times*, Nov. 11, 1973.

58. Interview with a White House official; Kissinger, *Years of Upheaval*, pp. 688–97.

59. Interview with John Holdridge; *NYT*, Mar. 3, 1973.

60. Interviews with U.S. government officials; *WP*, May 17, 1973; Kissinger, *Years of Upheaval*, p. 688.

61. Oksenberg, "Dynamics of Sino-American Relations," p. 58; interviews with U.S. government officials; Solomon, *U.S.–PRC Political Negotiations*, p. 42.

62. Interview with Roger Sullivan.

63. Kissinger, *Years of Upheaval*, pp. 689–94.

64. Interview with Roger Sullivan.

65. Oksenberg, "Decade of Sino-American Relations," p. 180. Zhou first made this charge in June 1973. Solomon, *U.S.–PRC Political Negotiations*, p. 34.

66. Xue, ed., *Dangdai Zhongguo waijiao*, p. 223; Solomon, *U.S.–PRC Political Negotiations*, pp. 36–38, 41.

67. Interview with U.S. government official; Solomon, *U.S.–PRC Political Negotiations*, pp. 43–44, 46.

68. Interviews with William Gleysteen and White House officials. Reporters accompanying Kissinger allegedly found maps of China that included Vladivostok within the Chinese boundary in their hotels. Terrill, *Mao*, p. 414.

69. Xue, ed., *Dangdai Zhongguo waijiao*, p. 226.

70. Interview with John Holdridge and with other U.S. government officials. Note that the statement is very brief, making no mention of a Chinese invitation or of Chairman Mao's interest in meeting the U.S. president. *NYT*, Nov. 30, 1974.

71. Interviews with White House and State Department officials.

72. *NYT*, Sept. 2, 1973; Sept. 4, 1973; Nov. 14, 1973; June 8, 1975.

73. *NYT*, May 19, 1974; June 8, 1975.

74. Interview with Harvey Feldman.

75. *WP*, June 1, 1975; *NYT*, Oct. 16, 1975; *WP*, Dec. 1, 1975. For Goldwater's earlier comments, see *Congressional Record*, Feb. 18, 1975, pp. 3310–11. For Thurmond's remarks, see, e.g., ibid., May 5, 1975, p. 12904. For Helm's remarks, see, e.g., ibid., Feb. 5, 1975, p. 2567. The poll results are reported in ibid., Feb. 3, 1875, pp. 2082–83, and Dec. 12, 1975, p. 40386.

76. Interview with a White House official.

77. *NYT*, Oct. 19, 1975; Solomon, *U.S.–PRC Political Negotiations*, p. 51; Solomon, *Chinese Political Negotiating Behavior*, pp. 34, 81.

78. Interviews with White House and State Department officials; Solomon, *U.S.–PRC Political Negotiations*, p. 54. See also Bush, *Looking Forward*, pp. 142–44.

79. Interviews with White House and State Department officials; Solomon, *U.S.–PRC Political Negotiations*, p. 48. See also *NYT*, Oct. 23, 1975; Oct. 24, 1975; Nov. 30, 1975.

80. Interviews with White House and State Department officials; Solomon, *U.S.–PRC Political Negotiations*, p. 55.

81. Interview with an administration official; Bush, *Looking Forward*, p. 146; *WP*, Oct. 22, 1975.

82. Interview with a State Department official. See also *NYT*, Nov. 5, 1975.

83. Interviews with White House and State Department officials.

84. *NYT*, Nov. 5, 1975; Solomon, *U.S.–PRC Political Negotiations*, pp. 55–56.

85. Interview with White House official. On Bush, see *WP*, Feb. 7, 1975.

86. Gates and Geelhoed, *Dragon and the Snake*, p. 11.

87. Interview with William Gleysteen and a White House official.

88. See, e.g., Kissinger's press conference in *SD Bull.*, Dec. 29, 1975, pp. 929–32.

89. Hu Sheng, ed., *Zhongguo Gongchandang de qishi nian*, p. 446.

90. Xue, ed., *Dangdai Zhongguo waijiao*, p. 226; interview with Gerald Ford.

91. Xue, ed., *Dangdai Zhongguo waijiao*, p. 226. The administration carried out its troop-withdrawal commitment, and in June 1976 it also withdrew its advisers from the offshore islands of Quemoy and Matsu, removing the American "trip-wire" defense of the islands. *NYT*, June 24, 1976.

92. Interviews with Gerald Ford and Michel Oksenberg.

93. Interviews with James Lilley and U.S. State Department officials. For discussion of the 1962 episode, see Whiting, *Chinese Calculus*, pp. 62–72.

94. Gates and Geelhoed, *Dragon and the Snake*, pp. 53–55.

95. Ibid., pp. 55–56, 60–62; U.S. Senate, *United States and China*, pp. 2–3, 16, 18.

96. Gates and Geelhoed, *Dragon and the Snake*, pp. 104–5.

97. *WP*, Feb. 28, 1975; Mar. 6, 1975. For the 1976 trade statistics, see Barnett, *China's Economy*, p. 507. For an interpretation of these developments, see Robert S. Ross, "From Lin Biao to Deng Xiaoping."

98. See, e.g., *SD Bull.*, Feb. 24, 1975, p. 247; *NYT*, Oct. 19, 1975; *SD Bull.*, Dec. 29, 1975, pp. 926–30.

99. Interviews with Benjamin Huberman, Roger Sullivan, other State Department officials, and James Lilley.

100. *WP*, Jan. 16, 1974; *NYT*, Oct. 4, 1975; Apr. 12, 1976; Oct. 29, 1976; Oct. 30, 1976. The best analysis of this episode is in Garrett, "U.S. Bureaucratic Politics and the Strategic Triangle."

101. See the report of the NSC decision memorandum in *Aviation Week and Technology Review*, Oct. 25, 1976, p. 18.

102. Interviews with White House and State Department officials. For the report of the computer decision, see *NYT*, Oct. 29, 1976.

103. *SD Bull.*, Nov. 8, 1976, p. 579; *NYT*, Oct. 19, 1976; *SD Bull.*, Nov. 15, 1976, pp. 608–09. Kissinger made a similar statement in May 1976 before Congress. See *NYT*, Oct. 19, 1976.

Chapter 4

1. See Brzezinski, *Power and Principle*, pp. 53–54.

2. U.S. Department of State, *American Foreign Policy: Basic Documents, 1977–1980* (hereafter cited as *Basic Docs.*), pp. 154–55; Brzezinski, *Power and Principle*, p. 307. See also Garthoff, *Détente and Confrontation*, pp. 786–87.

3. Carter's announcement of the B-1 and neutron bomb decisions are in *Basic Docs.*, pp. 107–8, 111–12. On the Minuteman III, see Garthoff, *Détente and Confrontation*, p. 701.

4. *Basic Docs.*, pp. 169–71, 185–86.

5. Ibid., pp. 6–9.

6. "The Past and the Future in Soviet-American Relations," in *Basic Docs.*, pp. 561–65.

7. *Basic Docs.*, pp. 18–20.

8. Ibid., p. 1131.

9. *SD Bull.*, July 4, 1977, p. 9.

10. *Basic Docs.*, p. 1408–1412.

11. U.S. Senate, *U.S. MIAs in Southeast Asia.*

12. Garthoff, *Détente and Confrontation*, pp. 579, 632–33; Shelton, "Sino-Soviet Split," p. 79; Legum, "Angola," pp. 615–16; Vance, *Hard Choices*, p. 73.

13. Legum, "Angola," p. 616; Shelton, "Sino-Soviet Split," pp. 79–80; Garthoff, *Détente and Confrontation*, p. 639; Vance, *Hard Choices*, pp. 74, 85.

14. Brzezinski, *Power and Principle*, pp. 178–79, 183–84; Vance, *Hard Choices*, pp. 74, 84–85.

15. Zheng et al., eds., *Xin Zhongguo jishi*, p. 604; Shao et al., eds., *Zhongguo Gongchandang lishi jiangyi*, p. 337; He Qin et al., eds., *Zhonggongdang li jiangyi*, p. 199; Zheng and Zhu, eds., *Zhongguo Gongchandang lishi jiangyi*, 2:243–44.

16. Chinese analysis of Soviet motives is in "Dangqian Suxiu Dui Hua zhengce de dongxiang," pp. 11–14. Note also Beijing's charge that "Moscow even haughtily demanded that we change our policy." Cited in FBIS, *Trends*, Jan. 5, 1977, p. 9. For a Soviet discussion of Moscow's initiatives, see Gromyko and Ponomarev, eds., *Soviet Foreign Policy*, 2:565–66.

17. On the negotiations and the brief lull in Chinese polemics, see FBIS, *Trends*, Dec. 22, 1976, p. 12. Hua's Dazhai speech is in *Xinhua*, Dec. 28, 1976, in *FBIS/PRC*, Dec. 28, 1976, pp. E2–15. See also Li Xiannian's many comments in late 1976 and early 1977 criticizing Soviet overtures. Soviet nuclear intimidation is discussed in "Down with Nuclear Superstition," *Renmin ribao*, May 13, 1977, in *FBIS/PRC*, May 13, 1977, pp. E26–27.

18. Oksenberg, "Decade of Sino-American Relations," p. 183; FBIS, *Trends*, Mar. 9, 1977, p. 6; ibid., Apr. 6, 1977, p. 5.

19. *Xinhua*, Sept. 29, 1977, in *FBIS/PRC*, Sept. 30, 1977, pp. A5–6; FBIS, *Trends*, Oct. 27, 1977, pp. 2–3; Jen Ku-ping, "The Munich Tragedy and Contemporary Appeasement," *Renmin ribao*, Nov. 26, 1977, in *Peking Review* 20, no. 50 (Dec. 9, 1977): 6–11. See also FBIS, *Trends*, Nov. 30, 1977, pp. 8–9.

20. *WP*, Aug. 16, 1977.

21. Moscow in English to South and Southeast Asia, June 27, 1977, in U.S. National Technical Information Service, Foreign Broadcast Information Service, *FBIS Daily Report: Soviet Union* (hereafter cited as *FBIS/SU*), June 28, 1977, p. L1; Moscow Radio Peace and Progress, in English to Asia, June 29, 1977, in *FBIS/SU*, June 30, 1977, p. L1.

22. *Krasnaya zvezda*, Mar. 22, 1977, *FBIS/SU*, Mar. 24, 1977, p. L1; Hanoi Domestic Service, May 4, 1977, *FBIS/SU*, May 5, 1977, p. L1; Chanda, *Brother Enemy*, p. 190.

23. "Memorandum on Vice Premier Li Xiannian's Talks with Premier Pham Van Dong," *Beijing Review*, Mar. 30, 1979, p. 22.

24. For a discussion of this visit, see Robert S. Ross, *Indochina Tangle,* pp. 149–50.

25. See the text of the treaty in *Khao San Pathet Lao,* July 19, 1977, in *FBIS, Asia Pacific,* July 19, 1977, pp. I8–11. On Soviet support for Vietnam's Laos policy, see S. Alfonin, "Vietnam's Radiant Horizons," *International Affairs* (Moscow), no. 4 (1977): 25; Aleksandr Serbin, "Friendship and Solidarity," *Pravda,* July 26, 1977, in *FBIS/SU,* July 29, 1977, p. L1.

26. Commentary, "Why Is the Soviet Union Spreading Lies and Slanders on the Incident of Armed Conflicts in Cambodia?" *Xinhua,* Jan. 19, 1978, in *FBIS/PRC,* Jan. 19, 1978, p. A9; *Xinhua,* Feb. 9, 1978, in *FBIS/PRC,* Feb. 10, 1978, pp. A4–5. For an in-depth discussion of Cambodian-Vietnamese relations during this period and of Chinese involvement, see Robert S. Ross, *Indochina Tangle,* chs. 5 and 6.

27. *SD Bull.,* Feb. 21, 1977, pp. 153–54; *NYT,* Feb. 3, 1977; Vance, *Hard Choices,* p. 78.

28. U.S. Senate, *United States and China,* p. 2; *Xinhua,* Nov. 14, 1976, *FBIS/PRC,* Nov. 15, 1976, p. A3; Agence France-Presse (hereafter cited as AFP), Nov. 22, 1976, *FBIS/PRC,* Nov. 22, 1976, p. A5.

29. FBIS, *Trends,* Sept. 22, 1976, p. 7; Peking Domestic Service, Jan. 11, 1977, *FBIS/PRC,* Jan. 13, 1977, pp. E9–10. See Hua's eulogy for Mao in *Xinhua,* Sept. 18, 1976, in *FBIS/PRC,* Sept. 20, 1976, pp. A7–11.

30. FBIS, *Trends,* Mar. 2, 1977, pp. 7–9; ibid., July 7, 1977, pp. 3–4.

31. Interview with William Gleysteen and other State Department officials; *NYT,* Feb. 11 and 16, 1977.

32. Interview with William Gleysteen and other State Department officials; *NYT,* May 2, 1977.

33. Brzezinski, *Power and Principle,* pp. 51–52, 197.

34. Oksenberg, "Decade of Sino-American Relations," p. 181.

35. Brzezinski, *Power and Principle,* p. 200.

36. *WP,* Feb. 9, 1979.

37. Brzezinski, *Power and Principle,* pp. 197–99.

38. Ibid., p. 200–201.

39. Interviews with Paul Kreisberg, Richard Holbrooke, and other State Department officials.

40. Interviews with William Gleysteen and Richard Holbrooke; Vance, *Hard Choices,* p. 79.

41. See the memoirs of Vance, *Hard Choices,* p. 79, and Brzezinski, *Power and Principle,* pp. 200–201.

42. Interviews with Cyrus Vance and Leonard Woodcock.

43. Interview with Benjamin Huberman.

44. *Basic Docs.,* p. 913; *NYT,* Aug. 17, 1977. Vance and Assistant Secretary of State Richard Holbrooke recall that this line in the speech was aimed at Beijing to prepare it for a tough U.S. negotiating position. Interviews with Cyrus Vance and Richard Holbrooke.

45. Carter, *Keeping Faith,* p. 189; *WP,* July 5, 1977.

46. Interviews with Michel Oksenberg, William Gleysteen, and other U.S. officials; Xue, ed., *Dangdai Zhongguo waijiao*, pp. 227–28; Tian, ed., *Gaige kaifang yilai de Zhongguo waijiao*, p. 382.

47. Michel Oksenberg, Richard Holbrooke, and Alan Romberg concurred that this was an important meeting, and that Huang Hua's initial response suggested Chinese flexibility, and thus progress toward normalization. Interview with Michel Oksenberg.

48. Xue, ed., *Dangdai Zhongguo waijiao*, pp. 227–28; Vance, *Hard Choices*, pp. 81–82; interviews with Michel Oksenberg and with William Gleysteen and other State Department officials; Vance's response to Deng's accusation was that the Ford administration had agreed to the Japan formula *if* it could resolve the Taiwan issue. But Vance's explanation is disingenuous, for the Japan formula was precisely a formula to resolve the issue of representation on Taiwan following normalization. Vance, *Hard Choices*, p. 82. Note also that the Carter administration review of the negotiating record did not find a U.S. *commitment* to normalize relations. Interview with Michel Oksenberg; *NYT*, Mar. 4, 1977. Oksenberg stresses that the phrase "under unofficial arrangements" begged for further probing by China, and that it was unfortunate that China did not seek clarification of the U.S. position. But he acknowledges that the U.S. proposal regarding an official presence in Taiwan after normalization was contrary to the Japan formula and thus a retreat from the position of the Ford administration.

49. Xue, ed., *Dangdai Zhongguo waijiao*, pp. 227–28.

50. Woodcock oral history.

51. The report is in the *Boston Herald American*, Aug. 26, 1977; interview with Samuel Huntington.

52. *NYT*, Sept. 7, 1977.

53. Vance, *Hard Choices*, pp. 82–83; interview with William Gleysteen.

54. Carter, *Keeping Faith*, p. 192; *NYT*, Aug. 28, 1977; interview with Cyrus Vance.

55. This and the next four paragraphs are based on interviews with Leonard Woodcock.

56. Ibid.; Woodcock oral history.

57. Interview with Leonard Woodcock; Woodcock oral history.

58. Ibid.

59. Brzezinski, *Power and Principle*, pp. 202–3.

60. Ibid.; Oksenberg, "Ten Years of U.S.–China Relations."

61. Interview with Cyrus Vance. Note that Brzezinski agrees that he used the invitation to establish a greater presence in the policy-making process, and that Vance's opposition arose over disagreement regarding Soviet policy. Brzezinski, *Power and Principle*, pp. 203–4.

62. Woodcock oral history.

63. Interview with Leonard Woodcock; Woodcock oral history.

64. Oksenberg and Perkins, "China Policy of Henry Jackson," p. 162.

65. Interview with Leonard Woodcock. Li's comment is in _NYT_, Aug. 30, 1977.

66. Vance, _Hard Choices_, pp. 78–79; _NYT_, June 24, 1977; interview with Michel Oksenberg; Solomon, _U.S.–PRC Political Negotiations_, p. 63.

67. _NYT_, Sept. 11, 1977.

68. Interview with Harold Brown; Brzezinski, _Power and Principle_, p. 203; _NYT_, Jan. 4, 1978.

69. Interviews with Cyrus Vance and Michel Oksenberg; Woodcock oral history; Vance, _Hard Choices_, p. 114; Brzezinski, _Power and Principle_, p. 203; _NYT_, Jan. 4, 1978. See also Vance's comments at a January news conference, _NYT_, Jan. 12, 1978. For public reports of Chinese interest, see _NYT_, Feb. 28, 1977.

70. This paragraph is based on Barnett, _China's Economy_, pp. 508–10.

Chapter 5

1. Interview with Samuel Huntington; _Basic Docs._, pp. 20–24.

2. Interview with Samuel Huntington; Garthoff, _Détente and Confrontation_, p. 899.

3. President Carter's May 25, 1978, news conference, in _SD Bull._, July 1978, pp. 18–19. See also Carter's news conference of June 14, 1978, in _SD Bull._, Aug. 1978, pp. 6–7. See also Garthoff, _Détente and Confrontation_, p. 624–26.

4. Garthoff, _Détente and Confrontation_, pp. 625–26; Vance, _Hard Choices_, pp. 100, 102–3.

5. _Basic Docs._, pp. 565–68; Vance, _Hard Choices_, pp. 101–2. There is much controversy over this speech. Vance and Brzezinski presented Carter with distinctly different drafts. Carter combined the two different drafts, thus producing a mixed signal. Nonetheless, Brzezinski reports that the references to totalitarianism and repression and the other hard-line ideological references were Carter's own insertions. Brzezinski, _Power and Principle_, pp. 320–21. Moreover, the main thrust of the speech was hard-line and pessimistic.

6. Creekman, "Sino-Soviet Competition in the Yemens," pp. 78–79.

7. Carter, _Keeping Faith_, p. 384.

8. See Garthoff, _Détente and Confrontation_, pp. 856–57. This view was widely shared in the administration. See Vance, _Hard Choices_, p. 64.

9. _SD Bull._, July 1978, p. 20.

10. _Basic Docs._, p. 478. The January 1978 speech is inibid., pp. 476–78.

11. Brzezinski, _Power and Principle_, pp. 307–8.

12. Interview with Harold Brown. Brown recalls that Carter's understanding of improving Soviet ICBM accuracy affected his perception of Soviet intentions. Brzezinski, _Power and Principle_, pp. 332–33; Collins, _American and Soviet Military Trends_, pp. 94–95, 120 n. 69, 121 n. 72; Garthoff, _Détente and Confrontation_, pp. 791–93; Talbott, _Endgame_, pp. 101–2.

13. _Basic Docs._, pp. 20–24; ibid., pp. 565–68;

14. Brzezinski, *Power and Principle*, p. 335.

15. Interview with Harold Brown.

16. "My Opinion of the Russians Has Changed Most Dramatically," *Basic Docs.*, pp. 811–12.

17. Carter, *Keeping Faith*, p. 483; Brzezinski, *Power and Principle*, p. 444.

18. Gelman, *Soviet Far East Buildup*, pp. 75–77; Garthoff, *Détente and Confrontation*, p. 698; *Asian Security*, pp. 42–46; International Institute for Strategic Studies, *Strategic Survey, 1978*, p. 45;. Jacobson, "Developments in the Far East," p. 146; Japanese Defense Agency, *Defense of Japan, 1979*, pp. 33–35; *NYT*, Apr. 6, 1978.

19. Xu Xiangqian, "Heighten Vigilance, Be Ready to Fight," *Red Flag*, no. 8 (Aug. 1978), in Joint Publications Research Service (henceforth cited as JPRS), *Translations from "Red Flag,"* no. 71961, p. 64. For a discussion of this article, see FBIS, *Trends*, Aug. 2, 1978, pp. 11–12.

20. Chu Yu, commentary, *Red Flag*, no. 4 (1978), in JPRS, *Translations from "Red Flag,"* no. 71314, pp. 174–77; Xu Xiangqian, "Heighten Vigilance, Be Ready to Fight," p. 61.

21. The discussion in the following paragraphs on Indochina draws from Robert S. Ross, *Indochina Tangle*, ch. 7.

22. See the *Xinhua* interview with the spokesperson of the Overseas Chinese Affairs Office and Zhong Xidong's speech at the Sino-Vietnamese negotiations in *On Vietnam's Expulsion of Chinese Residents* (Beijing: Foreign Language Press, 1978), pp. 23–25, 54–55. For the Soviet reaction, see TASS, Apr. 20, 1978, in *FBIS/SU*, Apr. 28, 1978, p. L1; M. Ilinskiy, "The Light of Freedom," *Izvestiya*, Apr. 29, 1978, in *FBIS/SU*, May 9, 1978, p. L2; V. Skvortsov, "Bright Horizons," *Pravda*, Apr. 30, 1978, in *FBIS,/*, May 5, 1978, p. L3.

23. Deng Xiaoping remarked to a "foreign dignitary" that there was a connection between the naval movement and Sino-Vietnamese relations. See AFP, June 1, 1978, in *FBIS/PRC*, June 2, 1978, p. A12. Liao's comments are from AFP, June 2, 1978, in *FBIS/PRC*, June 2, 1978, p. A18. Deng's subsequent remarks are in *Nation Review* (Bangkok), June 9, 1978, in *FBIS/PRC*, June 9, 1978, pp. A11–15.

24. Commentator, "Who Is the Instigator?" *Renmin ribao*, June 17, 1978, in *FBIS/PRC*, June 19, 1978, pp. A3–6.

25. Commentator, "The Plotter of a Siege Is Being Besieged," *Red Flag*, No. 11, 1978, in *FBIS/PRC*, Nov. 29, 1978, p. A10; Kyodo News Service, June 5, 1978, in *FBIS/PRC*, June 5, 1978, p. 8.

26. Oksenberg, "Decade of Sino-American Relations," p. 183. For a Chinese appraisal of the bureaucratic struggle, see, e.g., "The Fierce Debate in the United States on U.S. Policy Toward the Soviet Union," Beijing Domestic Service, Apr. 18, 1978, in *FBIS/PRC*, Apr. 19, 1978, pp. A1–4. See also FBIS, *Trends*, June 1, 1978, pp. 6–7; Mei Ping, "What Does the U.S.–Soviet Quarrel Show," *Renmin ribao*, July 27, 1978, in *FBIS/PRC*, Aug. 2, 1978,

p. A2; Fang Min, "'What Is Reasonable' and 'What Is Unreasonable,'" *Renmin ribao*, Aug. 10, 1978, in *FBIS/PRC*, Aug. 17, 1978, pp. A3–4.

27. Commentator, "The Cuban Mercenary Troops Are a Product of the Policy of Soviet Social-Imperialism," *Red Flag*, no. 10 (Oct. 1978), in JPRS, *Translations from "Red Flag,"* no. 72318, p. 132; FBIS, *Trends*, Oct. 25, 1978, pp. 2–3.

28. Interviews with Zbigniew Brzezinski and Michel Oksenberg.

29. Interviews with Cyrus Vance, Zbigniew Brzezinski, and Leonard Woodcock; Brzezinski, *Power and Principle*, p. 563. See Vance's discussion of Vietnam and the intelligence report in *Hard Choices*, p. 122.

30. Interviews with Zbigniew Brzezinski and Cyrus Vance; Brzezinski, *Power and Principle*, pp. 203–4; Vance, *Hard Choices*, p. 114.

31. Interview with Harold Brown; Brzezinski, *Power and Principle*, p. 206.

32. Interview with Zbigniew Brzezinski.

33. The text of Carter's instructions is in Brzezinski, *Power and Principle*, annex I.

34. Ibid.; emphasis added. Note that Brzezinski was instructed to encourage Chinese assistance to Somalia in its conflict with Ethiopia. On the Gromyko visit, see Brzezinski, *Power and Principle*, p. 208.

35. Interviews with Harold Brown and Cyrus Vance. Once again, Brown's position had hardened. He now believed that Washington should not allow Moscow to dictate U.S. China policy. He further believed that better relations with China would not damage superpower relations but might give Washington an additional and needed lever in U.S.–Soviet relations. Interview with Harold Brown.

36. Brzezinski, *Power and Principle*, pp. 207–8; interview with Leonard Woodcock.

37. Interview with Cyrus Vance; Vance, *Keeping Faith*, p. 115–16; Oksenberg, "Decade of Sino-American Relations," p. 185.

38. *WP*, Apr. 27, 1978; interview with Michel Oksenberg.

39. Xue, ed., *Dangdai Zhongguo waijiao*, p. 228.

40. Interview with Benjamin Huberman.

41. Interviews with Morton Abramowitz, Samuel Huntington, and Benjamin Huberman. Huberman also carried with him a piece of the moon and a letter from President Carter to Chairman Hua Guofeng on the significance of the gift. Hua and his colleagues were genuinely excited by the gift.

42. *NYT*, May 23 and 28, 1978; Brzezinski, *Power and Principle*, pp. 211–12.

43. Brzezinski, *Power and Principle*, p. 214; Xue, ed., *Dangdai Zhongguo waijiao*, p. 228. On the three conditions, see Brzezinski, *Power and Principle*, p. 225.

44. Interview with Leonard Woodcock; Oksenberg, "Decade of Sino-American Relations," pp. 185–86.

45. Oksenberg, "Decade of Sino-American Relations," pp. 185–86; Woodcock Oral History.

46. Brzezinski, *Power and Principle*, p. 229; interview with Roger Sullivan.

47. Interview with Harvey Feldman.

48. Interviews with Richard Holbrooke and Harvey Feldman.

49. Interviews with Zbigniew Brzezinski and Michel Oksenberg.

50. Interview with Harvey Feldman.

51. Brzezinski, *Power and Principle*, p. 197.

52. Interview with Leonard Woodcock; Woodcock Oral History; Solomon, *U.S.–PRC Political Negotiations*, p. 69.

53. Dou, ed., *Zhongguo Renmin Gongheguo duiwai guanxi gaishu*, p. 109; Oksenberg, "Decade of Sino-American Relations," p. 187.

54. Woodcock Oral History.

55. Interviews with Leonard Woodcock and Roger Sullivan; Vance, *Hard Choices*, p. 117.

56. Interview with Roger Sullivan.

57. Interview with Ambassador Leonard Woodcock; Woodcock Oral History. Note that the dates of final normalization discussions are all based on the Washington, D.C., time zone.

58. Vance, *Hard Choices*, p. 118; Brzezinski, *Power and Principle*, p. 230; Oksenberg, "Decade of Sino-American Relations," pp. 187–88. Brzezinski gives greater importance to his meeting with Chai than warranted, given Deng's prior decision to participate in the negotiations.

59. Interviews with Leonard Woodcock and Roger Sullivan.

60. Oksenberg, "Decade of Sino-American Relations," p. 188; Vance, *Hard Choices*, pp. 109–10, 118–19; interview with Cyrus Vance.

61. Interview with Leonard Woodcock.

62. Woodcock oral history.

63. Interviews with Leonard Woodcock and Roger Sullivan. For the White House's concern, see Brzezinski, *Power and Principle*, p. 231.

64. For a discussion of the dates of the workshop and Deng's speech and of the workshop's agenda, see Lieberthal and Dickson, *Research Guide*, pp. 258–59.

65. Brzezinski, *Power and Principle*, p. 227.

66. This and the following paragraphs on Indochina draw from Robert S. Ross, *Indochina Tangle*, ch. 8.

67. "Zhonggong zhongyang guanyu dui Yue jinxing ziwei fanji, baowei bianjing zhandou de tongzhi," in Research Office of the Central Committee of the Chinese Communist Party, ed., *San zhongquanhui yilai wenxian xuanbian*, 1:66.

68. Interview with Leonard Woodcock; *Xinhua*, Dec. 16, 1978, in *FBIS/PRC*, Dec. 18, 1978, p. A6; FBIS, *Trends*, Dec. 20, 1978, p. 2.

69. *Time*, Feb. 5, 1979, p. 34.

70. Downen, *Taiwan Pawn*; U.S. Senate, *Executive-Legislative Consultations*, pp. 8, 20–21; interviews with Leonard Woodcock and Cyrus Vance.

71. Interviews with Richard Holbrooke, Michel Oksenberg, Roger Sullivan, and Cyrus Vance.

72. On congressional attitudes toward the handling of normalization, see the statements by members of Congress in U.S. House, *Taiwan Legislation*; U.S. Senate, *Taiwan*. For a full discussion of the congressional reaction to the administration's handling of normalization and to its treatment of the Taiwan issue, see Sutter, *China Quandary*, ch. 4.

73. Downen, *Taiwan Pawn*; interview with Roger Sullivan.

74. Brzezinski, *Power and Principle*, pp. 415–16; interview with Roger Sullivan.

75. Note that Senate leaders later protested without success that this was not their intention and that they had believed that the act had granted them authority to decide arms sales to Taiwan. Interviews with Roger Sullivan and Carl Ford. The president's statement is in *Basic Docs.*, pp. 988–89.

76. U.S. Senate, *Executive-Legislative Consultations*, p. 3.

77. For a discussion of the importance of institutions in promoting long-term stability in U.S.–China cooperation, see Oksenberg, "Dynamics of the Sino-American Relationship."

78. Brzezinski, *Power and Principle*, pp. 345, 414. As in the past, Vance opposed such developments. He tried to persuade the president to cancel Secretary of the Treasury Michael Blumenthal's February visit to China in order to distance the United States from China's invasion of Vietnam. Interview with Roger Sullivan.

79. Interviews with Frank Press and Ben Huberman.

80. Brzezinski, *Power and Principle*, pp. 419–21.

81. Ibid., p. 421; Solomon, *U.S.–PRC Political Negotiations*, p. 76; *NYT*, Aug. 28, 1979; Pollack, *Lessons of Coalition Politics*, p. 41; U.S. Senate, *United States, China, and Japan*, p. 15.

82. Vance, *Hard Choices*, p. 390; Brzezinski, *Power and Principle*, pp. 422–23.

83. *NYT*, May 9 and June 9, 1978; Brzezinski, *Power and Principle*, pp. 203, 219, 421.

84. Vance, *Hard Choices*, p. 117; Brzezinski, *Power and Principle*, p. 420.

85. Garthoff, *Détente and Confrontation*, p. 750; Vance, *Hard Choices*, p. 390; Brzezinski, *Power and Principle*, pp. 424–25, 431; interview with Benjamin Huberman.

86. Interviews with Harold Brown and Roger Sullivan; Vance, *Hard Choices*, pp. 390–91; Brzezinski, *Power and Principle*, pp. 424, 431; *NYT*, Jan. 9, 1980; *WP*, June 25, 1980; Solomon, *U.S.–PRC Political Negotiations*, p. 78.

87. Vance, *Hard Choices*, p. 394; Brzezinski, *Power and Principle*, p. 437.

88. U.S. House, *United States and the People's Republic of China*, pp. 2–6. A copy of Munitions Control Newsletter no. 81 is in ibid., p. 163.

89. Interview with Ben Huberman.

90. *China Business Review*, Mar.–Apr. 1980, p. 7; ibid., July–Aug. 1980, pp. 23–24; Brzezinski, *Power and Principle*, p. 424. For a discussion of the helicopter deal, see *NYT*, Feb. 22, 1980. The discussion of the Perry visit is

based on *NYT*, Sept. 7, 1980; interview with Roger Sullivan. Carter's statement is in *NYT*, July 10, 1980.

91. Brzezinski, *Power and Principle*, p. 420; *WP*, Apr. 20, 1979; *NYT*, June 18, 1981; U.S. Senate, *United States, China, and Japan*, p. 15; *WP*, June 25, 1980.

92. See Bernstein, *Negotiations to Normalize U.S.–China Relations*, pp. 15–16.

93. Oksenberg, "Dynamics of Sino-American Relations," pp. 58–9; *China Business Review*, May–June, 1979, p. 16; *NYT*, Apr. 4, 1979; *WP*, May 11 and 15, 1979.

94. Carter, *Keeping Faith*, p. 209. For the administration's full justification for granting China MFN status, see U.S. House, *United States–China Trade Agreement*, pp. 40–42; U.S. Senate, *Agreement on Trade Relations Between the United States and China*, pp. 28–54. See also *China Business Review*, Nov.–Dec. 1979, pp. 9–10, for a discussion of other aspects of PRC emigration policy suggesting compliance with the Jackson-Vanik amendment.

95. Oksenberg, "Dynamics of Sino-American Relations," p. 189.

96. *WSJ*, May 15, 1979; *WP*, May 15, 1979; *NYT* July 8, 1978; *WP*, July 4, 1978; *WSJ*, July 9, 1979. See also Oksenberg, "Decade of Sino-American Relations," p. 189; Brzezinski, *Power and Principle*, pp. 418–19.

97. *NYT*, May 15, 1979; *WP*, May 16, 1979.

98. *China Business Review*, Nov.–Dec. 1979, pp. 9–11; *WSJ*, Oct. 24, 1979.

99. Interviews I have had with numerous textile negotiators indicate that there was a consensus that China should have been granted immediate high-level access to the U.S. textile market.

100. Interview with Michael B. Smith, U.S. textile negotiator in 1978–79.

101. Ibid.; *WSJ*, June 1, 1979; *WP*, June 2, 1979.

102. Interview with H. Reiter Webb, U.S. textile negotiator, 1979–80.

103. Ibid.

104. Ibid.

105. Ibid. For a discussion of the agreement, see *WSJ*, July 25, 1980; *NYT*, May 21, and Sept. 18 and 19, 1980.

106. The only issue here would be China's use of U.S. high-technology physics programs to train future Chinese military scientists. But the only methods available to Washington to prevent this—controlling U.S. educational institutions or disrupting educational exchanges—would impose far greater damage than the original problem.

107. Interview with Benjamin Huberman; Brzezinski, *Power and Principle*, p. 226.

108. Interviews with Benjamin Huberman, Frank Press, Michel Oksenberg, and Roger Sullivan; Woodcock Oral History. For a discussion of the delegation and its agenda, see *NYT*, June 28, 1978.

109. Interview with Benjamin Huberman; Lampton, *Relationship Restored* pp. 31–32, 62.

110. These issues are discussed in Lampton, *Relationship Restored*, ch. 7.

111. Interview with Benjamin Huberman.

112. Siddiqi, Jin, and Shi, *China–USA Governmental Cooperation*; interviews with Frank Press and Benjamin Huberman.

113. The English-language text of the communiqué is in *Basic Docs.*, pp. 967–68. The Chinese-language text of the normalization communiqué is in Xue, ed., *Dangdai Zhongguo waijiao*, p. 429.

Chapter 6

1. See Reagan, *Ronald Reagan*, p. 361.

2. *American Foreign Policy: Current Documents* [hereafter cited as *Current Docs.*], *1981*, p. 545. See also, e.g.,*Current Docs.*, *1982*, p. 132.

3. *Current Docs.*, *1981*, pp. 89–90; *SD Bull.*, May 5, 1982, p. 29.

4. *SD Bull.*, Nov. 1981, pp. 22–23; ibid., Dec. 1981, pp. 22–23.

5. For the administration's position, see *SD Bull.*, May 1982, pp. 31–32; *Current Docs.*, *1982*, pp. 469–70.

6. See Haig's account of the Polish situation in *Caveat*, ch. 12.

7. *Current Docs.*, *1982*, p. 16; *Current Docs.*, *1981*, pp. 602–3.

8. *SD Bull.*, Sept. 1981, p. 16; *SD Bull.*, June 1981, p. 5; *Current Docs.*, *1981*, pp. 28–30.

9. *SD Bull.*, June 1981, p. 5.

10. For a discussion of U.S. defense spending during the first years of the Reagan administration, see William W. Kaufman, *Reasonable Defense*.

11. Caspar Weinberger, "Rearming America," in *Current Docs.*, *1981*, p. 32.

12. *Current Docs.*, *1981*, pp. 166–67. See also, e.g., ibid., pp. 28–29. See also Reagan's interview in ibid., pp. 149–50. An excellent source on the early Reagan administration's attitude to arms control is Strobe Talbott, *Deadly Gambits*.

13. *Current Docs.*, *1981*, p. 366; *Current Docs.*, *1982*, pp. 14–19.

14. Haig, *Caveat*, p. 194; interview with State Department officials. See also Haig's statements in *NYT*, Mar. 22, 1981; *Current Docs.*, *1981*, pp. 948–49.

15. Interviews with Richard Allen, Bill Rope, Gaston Sigur, and other administration officials. See Reagan's formal campaign statement on Taiwan, which was written by Richard Allen, in Robert L. Downen, *Of Grave Concern*, 59–64.

16. Zeng, "Meiguo dui Su zhanlue de dongxiang," p. 5.

17. Zhuang, "Meiguo dui Mei Su junshi liliang duibi de jizhong kanfa," pp. 14–15.

18. Zhuang, "Meiguo dui Su zhengce de xin qushi," pp. 2–3; and Hu and Zhuang, "Meiguo weishenma xiuding hezhanlue," pp. 10–11.

19. Jun Xiang, "New Development of U.S. Military Posture Toward the Soviet Union," *Renmin ribao*, Mar. 25, 1980, in *FBIS/PRC*, Mar. 27, 1980, pp. B1–4.

20. Cited in Pollack, *Lessons of Coalition Politics*, pp. 76–77.

21. Assessment of the seriousness of the meetings is based on an interview with a Chinese official posted at the Soviet embassy. Commentary, "New 'Proposal,' Old Tricks," *Xinhua*, May 24, 1980, in *FBIS/PRC*, June 30, 1980, pp. C1–2. See also Chen Xiong, "Dangqian Su Mei zhanlue taishi," pp. 1–5.

22. Hyland, "Sino-Soviet Conflict," pp. 141–45: Kyodo News Service, Oct. 18, 1979, in *FBIS/PRC*, Oct. 18, 1979, p. C1; Mills, *Sino-Soviet Interactions*, pp. 248–50. For a full discussion of China's response to the Soviet invasion of Afghanistan, see Segal, "China and Afghanistan."

23. Yi, *Cong Haolaiwu dao Baigong*, pp. 56–59.

24. Zhuang, "Ligen de Waijiao qiju," pp. 2–3; emphasis in original. On Reagan's arms control policy, see Talbott, *Deadly Gambits*.

25. Wang Qianqi, "Ligen zhengfu de junshi zhanlue," p. 22. See also Gao and Yu "Sulian nanxia zhanlue ji qi mianlin de zuli," pp. 12–15.

26. Yuan Xianlu, "A New Round of Struggle," *Renmin ribao*, Sept. 27, 1981, in *FBIS/PRC*, Sept. 28, 1981, pp. B1–2.

27. Fang Min, "On the Eve of the U.S.–Soviet Nuclear Talks," *Renmin ribao*, Nov. 30, 1981, in *FBIS/PRC*, Nov. 30, 1981, pp. A1–2.

28. Lu Shipu, "A New Round of the Arms Race Between the Soviet Union and the United States," *Renmin ribao*, June 2, 1982, in *FBIS/PRC*, June 3, 1982, pp. A1–3. See also, e.g., Chen Weibin, "A Prolonged and Fruitless Process," *Xinhua*, Jan. 12, 1982, in *FBIS/PRC*, Jan. 13, 1982, p. A1; Fang Min, "Reasons for Reagan's Disarmament Statement and His Stand," *Renmin ribao*, Apr. 7, 1982, in *FBIS/PRC*, Apr. 2, 1982, pp. B1–3; Fang Min, "special commentary," "U.S. Dual Tactics Toward the Soviet Union," *Renmin ribao*, June 29, 1982, in *FBIS/PRC*, June 29, 1982, pp. B1–3.

29. Jin Junhui, "Ligen zhengfu de duiwai zhengce," p. 3.

30. Wang Baoqin, "Ligen zhengfu dui Su zhengci de tiaozheng he qushi," p. 8, 11. See also, e.g., Wang Qianqi, "Ligen zhengfu de junshi zhanlue," p. 22; Gao and Yu "Sulian nanxia zhanlue ji qi mianlin de zuli," pp. 12–15.

31. Wang Shuzhong, "Su Mei zhengba de zhanlue yanbian he dangqian de zhanlue xingshi," p. 7.

32. Zhang Yebai, "Commenting on the Contradictions in the Reagan Administration's Foreign Policy," *Renmin ribao*, July 31, 1982, in *FBIS/PRC*, Aug. 2, 1982, pp. B1–6. Zhang repeatedly emphasized Washington's "passive position." See also, e.g., Mu Youlin, "Opposing Hegemonism," *Beijing Review*, Aug. 9, 1982, p. 3.

33. Zhuang, "Ligen de waijiao qiju"; Wang Shuzhong, "Su Mei zhengba de zhanlue yanbian he dangqian de zhanlue xingshi," p. 7; Wang Baoqin, "Ligen zhengfu dui Su zhengci de tiaozheng he qushi," p. 11.

34. For an early Chinese view of Soviet economic difficulties, see *Renmin ribao*, Jan. 11, 1981, in *FBIS/PRC*, June 23, 1981, pp. C2–5.

35. On this and other developments in Sino-Soviet relations, see Barnett, *FX Decision*, p. 29; Zagoria, "Moscow-Beijing Détente," p. 856; Barnett, "China's International Posture," pp. 92–93.

36. "Quarterly Chronicle and Documentation," *China Quarterly*, no. 91 (Sept. 1982): 564–65; Barnett, "China's International Posture," p. 90.

37. *WP*, Mar. 25 and Apr. 20, 1979; *NYT*, Apr. 20, 1979.

38. *WP*, Apr. 20, 1979.

39. Commentary, "Do No Harm to Sino–U.S. Relations," *Xinhua*, June 20, 1980, in *FBIS/PRC*, June 23, 1980, pp. B2–3. See also FBIS, *Trends*, June 25, 1980, pp. 7–8. For a later indirect threat of greater conflict with the United States, see the pro-PRC Hong Kong newspaper *Wen wei po*, Oct. 22, 1980, in *FBIS/DR*, Oct. 27, 1980, pp. U1–2. For detailed accounts of the FX issue during this period, see Barnett, *FX Decision*; Sutter, *China Quandary*, p. 81.

40. On the protest note, see *Xinhua*, Oct. 15, 1980, in *FBIS/PRC*, Oct. 16, 1980, p. B1; AFP, Oct. 11, 1980, in *FBIS/PRC*, Oct. 14, 1980, p. B1. For the Commentator article, see "An Inadvisable Move," *Renmin ribao*, Oct. 9, 1980, in *FBIS/PRC*, Oct. 9, 1980, pp. B1–2. *Shijie zhishi* issued a similar warning. See Wen, "Sunhai Zhongmei guanxi de Meiguo 'Yu Taiwan Guanxifa,'" pp. 14–15.

41. Oksenberg, "Decade of Sino-American Relations," p. 191.

42. See *NYT*, Aug. 26 and Dec. 4, 1980. And see the text of Reagan's official campaign statement on Taiwan in Downen, *Of Grave Concern*, pp. 59–64.

43. Interviews with Richard Allen and James Lilley; *WP*, Jan. 15, 1981; Haig, *Caveat*, pp. 199–200; *WP*, May 29, 1981; *Xinhua*, May 13, 1981, in *FBIS/China*, May 14, 1981.

44. Interview with John Holdridge; *NYT*, Mar. 22, 1981; *Current Docs., 1981*, pp. 948–49; *NYT*, Apr. 5, 1981; *WP*, Apr. 5, 1981. See also DOD, *Annual Report: FY 1982*, pp. 88–89.

45. Ren Yi, "The Taiwan Lobby in the United States," *Shijie zhishi*, Mar. 10, 1981, in *FBIS/PRC*, Mar. 10, 1981, pp. B1–4. See also, e.g., *Xinhua*, May 5, 1981, in *FBIS/PRC*, May 5, 1981, p. B1; *NYT*, June 5, 1981.

46. Recall Zhuang Qubing's observation that the Reagan administration "takes resistance to Soviet expansion as the central link of its foreign policy." Zhuang, "Ligen de waijiao qiju," pp. 2–3.

47. *NYT*, Jan. 18 and Feb. 28, 1981. Afterward, Chinese officials frequently referred to Beijing's response to the Dutch arms sales, and U.S. officials understood the threat. Interview with senior U.S. official.

48. Interview with a former Chinese Foreign Ministry official.

49. Interviews with James Lilley, Bill Rope, and John Holdridge; Haig, *Caveat*, p. 199.

50. Interview with Richard Allen and a senior State Department official; Haig, *Caveat*, pp. 199, 203–4; interview with Richard Armitage; FBIS, *Trends*, Feb. 11, 1981, p. 10; *NYT*, Mar. 22, 1981; *Xinhua*, Mar. 20, 1981, in

FBIS/PRC, Mar. 20, 1981, p. B2; interview with President Gerald Ford; *SD Bull.*, Oct. 1982, p. 23.

51. Haig, *Caveat*, pp. 205–6; *NYT*, May 13, 1981; interview with Benjamin Huberman;

52. Haig, *Caveat*, pp. 205–6; *NYT*, June 17, 1981; *SD Bull.*, Oct. 1981, p. 23; *NYT*, May 14, 1981. Interviews with Richard Armitage and Ambassador Arthur Hummel; *NYT*, June 13, 1981; *SD Bull.*, Aug. 1981, p. 34.

53. *Xinhua*, Mar. 12, 1981, *FBIS/PRC*, Mar. 12, 1981, pp. B1–2.

54. Commentary, Hua Xiu, "A Move Doomed to Failure," *Xinhua*, June 11, 1981, in *FBIS/PRC*, June 12, 1981, pp. B1–2. See also the later *Xinhua* commentary asserting that such a proposal for a trade-off was actually suggested by Haig. Commentary, Hua Xiu, "What Is the Way Out," *Xinhua*, Nov. 24, 1981, in *FBIS/PRC*, Nov. 25, 1981, p. B1. See also Zhang Ruizhuang, "Meiguo xiang Taiwan xian chushou wuqi de lishi yu xianzhuang," p. 29.

55. Haig, *Caveat*, p. 206; interview with Ambassador Arthur Hummel; *SD Bull.*, Aug. 1981, pp. 35–36.

56. Xue, ed., *Dangdai Zhongguo waijiao*, pp. 235–36.

57. Tian, ed., *Gaige kaifang yilai de Zhongguo waijiao*, pp. 387–88; *NYT*, June 14, 1981; *WP*, June 17, 1981; Haig, *Caveat*, p. 207; *SD Bull.*, Oct. 1982, p. 23.

58. Xue, ed., *Dangdai Zhongguo waijiao*, p. 36.

59. *NYT*, June 22, 1981; interviews with Richard Armitage, James Lilley, William Rope, and with Defense Intelligence Agency officials.

60. Interview with Bill Rope. The "wish list" is discussed in Weinberger, *Fighting for Peace*, p. 272.

61. Interview with William Rope, who promoted this idea within the State Department and the Pentagon.

62. *SD Bull.*, Aug. 1981, p. 35; Commentary, "A Key Link in the Development of Sino-American Relations," *Xinhua*, June 18, 1981, in *FBIS/PRC*, June 19, 1981, pp. B1–2; Haig, *Caveat*, p. 208; interview with Bill Rope; *Ming bao* (Hong Kong), Aug. 25 1981, in *FBIS/PRC*, Aug. 25, 1981, p. W6; Haig, *Caveat*, p. 208. Note that the *Ming bao* interview with Deng was conducted on July 18 and publication was delayed until Aug. 25. Beijing presumably delayed the publication until it was thought necessary for Deng to commit his personal prestige to the conflict. Note also that in late August or early September, the Chinese vice foreign minister, Zhang Wenjin, told Haig that U.S. arms sales to Taiwan "[cast] a shadow" over U.S.–China relations. Haig, *Caveat*, pp. 208–9.

63. Haig, *Caveat*, pp. 209–11; Solomon, *U.S.–PRC Political Negotiations*, pp. 89, 91; interview with a former Chinese Foreign Ministry official; Xue, ed., *Dangdai Zhongguo waijiao*, p. 236; interview with William Rope; *NYT*, Oct. 16, 1981; *Current Docs., 1981*, p. 962. One report, citing administration officials, says that Huang Hua demanded an end to arms sales within five years. *NYT*, Nov. 15, 1981.

64. Tian, ed., *Gaige kaifang yilai de Zhongguo waijiao*, p. 388; Xue, ed.,

Dangdai Zhongguo waijiao, p. 236; interview with a former Chinese Foreign Ministry official.

65. Interview with William Rope; *WP*, Jan. 11 and 14, 1981.

66. Haig, *Caveat*, p. 211.

67. Interviews with DOD and State Department officials.

68. Note that the year before, the CIA had concluded that Taiwan did not have air superiority over the mainland. Overall, however, as the Pentagon concluded in 1981, the mainland still lacked the ability to launch a successful invasion of Taiwan. *NYT*, Oct. 16, 1981; interviews with James Lilley, Richard Armacost, Carl Ford, and other DOD officials.

69. *NYT*, Nov. 10, 1981; *Xinhua*, Nov. 12, 1981, in *FBIS/PRC*, Nov. 12, 1981; *NYT*, Nov. 12, 1981; Hua Xiu, "What Is the Way Out," *Xinhua*, Nov. 24, 1981, in *FBIS/PRC*, Nov. 25, 1981, p. B1.

70. FBIS, *Trends*, Nov. 25, 1981, p. 4; *WP*, Dec. 30, 1981; *Xinhua*, Dec. 18, 1981, in *FBIS/PRC*, Dec. 21, 1981, p. B1.

71. *SD Bull.*, July 1982, p. 51; *SD Bull.*, Oct. 1982, p. 25; Haig, *Caveat*, p. 211.

72. Interviews with William Rope, Mark Pratt, and other State Department officials.

73. Gong, "Zhong Mei '817' gongbao de chansheng," p. 74; Zhang Ruizhuang, "Meiguo xiang Taiwan xian chushou wuqi de lishi yu xianzhuang," pp. 29–30; *Current Docs., 1981*, p. 968; *Current Docs., 1982*, pp. 1029–30; interview with William Rope and other State Department officials.

74. *Current Docs., 1983*, suppl., pt. 2, *Department of State Daily Briefings*, Jan. 11, 1982, pp. 1–9.

75. Interviews with William Rope and other State Department officials; Gong, "Zhong Mei '817' gongbao de chansheng," p. 74.

76. Zhang Ruizhuang, "Meiguo xiang Taiwan xian chushou wuqi de lishi yu xianzhuang," p. 30; interviews with John Holdridge, Richard Armitage, William Rope, other members of the Holdridge mission, and with a senior State Department official; *Current Docs., 1983*, suppl., pt. 2, *Department of State Daily Briefings*, Feb. 1, 1982.

77. Commentary, Mei Ping, "Going Too Far," *Xinhua*, Jan. 13, 1982, in *FBIS/PRC*, Jan. 15, 1982, pp. B1–2.

78. *Xinhua*, Jan. 24, 1982, in *FBIS/PRC*, Jan. 25, 1982, pp. K2–3. See also the December report that Li commented, "If we should make all the concessions, all leaders, including Zhao Ziyang, would have to resign." Kyodo News Service, Dec. 24, 1989, in *FBIS/PRC*, Jan. 5, 1982, p. B1.

79. Interviews with William Rope and other State Department officials. The public announcement was made in April by Alan Romberg, acting State Department Spokesman. *Current Docs., 1982*, pp. 1029–30.

80. Zhang Ruizhuang, "Meiguo xiang Taiwan xian chushou wuqi de lishi yu xianzhuang," pp. 29–30.

81. Interviews with Richard Allen, James Lilley, and William Rope. Note this perspective is shared by both White House and State Department officials. James Lilley recalls that by the end of 1981, the NSC did not receive

the cable traffic from the U.S. embassy in Beijing, and that Haig was in full control of China policy.

82. Zhang Ruizhuang, "Meiguo xiang Taiwan xian chushou wuqi de lishi yu xianzhuang," p. 30. On the importance of the conservative, pro-Taiwan group in the administration's Taiwan policy, see also, e.g., Wang Baoqin, "Ligen zhengfu dui Su zhengci de tiaocheng he qushi," p. 11.

83. Xue, ed., *Dangdai Zhongguo waijiao,* p. 236–37; interviews with William Rope and senior State Department officials. See also President Ronald Reagan's April 5, 1982, letter to Premier Zhao Ziyang in *Current Docs., 1982,* pp. 1028–29; *NYT,* Apr. 6, 1982; Haig, *Caveat,* p. 211; *NYT,* Apr. 1, 1982.

84. Interviews with William Rope and other State Department officials.

85. Interview with a senior State Department official; *Current Docs., 1982,* pp. 1027–28.

86. *Current Docs., 1982,* p. 1026; interview with Deng Xiaoping, *Liaowang,* March 1982, in FBIS, *Trends,* Mar. 31, 1982; commentator, *Xinhua,* Mar. 1, 1982, in *FBIS/PRC,* Mar. 2, 1982, p. B1; Benkan teyue pinglunyuan (special commentator), "Zhong Mei guanxi de zhenjie hezai?" pp. 6–7; *NYT,* Mar. 26, 1982; *Current Docs., 1982,* suppl., pt. 2, *Department of State Daily Briefings,* Aug. 17, 1982, p. 9 (the senior official was probably Assistant Secretary of State Holdridge); Haig, *Caveat,* p. 212. Interview with John Holdridge. For additional Chinese warnings, see Deputy Foreign Minister Zhong Xidong's February observation that "relations are at a crisis." *Xinhua,* Feb. 5, 1981, in *FBIS/PRC,* Feb. 8, 1982, p. B2.

87. Reagan's letters are in *Current Docs., 1982,* p. 1028–29.

88. Commentary, "He Who Ties the Knot Should Untie It," *Renmin ribao,* May 2, 1981, in *FBIS/PRC,* May 3, 1981, p. B1.

89. Interview with William Rope and senior State Department officials; Gong, "Zhong Mei '817' gongbao de chansheng," p. 75; Tian Zengpei, ed. *Gaige kaifang yilai de Zhongguo waijiao,* p. 390; Xue, ed., *Dangdai Zhongguo waijiao,* pp. 237–38; *SD Bull.,* Aug. 1982, p. 45; Haig, *Caveat,* pp. 213–14. Throughout 1981 and 1982, Ambassador Hummel arranged for other leading U.S. statesmen, including former Vice President Walter Mondale and former Secretary of Defense Harold Brown of the Carter administration, to convey similar messages to Chinese leaders in order to "educate" them about the limits to U.S. flexibility.

90. Gong, "Zhong Mei '817' gongbao de chansheng," p. 75; interview with a former Chinese foreign ministry official.

91. Gong, "Zhong Mei '817' gongbao de chansheng," p. 75; interview with a former Chinese foreign ministry official.

92. Interviews with Alexander Haig, James Lilley, Mark Pratt, William Rope, and another State Department official.

93. Interviews with Richard Allen, William Rope, Richard Armitage, and senior State Department officials; *NYT,* July 29, 1982. Cf. Haig, *Caveat,* pp. 213–15.

94. Interviews with Arthur Hummel and John Holdridge; *NYT*, July 17, 1982.

95. Interviews with William Rope and senior U.S. government officials.

96. Interview with John Holdridge.

97. Interviews with John Holdridge, Arthur Hummel, William Rope, and senior State Department officials. The Chinese-language version uses the characters *zhubu*, which can be translated as "step-by-step" or "progressively," implying a steady, uninterrupted decline. For the Chinese version, see Shanghai Institute of International Affairs, ed., *Guoji xingshi nianjian, 1983*, pp. 365–66.

98. Interview with William Rope.

99. Interview with John Holdridge.

100. *Current Docs., 1982*, suppl., part 2, *Department of State Daily Briefings*, Aug. 17, 1982, pp. 1–5, 13; interviews with William Rope and a senior State Department official.

101. *China Business Review*, May–June 1984, p. 60.

Chapter 7

1. For a detailed look at this shift, see Dallin and Lapidus, "Reagan and the Russians."

2. *Current Docs., 1983*, p. 100.

3. Ibid., pp. 1411–12.

4. Ibid., pp. 249–50; 455–57; *SD Bull.*, Mar. 1984, p. 2.

5. See the December 1983 report by the State Department's Bureau of Intelligence and Research in *Current Docs., 1983*, pp. 855–65. Shultz's comment is in ibid, p. 17.

6. *Current Docs., 1984*, p. 414–15.

7. *SD Bull.*, Apr. 1983, p. 41. See also Under Secretary for Political Affairs Lawrence Eagleburger's statement in *SD Bull.*, Mar. 1983, pp. 81–83.

8. *SD Bull.*, Oct. 1983, p. 27; *Current Docs., 1983*, p. 105.

9. *SD Bull.*, Feb. 1984, pp. 1–2.

10. *Current Docs., 1984*, p. 8.

11. Interviews with Richard Armitage, Gaston Sigur, Paul Wolfowitz, and other State Department officials. For Shultz's public statements to this effect, see, e.g., *Current Docs., 1983*, pp. 922–27; *WP*, Feb. 19, 1983. Assistant Secretary of State Wolfowitz made similar statements. See, e.g., *China News Analysis* (Taipei), Apr. 16, 1983, in *FBIS/PRC*, Apr. 20, 1983, pp. V1–3. Haig's statement is in Haig, *Caveat*, p. 194.

12. Jin Zujie, "Meiguo de jin Tai baoshou lishi," p. 10. See also Wang Yan's September 1982 article, "Dangqian Mei Su dui Hua zhengce de bijiao yanjiu," pp. 7–11, which argued that in the U.S.–Soviet struggle, the *"only advantageous choice"* for the United States was *"to unite with China to resist the Soviet Union,"* calling China's overall position in the triangular relationship *"extremely beneficial"* (emphasis in original).

13. Wang and Xu, "Ligen zhengfu de dui Su zhanlue," p. 24. For additional

analyses stressing U.S. strategic weakness, see, e.g., Dai Zengzhi, "The Contradiction-Ridden U.S. Diplomacy," *Ban yue tan*, Aug. 25, 1982, in *FBIS/ PRC*, Sept. 10, 1982, pp. B1–3; Wu Jin, "The United States Has Not Realized Its Wish of Rebuilding Its Strength," *Liaowang*, Dec. 20, 1983, in *FBIS/ PRC*, Jan. 24, 1983, pp. A1–2.

14. Ding, "Mei Su kangheng zhong Meiguo ruhe kan 'Zhongguo yinsu'," pp. 24–25.

15. Wang Shuzhong, "Mei Su zhengba zhong de Meiguo dui Hua zhanlue," pp. 11–12, 27.

16. Li Ning, "Gengjia jinjiang dongdang de yi nian," pp. 3–11. See also the article by Jin Junhui, also from the Institute of International Studies, "Kunjing de chanwu," pp. 7–8.

17. Beijing Domestic Service, Jan. 3, 1983, in *FBIS/PRC*, Jan. 14, 1983, pp. A5–6. See also, e.g., He Fang, "Guoji xingshi de huigu he zhanwang," pp. 2–4; and the conclusions of analysts at the Shanghai Institute of International Studies in *Guoji xingshi nianjian, 1983*, pp. 7–10.

18. Zong, "Guoji xingshi de bianhua yu fazhan qushi," p. 5. This article went to press on May 23. See also, e.g., Xie, "Su Mei: Zhengdou de xin tedian," pp. 10–12; Qi, "Xi Ou dui Meiguo de duli zuzhu qingxiang," pp. 10–12. For a closer look at China's view of the superpower stalemate in mid 1983 based on interviews with Huan Xiang and other Chinese analysts, see Garrett and Glaser, *War and Peace*, pp. 69–71.

19. See Segal, *Sino-Soviet Relations After Mao*, pp. 11–12.

20. Wang, Yan, and Liu, "Bashi niandai de Zhong, Mei, Su guanxi chutan," pp. 36–37. Although this article appeared after the peak of this trend in Chinese strategic thinking, its analysis of the implications for Chinese security of the superpower stalemate applies to the earlier period. The mention of the "three strategic tasks" is a reference to the January 1980 speech in which Deng Xiaoping laid out these three items as China's primary concerns for the 1980s. See *Deng Xiaoping wenxuan*, pp. 203–4.

21. *Xinhua*, Apr. 15, 1983, in *FBIS/PRC*, Apr. 20, 1983, p. A1.

22. *Xinhua*, May 31, 1983, in *FBIS/PRC*, June 3, 1983, p. A1. For a later report offering a similar view, see Jiang, "Xinping jiujiu—Ping Andeluopofu de caijun jianyi," p. 5. See also the discussion of West German Chancellor Helmut Kohl's July visit to Moscow in *Guangming ribao*, July 11, 1983, in *FBIS/PRC*, July 19, 1983, pp. A1–2.

23. Zhang Dezhen, "MX Missiles and U.S.–Soviet Nuclear Talks," *Renmin ribao*, Aug. 24, 1983, in *FBIS/PRC*, Aug. 25, 1983, p. A1.

24. Huang, "Huan Xiang zongtang dangqian guoji xingshi," pp. 2–4. For a similar analysis strongly stressing U.S. initiative, see Zhang Dezhen, special commentary, "Superpowers' Arms Race Threatens World Peace," *Renmin ribao*, Oct. 11, 1983, in *FBIS/PRC*, Oct. 12, 1983, pp. A1–3, which argued that modernization of nuclear weapons in the United States was "in full bloom" and emphasized the magnitude of increased U.S. defense spending. See also Fang Min, "The Checkered Strategic Nuclear Arms Talks," *Renmin ribao*, June 8, 1983, in *FBIS/PRC*, June 9, 1983, pp. A4–5.

25. Huang, "Huan Xiang zongtang dangqian guoji xingshi."

26. Ding, "Meiguo Zhengfu dui Yazhou zhengce de tiaozheng," p. 3.

27. *Xinhua*, Nov. 5, 1983, in *FBIS/PRC*, Nov. 7, 1983, p. B4; *Xinhua*, Nov. 9, 1983, in *FBIS/PRC*, Nov. 9, 1983, pp. J1–2.

28. He Fang, "Lun Mei Su zhengdou de xin taishi," pp. 1–3.

29. Li Ning, "Mei Su dangqian de zhengdou taishi ji tamen dui Zhongguo zuoyong de jiliang," pp. 27–28 (my emphasis). The *gongkai* analysis is in id., "Mei Su zhengdou jihua he guoji jinzhang jushi," pp. 1–6. Note also the *gongkai* analyses by Li's institute colleagues: Zhuang Qubing, "Cong Ligen Guoqing ziwen kan Meiguo de waijiao zhengce," pp. 8–9 (compare Zhuang's appraisal of Reagan's 1984 speech with Jin Junhui's highly negative assessment of the 1983 speech); and Li Dai, "1983 nian guoji xingshi de tedian," p. 4. And note that this consensus was shared by analysts at the influential Institute of Contemporary International Relations: Zhou Jirong, Wang Baoqin, and Gu Guanfu, "Su Mei zhengba taishi de bianhua yu qianjing," *Shijie zhishi*, no. 23 (Dec. 1, 1983): 2–5; and Zhou Jirong, Wang Baoqin, and Gu Guanfu, "Su Mei zhengba taishi de bianhua yu qianjing," *Xiandai guoji guanxi*, no. 6 (Mar. 1984), where it was argued that there had been a "conspicuous change in the U.S.–Soviet struggle for hegemony. The U.S. counterattack has clearly increased, and the Soviet offensive has weakened because of the increase in its internal and external difficulties." See also the analysis in Shanghai Institute of International Studies, ed., *Guoji xingshi nianjian, 1984*, p. 4.

30. Zhang Dezhen, "From Exploratory Moves to the Drawing of Swords—A Year of Acute U.S.–Soviet Tension," *Renmin ribao*, Dec. 13, 1983, in *FBIS/PRC*, Dec. 14, 1983, pp. A1–4. On the situation in Europe, see also *Xinhua*, Dec. 28, 1983, in *FBIS/PRC*, Dec. 29, 1983, p. A1.

31. Li Ning, "Mei Su dangqian de zhengdou taishi ji tamen dui zhongguo zuoyong de jiliang," p. 29.

32. He Fang, "Lun Mei Su zhengdou de xin taishi," pp. 3, 5.

33. For an extended discussion of this development, see Harding, *Fragile Relationship*, pp. 119–25.

34. Interview with Thomas Shoesmith, who also recalled that "illegal" Taiwan behavior at the most local level in the United States on the most obscure occasion would elicit a PRC protest.

35. Interview with a State Department official.

36. "Yanshou xieyi, paichu zhang'ai," *Renmin ribao*, Aug. 18, 1982, p. 1.

37. *Xinhua*, Aug. 25, 1982, in *FBIS/PRC*, Aug. 26, 1982, p. B1.

38. *Xinhua*, Oct. 7, 1982, in *FBIS/PRC*, Oct. 8, 1982, p. B2.

39. Commentary, "There Can Be No Preconditions for Implementing the Sino–U.S. Joint Communiqué," *Renmin ribao*, Oct. 10, 1982, in *FBIS/PRC*, Oct. 12, 1982, pp. B1–2. For additional incidents eliciting a harsh PRC response, see, e.g., *Xinhua*, Oct. 22, 1982, in *FBIS/PRC*, Oct. 25, 1982, p. B1.

40. *Xinhua*, Dec. 17, 1982, in *FBIS/PRC*, Dec. 17, 1982, p. B1. The meeting adjourned with no new agreements.

41. Interviews with Paul Wolfowitz and Richard Armitage.

42. For Chinese praise for Shultz's "patience," see Assistant Secretary of State Wolfowitz's account of Shultz's visit in U.S. House, *United States–China Relations Eleven Years After the Shanghai Communiqué*, p. 12. For media reports of Shultz's conversations with PRC leaders, see *Xinhua*, Feb. 6, 1983, in *FBIS/PRC*, Feb. 7, 1983, pp. B7–9; *Xinhua*, Feb. 5, 1982, in *FBIS/PRC*, Feb. 7, 1983, pp. B4–5; *Xinhua*, Feb. 3, 1983, in *FBIS/PRC*, Feb. 3, 1983, pp. B3–4; *Xinhua*, Feb. 4, 1983, in *FBIS/PRC*, Feb. 4, 1983, pp. B2–3. On Shultz's lack of initiatives, see also *NYT*, Feb. 2, 1983, p. 3.

43. *Renmin ribao*, Feb. 7, 1983, in *FBIS/PRC*, Feb. 8, 1983, p. B3.

44. See *WP*, Feb. 13, 1983, p. 25; *NYT*, Feb. 6, 1983, pp. 1, 8.

45. Interviews with Paul Wolfowitz, Thomas Shoesmith, and Richard Armitage.

46. *Current Policy*, no. 459; *WP*, Feb. 19, 1983, p. 5. Similar statements were later made by Assistant Secretary of State Wolfowitz. See *China News Analysis* (Taipei), Apr. 16, 1983, in *FBIS/PRC*, Apr. 20, 1983, pp. V1–3.

47. Interviews with Paul Wolfowitz and James Lilley. For a Chinese analysis expressing sensitivity to the U.S. reappraisal, see Zhang Jialin, "New Romanticism." See Shultz's speech in *Current Docs., 1983*, pp. 922–27. See the coverage in *WP*, Feb. 19, 1983, and the *Far Eastern Economic Review* (hereafter cited as *FEER*), Apr. 21, 1983. Assistant Secretary of State Wolfowitz made similar statements. See, e.g., *China News Analysis* (Taipei), Apr. 16, 1983, in *FBIS/PRC*, Apr. 20, 1983, pp. V1–3.

48. *Current Docs., 1983*, pp. 1000–1002; interview with Mark Pratt. The decision was made at meeting chaired by Lawrence Eagleburger, where it was decided that with a starting point of $800 million, an annual reduction $20 million would be slow enough to permit the United States sufficient flexibility, allowing arms sales to continue for 40 years. Interview with a State Department official.

49. Interview with Arthur Hummel.

50. FBIS, *Trends*, Mar. 2, 1983, pp. 1–2; commentary, "A Serious Retrogression," *Xinhua*, Feb. 25, 1983, in *FBIS/PRC*, Feb. 28, 1983, pp. B1–2; AFP, Mar. 21, 1983, in *FBIS/DR*, Mar. 21, 1983, p. B1; *Xinhua*, Mar. 23, 1983, p. B1, in *FBIS/PRC*, Mar. 22, 1983.

51. *Xinhua*, Mar. 29, 1983, and Mar. 30, 1983, *FBIS/PRC*, Mar. 30, 1983, p. B1. For additional statements by Zhao, see, e.g., *Xinhua*, May 11, 1983, in *FBIS/PRC*, May 11, 1983, p. B1.

52. Peng Di, "Whither U.S. China Policy?" *Liaowang*, no. 26 (May 20, 1983), in *FBIS/PRC*, Aug. 4, 1983, pp. B1–3. Zhao's comments are in *NYT*, Mar. 16, 1983.

53. *WP*, May 21, 1983.

54. Interviews with Lionel Olmer, Richard Armitage, William Abnett, Gaston Sigur, and a State Department official; *WP*, June 21, 1983.

55. *WP*, June 21, 1983, p. 8. The PRC report on the meeting is in *Xinhua*, May 26, 1983, *FBIS/PRC*, May 27, 1983, pp. B1–2; interviews with Chinese officials.

56. Interview with Lionel Olmer. See also Garrett and Glaser, *War and Peace*, pp. 88–90.

57. On China's ongoing opposition to various aspects of U.S. policy, see also FBIS, *Trends*, June 2, 1983, pp. 6–8.

58. Zhao Ziyang, "Report on the Work of the Government," in *The First Session of the Sixth National People's Congress (June 1983)* (Beijing: Foreign Languages Press, 1983), pp. 62–63.

59. *Xinhua*, July 23, 1983, in *FBIS/PRC*, July 25, 1983, pp. B1–2. Recall, too, that in June that China threatened that Pan Am service to Taiwan would "inevitably cause damage" to U.S.–PRC relations.

60. *Xinhua*, Aug. 1, 1983, in *FBIS/PRC*, Aug. 2, 1983, p. B1.

61. Interview with Paul Wolfowitz; Solomon, *U.S.–PRC Political Negotiations*, p. 110. See also the *WP*, Sept. 22, 1983.

62. U.S. officials recognized China's changing attitude toward the Reagan administration from diplomatic cables. Interviews with Paul Wolfowitz and Richard Armitage.

63. Solomon, *U.S.–PRC Political Negotiations*, p. 109; Weinberger, *Fighting for Peace*, p. 280; *NYT*, Sept. 30, 1983; interviews with Edward Ross and Eden Woon.

64. Interview with Paul Wolfowitz; Weinberger, *Fighting for Peace*, pp. 271–72. See also *NYT*, Sept. 27 and 28, 1983.

65. Deng's remarks are in *Xinhua*, Sept. 28, 1983, in *FBIS/PRC*, Sept. 28, 1983, pp. B3–4. Zhao's statement is in *Renmin ribao*, Sept. 28, 1983, in *FBIS/PRC*, Sept. 28, 1983, p. B1, and is discussed in Weinberger, *Fighting for Peace*, pp. 271–72; interview with a U.S. embassy official; *NYT*, Sept. 28, 1983.

66. Interviews with Paul Wolfowitz and James Kelly; Weinberger, *Fighting for Peace*, p. 273. For the negative press, see, e.g., *NYT*, Sept. 30, 1098; *WP*, Oct. 9, 1983.

67. *NYT*, Sept. 28, 1983, p. 3; *Renmin ribao*, Sept. 28, 1983, and *Xinhua*, Sept. 27, 1983, in *FBIS/PRC*, Sept. 28, 1983, pp. B2–4; *NYT*, Sept. 27, 1983.

68. *Renmin ribao*, Sept. 28, 1983, in *FBIS/PRC*, Sept. 28, 1983, pp. B5–6 (emphasis added); *Current Docs., 1983*, pp. 1008–9.

69. *Xinhua*, Oct. 12, 1983, in *FBIS/PRC*, Oct. 12, 1983, pp. B2–3; *Current Docs., 1983*, document no. 474, pp. 1008–10; *Xinhua*, Oct. 15, 1983, in *FBIS/PRC*, Oct. 17, 1983, pp. B1–2; *WP*, Oct. 11, 1983, p. 7.

70. *Xinhua*, Nov. 18, 1983, in *FBIS/PRC*, Nov. 21, 1983, p. B1.

71. Hu Yaobang's comment is in *Xinhua*, Nov. 26, 1983, in *FBIS/PRC*, Nov. 28, 1983, p. B1. Also note that Hu Yaobang was the only Chinese leader that did not offer a positive appraisal of his meeting with President Reagan, stressing instead that his conversation with the president had been "frank." Solomon, *U.S.–PRC Political Negotiations*, p. 111. President Li's position is based on an interview with a former Chinese Foreign Ministry analyst. For an extended discussion of the suggestion that the White House failure to respond adequately to Chinese complaints might jeopardize the summit, see FBIS, *Trends*, Nov. 23, 1983, pp. 14–15.

72. *Xinhua*, Dec. 7, 1983, in *FBIS/PRC*, Dec. 8, 1983, pp. K13–15; *Xinhua*, Dec. 6, 1983, in *FBIS/PRC*, Dec. 6, 1983, pp. B1–2.

73. *Renmin ribao*, Jan. 12, 1984, in *FBIS/PRC*, Jan. 13, 1984, p. B1. Emphasis added.

74. *Xinhua*, Jan. 12, 1984, in *FBIS/PRC*, Jan. 12, 1984, p. B8.

75. *Xinhua*, Jan. 16 and 17, 1984, in *FBIS/PRC*, Jan. 17, 1984, pp. B9–11. See also editorial, "A Significant Visit," *Renmin ribao*, Jan. 18, 1984, in *FBIS/PRC*, Jan. 18, 1984, pp. B3–5.

76. Cannon, *President Reagan*, p. 481; testimony by Assistant Secretary of State Paul Wolfowitz in U.S. House, *United States–China Relations*, pp. 187, 190, 230–31. Wolfowitz surmised that China was seeking an annual reduction of $100 million in U.S. arms sales to Taiwan.

77. See the account of Reagan's speech at the welcoming banquet hosted by President Li Xiannian in *Xinhua*, Apr. 26, 1984, in *FBIS/PRC*, Apr. 26, 1984, pp. B4–5. *Xinhua*, Apr. 27, 1984, in *FBIS/PRC*, Apr. 27, 1984, p. B5. Zhao's banquet speech and Deng's remarks are in *Xinhua*, Apr. 28, 1984, in *FBIS/PRC*, Apr. 30, 1984, pp. B13–14, 16–18 (emphasis added). The warning that U.S.–Taiwan relations might disrupt relations in the future evolved into the PRC's standard treatment of the issue. See, e.g., Deng's statement reported in *NYT*, Oct. 2, 1984. The meetings with Deng and Li are discussed in U.S. House, *United States–China Relations*, pp. 190, 230–31.

78. *Xinhua*, Feb. 9, 1983, in *FBIS/PRC*, Feb. 9, 1983, pp. B1–2; *WP*, Aug. 19, 1983, p. 2. The court agreed with the PRC and set aside the U.S. $43 million judgment. *WP*, Feb. 29, 1984, p. C1; interview with Arthur Hummel.

79. *Xinhua*, Feb. 12, 1983, in *FBIS/PRC*, Feb. 14, 1983, p. B1.

80. For a serious and authoritative treatment of the issue, see Liu Daqun, "The Odious Nature of the Huguang Railway Loan," *Guoji wenti yanjiu*, no. 4, 1983, in *Renmin ribao*, Sept. 13, 1983, in *FBIS/PRC*, Sept. 14, 1983, pp. B1–7; *WP*, Aug. 19, 1983, p. 2.

81. Interviews with Mark Pratt and other U.S. officials.

82. *WP*, Apr. 18, 1983, p. 15; *Xinhua*, June 16, 1983, in *FBIS/PRC*, June 16, 1983, p. B1.

83. *Xinhua*, June 16, 1983, in *FBIS/PRC*, June 16, 1983, p. B2. Interviews with Arthur Hummel and other U.S. government officials. See also *WP*, Apr. 18, 1983, p. 15; AFP, Sept. 14, 1983, in *FBIS/PRC*, Sept. 15, 1983, p. B1; *WP*, June 17, 1983, pp. 21, 29.

84. Interviews with Eliott Abrams, Thomas Shoesmith, Arthur Hummel, Mark Pratt, a senior State Department official, and other State Department officials; *NYT*, Apr. 5, 1983, pp. 1, 10; *WP*, Apr. 5, 1983.

85. AFP, Aug. 4, 1982, in *FBIS/PRC*, Aug. 4, 1982, pp. B1–2; see the PRC Foreign Ministry note in *Xinhua*, Apr. 6, 1983, in *FBIS/PRC*, Apr. 7, 1983, pp. B1–2.

86. *FEER*, Apr. 21, 1987, p. 10; interview with a Chinese Foreign Ministry official.

87. *Xinhua*, Apr. 6, 1983, in *FBIS/PRC*, Apr. 7, 1983, pp. B1–2; *NYT*, Apr. 7, 1983, p. 4.

88. The cancelled exchanges are reported in *Xinhua*, Apr. 7, 1983, in *FBIS/PRC*, Apr. 7, 1983, pp. B2–3. Note that although Washington refused to compromise, it tried to minimize any appearance of political overtones. See Shultz's comments in *Current Docs., 1983*, p. 1002. "Yet Another Instance of Endangering Sino–U.S. Relations," short commentary, *Renmin ribao*, Apr. 9, 1983, in *FBIS/PRC*, Apr. 11, 1983, pp. B2–3.

89. *WP*, Oct. 14, 1983; *NYT*, Oct. 15, 1983; *NYT*, Dec. 30, 1983, p. 5. From that time through June 4, 1989, the United States approved numerous Chinese political asylum requests on a variety of grounds, and Beijing did not issue any serious protests.

90. *Xinhua*, Apr. 26, 1983, in *FBIS/PRC*, Apr. 26, 1983, p. A1; *Xinhua*, Mar. 8, 1983, in *FBIS/PRC*, Mar. 8, 1983, p. A1.

91. Interview with Thomas Shoesmith and Mark Pratt.

92. *Xinhua*, Mar. 23, 1983, in *FBIS/PRC*, Mar. 23, 1983, p. B1.

93. Chen Tiqiang, "It Is Impermissible for the Taiwan Authorities to Continue to Usurp the Seat in the Asian Development Bank," *Renmin ribao*, May 4, 1983, in *FBIS/PRC*, May 4, 1983, pp. U1–2.

94. Mu Yaolin, "China Should Become a Member of Asian Bank," *Beijing Review*, no. 20 (May 16, 1983): 4.

95. *Xinhua*, Nov. 25, 1983, in *FBIS/PRC*, Nov. 25, 1983, p. B1.

96. "Do Not Play a Dangerous Game that Damages Sino–U.S. Relations," commentary, *Renmin ribao*, Nov. 27, 1983, in *FBIS/PRC*, Nov. 28, 1983, pp. B1–2.

97. *Weekly Compilation of Presidential Documents*, Dec. 5, 1983, p. 1627; *Xinhua*, Dec. 1, 1983, in *FBIS/PRC*, Dec. 1, 1983, pp. B3–4.

98. "Yingdang yan er youxin," commentary, p. 6 (emphasis added). See also Kyodo News Service, Nov. 30, 1983, in *FBIS/PRC*, Nov. 30, 1983, p. A1; *Xinhua*, Jan. 16, 1984, in *FBIS/PRC*, Jan. 17, 1984, p. B9. The precise name that Taiwan used in the bank, however, remained in dispute.

99. *Xinhua*, Dec. 7, 1983, in *FBIS/PRC*, Dec. 8, 1983, pp. K13–15.

100. In fact, U.S. officials held up the plane's departure to reach final agreement with Chinese negotiators. Interviews with Arthur Hummel and Yoshi Ogawa; *WSJ*, Mar. 5, 1984.

101. Interviews with James Lilley and Mark Pratt. The term "creative application" is Lilley's.

102. Interviews with Paul Wolfowitz, James Kelly, James Lilley, Carl Ford, Mark Pratt, and other State Department officials; *FEER*, June 8, 1989, p. 23. On the technology purchases, see *FEER*, May 8, 1986, and July 30, 1987. The license review process was managed by a Taiwan policy group that met in the White House approximately every four to six weeks. For Chinese opposition to this policy, see, e.g., Huang Xiang, "Sino–U.S. Relations over the Past Year," *Beijing Review*, Feb. 15, 1988.

103. DOD, *Foreign Military Sales*, pp. 2–3, 16–17, 52–53.

104. Zhang Jingxu, "A Preliminary Analysis of the 'Taiwan Straits' Mili-

tary Power Balance' Theory," *Liaowang*, no. 30 (July 28, 1986), in *FBIS/PRC*, Aug. 1, 1986, pp. B2–4; *WP*, Apr. 25, 1986.

105. Beijing Domestic Service, Mar. 5, 1987, in *FBIS/PRC*, Mar. 6, 1987, p. B1.

106. For a discussion of the less obvious but important aspects of military cooperation, see Edward W. Ross, "U.S.–China Military Relations."

107. For a discussion of the high-level exchanges and the Weinberger visits, see Edward W. Ross, "U.S.–China Military Relations"; Woon, "Chinese Arms Sales and U.S.–China Military Relations"; Weinberger, *Fighting for Peace*, pp. 284–85; interview with James Kelly.

108. Edward W. Ross, "U.S.–China Military Relations."

109. Ibid.; interview with Paul Wolfowitz.

110. Edward W. Ross, "U.S.–China Military Relations," Woon, "Chinese Arms Sales and U.S.–China Military Relations."

111. Persico, *Casey*, pp. 366–67; North, *Under Fire*, pp. 306–7; *WP*, June 25, 1989; July 19, 1992.

112. Interview with Lionel Olmer. For an extended discussion of the new regulations, see Endsley, "New Technology Transfer Regulations for the People's Republic of China."

113. For a discussion of the developments in U.S. technology export policy and U.S.–China trade relations, see U.S. House, *Technology Transfer to China*.

114. Lardy, *China's Entry*, pp. 22–26; Kleinberg, *China's Opening*, ch. 7–9.

115. See *Cost of Removing MFN from China*.

116. Material for this the next two paragraphs draws from Brenner, *U.S.–China Nuclear Bilateral Accord*, pp. 15–42.

117. Solomon, *U.S.–PRC Political Negotiations*, p. 85.

118. Given the importance of Pakistan in resisting Soviet occupation of Afghanistan and its vulnerability to Soviet forces in Afghanistan, the Reagan administration may well have welcomed Chinese nuclear assistance as a strategic contribution to its Soviet policy.

119. Lampton, *Relationship Restored*, pp. 30–37; Rosen, "Students," p. 100.

120. On the U.S. response to Chinese arms sales, see *NYT*, Oct. 22, 1987. On human rights issues, see *NYT*, Oct. 7 and 18, 1987.

Chapter 8

1. For a discussion of China's perspective on its role in superpower relations, see Yahuda, "Significance of Tripolarity."

2. On China's incorporation of its American domestic politics in policy making and the contrast to the importance of Chinese domestic politics in U.S. policy making, see Solomon, *Chinese Political Negotiating Behavior*, pp. 22–29; Ross, "Two-Level Games and Unexpected Outcomes."

3. Nevertheless, ideological considerations did influence China's Soviet policy during this period. See Su, "Strategic Triangle."

4. *Time*, Feb. 5, 1979, p. 34.

5. For a discussion of these different approaches, see Craig and George, *Force and Statecraft*, pp. 163–64.

6. These findings support those of Pye, *Chinese Commercial Negotiating Style*, pp. 68–70; Solomon, *Chinese Political Negotiating Style*. Also see Lavin, "Negotiating with the Chinese," for a discussion of the contrasting approaches in economic negotiations and the utility of U.S. resistance to concessions and the associated risk of conflict escalation to reaching agreements.

7. Interview with a former Chinese Foreign Ministry official.

8. Pye, *Chinese Commercial Negotiating Style*, pp. 78–79.

9. Apparently Henry Kissinger fell victim to Zhou Enlai's celebrated charm, for he concluded that Chinese leaders eschewed "salami" tactics in favor of an approach in which Chinese negotiators readily accommodated themselves to the limits of their counterpart's flexibility. Kissinger, *White House Years*, p. 752.

10. Haig, *Caveat*, pp. 213–14.

11. For a discussion of the breakdown of relations, see Robert S. Ross, "National Security, Human Rights, and Domestic Politics."

Works Cited

U.S. Government Documents

Congressional Record. Washington, D.C. Various issues.

U.S. Congress. House. Committee on Foreign Affairs. *Executive-Legislative Consultations on China Policy, 1978–79.* Washington, D.C.: GPO, 1980.

———. *Taiwan Legislation.* Washington, D.C.: GPO, 1979.

U.S. Congress. House. Committee on Foreign Affairs. Subcommittee on Asian and Pacific Affairs. *The United States and the People's Republic of China: Issues for the 1980's.* Washington, D.C.: GPO, 1980.

———. *United States–China Relations.* Washington, D.C.: GPO, 1984.

———. *United States–China Relations Eleven Years After the Shanghai Communiqué.* Washington D.C.: GPO, 1983.

U.S. Congress. House. Committee on Foreign Affairs. Subcommittee on International Economic Policy and Trade. *Technology Transfer to China.* Washington, D.C.: GPO, 1989.

U.S. Congress. House. Committee on Ways and Means. Subcommittee on Trade. *United States–China Trade Agreement.* Washington, D.C.: GPO, 1980.

U.S. Congress. Senate. Committee on Finance. Subcommittee on International Trade. *Agreement on Trade Relations Between the United States and China.* Washington, D.C.: GPO, 1980.

U.S. Congress. Senate. Committee on Foreign Relations. *Taiwan.* Washington, D.C.: GPO, 1979.

———. *The United States and China.* Washington D.C.: GPO, 1976.

———. *The United States, China and Japan.* Washington, D.C.: GPO, 1979.

———. *U.S. MIAs in Southeast Asia.* Washington, D.C.: GPO, 1977.

U.S. Congress. Senate. Committee on International Relations. Subcommittee on African Affairs. *Angola.* Washington, D.C.: GPO, 1976.

U.S. Department of Defense [DOD]. *Defense Program and Budget: FY 1971.* Washington, D.C.: GPO, 1970.

———. *Annual Report: FY 1973.* Washington, D.C.: GPO, 1972.

———. *Annual Report: FY 1975.* Washington, D.C.: GPO, 1974.

———. *Annual Report: FY 1976.* Washington, D.C.: GPO, 1975.

———. *Annual Report: FY 1977.* Washington, D.C.: GPO, 1976.

———. *Annual Report: FY 1982.* Washington, D.C.: GPO, 1981.

U.S. Department of Defense. Security Assistance Agency. *Foreign Military Sales, Foreign Military Construction Sales and Military Assistance Facts: As of September 30, 1992.* Washington, D.C.: Foreign Military Sales Control and Reports Division, Defense Security Assistance Agency, 1992.

U.S. Department of State. *American Foreign Policy: Basic Documents, 1977–1980.* Washington, D.C.: GPO, 1983.

———. *American Foreign Policy: Current Documents, 1981.* Washington, D.C.: GPO, 1984.

———. *American Foreign Policy: Current Documents, 1982.* Washington, D.C.: GPO, 1985.

———. *American Foreign Policy: Current Documents, 1983.* Washington, D.C.: GPO, 1985.

———. *State Department Bulletin.*

U.S. National Archives. *Public Papers of the Presidents of the United States: Richard Nixon, 1969.* Washington, D.C.: GPO, 1970.

———. *Public Papers of the Presidents of the United States: Richard Nixon, 1970.* Washington, D.C.: GPO, 1971.

———. *Public Papers of the Presidents of the United States: Richard Nixon, 1971.* Washington, D.C.: GPO, 1972.

———. *Public Papers of the Presidents of the United States: Richard Nixon, 1972.* Washington, D.C.: GPO, 1974.

———. *Public Papers of the Presidents of the United States: Richard Nixon, 1973.* Washington, D.C.: GPO, 1975.

U.S. National Technical Information Service. Foreign Broadcast Information Service. *Trends in Communist Media.*

———. *Daily Report: Asia Pacific.* Washington, D.C., various years.

———. *Daily Report: China.* Washington, D.C., 1969–88.

———. *Daily Report: Soviet Union.* Washington, D.C., various years.

Weekly Compilation of Presidential Documents. Washington, D.C.: GPO. Various years.

Books and Articles

Art, Robert J. "Bureaucratic Politics and American Foreign Policy—A Critique." *Policy Sciences* 4, no. 4 (Dec. 1973).

Asian Security. Tokyo: Research Institute for Peace and Security, 1979.

Barnett, A. Doak. *China and the Major Powers in East Asia.* Washington, D.C.: Brookings Institution, 1977.

———. *China's Economy in Global Perspective.* Washington, D.C.: Brookings Institution, 1981.

———. "China's International Posture." In *China Briefing, 1982,* ed. Richard C. Bush. New York: Asia Society, 1983.

———. *The FX Decision.* Washington, D.C.: Brookings Institution: 1981.

Benkan teyue pinglunyuan [special journal commentator]. "Zhong Mei guanxi de zhenjie hezai?" (Wherein Lies the Crux of Sino-American Relations?) *Guoji wenti yanjiu* (Journal of International Studies), no. 2 (1982).

Bernstein, Thomas P. *The Negotiations to Normalize U.S.–China Relations.* Pew Case Studies in International Affairs, case 426. Washington, D.C.: Institute for the Study of Diplomacy, Georgetown University, 1988.

Brenner, Michael. *The U.S.–China Nuclear Bilateral Accord.* Pew Case Studies in International Affairs, case 106. Washington, D.C.: Institute for the Study of Diplomacy, Georgetown University, 1986.

Brzezinski, Zbigniew. *Power and Principle: Memoirs of the National Security Advisor, 1977–1981.* New York: Farrar, Straus & Giroux, 1983.

Bush, George. *Looking Forward: Autobiography.* New York: Bantam Books, 1987.

Buszynski, Leszek. *Soviet Foreign Policy and Southeast Asia.* New York: St. Martin's Press, 1986.

Cannon, Lou. *President Reagan: The Role of a Lifetime.* New York: Simon & Schuster, 1991.

Carter, Jimmy. *Keeping Faith: Memoirs of a President.* New York: Bantam Books, 1982.

Chanda, Nayan. *Brother Enemy: The War After the War.* New York: Harcourt Brace Jovanovich, 1986.

Chang, Gordon H. *Friends and Enemies: The United States, China, and the Soviet Union, 1948–1972.* Stanford: Stanford University Press, 1990.

———. "To the Nuclear Brink: Eisenhower, Dulles, and the Quemoy-Matsu Crisis." *International Security* 12, no. 4 (Spring 1988).

Chen Dunde. *Mao Zedong—Nikesen zai 1972* (Mao Zedong and Nixon in 1972). Beijing: Kunlun Press, 1988.

Chen Xiong. "Dangqian Su Mei zhanlue taishi" (The Current Soviet–U.S. Strategic Situation). *Shijie zhishi,* no. 12 (June 16, 1979).

"Chiang Ch'ing's Address to Diplomatic Cadres." *Classified Chinese Documents: A Selection.* Taipei: Institute of International Relations, 1978.

"Chou En-Lai's Reports on the International Situation." *Issues and Studies* 13, no. 1 (January 1977).

Christensen, Thomas J. "Domestic Mobilization and International Conflict: Sino-American Relations in the 1950s." Ph.D. diss., Columbia University, 1993.

———. "Threats, Assurances, and the Last Chance for Peace." *International Security* 17, no. 1 (Summer 1992).

Collins, John M. *American and Soviet Military Trends Since the Cuban*

Missile Crisis. Washington, D.C.: Center for Strategic and International Affairs, 1978.

The Cost of Removing MFN from China. Washington D.C.: U.S.–China Business Council, 1990.

Craig, Gordon A., and Alexander George. *Force and Statecraft: Diplomatic Problems of Our Time*. New York: Oxford University Press, 1983.

Creekman, Charles T. "Sino-Soviet Competition in the Yemens." *Naval War College Review* 30, no. 4 (June–July 1979).

Dallin, Alexander, and Gail W. Lapidus. "Reagan and the Russians: American Policy Toward the Soviet Union." In *Eagle Resurgent: The Reagan Era in American Foreign Policy*, ed. Kenneth A. Oye, Robert J. Lieber, and Donald Rothchild. Boston: Little, Brown, 1987.

"Dangqian Suxiu dui Hua zhengce de dongxiang." *Sulian qingkuang* (Soviet Situation) (*jimi*), no. 101 (Nov. 29, 1976).

Deng Xiaoping wenxuan: 1975–1982 (Selected Works of Deng Xiaoping: 1975–1982). Beijing: Renmin Chubanshe, 1983.

Ding Xinghao. "Mei Su kangheng zhong Meiguo ruhe kan 'Zhongguo yinsu'" (How the United States Sees the "China factor" in the U.S.–Soviet Contention). *Shijie jingji yu zhengzhi neican* (*neibu*), no. 2 (1983).

———. "Meiguo zhengfu dui Yazhou zhengce de tiaozheng" (Adjustment in the U.S. Government's Asia Policy). *Shijie jingji yu zhengzhi neican* (*neibu*), no. 8 (1983).

Diplomatic History Research Office, Foreign Ministry of the People's Republic of China, ed. *Xin Zhongguo waijiao fengyun, dier ji* (Diplomatic Turbulence of New China, vol. 2). Beijing: Shijie Zhishi Chubanshe, 1991.

———. *Xin Zhongguo waijiao fengyun, disan ji* (Diplomatic Turbulence of New China, vol. 3). Beijing: Shijie Zhishi Chubanshe, 1994.

———. *Zhou Enlai waijiao huodong dashiji, 1949–1975* (Chronology of Zhou Enlai's Diplomatic Activities, 1949–1975). Beijing: Shijie Zhishi Chubanshe, 1993.

Dong Mei. *Zhong Mei guanxi ciliao xuanbian (1971.7–1981.7)* (Selected Compilation of Materials on U.S.–China Relations: July 1971–July 1981) (*neibu*). Beijing: Shishi Chubanshe, 1982.

Dou Hui, ed. *Zhongguo Renmin Gongheguo duiwai guanxi gaishu* (A General View of the Foreign Relations of the People's Republic of China). Shanghai: Shanghai Foreign Language and Education Press, 1989.

Downen, Robert L. *Of Grave Concern: U.S.–Taiwan Relations on the Threshold of the 1980s*. Washington, D.C.: Center for Strategic and International Studies, 1981.

———. *The Taiwan Pawn in the China Game: Congress to the Rescue*. Washington, D.C.: Center for Strategic and International Affairs, 1979.

Editorial and Writing Organization of the Academy of Military Science. *Ye Jianying zhuanlue* (*neibu*) (The Strategy of Ye Jianying). Beijing: Junshi Kexue Chubanshe, 1987.

Editorial Group of the Collected Essays of the Academic Seminar on Research on Zhou Enlai, ed. *Zhou Enlai yanjiu xueshu taolunhui lunwenji* (Collected Essays of the Academic Seminar on Research on Zhou Enlai). Beijing: Zhongyang Wenxian Chubanshe, 1988.

Freedman, Lawrence. *U.S. Intelligence and the Soviet Strategic Threat.* 2d ed. Princeton, N.J.: Princeton University Press, 1986.

Gaddis, John Lewis. *Strategies of Containment: A Critical Appraisal of Postwar American National Security Policy.* New York: Oxford University Press, 1982.

Garrett, Banning N. "The 'China Card' and Its Origins: U.S. Bureaucratic Politics and the Strategic Triangle." Ph.D. diss., Brandeis University, 1983.

———. "The Strategic Basis of Learning in U.S. Policy Toward China, 1949–1988." In *Learning in U.S. and Soviet Foreign Policy*, eds. George W. Breslauer and Philip E. Tetlock. Boulder, Colo.: Westview Press, 1991.

Garrett, Banning N., and Bonnie S. Glaser. *War and Peace: The Views from Moscow and Beijing.* Berkeley: Institute of International Studies, University of California, Berkeley, 1984.

Garthoff, Raymond. *Détente and Confrontation: American-Soviet Relations from Nixon to Reagan.* Washington, D.C.: Brookings Institution, 1985.

Garver, John. *China's Decision for Rapprochement with the United States, 1969–1971.* Boulder, Colo.: Westview Press, 1982.

Gates, Millicent Anne, and E. Bruce Geelhoed. *The Dragon and the Snake: An American Account of the Turmoil in China, 1976–1977.* Philadelphia: University of Pennsylvania Press, 1986.

Gelman, Harry. *The Brezhnev Politburo and the Decline of Détente.* Ithaca, N.Y.: Cornell University Press, 1984.

———. *The Soviet Far East Buildup and Soviet Risk-Taking Against China.* Santa Monica, Calif.: RAND Corporation, 1982.

Gao Bo and Yu Lei. "Sulian nanxia zhanlue ji qi mianlin de zuli" (The Soviet Strategy of Thrusting Southward and the Impediments It Faces). *Xiandai guoji guanxi*, no. 1 (1981).

Goncharov, Sergei N., John W. Lewis, and Xue Litai. *Uncertain Partners: Stalin, Mao, and the Korean War.* Stanford: Stanford University Press, 1993.

Gong Li. *Kuayue: 1969–1979 nian Zhong Mei guanxi de yanbian* (Across the Chasm: The Evolution of China–U.S. Relations, 1969–1979). Henan: Henan People's Press, 1992.

———. "Zhong Mei '817' gongbao de chansheng" (The Emergence of the 8/17 Communiqué). *Zhonggong Dang shi yanjiu* (Research on Chinese Communist Party History), no. 3 (May 25, 1994).

Gromyko, A. A., and B. N. Ponomarev, eds. *Soviet Foreign Policy*, vol. 2: *1945–1980.* 4th rev., enlarged ed. Moscow: Progress Publishers, 1981.

Guan Fengrui. "Zhou Enlai tongzhi zai Woguo waijiao shijian zhong dui

Mao Zedong sixiang de zhuoyue gongxian. (Comrade Zhou Enlai's Outstanding Contribution to Mao Zedong Thought in China's Diplomatic Affairs). *Liaoning Daxue xuebao* (Liaoning University Journal), no. 5, 1986. In *Fuyin baokan ziliao: Zhongguo waijiao* (Duplication of Materials from Newspapers and Periodicals: Chinese Foreign Policy), no. 10 (1986).

Gurtov, Melvin. "The Taiwan Strait Crisis Revisited: Politics and Foreign Policy in Chinese Motives." *Modern China* 2, no. 1 (Jan. 1976).

Haig, Alexander. *Caveat: Realism, Reagan, and American Foreign Policy*. New York: Macmillan, 1984.

Han Xu et al. "Wei Zhong Mei guanxi zhengchanghua puping daolu de shizhe" (The Envoy Who Paved the Way for Sino-American Normalization). *Jiangjun, waijiaojia, yishujia: Huang Zhen jinian wenji* (General, Diplomat, Artist: Collected Works in Memory of Huang Zhen), ed. Yao Zhongmin, Xie Wushen, and Pei Jianzhang. Beijing: Jiefangjun Chubanshe, 1992.

Hao Mengbi and Duan Haoran, eds. *Zhongguo Gongchandang liushinian* (Sixty Years of the Chinese Communist Party). Beijing: Jiefangjun Chubanshe, 1984.

Harding, Harry. *A Fragile Relationship*. Washington, D.C.: Brookings Institution, 1992.

———. "Political Trends in China Since the Cultural Revolution." *Annals of the American Academy of Political and Social Science* 402 (July 1972).

Harsanyi, John C. "Advances in Understanding Rational Behavior." In *Rational Choice*, ed. Jon Elster. New York: New York University Press, 1986.

He Fang. "Guoji xingshi de huigu he zhanwang" (Review and Outlook on the International Situation). *Shijie zhishi*, no. 1 (Jan. 1, 1983).

———. "Lun Mei Su zhengdou de xin taishi" (On the New Situation in the U.S.–Soviet Contention). *Shijie jingji yu zhengzhi neican* (neibu), no. 11 (1983).

He Qin, Zhang Jingru, Zhou Chen'gen, and Wen Lishu, eds. *Zhonggongdang li jiangyi* (Teaching Materials of the History of the Chinese Communist Party). Beijing: Chinese People's University Press, 1984.

He Xiaolu. *Yuanshuai waijiaojia: Chen Yi wenxue zhuanyi zhi shiyi* (Marshal Diplomat: Eleven Literary Biographies of Chen Yi). Beijing: Liberation Army Literature and Art Press, 1985.

Herring, George C. *America's Longest War: The United States and Vietnam, 1950–1975*. New York: John Wiley & Sons, 1979.

Hersh, Seymour M. *The Price of Power: Kissinger in the Nixon White House*. New York: Summit Books, 1983.

Hu Sheng, ed. *Zhongguo gongchandang de qishi nian* (Seventy Years of the Chinese Communist Party). Beijing: Zhonggong Dangshi Chubanshe, 1991.

Hu Shiyan et al., eds. *Chen Yi zhuan* (Biography of Chen Yi). Beijing: Dangdai Zhongguo Chubanshe, 1991.

Hu Zhengqing and Zhuang Qubing. "Meiguo weishenma xiuding he zhanlue?" (Why Did the U.S. Revise Its Nuclear Strategy?). *Shijie zhishi*, no. 18 (Sept. 16, 1980).

Huang Shuhai. "Huan Xiang zongtang dangqian guoji xingshi" (Huan Xiang Talks Freely on the Current International Situation). *Shijie zhishi*, no. 16 (Aug. 16, 1983).

Hyland, William. "The Sino-Soviet Conflict: Dilemmas of the Strategic Triangle." In *The China Factor*, ed. Richard Solomon. Englewood Cliffs, N.J.: Prentice-Hall, 1981.

Ikle, Fred Charles. *How Nations Negotiate*. New York: Harper & Row, 1964.

International Institute for Strategic Studies. *Strategic Survey, 1978*. London: IISS, 1979.

Jackson, Karl. "Thai–U.S. Security Relations." In *United States–Thailand Relations*, ed. Karl Jackson and Wiwat Mungkandi. Berkeley: Institute of East Asian Studies, University of California, Berkeley, 1986.

Jackson, Karl, and Wiwat Mungkandi, eds. *United States–Thailand Relations*. Berkeley: Institute of East Asian Studies, University of California, Berkeley, 1986.

Jackson, Robert. *South Asian Crisis: India, Pakistan, Bangladesh*. London: Chatto & Windus, 1975.

Jacobson, Carl G. "Developments in the Far East." In *Soviet Armed Forces Review Annual*, vol. 3: *1979*, ed. David R. Jones. Gulf Breeze, Fl.: Academic International Press, 1979.

Japanese Defense Agency. *Defense of Japan, 1979*. Tokyo: JDA, 1979.

Jervis, Robert. *The Logic of Images in International Relations*. Princeton, N.J.: Princeton University Press, 1976.

Jia Ennan. *Mao Zedong renji jiaowang shilu* (True Record of Mao Zedong's Interpersonal Contacts). Nanjing: Jiangsu Wenyi Chubanshe, 1990.

Jiang Bo and Li Qing, eds. *Lin Biao: 1959 nian yihou* (Lin Biao: After 1959) (*neibu*). Chengdu: Sichuan Renmin Chubanshe, 1993.

Jiang Zhongren. "Xinping jiujiu—Ping Andeluopofu de caijun jianyi" (Old Wine in a New Bottle: On Andropov's New Disarmament Proposal). *Shijie zhishi*, no. 19 (Oct. 1, 1983).

Jin Junhui. "Kunjing de chanwu" (Outcome of a Predicament). *Shijie zhishi*, no. 6 (Mar. 16, 1983).

———. "Ligen zhengfu de duiwai zhengce" (The Foreign Policy of the Reagan Administration). *Guoji wenti yanjiu*, no. 1 (1982).

Jin Zujie. "Meiguo de jin Tai baoshou lishi" (The History of America's Pro-Taiwan Conservatives). *Shijie jingji yu zhengzhi neican* (*neibu*), no. 10, 1982.

Kalb, Marvin, and Bernard Kalb. *Kissinger*. Boston: Little, Brown, 1974.

Kallgren, Joyce K., Noordin Sopiee, and Soedjati Djiwandono, eds. *ASEAN and China: An Evolving Relationship*. Berkeley: Institute of East Asian Studies, University of California, Berkeley, 1988.

Kao, Michael Y. M., ed. *The Lin Piao Affair: Power Politics and Military Coup*. White Plains, N.Y.: International Arts and Sciences Press, 1975.

Kaplan, Stephen S., ed. *Diplomacy of Power: Soviet Armed Forces as a Political Instrument.* Washington, D.C.: Brookings Institution, 1981.

Kaufman, William W. *A Reasonable Defense.* Washington, D.C.: Brookings Institution, 1986.

Keohane, Robert O. *After Hegemony: Cooperation and Discord in the World Political Economy.* Princeton: Princeton University Press, 1984.

——, ed. *Neorealism and Its Critics.* New York: Columbia University Press, 1986.

Kissinger, Henry. *The White House Years.* Boston: Little, Brown, 1979.

——. *Years of Upheaval.* Boston: Little, Brown, 1982.

Kleinberg, Robert. *China's Opening to the Outside World: The Experiment with Foreign Capitalism.* Boulder, Colo.: Westview Press, 1990.

Lampton, David. *A Relationship Restored: Trends in U.S.–China Educational Exchanges, 1978–1984.* Washington, D.C.: National Academy Press, 1986.

Lardy, Nicholas R. *China's Entry into the World Economy.* Lanham, Md.: University Press of America, 1987.

Larson, Deborah Welch. "The Crisis Prevention and the Austrian State Treaty." *International Organization* 41, no. 1 (Winter 1987).

Lavin, Franklin L. "Negotiating with the Chinese." *Foreign Affairs* 73, no. 4 (July/August 1994).

Lawson, Eugene K. *The Sino-Vietnamese Conflict.* New York: Praeger, 1984.

Legum, Colin. "Angola and the Horn of Africa." In *Diplomacy of Power: Soviet Armed Forces as a Political Instrument,* ed. Stephen S. Kaplan. Washington, D.C.: Brookings Institution, 1981.

Li Dai. "1983 nian guoji xingshi de tedian" (Characteristics of the 1983 International Situation). *Shijie zhishi,* no. 1 (Jan. 1, 1983).

Li Ning. "Gengjia jinjiang dongdang de yi nian" (A Year of Increased Tension and Turbulence). *Guoji wenti yanjiu,* no. 1 (1983).

——. "Mei Su dangqian de zhengdou taishi ji tamen dui Zhongguo zuoyong de jiliang (The Current Situation in the U.S.–Soviet Contention and Their Evaluation of China's Impact). *Shijie jingji yu zhengzhi neican (neibu),* no. 12 (1983).

——. "Mei Su zhengdou jihua he guoji jinzhang jushi" (Intensified U.S.–Soviet Contention and the Tense World Situation). *Guoji wenti yanjiu,* no. 1 (1984).

Li Ping. "'Wenhua Da Geming' zhong de Zhou Enlai" (Zhou Enlai During the 'Cultural Revolution'). In *Wenhua Da Geming zhong de Zhou Enlai* (Zhou Enlai During the Cultural Revolution), ed. Shen Danying. Beijing: Zhonggong Zhongyang Dangjiao Chubanshe, 1991.

Li Zhisui, *The Private Life of Chairman Mao.* New York: Random House, 1994.

Lieberthal, Kenneth. *Sino-Soviet Conflict in the 1970s: Its Evolution and Implications for the Strategic Triangle.* Santa Monica, Calif.: RAND Corporation, 1978.

Lieberthal, Kenneth G., and Bruce J. Dickson. *A Research Guide to Central Party and Government Meetings in China, 1949–1986.* Armonk, N.Y.: M. E. Sharpe, 1989.

Lin Qing. *Zhou Enlai zaixiang shengya* (The Career of Prime Minister Zhou Enlai). Hong Kong: Changcheng Wenhua Chubanshe, 1991.

Litwak, Robert S. *Détente and the Nixon Doctrine: American Foreign Policy and the Pursuit of Stability, 1969–1976.* New York: Cambridge University Press, 1984.

Lu Zhikong. *Waijiao jubu* (Diplomatic Authority). Henan People's Press, 1989.

MacFarquhar, Roderick. "The Succession to Mao and the End of Maoism." In *The Politics of China, 1949–1989,* ed. Roderick MacFarquhar. New York: Cambridge University Press, 1993.

Mills, William deB. "Sino-Soviet Interactions, May 1977–June 1980." Ph.D. diss., University of Michigan, 1981.

Morris, Roger. *Uncertain Greatness: Henry Kissinger and American Foreign Policy.* New York: Harper & Row, 1977.

Mozingo, David, and Thomas Robinson. *Lin Piao on People's War: China Takes a Second Look at Vietnam.* Santa Monica, Calif.: RAND Corporation, 1965.

Nalebuff, Barry. "Rational Deterrence in an Imperfect World." *World Politics* 43, no. 3 (Apr. 1991).

Naughton, Barry. "The Third Front: Defence Industrialization in the Chinese Interior." *China Quarterly,* no. 115 (Sept. 1988).

Nelson, Harvey. *Power and Insecurity: Beijing, Moscow & Washington, 1949–1988.* Boulder, Colo.: Lynne Rienner Publishers, 1989.

Newhouse, John. *Cold Dawn: The Story of SALT.* New York: Holt, Rinehart & Winston, 1973.

Nixon, Richard. "Asia After Vietnam." *Foreign Affairs* 46, no. 1 (Oct. 1967).

———. *RN: The Memoirs of Richard Nixon.* New York: Grosset & Dunlap, 1978.

North, Oliver. *Under Fire: An American Story.* New York: HarperPaperbacks, 1991.

Oksenberg, Michel. "A Decade of Sino-American Relations." *Foreign Affairs* 61, no. 1 (Fall 1982).

———. "The Dynamics of the Sino-American Relationship." In *The China Factor,* ed. Richard Solomon. Englewood Cliffs, N.J.: Prentice-Hall, 1981.

Oksenberg, Michel, and Dwight H. Perkins. "The China Policy of Henry Jackson." In *Staying the Course: Henry M. Jackson and National Security,* ed. Dorothy Fosdick. Seattle: University of Washington Press, 1987.

Oye, Kenneth A., Robert J. Lieber, and Donald Rothchild, eds. *Eagle in a New World: American Grand Strategy in the Post-Cold War Era.* New York: Harper Collins, 1992.

———. *Eagle Resurgent: The Reagan Era in American Foreign Policy.* Boston: Little, Brown, 1987.

Party History Research Office of the Chinese Central Committee. *Zhong-guo Gongchandang lishi dashiji* (Chronology of the History of the Chinese Communist Party). Beijing: Renmin Chubanshe, 1991.

Pei Jianzhang. *Yanjiu Zhou Enlai: Waijiao sixiang yu shijian* (Researching Zhou Enlai: Diplomatic Thought and Practice). Beijing: Shijie Zhishi Chubanshe, 1989.

Persico, Joseph E. *Casey: From the OSS to the CIA*. New York: Penguin Books, 1990.

Pollack, Jonathan. *The Lessons of Coalition Politics: Sino-American Security Relations*. Santa Monica, Calif.: RAND Corporation, 1984.

Prados, John. *The Soviet Estimate: U.S. Intelligence Analysis and Soviet Strategic Forces*. Princeton: Princeton University Press, 1982.

Putnam, Robert. "Diplomacy and Domestic Politics: The Logic of Two-Level Games." *International Organization* 42, no. 3 (Summer 1988).

Pye, Lucian. *Chinese Commercial Negotiating Style*. Santa Monica, Calif.: RAND Corporation, 1982.

Qi Wenhuan. "Xi Ou dui Meiguo de duli zuzhu qingxiang" (The Trend of Western European Independence and Initiative Toward the United States). *Shijie zhishi*, no. 8 (Apr. 16, 1983).

Qian Jiang. *"Pingpang waijiao": Shimo* ("Ping-pong Diplomacy": The Beginning and End). Beijing: Dongfang Chubanshe, 1987.

Reagan, Ronald. *Ronald Reagan: An American Life*. New York: Pocket Books, 1990.

Research Office of the Central Committee of the Chinese Communist Party, ed. *San zhongquanhui yilai wenxian xuanbian* (Selection of Important Documents Since the Third Plenum) (*neibu*). Vol. 1. Beijing: Renmin Chubanshe, 1982.

Robinson, Thomas. "The Sino-Soviet Border Dispute: Background, Development, and the March 1969 Clashes." *American Political Science Review* 66, no. 4 (1972).

Rosen, Stanley. *Students*. In *China Briefing, 1988*, ed. Anthony J. Kane. Boulder, Colo.: Westview Press, 1988.

Ross, Edward W. "U.S.–China Military Relations." In *ASEAN and China: An Evolving Relationship*, ed. Joyce K. Kallgren, Noordin Sopiee, and Soedjati Djiwandono. Berkeley: Institute of East Asian Studies, University of California, Berkeley, 1988.

Ross, Robert S. "From Lin Biao to Deng Xiaoping: Elite Instability and China's U.S. Policy." *China Quarterly*, no. 118 (June 1989).

———. *Indochina Tangle: China's Vietnam Policy, 1975–1979*. New York: Columbia University Press, 1988.

———. "International Bargaining and Domestic Politics: U.S.–China Relations Since 1971." *World Politics* 38, no. 2 (Jan. 1986).

———. "National Security, Human Rights, and Domestic Politics: The Bush Administration and China." In *Eagle in a New World: American Grand Strategy in the Post–Cold War Era*, ed. Kenneth A. Oye, Robert J. Leiber, and Donald Rothchild. New York: Harper Collins, 1992.

———. "Two-Level Games and Unexpected Outcomes: U.S.–China Relations During the Bush Administration." Forthcoming.

Safire, William. *Before the Fall: An Inside View of the Pre-Watergate White House*. New York: Doubleday, 1975.

Segal, Gerald. "China and Afghanistan." *Asian Survey* 21, no. 11 (Nov. 1981).

———. *Sino-Soviet Relations After Mao*. Adelphi Papers, no. 202. London: International Institute for Strategic Studies, 1985.

Shambaugh, David L. *Beautiful Imperialist: China Perceives America, 1972–1990*. Princeton, N.J.: Princeton University Press, 1991.

———. "China's National Security Research Bureaucracy." *China Quarterly*, no. 110 (June 1987).

Shanghai Institute of International Studies, ed. *Guoji xingshi nianjian, 1983* (Yearbook of the International Situation, 1983). Shanghai: Zhongguo Dabaike Quanshu Chubanshe, 1983.

———, ed. *Guoji xingshi nianjian, 1984* (Yearbook of the International Situation, 1984). Shanghai: Zhongguo Da Baike Quanshu Chubanshe, 1984.

Shao Pengwen et al., eds. *Zhongguo Gongchandang lishi jiangyi* (Teaching Materials of the History of the Chinese Communist Party). Changchun: Jilin University Press, 1984.

Shelton, L. G. "The Sino-Soviet Split: The Horn of Africa, November 1977 to February 1979." *Naval War College Review* 32, no. 3 (May–June 1979).

Shen Danying, ed. *Wenhua Da Geming zhong de Zhou Enlai* (Zhou Enlai in the Cultural Revolution). Beijing: Zhonggong Zhongyang Dangjiao Chubanshe, 1991.

Shi Lin, ed. *Dangdai Zhongguo de duiwai jingji hezuo* (Contemporary Chinese Foreign Economic Cooperation). Beijing: Zhongguo Shehui Kexueyuan Chubanshe, 1989.

Siddiqi, Toufiq A., Jin Xiaoming, and Shi Minghao. *China–USA Governmental Cooperation in Science and Technology*. Occasional Papers of the East-West Environment and Policy Institute, no. 1. Honolulu: East-West Center, 1987.

Smith, Gerard. *Doubletalk: The Story of SALT I*. Lanham, Md.: University Press of America, 1985.

Snow, Edgar. *The Long Revolution*. New York: Random House, 1972.

Snyder, Glenn H. "The Security Dilemma in Alliance Politics." *World Politics* 36, no. 4 (July 1984).

Snyder, Glenn H., and Paul Diesing. *Conflict Among Nations*. Princeton, N.J.: Princeton University Press, 1977.

Solomon, Richard. *Chinese Political Negotiating Behavior, 1967–1984: An Interpretive Assessment*. Santa Monica, Calif.: RAND Corporation, 1985. Declassified by the U.S. Central Intelligence Agency and available from that agency.

———. *Chinese Political Negotiating Style: A Briefing Analysis*. Santa Monica, Calif.: RAND Corporation, 1985.

————. *U.S.–PRC Political Negotiations, 1967–1984: An Annotated Chronology*. Santa Monica, Calif.: RAND Corporation, 1985. Declassified by the U.S. Central Intelligence Agency and available from that agency.

Stein, Arthur A. *Why Nations Cooperate: Circumstance and Choice in International Relations*. Ithaca, N.Y.: Cornell University Press, 1990.

Stolper, Thomas E. *China, Taiwan and the Offshore Islands*. Armonk, N.Y.: M. E. Sharpe, 1985.

Su, Chi. "The Strategic Triangle and China's Soviet Policy." In *China, the United States, and the Soviet Union: Tripolarity and Policy Making in the Cold War*, ed. Robert S. Ross. Armonk, N.Y.: M. E. Sharpe, 1993.

Sutter, Robert G. *The China Quandary: Domestic Determinants of U.S. China Policy, 1972–1982*. Boulder, Colo.: Westview Press, 1983.

————. *China-Watch: Toward Sino-American Reconciliation*. Baltimore: Johns Hopkins University Press, 1978.

Szulc, Tad. *The Illusion of Peace: Foreign Policy in the Nixon Years*. New York: Viking Press, 1978.

Talbott, Strobe. *Deadly Gambits: The Reagan Administration and the Stalemate in Nuclear Arms Control*. New York: Random House, Vintage Books. 1984.

————. *Endgame: The Inside Story of SALT II*. New York: Harper & Row, 1979.

Terrill, Ross. *Mao: A Biography*. New York: Touchstone, 1980.

————. *White-Boned Demon: A Biography of Madam Mao Zedong*. New York: William Morrow, 1984.

Tian Zengpei, ed. *Gaige kaifang yilai de Zhongguo waijiao* (Chinese Diplomacy Since Reform and Opening). Beijing: Shijie Zhishi Chubanshe, 1993.

Tsou, Tang. "Mao's Limited War in the Taiwan Strait." *Orbis* 3, no. 3 (Fall 1959).

Turley, William S. *The Second Indochina War: A Short Political and Military History, 1954–1975*. New York: New American Library, 1987.

Valenti, Jiri. "Soviet Decision-Making on the Intervention in Angola." In *Communism in Africa*, ed. David E. Albright. Bloomington: Indiana University Press, 1980.

Vance, Cyrus. *Hard Choices: Critical Years in America's Foreign Policy*. New York: Simon & Schuster, 1983.

Vertzberger, Yaacov Y. I. *China's Southwestern Strategy: Encirclement and Counterencirclement*. New York: Praeger, 1985.

Walters, Vernon. *Silent Missions*. New York: Doubleday, 1978.

Wang Baoqin. "Ligen zhengfu dui Su zhengci de tiaozheng he qushi" (Adjustments and Trends in the Reagan Administration Policy Toward the Soviet Union). *Shijie jingji yu zhengzhi neican (neibu)*, no. 1 (1982).

Wang Baoqin and Xu Lei. "Ligen zhengfu de dui Su zhanlue" (The Reagan Administration's Strategy Toward the Soviet Union). *Shijie jingji yu zhengzhi neican (neibu)*, no. 11 (1982).

Wang Baoqin, Yan Yumei, and Liu Liandi. "Bashi niandai de Zhong, Mei,

Su guanxi chutan" (Preliminary Discussion of China–U.S.–Soviet Relations in the 1980s). *Shijie jingji yu zhengzhi neican (neibu)*, no. 11 (1983).

Wang Jingke, *Chen Yi de waijiao yishu* (The Diplomatic Art of Chen Yi). Jinan: Shandong Daxue Chubanshe, 1994.

Wang Li and Qiu Chengyun. "Lishi de gongxun—Zhou Enlai yu dakai Zhong Mei guanxi damen de jincheng" (Historical Exploit: Zhou Enlai and the Process of Opening the Door of China–U.S. Relations). In *Yanjiu Zhou Enlai: Waijiao sixiang yu shijian* (Researching Zhou Enlai: Diplomatic Thought and Practice), ed. Pei Jianzhang. Beijing: Shijie Zhishi Chubanshe, 1989.

Wang Qianqi. "Ligen zhengfu de junshi zhanlue" (The Military Strategy of the Reagan Administration). *Xiandai guoji guanxi*, no. 1 (Oct. 1981).

Wang Shuzhong. "Mei Su zhengba zhong de Meiguo dui Hua zhanlue" (U.S. Strategy Toward China in the U.S.–Soviet Struggle for Hegemony). *Shijie jingji yu zhengzhi neican (neibu)*, no. 3 (1983).

———. "Su Mei zhengba de zhanlue yanbian he dangqian de zhanlue xingshi" (The Strategic Evolution and Current Strategic Situation of the U.S.–Soviet Struggle for Hegemony). *Shijie jingji yu zhengzhi neican (neibu)*, no. 1 (1982).

Wang Yan. "Dangqian Mei Su dui Hua zhengce de bijiao yanjiu" (Comparative Study of Current U.S. and Soviet Policy Toward China). *Shijie jingji yu zhengzhi neican (neibu)*, no. 9 (Sept. 1982).

Wei Shiyen, "Jixinge dier ci fang Hua" (Kissinger's Second Visit to China). In Diplomatic History Research Office, Foreign Ministry of the People's Republic of China, ed., *Xin Zhonguo waijiao fengyun, disan ji* (Diplomatic Turbulence of New China, vol. 3). Beijing: Shijie Zhishi Chubanshe, 1994.

———. "Jixinge mimi fang Hua neimu" (Inside Information on Kissinger's Secret Visit to China). In Diplomatic History Research Office, Foreign Ministry of the People's Republic of China, ed., *Xin Zhonguo waijiao fengyun, dier ji* (Diplomatic Turbulence of New China, vol. 2). Beijing: Shijie Zhishi Chubanshe, 1991.

———. "Nikesen Zongtong fang Hua" (President Nixon's Visit to China). In Diplomatic History Research Office, Foreign Ministry of the People's Republic of China, ed., *Xin Zhonguo waijiao fengyun, disan ji* (Diplomatic Turbulence of New China, vol. 3). Beijing: Shijie Zhishi Chubanshe, 1994.

Weinberger, Caspar. *Fighting for Peace: Seven Critical Years in the Pentagon*. New York: Warner Books, 1990.

Wen Fu. "Sunhai Zhong Mei guanxi de Meiguo 'Yu Taiwan Guanxi Fa'" (The United States 'Taiwan Relations Act,' Which Harms U.S.–China Relations). *Shijie zhishi*, no. 21 (Nov. 1, 1980).

Whiting, Allen S. *China Crosses the Yalu: The Decision to Enter the Korean War*. Stanford: Stanford University Press, 1960.

———. *The Chinese Calculus of Deterrence: India and Indochina*. Ann Arbor: University of Michigan Press, 1975.

———. "Sino-American Détente." *China Quarterly*, no. 82 (June 1980).

Wich, Richard. *Sino-Soviet Crisis Politics: A Study of Political Change and Communication.* Cambridge, Mass.: Council on East Asia Relations, Harvard University, and Harvard University Press, 1980.

Woon, Eden Y. "Chinese Arms Sales and U.S.–China Military Relations." *Asian Survey* 29, no. 6. (June 1989).

Xie Xiaochuan. "Su Mei: Zhengdou de xin tedian" (The Soviet Union and the United States). *Shijie zhishi*, no. 3 (Feb. 1, 1983).

Xiong Xianghui. "Dakai Zhong Mei guanxi damen de qianzou" (Prelude to the Opening of the Door to China–U.S. Relations). *Liaowang*, no. 35 (Aug. 31, 1992).

———. "Dakai Zhong Mei guanxi de qianzou: 1969 nian siwei laoshuai dui guoji xingshi yanjiu he jianyi de qianqian houhou" (Prelude to Opening Sino-American Relations: The Before and After of the 1969 Research and Proposals of the Four Veteran Marshals Regarding the International Situation). *Zhonggong dangshi ziliao* (Materials on Chinese Communist Party history), no. 42 (1992).

Xue Mouhong, ed. *Dangdai Zhongguo waijiao* (Contemporary Chinese Diplomacy) (*neibu*). Beijing: Shehui Kexue Chubanshe, 1987.

Yahuda, Michael. "The Significance of Tripolarity in China's Policy Toward the United States Since 1972." In *China, the United States, and the Soviet Union: Tripolarity and Policy Making in the Cold War*, ed. Robert S. Ross. Armonk, N.Y.: M. E. Sharpe, 1993.

Yao Zhongmin, Xie Wushen, and Pei Jianzhang, eds. *Jiangjun, waijiaojia, yishujia: Huan Zhen jinian wenji* (General, Diplomat, Artist: Collected Works in Memory of Wang Zhen). Beijing: Jiefangjun Chubanshe, 1992.

Ye Yonglie, "Jiefang hou de Jiang Qing" (Jiang Qing After Liberation), *Nanfang zhoumo*, Oct. 14, 1994.

Yi Bianzhu. *Cong Haolaiwu dao Baigong* (From Hollywood to the White House). Beijing: Shishi Chubanshe, 1981.

Yin Jiamin, "Bali de mimi" (The Secrets of Paris). *Zhongguo waijiao miwen* (Secret News of Chinese Diplomacy), ed. Ying Zi. Beijing: Tuanjie Chubanshe, 1993.

Ying Zi, ed. *Zhongguo waijiao miwen* (Secret News of Chinese Diplomacy). Beijing: Tuanjie Chubanshe, 1993.

"Yingdang yan er youxin" (Words Should Be Trustworthy). Commentary. *Renmin ribao*, Dec. 6, 1983.

Zagoria, Donald. "The Moscow-Beijing Détente." *Foreign Affairs* 61, no. 4 (Spring 1983).

———. *The Sino-Soviet Conflict, 1956–1961.* New York: Atheneum, 1964.

Zeng Qing. "Meiguo dui Su zhanlue de dongxiang" (The Trend in U.S. Strategy Toward the Soviet Union). *Shijie zhishi*, no. 6 (Mar. 16, 1979).

Zhang Jialin. "The New Romanticism in the Reagan Administration's Asia Policy." *Asian Survey* 24, no. 10 (Oct. 1984).

Zhang Ping. "Zhou Enlai zhong wai wenhua jiaoliu sixiang chutan" (Preliminary Discussion of Zhou Enlai's Thinking on Sino-Foreign Cultural

Exchanges). In *Zhou Enlai yanjiu xueshu taolunhui lunwenji*, ed. Editorial Group of the Academic Seminar on Research on Zhou Enlai. Beijing: Zhongyang Wenxian Chubanshe, 1988.

Zhang Ruizhuang. "Meiguo xiang Taiwan xian chushou wuqi de lishi yu xianzhuang" (The History and Present Situation of U.S. Arms Sales to Taiwan Province). *Shijie jingji yu zhengzhi neican (neibu)*, no. 5 (1982).

Zhang Shuguang. "'Preparedness Eliminates Mishaps'": The CCP's Security Concerns in 1949–1950 and the Origins of the Sino-American Confrontation." *Journal of American–East Asian Relations* 1, no. 1 (Spring 1992).

Zheng Derong, Shao Pengwen, Zhu Yang, and Gu Min,, eds. *Xin Zhongguo jishi, 1949–1984* (Record of New China, 1949–1984). Jilin: Dongbei Shifan Daxue Chubanshe, 1986.

Zheng Derong, Zhu Yang, et al., eds. *Zhongguo Gongchandang lishi jiangyi* (Teaching Materials of the History of the Chinese Communist Party). Vol. 2. 5th ed. Jilin: Jilin People's Press, 1986.

"Zhonggong zhongyang guanyu dui Yue jinxing ziwei fanji, baowei bianjing zhandou de tongshi" (Bulletin of the Central Committee of the Chinese Communist Party on Carrying Out the Self-Defense Counterattack, Defend the Border Battle Against Vietnam). In *San zhongquanhui yilai wenxian xuanbian (neibu)*, vol. 1, ed. Research Office of the Central Committee of the Chinese Communist Party. Beijing: Renmin Chubanshe, 1982.

Zhou Jirong, Wang Baoqin, and Gu Guanfu. "Su Mei zhengba taishi de bianhua yu qianjing" (Change and Prospect in the U.S.–Soviet Struggle for Hegemony). *Shijie zhishi*, no. 23 (Dec. 1, 1983).

———. "Su Mei zhengba taishi de bianhua yu qianjing" (Change and Prospect in the U.S.–Soviet Struggle for Hegemony). *Xiandai guoji guanxi*, no. 6 (1984).

Zhu Lin. *Dashi furen huiyilu: Xiongyali, Yinni, Faguo, Meiguo* (Memoirs of an Ambassador's Wife: Hungary, Indonesia, France, the United States). Beijing: Shijie Zhishi Chubanshe, 1991.

Zhuang Qubing. "Cong Ligen Guoqing ziwen kan Meiguo de waijiao zhengce" (U.S. Foreign Policy Seen from Reagan's State of the Union Message). *Shijie zhishi*, no. 4 (Feb. 16, 1984).

———. "Ligen de waijiao qiju" (Reagan's Diplomatic Chessboard). *Shijie zhishi*, no. 6 (Mar. 16, 1981).

———. "Meiguo dui Mei Su junshi liliang duibi de jizhong kanfa" (Various U.S. Views of the U.S.–Soviet Balance of Military Strength). *Shijie zhishi*, no. 2 (Jan. 16, 1979).

———. "Meiguo dui Su zhengce de xin qushi" (The New Trend in U.S. Policy Toward the Soviet Union). *Shijie zhishi*, no. 3 (Feb. 1, 1980).

Zong He. "Guoji xingshi de bianhua yu fazhan qushi" (The Trend in Changes and Developments in the International Situation). *Shijie zhishi*, no. 11 (June 1, 1983).

Index

In this index an "f" after a number indicates a separate reference on the next page, and an "ff" indicates separate references on the next two pages. A continuous discussion over two or more pages is indicated by a span of page numbers, e.g., "57–59." *Passim* is used for a cluster of references in close but not consecutive sequence.

Library of Congress Cataloging-in-Publication Data

Ross, Robert S.
  Negotiating cooperation: The United States and China, 1969–1989
/ Robert S. Ross.
  p. cm.
  Includes bibliographical references and index.
  ISBN 0-8047-2453-9 (cl.) : ISBN 0-8047-2454-7 (pb.)
  1. United States—Foreign relations—China. 2. China—Foreign
  relations—United States. I. Title.
  E183.8.C5R58 1995
  327.73051´09´047—dc20 94-34939 CIP